Mapping Linguistic Diversity in Multicultural Contexts

Mapping Linguistic Diversity in Multicultural Contexts

edited by
Monica Barni
Guus Extra

Mouton de Gruyter
Berlin · New York

Mouton de Gruyter (formerly Mouton, The Hague)
is a Division of Walter de Gruyter GmbH & Co. KG, Berlin.

∞ Printed on acid-free paper which falls within the guidelines
of the ANSI to ensure permanence and durability.

Library of Congress Cataloging-in-Publication Data

Mapping linguistic diversity in multicultural contexts / edited by
Monica Barni, Guus Extra.
　　p. cm. − (Contributions to the sociology of language ; 94)
Includes bibliographical references and index.
ISBN 978-3-11-019591-0 (hardcover : alk. paper)
ISBN 978-3-11-019621-4 (pbk. : alk. paper)
　　1. Linguistic minorities.　　2. Pluralism (Social sciences)　　I. Barni,
Monica.　　II. Extra, Guus.
　　P119.315.M37　　2008
　　306.44−dc22
　　　　　　　　　　　　　　　　　　　　　　　　　　　　　　　2008017060

ISBN 978-3-11-019621-4

Bibliographic information published by the Deutsche Nationalbibliothek

The Deutsche Nationalbibliothek lists this publication in the Deutsche
Nationalbibliografie; detailed bibliographic data are available in the Internet
at http://dnb.d-nb.de.

© Copyright 2008 by Walter de Gruyter GmbH & Co. KG, D-10785 Berlin
All rights reserved, including those of translation into foreign languages. No part of this
book may be reproduced in any form or by any means, electronic or mechanical, including
photocopy, recording or any information storage and retrieval system, without permission
in writing from the publisher.
Cover design: Martin Zech, Bremen.
　　　　　　　Image: picture-alliance/MAXPPP/FREDERIC CIROU.
Typesetting: PTP-Berlin GmbH, Berlin.
Printed in Germany.

Preface

The *European Science Foundation* in Strasbourg and the *Università per Stranieri di Siena* co-funded an international exploratory workshop on the theme of this book in September 2006 in Siena/Italy. The workshop was hosted by the University for Foreigners of Siena: a crossroads of Italians and foreigners, of (persons with) different languages, cultures and identities. A University that finds itself inside the City of Siena in which the first chair of Italian language was founded in 1588, something that had never existed before in a university on the Italian peninsula. It was essentially a chair designated for German students who chose to carry out their university studies in Tuscany. Connecting the two facts comes naturally. Although they are centuries apart in time, they are linked in witnessing the Italian language fulfilling its international destiny – through contact – at the moment it is taken as a subject of study.

Today, Italy, traditionally a country characterized by emigration, has become one of the European countries with the highest numbers of immigrants. The 3,7 million immigrants merge in the areas in which Italian is spoken – traditionally structured around the extremes of the Italian language and its varieties, and its 'dense forest of dialects' and the minority languages of historical settlement – a consistent factor of plurilingualism, including more than 130 languages of immigrants that are already rooted in several local communities. This neo-plurilingualism not only includes the languages of immigrants but the languages of minority groups as well, which by now are well-established among local communities: languages used systematically within groups, but also capable of displaying themselves to the entire collectivity, with the effect of profoundly modifying the semiotic and linguistic landscape of both our larger and smaller urban centres.

Tuscany is the fourth largest Italian region with the fourth highest number of immigrants in Italy. The province of Siena has seen major changes in its own demographic, social and linguistic structures as well. The vineyards of Brunello di Montalcino in the Chianti area are at this point in time cultivated by a growing number of immigrant workers from the Balkans and the Indian Subcontinent. Medieval buildings are being restored and modern structures are being built by Albanian, Romanian and North African workers. Elderly people are increasingly being nursed by young people from abroad. Strolling through Siena one could always hear the sounds of many languages: the languages of tourists and students in the City that has a distinct vocation as the centre of international university studies. Nowadays, walking around Siena, one could add the sounds and alphabets of new citizens. Signs, posters or spontaneous writings can be found in Chinese and Arabic, in Russian and Turkish. In schools throughout the province, the presence of children from immigrant or mixed families already represents a major challenge for school leaders and teachers.

Siena nowadays appears more and more like a laboratory, a city that typifies the general condition of the country, of Europe and of the entire globe. In such a laboratory, experiments are taking place involving advanced modalities in the elaboration of models adequate for describing and interpreting the new plurilingual reality of the globalized world, the new plurilingual identity of children who fill the schools of the City and the surrounding small towns, the new plurilingual profiles which accompany our daily lives. The Sienese workshop could not have emerged in any other Italian city: Siena is home to a University for Foreigners, and therefore the centre of choice, representative in the study and formative administration of plurilingualism; home to an Excellence Centre of research whose main purpose is to develop a Permanent Language Observatory for the diffusion of Italian among foreigners and immigrants in Italy.

We have gathered beautiful memories of the Sienese workshop, memories of an intense exchange of reflections of welcoming which only Tuscany and Siena can give. This is Siena, a model of *glocalization*, a City that has written on one of its gates: *Cor magis tibi Sena pandit*, that is, "Siena opens her heart to you once more". Once more from her gates Siena opens her heart to those who come from abroad and offers the history of her civil values to others. The others are, for Siena, today's immigrants. In September 2006, the participants were the most pleasant guests – new friends at the Sienese workshop. I would like to express my sincere thanks to all of our guests, to the *European Science Foundation*, and to the University's research staff and technical-administrative personnel, in remembrance of a high-profile scientific event of profound humanity.

Massimo Vedovelli
President of the University for Foreigners of Siena

Acknowledgements

This Volume is the follow-up to an international exploratory workshop on our topic of concern at the *Università per Stranieri di Siena* (Italy), held in September 2006 under the auspices of the *European Science Foundation* in Strasbourg. We want to thank the ESF and the University of Siena for their generous support in making this workshop and follow-up publication possible. We also want to express our thanks to Karin Berkhout at *Babylon, Centre for Studies of the Multicultural Society*, at Tilburg University (the Netherlands) for her dedicated support in the editing of this Volume, and to Simone Casini for the revision of the subject index.

Monica Barni and Guus Extra

Contents

Section IV. Mapping linguistic diversity abroad

Section I
Introduction

Mapping linguistic diversity in multicultural contexts: Cross-national and cross-linguistic perspectives

Guus Extra and Monica Barni

1. Aims and rationale of this book

The focus of this book is on mapping linguistic diversity in multicultural contexts. Both well-known and established approaches will be explored, coined as *demolinguistics* (De Vries 1990) and *geolinguistics* (Van der Merwe 1989). The term demolinguistics originated among Quebec demographers, probably during the 1970s (Lachapelle and Henripin 1980). Over the last three decades, the field has become an international crossing for demographers and linguists; the same holds for geolinguistics as the crossing for geographers and linguists. In addition, more recent approaches will be explored in terms of *linguistic landscaping* (Gorter 2006). Whereas geolinguistic and demolinguistic studies focus commonly on the spatial and temporal distribution and vitality of languages in the private domain of the home, linguistic landscaping has as its focus the public domain in the most literal sense, i.e., in terms of the visibility and distribution of languages on the streets. In this sense, the outcomes of linguistic landscaping research should be read with care: they do not intend to present a faithful mapping of the linguistic make-up of the population in a given place (see Barni, and Backhaus, this volume).

For each of these approaches, we will offer cross-national and cross-linguistic evidence on so-called "non-national" languages. Dependent on particular contexts or perspectives, such languages are often referred to as minority languages or dominated languages. Numerical classifications do not necessarily coincide with social classifications. According to the 2001 census outcomes in South Africa, (isi)Zulu is the most widely spoken home language and English functions commonly as *lingua franca* with all its power and prestige (see Van der Merwe and Van der Merwe, this volume). Whereas English is a minority language in the homes of South Africans, it is the dominant language in society.

In Western Europe, Turkish belongs to the major immigrant languages, and it is spoken in the homes of far more people than, e.g., any of the official state languages of the three Baltic States. (see Brizić and Yağmur, this volume).

In this book, cross-national and cross-linguistic perspectives will actually be offered on two major domains in which language transmission occurs, i.e., the domestic domain and the public domain. Prototypical of these two domains are the home and the school, respectively. At home, language transmission occurs between parents and children, at school this occurs between teachers and pupils. Viewed from the perspectives of majority language speakers *versus* minority language speakers, language transmission becomes a very different issue. In the case of majority language speakers, language transmission at home and at school is commonly taken for granted: At home, parents speak this language usually with their children and at school, this language is usually the only or major subject and medium of instruction. In the case of minority language speakers, there is usually a mismatch between the language of the home and the language of the school. Whether parents in such a context continue to transmit their language to their children is strongly dependent on the degree to which these parents, or the minority group to which they belong, conceive of this language as a core value of cultural identity.

Both demo/geolinguistic research and linguistic landscaping can be characterised as empirical approaches with a strong fascination for large data sampling and for the visual representation of the resulting outcomes in tabulated figures and language maps. In many regards, this book will show evidence of this fascination. This is not to say that the value of qualitative small-scale data, common in ethnographic research, should be under-estimated (see, e.g., Brizić and Yağmur, and Kipp, this volume). In particular in the domain of multilingualism in a multicultural context, there is a need for multidisciplinarity and complementarity of data collection methods. Table 1 gives an outline of complementary approaches or paradigms in ethnographic *versus* demo/geolinguistic research. Validity issues arise in each of these two approaches: in ethnographic research in terms of representativeness of the data and in terms of making generalisations, in demo/geolinguistic research in terms of a (mis)match between observed and reported data (see also section 7). To quote Hammersley (1992):

> We are not faced then, with a stark choice between words and numbers, or even between precise and imprecise data; but rather with a range from more to less precise data. Furthermore, our decisions about what level of precision is appropriate in relation to any particular claim should depend on the nature of what we are trying to describe, on the likely accuracy of our descriptions, on our purposes, and on the resources available to us; not on ideological commitment to one methodological paradigm or another.

Table 1. Complementary approaches or paradigms in ethnographic *versus* demo/geo-linguistic research

Research paradigms	Ethnographic research	Demo/geolinguistic research
Research methods	– Inductive / Heuristic – (Participating) observation – "Qualitative"	– Deductive – Distance between researcher and informants – "Quantitative"
Usual data	– Observed data in multiple contexts – Open-ended and in-depth interviews	– Reported data in single contexts – Selective set of questions in pre-designed questionnaires
Informants	– (Multiple) case studies – Single/few informants	– Large-scale studies – Many informants

A prominent concept in *geolinguistic* research is the spatial confinement of language groups to a particular geographical area. One should be aware that some language groups show a stronger degree of spatial confinement than other language groups. The former holds in particular for regional (minority) languages, the latter for immigrant (minority) languages. Taken from a dynamic perspective, regional languages may become (im)migrant languages within or across the borders of nation-states. Take the case of (isi)Xhosa as spoken in South Africa: it has its regional base ("centre of gravity") in the Eastern Cape but has started to move in the post-Apartheid era also to the Western Cape. As a result, Xhosa is gaining a strong appearance next to Afrikaans and English in Cape Town (see Van der Merwe and Van der Merwe, this volume). A similar awareness should hold for the concept of "language groups" itself. Although there are many reasons, including methodological reasons, for its popularity, one should be aware that this concept is problematic in any multicultural context. The language repertoire of people in such a context consists often of more than one language. In the European public and political discourse, this has led to the popularity of the reference to plurilingual people in multilingual societies (see also Lüdi, this volume). Taken from this perspective, plurilingualism refers to an ability of individuals to communicate in more than one language, whereas multilingualism refers to a key marker of societies at large.

In this book, we want to compare the European state of knowledge on mapping linguistic diversity with initiatives taken in other parts of the world. Over the last century, Europe has shifted from a continent of emigration to a continent of immigration. Demolinguistics is in particular a well-known and established field of research in non-European English-dominant immigration countries with a long history of population research in which census data have been collected and longitudinally compared, including census data on (home) language use. Apart from census data, other types of data, such as administrative population data and (*ad hoc*) survey data, may provide rich information sources on (home) language use (see Poulain, this volume).

Multicultural self-definitions have been created by former European immigrants in such non-European English-dominant immigration countries as Australia, Canada, the USA and South Africa (cf. also the concept of "rainbow nation"). A similar multicultural self-definition holds also for Europe at large: its identity is commonly described in terms of "celebrating cultural and linguistic diversity". A paradoxical phenomenon in the European public and political discourse is the absence of this celebration in the case of non-European immigrant groups and their languages. For Europeans, much can be learnt from the experiences abroad in dealing with multilingualism and multiculturalism, both in terms of public and political discourse and in terms of data provision and data analysis. The final objective of this book is to provide the European research community and policy makers with a variety of conceptual and methodological considerations and challenges for mapping linguistic diversity in multicultural contexts.

2.   The European constellation of languages

Europe's identity is determined to a great extent by cultural and linguistic diversity (Haarmann 1995). Table 2 serves to illustrate this diversity in terms of 30 current and candidate European Union (henceforward EU) nation-states with their estimated populations (ranked in decreasing order of millions) and official state languages.

As Table 2 makes clear, there are large differences in population size amongst EU nation-states. German, French, English, Italian, Spanish, and Polish belong to the six most widely spoken national languages in the present EU, whereas Turkish would come second to German in an enlarged EU. Table 1 also shows the close connection between nation-state references and official state language references. In 27 out of 30 cases, distinct languages are the clearest feature distinguishing one nation-state from its neighbours (Barbour 2000), the major exceptions (and for different reasons) being Belgium, Austria, and Cyprus. The same holds for Switzerland, a non-EU country where more than one language are official state languages (see also Lüdi, this volume). This match between

Table 2. Overview of 30 EU (candidate) nation-states with estimated populations and official state languages (EU figures for 2007)

Nr.	Nation-states	Population (in millions)	Official state language(s)
1	Germany	82.5	German
2	France	60.9	French
3	United Kingdom	60.4	English
4	Italy	58.8	Italian
5	Spain	43.8	Spanish
6	Poland	38.1	Polish
7	Romania	21.6	Romanian
8	The Netherlands	16.3	Dutch (Nederlands)
9	Greece	11.1	Greek
10	Portugal	10.6	Portuguese
11	Belgium	10.5	Dutch, French, German
12	Czech Republic	10.3	Czech
13	Hungary	10.1	Hungarian (Magyar)
14	Sweden	9.0	Swedish
15	Austria	8.3	German
16	Bulgaria	7.7	Bulgarian
17	Denmark	5.4	Danish
18	Slovakia	5.4	Slovak
19	Finland	5.3	Finnish
20	Ireland	4.2	Irish, English
21	Lithuania	3.4	Lithuanian
22	Latvia	2.3	Latvian
23	Slovenia	2.0	Slovenian
24	Estonia	1.3	Estonian
25	Cyprus	0.8	Greek, Turkish
26	Luxemburg	0.5	Luxemburgisch, French, German
27	Malta	0.4	Maltese, English
28	Turkey	72.5	Turkish
29	Croatia	4.4	Croatian
30	Macedonia	2.0	Macedonian

nation-state references and official state language references obscures the very existence of different types of minority languages that are actually spoken across

European nation-states. Many of these languages are indigenous minority languages with a regional base, many other languages stem from abroad without such a base. We will refer to these "other" languages of Europe as regional minority (henceforward RM) languages and immigrant minority (henceforward IM) languages, respectively (Extra and Gorter 2001).

A number of issues need to be kept in mind, however. Within and across EU nation-states, some RM and IM languages have larger numbers of speakers than some of the official state languages presented in Table 2. Moreover, RM or IM languages in one EU nation-state may be official state languages in another nation-state. Examples of the former result from language border crossing in adjacent nation-states, such as Finnish in Sweden or Swedish in Finland. Examples of the latter result from trans-national processes of migration and minorisation, in particular from Southern to Northern Europe, such as Portuguese, Spanish, Italian or Greek. In particular the context of migration and minorisation makes our proposed distinction between RM and IM languages ambiguous. We see, however, no better alternative. It should also be kept in mind that many, if not most, IM languages in particular European nation-states originate from countries outside Europe. In our opinion, the proposed distinction leads at least to awareness raising and may ultimately lead to an inclusive approach in the European conceptualisation of "minority" languages.

3. Phenomenological considerations

Contrary to many popular views, the concepts of "nation" and "nation-state" in the modern sense are relatively recent phenomena. Barbour (2000) discusses the distinction between these two concepts in terms of a population and a legally defined entity, respectively. Nations have frequently developed from ethnic groups, but nations and ethnic groups do not necessarily coincide. Ethnic groups are often subsets of nations or function as collective entities across the borders of nation-states. The construction and/or consolidation of nation-states across Europe has enforced the belief that an official state language should correspond to each nation-state, and that this language should be regarded as a core value of national identity. The equation of language and national identity, however, is based on a denial of the co-existence of majority and minority languages within the borders of any nation-state and has its roots in the German Romanticism at the end of the 18th and the early 19th century (see Fishman 1973: 39–85, 1989: 105–175, 270–287; Edwards 1985: 23–27; Joseph 2004: 92–131 for historical overviews). The equation of German and Germany was a reaction to the rationalism of the Enlightenment and was also based on anti-French sentiments. The concept of nationalism emerged at the end of the 18th century;

the concept of nationality only a century later. Romantic philosophers like Johan Gottfried Herder and Wilhelm von Humboldt laid the foundation for the emergence of a linguistic nationalism in Germany on the basis of which the German language and nation were conceived of as superior to the French ones. The French, however, were no less reluctant to express their conviction that the reverse was true. Although every nation-state is characterised by heterogeneity, including linguistic heterogeneity, nationalistic movements have always invoked this classical European discourse in their equation of language and nation (cf. revitalised references in Germany to such concepts as *Sprachnation*, *Urfolk* and *Leitkultur*). For recent studies on language, identity and nationalism in Europe we refer to Barbour and Carmichael (2000) and Gubbins and Holt (2002), and for a comparative study of attitudes towards language and national identity in France and Sweden to Oakes (2001).

The USA has not remained immune to this type of nationalism either. The English-only movement, *US English*, was founded in 1983 out of a fear of the growing number of Hispanics on American soil (Fishman 1988; May 2001: 202–224). This organisation resisted bilingual Spanish-English education from the beginning because such an approach would lead to "identity confusion". Similarly, attempts have been made to give the assignment of English as the official language of the USA a constitutional basis. This was done on the presupposition that the recognition of other languages (in particular Spanish) would undermine the foundations of the nation-state. This nationalism has its roots in a white, protestant, English-speaking elite (Edwards 1994: 177–178).

The relationship between language and identity is not a static but a dynamic phenomenon. During the last decades of the 20th century, this relationship underwent strong trans-national changes. Within the European context, these changes occurred in three different arenas (Oakes 2001):

– in the national arenas of the EU nation-states: the traditional identity of these nation-states has been challenged by major demographic changes (in particular in urban areas) as a consequence of migration and minorisation;
– in the European arena: the concept of a European identity has emerged as a consequence of increasing cooperation and integration at the European level;
– in the global arena: our world has become smaller and more interactive as a consequence of the increasing availability of information and communication technology.

Major changes in each of these three arenas have led to the development of concepts such as a trans-national citizenship and trans-national multiple identities. Inhabitants of Europe no longer identify exclusively with singular nation-states, but give increasing evidence of multiple affiliations. At the EU level, the notion of a European identity was formally expressed for the first time in the *Declaration on European Identity* of December 1973 in Copenhagen. Numerous institutions and documents have propagated and promoted this idea ever since. The most concrete and tangible expressions of this idea to date have been the introduction of a European currency in 2002 and the proposals for a European constitution in 2004. In discussing the concept of a European identity, Oakes (2001: 127–131) emphasizes that the recognition of the concept of multiple trans-national identities is a prerequisite rather than an obstacle for the acceptance of a European identity. The recognition of multiple trans-national identities not only occurs among the traditional inhabitants of European nation-states, but also among newcomers and IM groups in Europe. At the same time we see a strengthening of regional identities in many regions in Europe, in particular those where a RM language is in use.

Multiple trans-national identities and affiliations will require new competences of European citizens in the 21st century. These include the ability to deal with increasing cultural diversity and heterogeneity (Van Londen and De Ruijter 1999). Plurilingualism can be considered a core competence for such ability. In this context, processes of both convergence and divergence play a role. In the European and global arena, English has increasingly assumed the role of *lingua franca* for international communication (Oakes 2001: 131–136, 149–154). The rise of English has occurred at the cost of all other official state languages of Europe, including French. At the same time, a growing number of newcomers to the national arenas of the EU nation-states express the need of competence in the languages of their countries of origin and destination.

Europe has a rich diversity of languages. This fact is usually illustrated by reference to the official state languages of the EU. However, many more languages are spoken by the inhabitants of Europe. Examples of such languages are Welsh and Basque, or Arabic and Turkish. These languages are usually referred to as "minority languages", even when in Europe as a whole there is no one majority language because all languages are spoken by a numerical minority. The languages referred to are representatives of RM and IM languages, respectively. RM and IM languages have much in common, much more than is usually thought. On their sociolinguistic, educational and political agendas, we find issues such as their actual spread, their domestic and public vitality, the processes and determinants of language maintenance *versus* language shift towards majority languages, the relationship between language, ethnicity, and identity, and the status of minority languages in schools, in particular in the compulsory stages of primary and secondary education. The origin of most RM languages as *minority* languages lies in the 19th century, when, during the processes of state-formation in Europe, they found themselves excluded from the state level, in particular from general education. RM languages did not become official languages of the nation-states that were then established. Centralising tendencies and the ideology of *one language – one state* have threatened the continued existence of RM languages. The greatest threat to RM languages, however, is lack of inter-generational transmission. When parents stop speaking the ancestral language with their children, it becomes almost impossible to reverse the ensuing language shift. Education can also be a major factor in the maintenance and promotion of a minority language. For most RM languages, some kind of educational provisions have been established in an attempt at reversing ongoing language shift. Only in the last few decades have some of these RM languages become relatively well protected in legal terms, as well as by affirmative educational policies and programmes, both at the level of various nation-states and at the level of the EU at large.

There have always been speakers of IM languages in Europe, but these languages have only recently emerged as community languages spoken on a wide scale in urban Europe, due to intensified processes of migration and minorisation. Turkish and Arabic are good examples of so-called "non-European" languages that are spoken and learned by millions of inhabitants of the EU nation-states. Although IM languages are often conceived of and transmitted as core values by IM language groups, they are much less protected than RM languages by affirmative action and legal measures, for example, in education. In fact, the learning and certainly the teaching of IM languages are often seen by mainstream language speakers and by policy makers as obstacles to integration. At the European level, guidelines and directives regarding IM languages are scant and outdated. Despite the possibilities and challenges of comparing the status of RM and IM languages across European nation-states, amazingly few connections have been made in sociolinguistic, educational and political domains (Extra and Gorter 2001).

As yet, we lack a common referential framework for the languages under discussion. Publications which focus on both types of minority languages are rare: examples are the dual volumes on RM and IM languages by Alladina and Edwards (1991), and the integrated volumes by Gogolin et al. (1991), Fase et al. (1992, 1995), Ammon et al. (1995), Ammerlaan et al. (2001), and Extra and Gorter (2001). As all of these RM and IM languages are spoken by different language communities and not at state-wide level, it may seem logical to refer to them as community languages, thus contrasting them with the official languages of nation-states. However, the designation "community languages" leads to confusion at the surface level because this concept is already in use to refer to the official languages of the EU. In that sense the designation "community

Table 3. Nomenclature of the field (Extra and Yağmur 2004: 19)

Reference to the people

  National/historical/regional/indigenous minorities versus non-national/non-
  historical/non-territorial/non indigenous minorities

  Non-national residents

  Foreigners, étrangers, *Ausländer*

  (Im)migrants

  Newcomers, new Xmen (e.g., new Dutchmen)

  Co-citizens (instead of citizens)

  Ethnic/cultural/ethnocultural minorities

  Linguistic minorities

  Allochthones (e.g., in the Netherlands), allophones (e.g., in Canada)

  Non-English-speaking (NES) residents (in particular in the USA)

  Anderstaligen (Dutch: those who speak other languages)

  Coloured/black people, visible minorities (the latter in particular in Canada)

Reference to their languages

  Community languages (in Europe versus Australia)

  Ancestral/heritage languages (common concept in Canada)

  National/historical/regional/indigenous minority languages versus non-
  territorial/non-regional/non-indigenous/non-European minority languages

  Autochthonous versus allochthonous minority languages

  Lesser used/less widely used/less widely taught languages (in the EBLUL context)

  Stateless/diaspora languages (in particular used for Romani)

  Languages other than English (LOTE: common concept in Australia)

Reference to the teaching of these languages

  Instruction in one's own language (and culture)

  Mother tongue teaching (MTT)

  Home language instruction (HLI)

  Community language teaching (CLT)

  Regional minority language instruction versus immigrant minority language
  instruction

  Enseignement des Langues et Cultures d'Origine (ELCO: in French/Spanish
  primary schools)

  Enseignement des Langues Vivantes (ELV: in French/Spanish secondary
  schools)

  muttersprachlicher Unterricht (MSU: in German primary schools)

  muttersprachlicher Ergänzungsunterricht (in German primary/secondary
  schools)

  herkunftssprachlicher Unterricht (in German primary/secondary schools)

---

languages" is occupied territory. From an inventory of the different terms in use, we learn that there are no standardised designations for these languages across nation-states. Table 3 gives a non-exhaustive overview of the nomenclature of our field of concern in terms of reference to the people, their languages, and the teaching of these languages. The concept of "lesser used languages" has been adopted at the EU level; the *European Bureau for Lesser Used Languages* (EBLUL), established in Brussels and Dublin, speaks and acts on behalf of "the autochthonous regional and minority languages of the EU". Table 3 shows that the terminology varies not only across different nation-states, but also across different types of education.

4. Regional minority languages across EU nation-states

We will present basic information on different RM language groups in the EU. In some nation-states, there are fairly accurate figures because a language question has been included in the census several times; in other cases, we only have rough estimates by insiders to the language group (usually language activists who want to boost the figures) or by outsiders (e.g., state officials who quite often want to downplay the number of speakers). Figure 1 serves to illustrate our overview visually and is derived from the Mercator Education website (see also Extra and Gorter 2007).

Figures for numbers of speakers are almost always problematic. In only a few cases they are based upon recent census or survey outcomes. Many other figures are, due to the lack of other data, derived from informed estimates by experts (these are sometimes referred to as "disputed numbers"). Also, some languages would perhaps not be included according to certain criteria; others might be split up further. Figures on RM languages in (mainly Western) Europe can be found in Breatnach (1998), Euromosaic (1996), *Istituto della Enciclopedia Italiana* (1986), Siguan (1990) and Tjeerdsma (1998), as well as in the Ethnologue (2001). Derived from Extra and Gorter (2007), we will use a simple typology and distinguish between five categories of RM languages within the EU:

– unique RM languages, spoken in only one nation-state (e.g., Welsh in the United Kingdom, Frisian in the Netherlands or Breton in France; see Williams, Gorter and Caubet in this volume, respectively);
– RM languages spoken in more than one nation-state (e.g., Basque in Spain and France; see Cenoz, this volume);
– languages which are a RM language in one nation-state but the official mainstream language in a neighbouring state (e.g., Albanian and Croatian in Italy; see Barni, this volume);

Figure 1. Overview of RM languages across EU nation-states (Mercator Education, Fryske Akademy, Leeuwarden)

– historical non-territorial minority languages, which exist in smaller or larger numbers in almost all EU nation-states; the most prominent ones are Romani and Yiddish (see Extra and Yağmur, this volume);

– two languages with a special status, being official state languages of the EU but no official working languages of the EU; these are Luxemburgish, spoken in Luxembourg and France, and Irish, spoken in Ireland and Northern Ireland (UK) (see Table 2).

There are many publications on the status and use of RM languages, both in Europe and abroad (e.g., Gorter et al. 1990). Baetens Beardsmore (1993) focuses on RM languages in Western Europe, whereas Synak and Wicherkiewicz (1997), Bratt-Paulston and Peckham (1998), and Hogan-Brun and Wolff (2003) deal with RM languages in Central and Eastern Europe. In a number of European countries a periodical census includes one or a few questions on language and ethnicity, but in other countries no such questions are asked. An additional tool for obtaining data are sociolinguistic surveys. There are some RM language communities where such surveys are carried out with regular intervals. The Euromosaic (1996) project has provided a general overview of 48 language communities in the EU. In about half of those cases also data were collected through small-scale sociolinguistic surveys. The *European Language Survey Network* has developed a core module of 28 questions meant as a standard for questionnaires in any RM language community in Europe in order to obtain a basic overview of the language situation (ELSN 1996; Gorter 1997).

In Ireland and Wales, there is a tradition of both a regular census with language questions and regular sociolinguistic surveys (see Williams on Welsh, this volume). Spain has also a tradition of census with questions on the official languages of the Autonomous Communities in the Basque Country, Catalunya and Galicia (see Cenoz on Basque, this volume). In all contexts referred to, the focus is on regional languages, not on immigrant languages. The Netherlands has not had a census since 1971 and never had a language question; however, regular sociolinguistic surveys have been carried out on Frisian in the province of Friesland (see Gorter, this volume). In the United Kingdom, the next decennial census will be in 2011 and the Office for National Statistics carried out a household questionnaire in 2007 to test the planned procedures (*www.statistics.gov.uk/censustest*). Questions 12–15 refer to "national identity", ethnicity, religion and language skills, respectively. With respect to the latter, a distinction is made between English, Welsh, Other language (to be specified in an open box), and British/Other Sign Language; in the first three cases, a further distinction is made between *no ability/understand/speak/read/write*. The format and nature of the 2011 UK census are still under negotiation. At the time of writing, no decision had been made on the number and type of language questions, neither on English nor on languages other than English.

5. The European discourse on "foreigners" and "integration"

In the European public discourse on IM groups, two major characteristics emerge: IM groups are often referred to as "foreigners" (*étrangers, Ausländer*) and as being in need of "integration". First of all, it is common practice to refer to IM groups in terms of *non-national* residents and to their languages in terms of *non-territorial, non-regional, non-indigenous* or *non-European* languages. The call for integration is in sharp contrast with the language of exclusion. This conceptual exclusion rather than inclusion in the European public discourse derives from a restrictive interpretation of the notions of citizenship and nationality. From a historical point of view, such notions are commonly shaped by a constitutional *ius sanguinis* (law of the blood) in terms of which nationality is based on descent, in contrast to *ius soli* (law of the soil) in terms of which nationality derives from the country of birth. When European emigrants left their continent in the past and colonised countries abroad, they legitimised their claim to citizenship by spelling out *ius soli* in the constitutions of these countries of settlement. Good examples of this strategy can be found in English-dominant immigration countries like the USA, Canada, Australia and South Africa. In establishing the constitutions of these (sub)continents, no consultation took place with native inhabitants, such as Indians, Inuit, Aboriginals and Zulus, respectively. At home, however, Europeans predominantly upheld *ius sanguinis* in their constitutions and/or perceptions of nationality and citizenship, in spite of the growing numbers of newcomers who strive for an equal status as citizens.

In this context, an interesting difference emerges between the American and European public discourse on ethnicity and nationality/citizenship. In the United States, word order constraints occur in such a way that ethnicity functions as modifier or adjective, and nationality/citizenship as head or noun (cf. references like *Latin/Afro/Anglo/Asian/Chinese/Dutch American*). In Europe, IM groups are often referred to by their source country instead of the target country of which they hold the nationality, resulting in such references as *Turks* instead of *Turkish Dutchmen*, or *Moroccans* instead of *Moroccan Frenchmen*. A remarkable phenomenon in the Israeli public discourse is the common way of referring to *Israeli Jews/Arabs* instead of *Jewish/Arab Israelis*: the former type of reference is focused upon difference in ethnicity, the latter upon similarity in citizenship.

A second major characteristic of the European public discourse on IM groups is the focus on *integration*. This notion is both popular and vague, and it may actually refer to a whole spectrum of underlying concepts that vary over space and time. Miles and Thränhardt (1995), Bauböck et al. (1996), and Kruyt and Niessen (1997) are good examples of comparative case studies on the notion of integration in a variety of EU countries that have been faced with increasing immigration since the early 1970s. The extremes of the spectrum range from assimilation to multiculturalism. The concept of assimilation is based on the premise that cultural differences between IM groups and established majority groups should and will disappear over time in a society which is proclaimed to be culturally homogeneous. On the other side of the spectrum, the concept of multiculturalism is based on the premise that such differences are an asset to a pluralist society, which actually promotes cultural diversity in terms of new resources and opportunities. Whereas the concept of assimilation focuses on unilateral tasks for *newcomers*, the concept of multiculturalism focuses on multilateral tasks for *all* inhabitants in changing societies (Taylor 1993; Cohn-Bendit and Schmid 1992). In practice, established majority groups often make strong demands on IM groups for integration in terms of assimilation and are commonly very reluctant to promote or even accept the notion of cultural diversity as a determining characteristic of an increasingly multicultural environment.

It is interesting to compare the underlying assumptions of "integration" in the European public discourse on IM groups at the national level with assumptions made at the level of trans-national cooperation and legislation. In the latter context, European politicians are eager to stress the importance of a proper balance between the loss and maintenance of "national" norms and values. A prime concern in the public debate on such norms and values is cultural and linguistic diversity, mainly in terms of the national languages of the EU. These languages are often referred to as core values of cultural identity. It is a paradoxical phenomenon that in the same public discourse IM languages and cultures are commonly conceived as sources of problems and deficits and as obstacles to integration, whereas national languages and cultures in an expanding EU are regarded as sources of enrichment and as prerequisites for integration.

The public discourse on integration of IM groups in terms of assimilation *versus* multiculturalism can also be noticed in the domain of education. Due to a growing influx of IM pupils, schools are faced with the challenge of adapting their curricula to this trend. The pattern of modification may be inspired by a strong and unilateral emphasis on learning (in) the language of the majority of society, given its significance for success in school and on the labour market, or by the awareness that the response to emerging multicultural school populations cannot be reduced to monolingual education programming (Gogolin 1994). In the former case, the focus will be on learning (in) the national language as a second language only, in the latter case on offering more than one language in the school curriculum.

6. Criteria for the identification of multicultural populations

Comparative information on population figures in EU member-states can be obtained from the Statistical Office of the EU in Luxemburg (*Eurostat*). For a variety of reasons, however, reliable and comparable demographic information on IM groups in EU countries is difficult to obtain. Seemingly simple questions like *How many Turkish residents live in Germany compared to France?* cannot easily be answered (see Poulain, this volume). For some groups or countries, no updated information is available or no such data have ever been collected. Moreover, official statistics only reflect IM groups with legal resident status. Another source of disparity is the different data collection systems being used, ranging from nation-wide census data to administrative registers or to more or less representative surveys. Most importantly, however, the most widely used criteria for IM status – nationality and/or country of birth – have become less valid over time because of an increasing trend toward naturalisation and births within the countries of residence. In addition, most residents from former colonies already have the nationality of their country of immigration. In the context of our reference to nation-states, we will refer to nationality rather than citizenship. Even if the two concepts are commonly used as synonyms nowadays, we should be aware of their historical and contextual difference in denotation. Nationals belong to a nation-state but they may not have all the rights linked with citizenship (e.g., voting rights); in this sense, citizenship is a more inclusive concept than nationality.

For a discussion of the role of censuses in identifying population groups in a variety of multicultural nation-states, we refer to Kertzer and Arel (2002). Alterman (1969) offers a fascinating account of the history of counting people from the earliest known records on Babylonian clay tables in 3800 BC to the USA census in 1970. Besides the methods of counting, Alterman discusses at length who has been counted, and how, who not, and why. The issue of mapping identities through nationwide periodical censuses by state institutions is commonly coupled with a vigorous debate between proponents and opponents about the following "ethnic dilemma": how can you combat discrimination if you do not measure diversity? (Kertzer and Arel 2002: 23–25). Both proponents and opponents of measuring diversity can be found (cf. Blum 2002 on this debate in France):

– proponents argue in terms of the social or scientific need for population data bases on diversity as prerequisites for affirmative action by government in such domains as labour, housing, health care, education or media policies;

– opponents argue in terms of the social or scientific risks of public or political misuse of such data bases for stereotyping, stigmatisation, discrimination or even removal of the "unwanted other".

Kertzer and Arel (2002: 2) show that the census does much more than simply reflect social reality; rather it plays a key role in the construction of that reality and in the creation of collective identities. At the same time, it should be acknowledged that the census is a crucial area for the politics of representation. Census data can make people aware of under-representation. Language rights are often a key demand for minority groups on the basis of (home) language databases.

Decennial censuses became a common practice in Europe and the New World colonised by Europeans in the first part of the 19th century. The USA became the first newly established nation-state with a decennial census since 1790. The first countries to include a language question in their census, however, were Belgium in 1846 and Switzerland in the 1850s, both being European countries with more than one official state language (see Table 2). At present, in many EU countries, only population data on nationality and/or birth country (of person and/or parents) are available. To illustrate this, Table 4 gives comparative statistics of population groups in the Netherlands, based on the birth-country (BC) criterion (of person and/or mother and/or father – PMF) *versus* the nationality criterion, as derived from the Dutch Central Bureau of Statistics (2000).

Table 4 shows strong criterion effects of birth country *versus* nationality. All IM groups are in fact strongly under-represented in nationality-based statistics. However, the combined birth-country criterion of person/ mother/father does not solve the identification problem either. The use of this criterion leads to non-identification in at least the following cases:

– an increasing group of third and further generations (cf. Indonesian/Moluccan and Chinese communities in the Netherlands);
– different ethnocultural groups from the same country of origin (cf. Turks and Kurds from Turkey or Berbers and Arabs from Morocco);
– the same ethnocultural group from different countries of origin (cf. Chinese from China and from other Asian countries);
– ethnocultural groups without territorial status (cf. Roma people).

From the data presented in Table 4, it becomes clear that collecting reliable information about the actual number and spread of IM population groups in EU countries is no easy enterprise. Krüger-Potratz et al. (1998) discuss the problem of criteria from a historical perspective in the context of the German *Weimarer*

Table 4. Population of the Netherlands based on the combined birth-country criterion (BC–PMF) versus the nationality criterion on January 1, 1999 (Antilleans are Dutch nationals; CBS 2000)

Groups	BC–PMF	Nationality	Absolute difference
Dutch	13,061,000	15,097,000	2,036,000
Turks	300,000	102,000	198,000
Moroccans	252,000	128,600	123,400
Surinamese	297,000	10,500	286,500
Antilleans	99,000	–	99,000
Italians	33,000	17,600	15,400
(former) Yugoslavs	63,000	22,300	40,700
Spaniards	30,000	16,800	13,200
Somalians	27,000	8,900	18,100
Chinese	28,000	7,500	20,500
Indonesians	407,000	8,400	398,600
Other groups	1,163,000	339,800	823,200
Total	15,760,000	15,760,000	–

Republik. In 1982, the *Australian Institute of Multicultural Affairs* recognised the above-mentioned identification problems for inhabitants of Australia and proposed including questions on birth country (of person and parents), ethnic origin (based on self-categorisation in terms of which ethnic group a person considers him/herself to belong to) and home language use in their censuses. As yet, different experiences have been gained in EU countries with periodical censuses, and, if such censuses have been held, with questions on ethnicity or (home) language use. Given the decreasing significance of nationality and birth-country criteria, collecting reliable information about population groups in increasingly multicultural European nation-states has become one of the most challenging tasks facing demographers. In Table 5, the four criteria mentioned are discussed in terms of their major (dis)advantage.

First of all, Table 5 reveals that there is no simple solution to the identification problem. Moreover, inspection of the criteria utilised for statistics on multicultural population groups is as important as the actual figures themselves. Taken from a European perspective, there is a top-down development over time in the utility and utilisation of different types of criteria, inevitably going from nationality and birth-country criteria in present statistics to self-categorisation and home language in the future. The latter two criteria are generally conceived as complementary criteria. Self-categorisation and home language references

Table 5. Criteria for the definition and identification of population groups in a multicultural society (P/F/M = person/father/mother) (Extra and Yağmur 2004: 31)

Criterion	Advantages	Disadvantages
Nationality (NAT) (P/F/M)	– objective – relatively easy to establish	– (inter-generational) erosion through naturalisation or dual NAT – NAT not always indicative of ethnicity/identity – some (e.g., ex-colonial) groups have NAT of immigration country
Birth country (BC) (P/F/M)	– objective – relatively easy to establish	– inter-generational erosion through births in immigration country – BC not always indicative of ethnicity/identity – invariable/deterministic: does not take account of dynamics in society (in contrast of all other criteria)
Self-categorisation (SC)	– affective (hearts and minds) – emancipatory: SC takes account of a person's own conception of ethnicity/identity	– subjective by definition: also determined by the language/ethnicity of the interviewer and by the mono/multi-cultural spirit of times – multiple SC possible – historically charged, especially by World War II experiences
Home language (HL)	– HL is most significant criterion of ethnicity in communication processes – HL data are prerequisite for government policy in areas such as public information or education	– complex criterion: who speaks what language to whom and when? – language is not always a core value of ethnicity/identity – useless in one-person households, because of absence of interlocutors

need not coincide, as languages may be conceived to variable degrees as core values of ethnocultural identity in contexts of migration and minorisation.

7. The importance of language for identifying population groups

Complementary or alternative criteria for identifying population groups in a multicultural society have been suggested and used in countries with a longer immigration history, and, for this reason, with a longstanding history of collecting census data on multicultural population groups (Kertzer and Arel 2002). This holds in particular for non-European English-dominant immigration countries like Australia, Canada, South Africa, and the USA. To identify the multicultural composition of their populations, these four countries employ a variety of questions in their periodical censuses. In Table 6, an overview of the kernel array of questions is provided; for each country the given census is taken as the norm.

Both the type and number of questions are different for each of these countries. Canada has a prime position with the highest number of questions. Only three questions have been asked in all countries whereas two questions have been asked in only one country. Four different questions have been asked about language. The operationalisation of questions also shows interesting differences, both between and within countries over time (see Clyne 1991 for a discussion of methodological problems in comparing the answers to differently phrased ques-

Table 6. Overview of kernel census questions in four multicultural contexts (Extra and Yağmur 2004: 67)

Kernel questions in the census	Australia	Canada	South Africa	USA	Coverage
	2001	2001	2001	2000	
1 Nationality of respondent	+	+	+	+	4
2 Birth country of respondent	+	+	+	+	4
3 Birth country of parents	+	+	−	−	2
4 Ethnicity	−	+	−	+	2
5 Ancestry	+	+	−	+	3
6 Race	−	+	+	+	3
7 Mother tongue	−	+	−	−	1
8 Language used at home	+	+	+	+	4
9 Language used at work	−	+	−	−	1
10 Proficiency in English	+	+	−	+	3
11 Religion	+	+	+	−	3
Total of dimensions	7	11	5	7	30

tions in Australian censuses from a longitudinal perspective; see also Williams, this volume).

Questions about ethnicity, ancestry and/or race have proven to be problematic in all of the countries under consideration (see also Spencer 2006; Ansell and Solomos 2008). In some countries, ancestry and ethnicity have been conceived of as equivalent, cf. USA census question 10 in 2000: *What is this person's ancestry or ethnic origin?* Or, take Canadian census question 17 in 2001: *To which ethnic or cultural group(s) did this person's ancestors belong?* Australian census question 18 in 2001 only involved ancestry and not ethnicity, cf. *What is the person's ancestry?* with the following comments for respondents: *Consider and mark the ancestries with which you most closely identify. Count your ancestry as far as three generations, including grandparents and great-grandparents.* As far as ethnicity and ancestry have been distinguished in census questions, the former concept related most commonly to current self-categorisation of the respondent and the latter to former generations. The diverse ways in which respondents themselves may interpret both concepts, however, remains a problem that cannot be solved easily.

According to Table 6, South Africa remains as the only country where a racial question is asked instead of a question on ethnicity and/or ancestry. The paradox in South Africa is that questions on ethnicity are often considered to be racist, whereas the racial question (in terms of *Black/White/Coloured/Indian*) from the earlier Apartheid era has survived. Although the validity of questions about ethnicity, ancestry and/or race is problematic, at least one question from this cluster is needed to compare its outcomes with those of questions on language. The reason for this has been mentioned in Table 5: language is not always a core value of ethnicity/identity and multiculturalism may become under-estimated if reduced to multilingualism. For this reason, one or more questions derived from cluster 4–6 in Table 6 are necessary complements of one or more questions derived from cluster 7–10.

Whereas, according to Table 6, "ethnicity" has been mentioned in recent censuses of only two countries, four language-related questions have been asked in one to four countries. Only in Canada has the concept of "mother tongue" been included (census question 7). It has been defined for respondents as *the language first learnt at home in childhood and still understood*, whereas questions 8 and 9 were related to the language *most often* used at home/work. Table 6 shows the added value of language-related census questions for the definition and identification of multicultural populations, in particular the added value of the question on home language use compared to questions on the more opaque concepts of mother tongue and ethnicity. Although the language-related census questions in the four countries under consideration differ in their precise formulation and commentary, the outcomes of these questions are generally conceived as cornerstones for educational policies with respect to the teaching of English as a first or second language and the teaching of languages other than English.

Table 6 also shows the importance of comparing different groups with equal criteria. Unfortunately, this is often not the case in public or political discourse. Examples of such unequal treatment are references to *Poles vs. Jews, Israelis vs. Arabs, Serbs* and *Croatians vs. Muslims, Dutchmen vs. Turks* (for Dutch nationals with Turkish ethnicity), *Dutchmen vs. Muslims,* or *Islam vs. the West* (where does the West end when is the world a globe?). Equal treatment presupposes reference to equal dimensions in terms of Table 6.

From this overview, it can be concluded that large-scale home language surveys are both feasible and meaningful, and that the interpretation of the resulting database is made easier by transparent and multiple questions on home language use. These conclusions become even more pertinent in the context of gathering data on multicultural *school* populations. European experiences in this domain have been gathered in particular in Great Britain and Sweden. In both countries, extensive municipal home language statistics have been collected through local educational authorities by asking school children and/or parents questions about their oral and written skills in languages other than the mainstream language, and about their need for education in these languages.

An important similarity in the questions about home language use in these surveys is that the outcomes are based on reported rather than observed facts. Answers to questions on home language use may be coloured by the language of the questions themselves (which may or may not be the primary language of the respondent), by the ethnicity of the interviewer (which may or may not be the same as the ethnicity of the respondent), by the (perceived) goals of the sampling (which may or may not be defined by central state or local authorities), and by the spirit of the times (which may or may not be in favour of multiculturalism). These problems become even more evident in a school-related context in which pupils are respondents. Apart from the problems mentioned, the answers may be coloured by peer-group pressure and they may lead to interpretation problems in attempts to identify and classify languages on the basis of the answers given. For a discussion of these and other possible effects, we refer to Nicholas (1988) and Alladina (1993). The problems referred to are inherent characteristics of large-scale data gathering through questionnaires about language-related behaviour and can only be compensated by small-scale data gathering through observing actual language behaviour. Such small-scale ethnographic research is not an alternative to large-scale language surveys, but a necessary complement, as outlined in section 1. For a discussion of (cor)relations between the reported and measured bilingualism of IM children in the Netherlands, we refer to Broeder and Extra (1998).

Throughout the EU, it is common practice to present data on RM groups on the basis of (home) language and/or ethnicity, and to present data on IM groups on the basis of nationality and/or country of birth. However, *convergence* between these criteria for the two groups appears over time, due to the increasing period of migration and minorisation of IM groups in EU countries. Due to their prolonged/permanent stay, there is strong erosion in the utility of nationality or birth-country statistics. Given the decreasing significance of nationality and birth-country criteria in the European context, the combined criteria of self-categorisation (ethnicity) and home language use are potentially promising alternatives for obtaining basic information on the increasingly multicultural composition of European nation-states. The added value of home language statistics is that they offer valuable insights into the distribution and vitality of home languages across different population groups and thus raise the awareness of multilingualism. Empirically collected data on home language use also play a crucial role in education. Such data will not only raise the awareness of multilingualism in multicultural schools; they are in fact indispensable tools for educational policies on the teaching of both the national majority language as a first or second language and the teaching of minority languages (see Extra and Yağmur, this volume).

8. Linguistic landscaping

A recent approach to mapping and measuring linguistic diversity in a given area is the so-called *linguistic landscape* approach. Although the concept of linguistic landscape can have several meanings (Gorter 2006), we refer here to the much-quoted definition given by Landry and Bourhis (1997) who introduced the concept in a paper on ethnolinguistic vitality in Quebec. Linguistic landscape concerns the way in which "the language of public road signs, advertising billboards, street names, place names, commercial shop signs, and public signs on government buildings combines to form the linguistic landscape of a given territory, region or urban agglomeration" (Landry and Bourhis 1997: 25). If we follow this definition, the study of linguistic landscape becomes a new dimension in mapping and measuring linguistic diversity.

As Gorter (2006) observes, the presence of languages around us is often neglected: we do not pay much attention to the linguistic landscape that surrounds us. But the conformation of the linguistic landscape can be assumed to be a contributing factor in describing the language use characteristics of a given territory. In the same seminal paper, Landry and Bourhis (1997: 29) state that "the linguistic landscape may act as the most observable and immediate index of the relative power and status of the linguistic communities inhabiting a given territory". This statement underlines the informative and symbolic functions that the linguistic make-up and its conformation in multicultural, and thus multilingual, areas can have. The way in which the linguistic landscape is structured has an informative function because it signals the presence of specific linguistic communities within a given territory, represents their sociolinguistic composition, indicates the languages that may be used there, and provides information regarding the power and status attained by the languages involved. Furthermore, the presence and visibility of a language fulfils a symbolic function: it indicates a positive attitude on the part of ethnolinguistic groups towards their identity of origin. In this sense, the linguistic landscape can also be linked to the concept of "ethnolinguistic vitality" (Giles et al. 1977). The use of a language for social communication can be a sign of its level of vitality, and therefore represents one of the factors contributing to its maintenance (Barker and Giles 2002).

The term *linguistic landscape* came into use only recently. Although linguistic landscaping is a fairly new branch within sociolinguistic and applied linguistic studies, it enjoys a growing interest. Indicative of this growing interest is the fact that in recent conferences, such as those organised by the *European Second Language Association* (San Sebastian, Spain, 2002), the *International Association of Applied Linguistics* (Madison, USA, 2005), and at the *16th Sociolinguistic Symposium* (Limerick, Ireland, 2006), there were sessions organised specifically on the subject. A whole issue of the *International Journal of Multilingualism*, edited by Gorter (2006), deals with research on linguistic landscaping in different societies.

The places analysed to date, including some pioneering work before this field of research was really founded by Landry and Bourhis, have mainly been urban areas with a high density of plurilingualism (see Backhaus 2006 for detailed references). Investigations have concentrated primarily on those cities where the presence and contact of several languages has led to political and social conflict, such as Brussels (Tulp 1978; Wenzel 1996); Montreal (Monnier 1989; *Conseil de la Langue Française* 2000); Jerusalem (Rosenbaum et al. 1977; Spolsky and Cooper 1991), San Sebastian and Leeuwarden (Cenoz and Gorter 2006). Since the publication of Landry and Bourhis's work, new studies have looked at cities that had already been analysed (such as Jerusalem: Ben-Rafael et al. 2004, 2006, in a comparative approach), but also in other urban areas, such as Lira Town in Uganda (Reh 2004), Hong Kong, Vienna, Beijing, Washington and Paris (Scollon and Scollon 2003); Tokyo (Backhaus 2006, 2007); Bangkok (Huebner 2006).

Some studies aim to shed light on the power relations between social groups sharing the same space, and between their languages, the use of which is often a source of conflict (the city of Jerusalem and the State of Israel as a whole are a good example). Other studies seek to examine the practical effects of language policies adopted by countries where plurilingualism is a constant feature (e.g., the Basque country). Few studies have been carried out to date on the presence of IM languages in the signs of social communication in areas where IM groups have settled. Furthermore, there are very few sociolinguistic studies looking into the effects of contact between languages in social communication (Huebner 2006), while in plurilingual environments it is precisely such contact that often leads to mixed use of more than one code.

These are the reasons why we decided to include the linguistic landscaping approach in a volume dealing with mapping and measuring linguistic diversity. Thus there are chapters on RM and IM languages, but also on majority languages and on English as a global language. What interests us is the consideration of the linguistic landscape as one of the levels at which linguistic diversity can be observed and measured. This means observing the presence and visibility of languages within a given territory, making them "speak" in their various manifestations, in order to analyse the conditions and ways in which one or more languages (can) become visible and used within a space in which they are not the dominant languages or to which they do not traditionally belong, and how, through contact, languages and cultures are recreated.

Being a relatively new branch of research, the linguistic landscaping approach still has to be developed further. Because a consolidated methodology has yet to be established, various research projects carried out in a range of contexts around the world have produced results that cannot easily be compared. Thus there is a clear necessity to define a shared methodological paradigm. There are questions that remain to be answered regarding various aspects of the approach: from the definition of the (textual) units of analysis or the observation and sampling methods to data analysis and classification procedures, so as to ensure the comparability of different data (Gorter 2006). A multidisciplinary approach is needed that, while taking into account the contribution of sociolinguistics, also makes use of the tools and techniques of other disciplines, including statistics, geography and information technology.

Analysis of the linguistic landscape is one of the ways to obtain a set of data from which a comprehensive portrayal of the linguistic space can be derived, for the same point, for several points or for a sequence of points at a given location. This kind of mapping entails constant monitoring of sociolinguistic dynamics, and thus needs to rely on methods suitable for "triangulated" data collection from different perspectives. By linking "triangulated data", the mapping enables us to portray linguistic contact profiles in various contexts such as large urban areas and specific zones within them, small and medium-sized centres, and isolated areas.

Measuring linguistic diversity implies taking into account many different factors concerning the languages of different groups, investigating their level of use, maintenance or loss to differing degrees according to generation, types and networks of use, their capacity to exert pressure on the local linguistic repertoire and the creation of new forms deriving from contact and linguistic assimilation; but also the attitudes and behaviour both of the local dominant community, in terms of the pressure it exerts on dominated groups and their languages, and of the dominated groups themselves towards the dominant language.

9. Promoting plurilingualism at school: an inclusive approach

In Europe, language policy has largely been considered a domain which should be developed within the boundaries of each EU nation-state. Proposals for an overarching EU language policy were laboriously achieved and are non-committal in character (Coulmas 1991). The most important declarations, recommendations or directives on language policy, each of which concepts carries a different charge in the EU jargon, show a hierarchy in the recognition of the status of official EU languages, "indigenous" or RM languages and "non-territorial" or IM languages (in the decreasing order mentioned).

Bilingual education in majority languages and RM languages has been an area of interest and research for a long time (Baker 2001). More recently, local and global perspectives are taken into consideration that go beyond bilingualism for RM Groups and focus on plurilingualism and plurilingual education. Apart from majority and RM languages, the focus is commonly on the learning and teaching of English as a third language, and in this way on promoting trilingualism from an early age on (Cenoz and Genesee 1998; Cenoz and Jessner 2000; Beetsma 2002; Ytsma and Hoffmann 2003).

In March 1998, the Council of Europe's *European Charter for Regional or Minority Languages* came into operation. The Charter functions as an international instrument for the comparison of legal measures and facilities of member-states in this policy domain (Craith 2003) and is aimed at the protection and the promotion of "the historical regional or minority languages of Europe". The concepts of "regional" and "minority" languages are not specified in the Charter and IM languages are explicitly excluded from the Charter.

It is remarkable that the teaching of RM languages is generally advocated for reasons of cultural diversity as a matter of course, whereas this is rarely a major argument in favour of teaching IM languages. The 1977 guideline of the Council of European Communities on education for "migrant" children (*Directive 77/486*, dated 25 July 1977) is now completely outdated. It needs to be put in a new and increasingly multicultural context and it needs to be extended to pupils originating from non-EU countries who form the large part of IM children at European primary schools. Allocating special rights to one group of minorities and denying the same rights to other groups is hard to relate to the principle of equal human rights for everyone. Besides, most of the so-called "migrants" in EU countries have taken up the citizenship of the countries in which they live, and in many cases they belong to second or third generation groups. Against this background, there is a growing need for overarching human rights for every individual, irrespective of his/her ethnic, cultural, religious or language background. For a similar inclusive approach to IM and RM language rights we refer to Grin (1995).

There is a great need for educational policies in Europe that take new realities of multilingualism into account. Processes of internationalisation and globalisation have brought European nation-states to the world, but they have also brought the world to European nation-states. This bipolar pattern of change has led to both convergence and divergence of multilingualism across Europe. On the one hand, English is on the rise as the *lingua franca* for international communication across the borders of European nation-states at the cost of all other official state languages of Europe, including French. In spite of many objections against the hegemony of English (Phillipson 2003), this process of convergence will be enhanced by the extension of the EU to Eastern Europe. Within the borders of European nation-states, however, there is an increasing divergence of home languages due to large-scale processes of global migration and intergenerational minorisation. Although these two processes of convergence and divergence seem to be contradictory trends, they can actually be counterbalanced (Fishman 1989: 220).

The call for differentiation of the monolingual *habitus* of primary schools across Europe originates not only *bottom-up* from IM parents or organisations, but also *top-down* from supra-national institutions which emphasize the increasing need for European citizens with a trans-national and multicultural affinity and identity. Plurilingual competencies are considered prerequisites for such an affinity and identity. Both the European Commission and the Council of Europe have published many policy documents in which language diversity is cherished as a key element of the multicultural identity of Europe – now and in the future. This language diversity is considered to be a prerequisite rather than an obstacle for a united European space in which all citizens are equal (but not the same) and enjoy equal rights (Council of Europe 2000). The maintenance of language diversity and the promotion of language learning and plurilingualism are seen as essential elements for the improvement of communication and for the reduction of intercultural misunderstanding.

The European Commission (1995) opted in a so-called *Whitebook* for trilingualism as a policy goal for all European citizens. Apart from the "mother tongue", each citizen should learn at least two "community languages". In fact, the concept of "mother tongue" referred to the official languages of particular nation-states and ignored the fact that for many inhabitants of Europe mother tongue and official state language do not coincide. At the same time, the concept of "community languages" referred to the official languages of two other EU nation-states. In later European Commission documents, reference was made to one foreign language with high international prestige (English was deliberately not referred to) and one so-called "neighbouring language". The latter concept related always to neighbouring countries, never to next-door neighbours. UNESCO also adopted the term "multilingual education" in 1999 (*General Conference Resolution* 12) for reference to the use of at least three languages, i.e., the mother tongue, a regional or national language, and an international language in education.

In a follow-up to the European Year of Languages in 2001, the heads of state and government of all EU member-states gathered in March 2002 in Barcelona and called upon the European Commission to take further action to promote plurilingualism across Europe, in particular by the learning and teaching of at least two additional languages from a very young age (Nikolov and Curtain 2000). The resulting *Action Plan 2004–2006*, published by the European Commission (2003), may ultimately lead to an inclusive approach in which IM languages are no longer denied access to Europe's celebration of language diversity. A recent initiative, supported by the Council of Europe and coordinated by the European Centre for Modern Languages in Graz (Austria), is the *Valeur* project (*Valuing all languages in Europe*; www.ecml.at/mtpz/valeur). Its ambitions are to bring together information about educational provision in different parts of Europe for these languages, to focus on the outcomes of this provision for students by the time they have left school, to identify good practices and draw conclusions abut how provision can be developed, to promote a greater awareness of the issues involved, and to create a network to take forward new initiatives.

In particular the plea for the learning of three languages by all EU citizens, the plea for an early start to such learning experiences, and the plea for offering a wide range of languages to opt from, open the door to the above-mentioned inclusive approach. Although this may sound paradoxical, such an approach can also be advanced by accepting the role of English as *lingua franca* for intercultural communication across Europe. Against this background, the following principles are suggested for the enhancement of plurilingualism at the primary school level (see also Extra and Yağmur 2004: 406).

1 In the primary school curriculum, three languages are introduced for all children:
    – the official standard language of the particular nation-state (or in some cases a region) as a major school subject and the major language of communication for the teaching of other school subjects;
    – English as *lingua franca* for international communication;
    – an additional third language opted from a variable and varied set of priority languages at the national, regional and/or local level of the multicultural society.
2 The teaching of all these languages is part of the regular school curriculum and subject to educational inspection.
3 Regular primary school reports contain information on the children's proficiency in each of these languages.
4 National working programmes are established for the priority languages referred to under (1) in order to develop curricula, teaching methods and teacher training programmes.
5 Some of these priority languages may be taught at specialised language schools.

This set of principles is aimed at reconciling *bottom-up* and *top-down* pleas in Europe for multilingualism, and is inspired by large-scale and enduring experiences with the learning and teaching of English (as L1 or L2) and one *Language Other Than English* (LOTE) for all children in the State of Victoria, Australia (see Extra and Yağmur 2004: 99–105). The *Victorian School of Languages* in Melbourne has led to an internationally recognised break-through in the conceptualisation of multilingualism in terms of making provisions feasible and mandatory for all children (including L1 English-speaking children), in terms of offering a broad spectrum of LOTE provision (in 2005, more than 40 languages were taught), and in terms of governmental support for this provision derived from multicultural policy perspectives (see also Kipp, this volume).

When in the European context each of the above mentioned languages should be introduced in the curriculum and whether or when they should be subject or medium of instruction, has to be spelled out according to particular national, regional or local demands. Derived from an overarching conceptual framework, priority languages could be specified in terms of both RM and IM minority languages for the development of curricula, teaching methods and teacher training programmes. Moreover, the increasing internationalisation of pupil populations in European schools requires that a language policy be introduced for *all* school children in which the traditional dichotomy between foreign language instruction for indigenous majority pupils and home language instruction for IM pupils is put aside. Given the experiences abroad (e.g., the Victorian School of Languages in Australia), language schools can become centres of expertise where a variety of languages are taught, if the students' demand is low and/or spread over many schools. In line with the proposed principles for primary schooling, similar ideas could be worked out for secondary schools where learning more than one language is already an established curricular practice. The above-mentioned principles would recognise plurilingualism in an increasingly multicultural environment as an asset for all children and for society at large. The EU, the Council of Europe, and UNESCO could function as leading trans-national agencies in promoting such concepts. The UNESCO *Universal Declaration of Cultural Diversity* (updated in 2002) is highly in line with the views expressed here, in particular in its plea to encourage linguistic diversity, to respect the mother tongue at all levels of education, and to foster the learning of more than one language from the youngest age.

10.   Structure and contents of this book

This book deals with methodological issues and empirical findings in the domain of mapping linguistic diversity in a variety of multicultural contexts, both in Europe and abroad, and both at the level of nation-states and at the level of metropolitan cities. The book is organised in four Parts.

Part I offers an outline of the aims and rationale of this book (the present Chapter). In addition, *Poulain* deals with European migration statistics in terms of definitions, data and challenges. From a demographic point of view, it is already a strong challenge to provide reliable and cross-nationally comparable data on international migration in terms of non-national or foreign-born residents of European nation-states. Three different data sources are discussed for identifying and characterising such residents: administrative registers, censuses and statistical surveys. The demographic challenge becomes even stronger when it comes to inter-generational statistics for which the criteria of nationality and birth-country (of persons and parents) have become meaningless. As yet, only few direct statistical data sources exist across European nation-states, which can support research on the linkage between migration and (home) language use.

Part II deals with the mapping of regional languages in Europe and offers case studies on Welsh, Basque, and Frisian. *Williams* goes into the methodology and outcomes of the 2001 UK census for Welsh, into patterns of language change between successive censuses, and into policy applications of the outcomes.

Cenoz deals with the status of Basque in the Basque country in terms of the rationale, goals, methods and outcomes of research in four domains: language use, bilingual education, attitudes and visibility of the Basque language. *Gorter* offers methodological considerations and empirical outcomes on the status of Frisian in the Netherlands and presents comparative perspectives on Basque, Frisian, Irish and Welsh across Europe.

Part III deals with the mapping of immigrant languages in Europe and offers case studies on the distribution and vitality of immigrant languages at the level of large multicultural cities and European nation-states. *Extra and Yağmur* present the rationale, methodology and kernel outcomes of the cross-national and cross-linguistic *Multilingual Cities Project* carried out, from Northern to Southern Europe, in Göteborg, Hamburg, The Hague, Brussels, Lyon and Madrid. *Caubet* offers a detailed documentation of languages other than French in France, in particular Maghrebi Arab and Berber, originating from the three Western Maghrebi countries Tunisia, Algeria and Morocco. Although France has a strong tendency to see itself as monolingual French, Caubet goes into the existence of what is referred to as the other languages of France. The focus is on comparing the methods and outcomes of the 1999 family survey on language practices with the available region-specific *baccalauréat* data of INALCO on Arabic and Berber. *Lüdi* deals with census data on immigrant languages in Switzerland, a non-EU country with a strong record in collecting and analysing census data on (home) language use, including immigrant languages. *Barni* goes into the methodology and outcomes of mapping immigrant languages in Italy in terms of linguistic landscaping. The focus of the study is on the visibility of languages other than Italian in the streets of metropolitan Rome.

Part IV offers case studies of mapping linguistic diversity abroad, i.e., in the non-European contexts of Turkey, South Africa, Australia and Japan. *Brizić and Yağmur* offer the linkage between Parts III and IV of this book by focusing on mapping linguistic diversity in Turkey and on the effects of this diversity in the immigration context of Austria. Both large-scale quantitative data on the languages of Turkey and small-scale qualitative data on Turkish children's language use in Austria/Vienna are presented and discussed. *Van der Merwe and Van der Merwe* present and discuss the objectives, methodology and organisation of the *Linguistic Atlas of South Africa*. They compare the findings of the 1991 and 2001 census data on home language use at the national level of South Africa and at the metropolitan level of Cape Town, with a focus at both levels on the distribution and shift patterns of Afrikaans. *Kipp* deals with community languages in Australia as an effect of immigration and immigration policies. Derived from the outcomes of successive national censuses in Australia, data on languages other than English (LOTE) are presented and discussed in terms of language maintenance and shift. In addition, the focus is on LOTE in education and on the question how LOTE provision matches demography. *Backhaus* goes into the methodology and kernel results of research on the linguistic landscape of Tokyo/Japan, led by three basic research questions, i.e., linguistic landscaping by whom, for whom and changes over time.

References

Alladina, S. and V. Edwards (eds.)
   1991   *Multilingualism in the British Isles* (Volume 1: The older mother tongues and Europe; Volume 2: Africa, the Middle East and Asia). London/New York: Longman.

Alladina, S.
   1993   South Asian languages in Britain. In: G. Extra and L. Verhoeven (eds.), *Immigrant Languages in Europe*, 55–65. Clevedon: Multilingual Matters.

Alterman, H.
   1969   *Counting People. The Census in History*. New York: Harcourt, Brace & World.

Ammerlaan, T., M. Hulsen, H. Strating and K. Yağmur (eds.)
   2001   *Sociolinguistic and Psycholinguistic Perspectives on Maintenance and Loss of Minority Languages*. Münster/New York: Waxmann.

Ammon, U., K. Mattheier and P. Welde (eds.)
   1995   Europaïsche Identität und Sprachenvielfalt. *Sociolinguistica* 9. Tübingen: Max Niemeyer.

Ansell, A. and J. Solomos
   2008   *Race & Ethnicity: Key Concepts*. London: Routledge.

Baetens Beardsmore, H.
   1993   *European Models of Bilingual Education*. Clevedon: Multilingual Matters.

Backhaus, P.
   2006   Multilingualism in Tokyo: A look into the linguistic landscape.In: D. Gorter (ed.), *Linguistic Landscape. A New Approach to Multilingualism*, 52–66. Clevedon: Multilingual Matters.

Backhaus, P.
   2007   *Linguistic Landscapes: A Comparative Study of Urban Multilingualism in Tokyo*. Clevedon: Multilingual Matters.

Baker, C.
   2001   *Foundations of Bilingual Education and Bilingualism*. Clevedon: Multilingual Matters.

Barbour, S. and C. Carmichael
2000   *Language and Nationalism in Europe.* Oxford: Oxford University Press.

Barbour, S.
2000   Nationalism, language, Europe. In: S. Barbour and C. Carmichael (eds.), *Language and Nationalism in Europe*, 1–17. Oxford: Oxford University Press.

Barker, V. and H. Giles
2002   Who supports the English-only movement?: Evidence for misconceptions about Latino group vitality. *Journal of Multilingual and Multicultural Development* 23 (2): 353–370.

Bauböck, R., A. Heller and A. Zolberg (eds.)
1996   *The Challenge of Diversity. Integration and Pluralism in Societies of Immigration.* Avebury: European Centre Vienna.

Beetsma, D. (ed.)
2002   *Trilingual Primary Education in Europe.* Ljouwert: Fryske Akademie.

Ben-Rafael, E., E. Shohamy, M. Hasan Amara and N. Trumper-Hecht
2004   *Linguistic Landscape and Multiculturalism: A Jewish-Arab Comparative Study.* Tel Aviv: Tami Steinmetz Center for Peace Research, Tel Aviv University.

Ben-Rafael, E., E. Shohamy, M. Hasan Amara and N. Trumper-Hecht
2006   Linguistic landscape as symbolic construction of the public space: The case of Israel.In: D. Gorter (ed.), *Linguistic Landscape. A new Approach to Multilingualism*, 7–30. Clevedon: Multilingual Matters.

Blum, A.
2002   Resistance to identity categorization in France. In: D. Kertzer and D. Arel, *Census and Identity. The Politics of Race, Ethnicity, and Language in National Censuses*, 121–147. Cambridge: Cambridge University Press.

Bratt-Paulston, C. and D. Peckham (eds.)
1998   *Linguistic Minorities in Central and Eastern Europe.* Clevedon: Multilingual Matters.

Breatnach, D. (ed.)
1998   *Mini Guide to Lesser Used Languages of the European Union.* Dublin: EBLUL.

Broeder, P. and G. Extra
1998   *Language, Ethnicity and Education. Case Studies on Immigrant Minority Groups and Immigrant Minority Languages.* Clevedon: Multilingual Matters.

Cenoz, J. and F. Genesee (eds.)
  1998   *Beyond Bilingualism. Multilingualism and Multilingual Education.* Clevedon: Multilingual Matters.

Cenoz, J. and D. Gorter
  2006   Linguistic landscape and minority languages. In: D. Gorter (ed.), *Linguistic Landscape. A new Approach to Multilingualism*, 67–80. Clevedon: Multilingual Matters.

Cenoz, J. and U. Jessner (eds.)
  2000   *English in Europe. The Acquisition of a Third Language.* Clevedon: Multilingual Matters.

Centraal Bureau voor de Statistiek (CBS)
  2000   *Allochtonen in Nederland 1999.* Voorburg: CBS.

Clyne, M.
  1991   *Community Languages: The Australian Experience.* Cambridge: Cambridge University Press.

Cohn-Bendit, D. and Th. Schmid
  1992   *Heimat Babylon. Das Wagnis der Multikulturellen Demokratie.* Hamburg: Hoffmann & Campe.

Conseil de la Langue Française
  2000   *La Langue de l'Affichage à Montréal de 1997 à 1999.* Québec: CLF.

Coulmas, F.
  1991   *A Language Policy for the European Community. Prospects and Quandaries.* Berlin/New York: Mouton de Gruyter.

Council of Europe
  2000   *Linguistic Diversity for Democratic Citizenship in Europe. Towards a Framework for Language Education Policies. Proceedings Innsbruck (Austria) May 1999.* Strasbourg: Council of Europe.

Craith, M.
  2003   Facilitating or generating linguistic diversity. The European charter for regional or minority languages. In: G. Hogan-Brun and S. Wolff (eds.), *Minority Languages in Europe. Frameworks, Status, Prospects*, 56–72. Hampshire: Palgrave Macmillan.

De Vries, J.
  1990   On coming to our census: a layman's guide to demolinguistics. *Journal of Multilingual and Multicultural Development* 11 (1–2): 57–76.

Directive 77/486
  1977   *Directive 77/486 of the Council of the European Communities on the Schooling of Children of Migrant Workers.* Brussels: CEC.

Edwards, J.
  1985   *Language, Society and Identity*. Oxford: Basil Blackwell.

Edwards, J
  1994   *Multilingualism*. London: Routledge.

ELSN
  1996   *European Language Survey Network. A Comparative Analysis of Four Language Surveys (Ireland, Friesland, Wales & the Basque Country)*. Dublin: ITE.

Ethnologue
  2001   *Ethnologue: Languages of the World, 14th edition. [www.ethnologue.org]*

Euromosaic
  1996   *The Production and Reproduction of the Minority Language Groups of the EU*. Luxembourg: Office for Official Publications of the European Communities. [*www.uoc.edu/euromosaic*]

European Commission
  1995   *Whitebook. Teaching and Learning: Towards a Cognitive Society*. Brussels: COM.

European Commission
  2003   *Promoting Language Learning and Linguistic Diversity. An Action Plan 2004–2006*. Brussels: COM. [*www.europa.eu.int/comm/education/ policies/lang/languages/actionplan_en.html.*]

Extra, G. and D. Gorter
  2007   Regional and immigrant minority languages in Europe. In: M. Hellinger and A. Pauwels (eds.), *Handbook of Language and Communication: Diversity and Change*. Handbook of Applied Linguistics, Vol. 9, 15–52. Berlin/New York: Mouton de Gruyter.

Extra, G. and D. Gorter (eds.)
  2001   *The Other Languages of Europe. Demographic, Sociolinguistic and Educational Perspectives*. Clevedon: Multilingual Matters.

Extra, G. and Yağmur, K. (eds.)
  2004   *Urban Multilingualism in Europe: Immigrant Minority Languages at Home and School*. Clevedon: Multilingual Matters.

Fase, W., K. Jaspaert and S. Kroon (eds.)
  1992   *Maintenance and Loss of Minority Languages*. Amsterdam/Philadelphia: John Benjamins.

Fase, W., K. Jaspaert and S. Kroon (eds.)
  1995   *The State of Minority Languages. International Perspectives on Survival and Decline*. Lisse/Exton: Swets & Zeitlinger.

Fishman, J.
    1973   *Language and Nationalism. Two Integrative Essays*. Rowly, Mass.: New-
            bury House.

Fishman, J.
    1988   "English only": Its ghosts, myths, and dangers. *International Journal of
            the Sociology of Language* 74: 125–140.

Fishman, J.
    1989   *Language and Ethnicity in Minority Sociolinguistic Perspective*. Cleve-
            don: Multilingual Matters.

Giles, H. (ed.)
    1977   *Language, Ethnicity and Intergroup Relations*. London: Academic Press.

Giles, H., R. Bourhis, and D. Taylor
    1977   Towards a theory of language in ethnic group relations.In: H. Giles (ed.),
            Language, Ethnicity and Intergroup Relations, 307–348. London: Aca-
            demic Press.

Gogolin, I,
    1994   *Der Monolinguale Habitus der Multilingualen Schule*. Münster/New
            York: Waxmann.

Gogolin, I., S. Kroon, M. Krüger-Potratz, U. Neumann and T. Vallen (eds.)
    1991   *Kultur- und Sprachenvielfalt in Europa*. Münster/New York: Waxmann.

Gorter, D. (ed.)
    2006   *Linguistic Landscape. A New Approach to Multilingualism*. Clevedon:
            Multilingual Matters.

Gorter, D.
    1997   Social surveys of minority language communities. In: B. Synak and T.
            Wicherkiewicz (eds.), *Language Minorities and Minority Languages in
            the Changing Europe*, 59–76. Gdansk: University of Gdansk.

Gorter, D., J. Hoekstra, L. Jansma and J. Ytsma (eds.)
    1990   *Fourth International Conference on Minority Languages* (Vol. 1: General
            papers; Vol. 2: Western and Eastern European papers). Clevedon: Multi-
            lingual Matters.

Grin, F.
    1995   Combining immigrant and autochthonous language rights: a territorial
            approach to multilingualism. In: T. Skutnabb-Kangas and R. Phillipson
            (eds.), *Linguistic Human Rights. Overcoming Linguistic Discrimination*,
            31–48. Berlin/New York: Mouton de Gruyter.

Gubbins, P. and M. Holt
    2002   *Beyond Boundaries. Language and Identity in Contemporary Europe*.
            Clevedon: Multilingual Matters.

Haarmann, H.
1995   *Europäische Identität und Sprachenvielfalt.* Tübingen: Max Niemeyer.

Hammersley, M.
1992   *What's Wrong with Ethnography? Methodological Explorations.* London: Routledge.

Hogan-Brun, G. and S. Wolff (eds.)
2003   *Minority Languages in Europe. Frameworks, Status, Prospects.* Hampshire: Palgrave Macmillan

Huebner, T.
2006   Bangkok's linguistic landscapes: Environmental print, codemixing and language change. In: D. Gorter (ed.) *Linguistic Landscape. A New Approach to Multilingualism,* 31–51. Clevedon: Multilingual Matters.

Istituto della Enciclopedia Italiana
1986   *Linguistic Minorities in Countries Belonging to the European Community.* Luxembourg: Office for Official Publications of the European Communities.

Joseph, J.
2004   *Language and Identity: National, Ethnic, Religious.* Basingstoke: Palgrave Macmillan.

Kertzer, D. and D. Arel
2002   *Census and Identity. The Politics of Race, Ethnicity, and Language in National Censuses.* Cambridge: Cambridge University Press.

Krüger-Potratz *et al.*
1998   *"Fremdsprachige Volksteile" und Deutsche Schule.* Münster/New York: Waxmann.

Kruyt, A. and J. Niessen
1997   Integration. In: H. Vermeulen (ed.), *Immigrant policy for a multicultural society. A comparative study of integration, language and religious policy in five Western European countries.* Brussels: Migration Policy Group.

Lachapelle, R. and J. Henripin
1980   *La Situation Démolinguistique au Canada. Évolution Passée et Prospective.* Montréal: Institut de recherches politiques.

Landry R. and R. Y. Bourhis
1997   Linguistic landscape and ethnolinguistic vitality. An empirical study. *Journal of Language and Social Psychology* 16 (1): 24–49.

May, S.
2001   *Language and Minority Rights. Ethnicity, Nationalism and the Politics of Language.* London: Longman.

Miles, R. and D. Thränhardt (eds.)
   1995   *Migration and European Integration. The Dynamics of Inclusion and Exclusion.* London: Pinter Publ.

Monnier, D.
   1989   *Langue d'Accueil et Langue de Service dans les Commerces à Montréal.* Québec: Conseil de la Langue Française.

Nicholas, J.
   1988   British language diversity surveys (1977–1987). A critical examination. *Language and Education* 2: 15–33.

Nikolov, M. and H. Curtain (eds.)
   2000   *An Early Start. Young Learners and Modern Languages in Europe and Beyond.* Strasbourg: Council of Europe.

Oakes, L.
   2001   *Language and National Identity. Comparing France and Sweden.* Amsterdam/ Philadelphia: John Benjamins.

Phillipson, R.
   2003   *English-only Europe? Challenging Language Policy.* London/New York: Routledge.

Reh, M.
   2004   Multilingual writing. A reader-oriented typology - with examples from Lira Municipality (Uganda). *International Journal of the Sociology of Language* 170: 1–41.

Rosenbaum, Y., E. Nadel, R.L. Cooper and J.A. Fishman
   1977   English on Keren Kayemet Street. In: J.A. Fishman, R.L. Cooper and A.W. Conrad (eds.), *The Spread of English*, 179–196. Rowley: Newbury House.

Scollon, R. and S.W. Scollon
   2003   *Discourse in Place: Language in the Material World.* London/New York: Routledge.

Siguan, M.
   1990   *Linguistic Minorities in the European Economic Community: Spain, Portugal, Greece (Summary of the report).* Luxembourg: Office for Official Publications of the European Communities.

Spencer, S.
   2006   *Race and Ethnicity. Culture, Identity and Representation.* London: Routledge

Spolsky, B. and R. Cooper
   1991   *The Languages of Jerusalem.* Oxford: Clarendon Press.

Synak, B. and T. Wicherkiewicz (eds.)
  1997   *Language Minorities and Minority Languages in the Changing Europe.*
          Gdansk: University of Gdansk.

Taylor, Ch.
  1993   *Multikulturalismus und die Politik der Anerkannung.* Frankfurt: Fischer.

Tjeerdsma, R.
  1998   *Mercator Guide to Organizations.* Leeuwarden: Mercator Educa-
          tion/Fryske Akademy.

Tulp, S.M.
  1978   Reclame en tweetaligheid: Een onderzoek naar de geografische verspreid-
          ing van franstalige en nederlandstalige affiches in Brussel. *Taal en Sociale
          Integratie* 1: 261–288.

Van der Merwe, I.J.
  1989   Geolinguistics of Afrikaans in the metropolitan area of Cape Town. *South
          African Journal of Linguistics* 7: 92–96.

Van Londen, S. and A. de Ruijter
  1999   Ethnicity and identity. In: M. Foblets and C. Pang (eds.), *Culture, Ethnicity
          and Migration*, 69–79. Leuven/Leusden: Acco.

Wenzel, V.
  1996   Reclame entweetaligheid in Brussel: Een empirisch onderzoek naar de
          spreiding van Nederlandstalige en Franstalige affiches. In: Vrije Univer-
          siteit Brussel (ed.), *Brusselse Thema's* 3, 45–74. Brussels: Vrije Univer-
          siteit.

Ytsma, J. and C. Hoffmann (eds.)
  2003   *Sociolinguistic Perspectives on Third Language Acquisition.* Clevedon:
          Multilingual Matters.

European migration statistics: Definitions, data and challenges

Michel Poulain

1. Introduction

Migration and language are clearly linked issues, as every immigrant arriving in a new country may be considered as an additional person speaking an immigrant language and commonly learning a new language. Accordingly, the spatial pattern of the use of immigrant languages is shaped by patterns of immigration and the distribution of immigrants across the territory. Some characteristics of immigrants such as country of birth, citizenship at birth, year of immigration, country of previous residence or current citizenship, including the possible effects of naturalisation are essential to analyse population groups with foreign background.

2. Defining migration flows and population stock with foreign background

Migration is an event in which a person changes his or her *place of usual residence*. The latter is defined as the place where the person spends most daily periods of rest. In the case of international migration the change of the place of residence means a change of the country of usual residence. Accordingly and statistically speaking, if a person changes the country where he or she spends most daily periods of rest, this will be registered as international migration. The UN recommendations on International Migration Statistics (United Nations 1998) fixed the following definition for a so-called "long-term migrant":

> "long-term migrant": A person who moves to a country other than that of his or her usual residence for a period of at least a year (12 months), so that the country of destination effectively becomes his or her new country of usual residence. From the perspective of the country of departure the person will be a long-term emigrant and from that of the country of arrival the person will be a long-term immigrant.

Recently, the European Office for Statistics (*Eurostat*) and the Directorate General for Justice, Freedom and Security (DG JLS), on behalf of the EU Commission, presented a regulation adopted in July 2007 and demanding that the EU Member States provide statistical data on international migration based on the following definitions (Regulation (EC) No 862/2007 of the European Parliament and of the Council of 11 July 2007):

– "usual residence" means the place at which a person normally spends the daily period of rest, regardless of temporary absences for purposes of recreation, holiday, visits to friends and relatives, business, medical treatment or religious pilgrimage; or, if not available, the place of legal or registered residence
– "immigration" means the action by which a person establishes his or her usual residence in the territory of a Member State for a period that is, or is expected to be, of at least twelve months, having previously been usually resident in another Member State or a third country
– "emigration" means the action by which a person, having previously been usually resident in the territory of a Member State, ceases to have his usual residence in that Member State for a period that is, or is expected to be, of at least twelve months
– "immigrant" means a person undertaking an immigration
– "emigrant" means a person undertaking an emigration

There are two different key concepts in the regulation, i.e., migration and migrant: the first concept is related to events while the second concerns the person who takes part in these events. The statistical figures describing these two concepts should be similar even if an immigrant or an emigrant may be found as having experienced more than one immigration or emigration during the period of observation while he/she will only be counted as a migrant once. In practice, all the proposed concepts and definitions are not easy to implement except by organising strict border checks and a complete registration of border crossings. Only data such as this would allow us to compute the duration of stay spent by immigrants in the country or emigrants outside the country. However, even if such information were recorded, data on entries cannot systematically be matched with data on exits, and consequently the duration of stay cannot be calculated. Recording international migration at border crossings is often replaced by administrative registration at the place of residence in the new country. As a result, we can only rely on information about the intended duration of stay. Thus, the identification of international migration or international migrants is dependent on administrative rules governing the right to enter and to stay in a given country. Actual data collection in this field is clearly a by-product of administrative data collection, with little or no consideration for the relevant international statistical recommendations.

The concepts presented above supply the methodological basis for calculating international migration as events and international migrants as individuals, both identified during a reference period that is usually a calendar year. These are data on *migration flows*. Data on immigration or immigrants entering a given country during a specific year is available in the Eurostat Database, for instance. Similar data is proposed on emigration and emigrants leaving the country.

There is another way to consider the impact of migration by looking at the population with an immigration background or more generally with a foreign background. *Population stock* data are fundamentally different from *migration flow* data. Basically, migration flow data may be compared with a video recording of every migration event during a given period, while population stock data provides photographs of a given population at a given moment. In most countries, population data allow us to characterise the situation on December 31 or January 1 of a given year. Broadly speaking, the population with an immigration background will consist of all persons that ever immigrated into the country, all of whom were born abroad. However, obviously not all persons born abroad should be included as citizens of the country in question that were born abroad should be excluded. The concept of population with immigration background should be replaced by the concept of population with foreign background. Indeed, people may have a foreign background without ever having experienced immigration. Therefore, foreign background may be a more appropriate concept than immigration background.

How to define a person with a foreign background? How to identify and characterise statistically the population with foreign background within a multicultural society? This population is supposed to differ more or less widely from the rest of the population. There are two indicators most commonly used to define the population with foreign background living in a given country at a given time: citizenship and country of birth. The group of persons not holding citizenship of that country is often referred to as "foreign population" and the group of persons born abroad as "foreign-born population". The above-mentioned EU Regulation defines "citizenship" as the *particular legal bond between an individual and his or her state, acquired by birth or naturalisation, whether by declaration, option, marriage or other means according to the national legislation*. However, some persons may have multiple citizenships and it is therefore better to define the population with foreign citizenship as effectively consisting of those not holding the citizenship of the given country. Along similar lines, the country of birth is defined as *the country of residence (in current borders, if available) of the mother at the time of birth, or, if not available, the country (in current borders, if available), in which the birth took place.*

In addition, cross-tabulation between the two discussed types of information would be very useful as well as additional information on the citizenship at birth and the country of birth of the parents. However, in the current situation of available statistical data in the Eurostat Database, only registration of the population by country of citizenship is proposed on an annual basis while the population by country of birth is available only through census data.

3.   Sources for collecting data on migration

Three different data sources are used in Europe for identifying and characterising population groups with foreign background: administrative registers, censuses and statistical surveys.

3.1.   Administrative registers

In many EU countries statistical data on international migration and on the characteristics of the population with foreign backgrounds are based on statistical data extracted from administrative registers. These may be centralised population registers, aliens' registers or residence permit databases. Administrative registers represent a major data source. However, the rules applied are strictly linked to administrative regulations and are not necessarily in accordance with international statistical recommendations. The following variables may be available at the individual level in administrative data sources and may serve to identify and characterise the population with foreign backgrounds:

– current citizenship or nationality;
– ethnic nationality or race;
– citizenship at birth;
– current citizenship of the parents and their citizenship at birth;
– country of birth;
– country of birth of the parents;
– year of and age at immigration;
– previous citizenship in case of naturalisation.

Information on (home) language use is rarely considered in administrative registers but some residence permit data files may include language data.

Most of the data are collected on the basis of official documents like passports, birth records or entry visas. Some evidence, e.g., on ethnicity, race or language, may only be based on self-reported data. In practice, administrative registers can provide a solid basis for the identification of international migrants and characteristics of the population with foreign background but in most cases no information on language will be available, i.e., neither on source country language skills nor on target country language skills.

3.2. Censuses

In contrast to administrative data sources, censuses are statistical data source and are expected to follow the UN recommendations specified for Europe by the UN Economic Commission for Europe jointly with Eurostat (UNECE 2006). The census does not allow direct identification of international migration as it describes the population at a given moment in time. While administrative registers may help to count events like international migrations, which relate to population flows, censuses only characterise population stocks. The following questions asked in censuses may be used to identify and characterise the population with foreign backgrounds:

- country of current citizenship;
- country of citizenship at birth;
- country of birth;
- country of birth of the parents;
- race or ethnicity;
- year of arrival or duration of stay in the country;
- country of previous residence;
- country where living at a fixed time in the past.

Unlike administrative registers, censuses may include information on language and people may be asked questions with respect to the following dimensions:

- "mother tongue", often defined as the first language spoken in early childhood at home;
- "main language", often defined as the language which the person commands best;
- language(s) most currently spoken at home and/or at work;
- knowledge of language(s), defined as the ability to understand, speak, read and/or write one or more designated languages.

The 2010 census recommendations (UNECE 2006) suggest that at least two of the above-mentioned dimensions should be on language. Many language groups are small. It is therefore recommended that at least an open answer box be included for indicating any other language than the ones specified. Countries should explain the chosen concepts and definitions, and document the classification procedures for languages in the census documentation and reports. Classifications should be comprehensive and include highly specific language groups, separate languages, regional dialects as well as artificial and sign languages.

3.3.   Statistical surveys

Statistical surveys may include questions on country of citizenship and country of birth or questions about language that make it possible to identify and characterise the population with foreign backgrounds. Among these, the regular *Labour Force Survey*, carried out in all EU Member States under the responsibility of Eurostat, is worth mentioning. In 2008, this European survey will include an additional *ad hoc* module on labour market integration of immigrants and their descendants. People will be asked about the following:

- citizenship of the person at birth;
- country of birth of the parents;
- nationality at birth of the parents;
- reasons for migration (employment, family reunion, studies, political refugee ...);
- residence status of migrants (temporary/permanent resident permit ...);
- time spent in the host country since migration/continuity of stay;
- participation in the educational system of the host country;
- language skills.

Table 1 summarises the pros and cons for each type of data source. In addition, it is important to mention that only the legal population is accounted for, which means that illegal or under-documented migrants (in French *sans-papiers*) are generally not included in administrative registers while they may be included in censuses and some surveys.

Table 1. Potentialities of data sources for measuring international migration flows and population stocks with foreign backgrounds

Data sources	Administrative registers	Censuses	Statistical surveys
International migration flows	Full coverage of international migration except for illegal immigrants and only with indirect variables concerning language	Limited information on migration flows with some variables for identifying immigrants and possibly direct questions on language skills	No information on flows except in border crossing surveys like the *International Passenger Survey* in the UK
Population stocks with foreign background	Full coverage except for illegal migrants and only with indirect variables concerning language	Full coverage but not systematically including asylum seekers and illegal migrants and few language questions	Sample of the whole population with possible inclusion of a full set of questions on language

4. Availability, reliability and comparability of data on international migration

The availability, reliability and comparability of statistical data in the field of international migration were the three major topics for assessing the quality of statistics in the EU within the THESIM research project. THESIM is an acronym for *Towards Harmonised European Statistics on International Migration*, an EU research project established within the 6th Framework Programme of the EU. All findings of the project can be found in Poulain, Perrin and Singleton (2006). Here are the main conclusions of this research project for the topic under concern.

4.1. Availability

The first main conclusion emerging from this in-depth investigation is the relatively limited level of availability of migration statistics.

As far as migration flows are concerned, the annual numbers of immigration/emigration or similarly of immigrants/emigrants, so-called "migration flow statistics", are systematically unknown in countries like Estonia, Greece and Bulgaria, while available figures are often only very partial or indirect estimations in several other countries (in particular in France, Ireland, Malta, Poland, Portugal and Romania).

As for populations with foreign background, usually, only the number of persons by country of citizenship is available. Moreover, in many countries, this information is collected only through censuses, as a result of which only rough estimations can be produced on an annual basis between census years (Greece, Estonia, France, Ireland, Latvia, Lithuania, Malta, Poland, Portugal, Cyprus, Bulgaria and Romania). Such estimations are not reliable enough for a rapidly changing phenomenon like migration. The foreign-born population is often only available in census results, while in a limited number of countries like Denmark, France, Belgium and The Netherlands more specific population groups with foreign background have been identified and appropriate statistical data are currently produced.

Table 2 shows the situation with respect to the 2000 censuses in the 46 countries that are part of UNECE (which also includes countries outside Europe such as Canada, the United States, Australia and New-Zealand). In this table, all potential variables allowing identification of international migration or charac-

Table 2. Questions on international migration in the 2000 census for the 46 UNECE countries (UNECE, unpublished information)

Questions	Frequency	Proportion
Place of residence one year before census	24	52,2%
Place of residence five years before census	10	21,7%
Place of residence at another point in time	8	17,4%
Year of arrival	30	65,2%
Country of birth	43	93,5%
Country of birth of mother only	2	4,3%
Country of birth of both parents	6	13,0%
Citizenship	42	91,3%
Multiple citizenship	20	43,5%
Year of naturalisation	2	4,3%
Citizenship at birth	3	6,5%
Subjective reason for immigration	8	17,4%
Legal reason for immigration	3	6,5%
Ethnic/national groups	29	63,0%
Race	2	4,3%
At least one question on language	35	76,1%
Mother tongue	21	45,7%
Main language (defined as best spoken)	3	6,5%
Most spoken language	11	23,9%
Knowledge of language(s)	19	41,3%
Other question(s) on language	2	4,3%

terisation of the population with foreign background are considered, including questions on language. Data on current citizenship and on country of birth are collected in 42 and 43 of the 46 countries, respectively. Year of immigration as well as multiple citizenship holders are identified in half of the countries. Only three countries asked for data on citizenship at birth, which is a very useful source of information. Finally, three fourths of the countries included information on language but as in the case of international migration, the level of harmonisation of the questions asked is limited.

4.2.   Reliability and comparability

Even if availability is the first problem with statistics on international migration, reliability is certainly the main element to be improved. Low reliability is evident at intra-EU level when data are compared on migration flows between pairs of EU Member States, reported by both the country of origin and the country of destination. In fact, data collection on international migration is unique in demography in the sense that the same phenomenon, the same events (international migration) and the same people (international migrants) are counted by two different countries using two completely different data collection systems. The emigration figures produced by the countries of origin and the immigration figures collected by the countries of destination would be similar if the two data collection systems were to use identical definitions and the data were to be fully reliable. The idea to compare these pairs of figures by using a double-entry matrix is more than thirty years old. Such double-entry matrices have been produced annually by UNECE since 1972 and more recently by Eurostat. The two main proponents of using this tool to estimate the level of harmonisation of international migration flows are Kelly (1987) and Poulain (1999).

In this double-entry matrix two figures are proposed in each cell M (i, j) for the migration flow between a specific pair of countries i and j: the figure on immigration in the country of destination and that on emigration in the country of origin. Figure 1 shows an example of comparison of statistics for the migration flows between Italy and Germany in 2003.

The double-entry matrix is a very interesting tool for studying the reliability of statistical data on a general basis, especially in a case where, as everybody will agree, the reliability problem is a major one. In the field of population analysis and forcast, reliable international migration data are urgently needed. From a European policy point of view, international migration is an increasingly common phenomenon. In this context, Eurostat, UNECE and other international bodies pay a great deal of attention to the improvement of the overall reliability and comparability of international migration data.

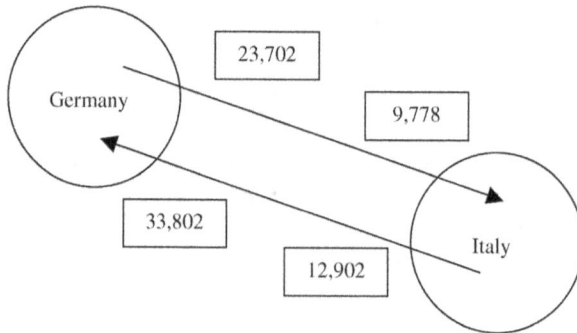

Figure 1. Migration flows between Italy and Germany in 2003: immigration in Germany (33,802) is compared with emigration in Italy (12,902) while emigration in Germany (23,702) is compared with immigration in Italy (9,778) (Eurostat Database)

This investigation of the intra-EU double-entry migration matrix demonstrates the weak comparability of the data. The same comparability problems probably affect data on the international migration of EU citizens outside the EU, as the same rules and practices apply. Fortunately, the immigration of non-EU citizens is better recorded in most EU Member States as a residence permit database may be used (directly or indirectly) to measure these flows. However, this is not valid for emigration.

How is it possible to explain so large differences between statistical figures supposed to describe the same migration flow? Despite existing international recommendations on harmonisation of definitions on international migration, the actually used definitions vary significantly between countries, within countries over time, and between sources of statistical information. Moreover, the definitions of immigration and emigration applied in a particular country do not necessarily match in terms of the time criterion. Consequently, the absence of harmonisation of definitions may be responsible for the poor comparability of data. Even if two countries are using the same definition to measure international migration flows, the problem of non-reliability of the data collection system may lead to very large differences between the two figures for the same migration flow. To assess the level of reliability we have to consider first of all the coverage of the data collection by identifying all sub-populations that are involved and those that are excluded. The latter will automatically lead to differences between corresponding statistical figures. It is also important to take into consideration that international migration refers to events that ideally should be reported by migrants themselves to local administrations when entering or leaving a country. For practical and financial reasons and in the absence of strict administrative rules, migrants may have particular reasons not to (want to) report. Accordingly, the figures for immigration and emigration will be under-estimated. In some countries, the level of under-registration may be as high as 90% for emigration. On another hand, immigration may be better registered for foreigners as there may be some advantages to registering, while for nationals returning to their home country registration may be useless.

By analysing these double-entry matrices, it becomes clear that in order to improve the overall comparability of international migration statistics the problem of poor reliability of international migration data collection systems in each country is certainly as important as that of the harmonisation of concepts. The reliability of migration flow statistics is very low in many EU Member States, and this explains why migration statistics are sometimes considered by experts as "less reliable social statistics". Because the comparability of international migration statistics is not guaranteed, it is difficult nowadays to produce comparative quantitative tables on international migration in Europe. Several international organisations such as UNECE, Eurostat and ILO launched initiatives in the last decades aimed at harmonising the main definitions (What is the usual resident population? What is an immigrant? What is an emigrant?). Recent improvements have been noticed, but the results are still limited and fundamental questions remain.

Stock data on population with foreign background are certainly more reliable and more comparable. However, data on population by country of citizenship cannot be directly compared between countries due to an obvious link between any national citizenship law and the size of the foreign population in each given country. There are countries that have a specific migration history like Latvia and Estonia or that have restrictive citizenship laws like Germany or Austria. In 1992, after the independence of Estonia and Latvia, an important part of the population did not apply for Estonian and Latvian citizenship, including people who were not citizens of another country, i.e., mainly members of the Russian minority. By contrast, there are relatively less foreigners in traditional countries of immigration with more liberal citizenship laws like France or the United Kingdom. Even if statistical data are available and reliable and even if statistical definitions are comparable, it may be difficult or nearly impossible to compare a basic indicator like the proportion of foreign citizens in EU Member States because the national legislations are often completely different for basic concepts like citizenship.

5.   What EU statistical data may reveal?

So far, only few global descriptive analyses of international migration flows concerning the EU have been developed. The weak reliability of the data as shown before is responsible for this and any comparative exercise would be incomplete and fragile. Even if the link between immigrant languages and international migration is evident, we have to restrict our investigations. We will focus on the main features that available statistical data on populations with foreign background will reveal. In order to identify such populations the key variable will be citizenship, even if there are certain comparability problems, as was explained before. The latest available data at the time of writing are summarised in Table 3 for 27 EU countries on January 1, 2005, including Bulgaria and Romania, even if these countries were not yet EU Member States at that time.

The data are extracted from the Eurostat Database and the figures in italics in the grey cells are our own estimations based on the only previous available figures, mostly derived from censuses (absolute figures are given in thousands of inhabitants). The first set of conclusions concerns foreign EU citizens living in another EU country, e.g., French citizens living in Germany.

– The smaller the country, the higher the proportion of foreign EU citizens living in this country. This is a common phenomenon as a smaller country will record relatively more international migrations than a large one.
– The central location of Belgium and Luxembourg in the EU and their respective roles in the EU account for the higher numbers of foreign EU citizens living in these countries.
– In contrast, countries like Greece, Portugal and Finland, which are the most distant from the geographical centre of the EU, clearly have lower proportions of foreign EU citizens. This may partly be explained by the fact that their geographical location involves more migrations with non-EU countries. Ireland, which was traditionally an emigration country, has recently been experiencing large immigration flows, mostly from new EU Member States, so that today it is showing an increasing proportion of foreign EU citizens compared to the proportion of non-EU citizens.
– The numbers of citizens of a given EU country living in all other EU countries can be compared to the number of foreign EU citizens living in that particular country itself (Table 4). As a direct consequence of the enlargement of the EU, Germany appears to be the most attractive country within Europe for people from other EU Member States. France, Spain and Belgium follow and precede the United Kingdom and Luxembourg. Sweden heads another group of countries that appear to be attractive at a slightly lower level. At

Table 3. Non-national populations in the EU Member States on January 1, 2005 (all absolute figures provided in thousands)

	Total population	Non-nationals	% Non-nationals	Foreign EU citizens	Foreign non-EU citizens	% Non-EU citizens	Largest foreign population	Largest non-EU population
Belgium	10,445.9	870.9	8.3	599.7	271.2	31.1	Italy	Morocco
Bulgaria	7,801.3	25.6	0.3	3.9	21.7	84.9	Russia	Russia
Czech Republic	10,220.6	254.3	2.5	87.3	167.0	65.7	Ukraine	Ukraine
Denmark	5,411.4	267.6	4.9	70.0	197.6	73.8	Turkey	Turkey
Germany	82,500.8	7,288.0	8.8	2,212.1	5,075.9	69.6	Turkey	Turkey
Estonia	1,347.0	250.0	18.6	5.0	245.0	98.0	Russia	Russia
Greece	11,075.7	900.0	8.1	157.1	742.9	82.5	Albania	Albania
Spain	43,038.0	3,371.4	7.8	1,070.7	2,300.7	68.2	Ecuador	Ecuador
France	60,561.2	3,500.0	z5.8	1,314.0	2,186.0	62.5	Portugal	Algeria
Ireland	4,109.2	295.0	7.2	200.0	95.0	32.2	UK	USA
Italy	58,462.4	2,402.2	4.1	470.9	1,931.3	80.4	Albania	Albania
Cyprus	749.2	98.1	13.1	58.9	39.2	40.0	Greece	Russia
Latvia	2,306.4	487.2	21.1	4.8	482.4	99.0	Russia	Russia
Lithuania	3,425.3	32.3	0.9	1.5	30.8	95.4	Russia	Russia
Luxembourg	455.0	177.4	39.0	152.9	24.5	13.8	Portugal	Serb/Mont.
Hungary	10,097.5	143.8	1.4	82.2	61.6	42.9	Romania	Ukraine
Malta	402.7	12.0	3.0	8.0	4.0	33.3	UK	India
Netherlands	16,305.5	699.4	4.3	233.1	466.3	66.7	Turkey	Turkey
Austria	8,206.5	788.6	9.6	235.1	553.5	70.2	Serb/Mont.	Serb/Mont.
Poland	38,173.8	700.0	1.8	16.0	684.0	97.7	Germany	Ukraine
Portugal	10,529.3	265.0	2.5	78.2	186.8	70.5	Capo Verde	Capo Verde
Romania	21,712.6	40.8	0.2	9.4	31.4	76.9	Moldova	Moldova
Slovenia	1,997.6	44.3	2.2	1.4	42.9	96.8	Bosn/Herz.	Bosn/Herz.
Slovakia	5,384.8	22.3	0.4	11.9	10.4	46.4	Czech Rep.	Ukraine
Finland	5,236.6	108.3	2.1	36.2	72.1	66.5	Russia	Russia
Sweden	9,011.4	481.1	5.3	212.1	269.0	55.9	Iraq	Iraq
UK	60,034.5	3,066.1	5.1	1,173.9	1,892.2	61.7	Ireland	India
EU 27	489,002.2	26,591.6	5.4	8,506.1	18,085.5	68.0		

Table 4. Comparison of the number of citizens of a given EU country living in another EU country and the number of foreign EU citizens living in that country (countries are ranked by decreasing Chi^2 differences between observed and expected figures)

	Citizens living in another EU country	Foreign EU citizens living in the country	Chi^2 differences
Immigration countries			
Germany	623,280	2,190,253	1,321
France	491,190	1,182,066	755
Spain	437,080	1,046,593	708
Belgium	180,635	599,640	671
United Kingdom	657,527	1,161,659	529
Luxembourg	17,019	136,450	431
Sweden	103,969	211,390	271
Czech Republic	65,182	87,000	79
Cyprus	29,877	36,745	38
Austria	227,325	233,795	13
Emigration countries			
Hungary	88,793	82,054	−23
Malta	7,491	4,000*	−46
Denmark	92,878	69,398	−82
Latvia	22,879	4,808	−154
Estonia	27,421	4,023	−187
Slovenia	31,857	1,418	−236
Netherlands	359,618	206,980	−287
Finland	137,960	36,104	−345
Lithuania	66,177	1,462	−352
Slovak Republic	116,349	11,843	−413
Ireland	409,968	146,369	−500
Greece	399,523	134,445	−513
Bulgaria	212,390	3,861	−634
Italy	1,179,657	465,698	−787
Poland	631,751	15,193	−1,084
Portugal	930,135	65,402	−1,226
Romania	773,242	5,889	−1,229

* Estimated figure as no data is officially available

the opposite end of the spectrum, Romania may be considered as the largest emigration country, before Portugal and Poland.

– Finally, the preference for citizens of a given EU country to live in another EU country may be assessed by comparing actual figures with expected figures obtained through a simple bi-proportional model. The estimated figure

Table 5. Largest Chi^2 differences between observed and expected figures of foreign EU citizens living in another EU country (in 2005)

	Country of citizenship	Country of residence	Chi^2 differences
1	Portugal	Luxemburg	17,121
2	Ireland	United Kingdom	13,506
3	Portugal	France	12,462
4	Finland	Sweden	7,536
5	Greece	Germany	5,948
6	Romania	Spain	5,353
7	Netherlands	Belgium	4,616
8	Italy	Germany	4,434
9	Belgium	Luxembourg	4,198
10	Italy	Belgium	4,147
11	Romania	Italy	3,973
12	Austria	Germany	3,806
13	United Kingdom	Ireland	3,760
14	Cyprus	Greece	3,487
15	Estonia	Finland	3,042

using the bi-proportional model is proportional to the product of the total population of the two countries concerned, so that the total number of expected figures will be equal to the total number of observed figures. The largest Chi^2 differences are presented in Table 5 and show that Portuguese citizens in Luxembourg and France, Irish citizens in the United Kingdom, and Finnish citizens in Sweden are the most extreme cases. Without considering neighbouring countries, we can also observe a preponderance of Italians and Greeks in Germany, Italians in Belgium and Romanians in Spain and Italy.

The second group of conclusions concerns the total number of non-EU citizens living in every EU country. When we compare the proportion of non-nationals in each EU country (Table 3), the figures show large differences, with the highest value for Luxembourg (39%) and the lowest values for Romania, Bulgaria, the Slovak Republic and Lithuania. For historical reasons, Latvia (21.1%) and Estonia (18.6%) also show high proportions due to their significant Russian communities. Three traditional immigration countries, i.e., Austria (9.6%), Germany (8.8%) and Belgium (8.3%), stand beside Luxembourg as other major immigration countries. Greece (8.1%) and Spain (7.8%), two new immigration countries, have joined this group. France (5.8%), Sweden (5.3%), Denmark (4.9%) and Italy (4.1%), another new immigration country, come next. When we consider

Table 6. Number of non-EU citizens living in the EU compared to the total population of each country in 2005 (The number of non-EU citizens is extracted from the Eurostat database while the total population figures were found on the UN Statistical Division website)

Country	Number of citizens living in the EU	Total population of the country	Ratio
Albania	784,845	3,129,678	25.1%
Cape Verde	72,088	506,807	14.2%
F.Y.R of Macedonia	194,155	2,034,060	9.5%
Bosnia and Herzegovina	337,901	3,907,074	8.6%
Croatia	332,368	4,551,338	7.3%
Serbia and Montenegro	756,911	10,502,224	7.2%
San Marino	1,831	28,117	6.5%
Iceland	18,352	294,561	6.2%
Sao Tome and Principe	8,039	156,523	5.1%
Morocco	1,522,130	31,819,881	4.8%
Ecuador	510,995	13,228,423	3.9%
Mauritius	45,581	1,244,663	3.7%
Barbados	9,450	269,556	3.5%
Seychelles	2,770	80,654	3.4%
Turkey	2,333,807	73,192,838	3.2%

the share among the non-nationals of EU citizens and non-EU citizens, the proportion of non-EU citizens is very low in Luxembourg (13.8%) and relatively low in Belgium (31.1%) and Ireland (32.2%). In all other EU countries, except for Malta, Cyprus and Hungary, this indicator is higher than 50% and peaks at over 95% in the three Baltic States, Poland and Slovenia.

If only non-EU citizens are taken into consideration, the number of people who are living in any of the EU Member States can be compared by considering the total population of the country of origin (Table 6).

Albania clearly has the largest part of the population that emigrated to the EU. The number of Albanese citizens in the EU amounts to one fourth of the total population of Albania. All former Yugoslavian Republics, except Slovenia, which nowadays is a EU Member State, have an average ratio of one citizen living in the EU to twelve citizens living in their home country. Some smaller islands like Capo Verde, Sao Tome and Principe, Iceland, Mauritius, Barbados and the Seychelles also have a high ratio. Also large populations, like those from Morocco, Ecuador and Turkey, figure also at the top of this ranking. These are clearly the three largest non-EU communities in the EU with 1.5, 0.5 and

Table 7. Largest *Chi²* differences between observed and expected numbers of non-EU citizens living in EU Member States in 2005

	Country of citizenship	Country of residence	Chi² differences
1	Albania	Greece	3,151
2	Russia	Estonia	2,359
3	Turkey	Germany	2,186
4	Ecuador	Spain	1,909
5	Algeria	France	1,497
6	Colombia	Spain	1,338
7	Capo Verde	Portugal	1,294
8	Bosnia Herzegovina	Austria	1,136
9	Serbia Montenegro	Austria	1,112
10	Serbia Montenegro	Germany	1,063
11	Argentina	Spain	1,031
12	Morocco	Spain	897
13	Norway	Sweden	853
14	Guinee Bisau	Portugal	815
15	Senegal	Luxembourg	733

2.3 million citizens, respectively, or in relative numbers 4.8%, 3.9% and 3.2% compared to the total populations of these countries.

Finally, the observed number of citizens from every non-EU country in every EU Member State can be compared with the expected number based on a simple proportional model. In the model, the expected number of citizens from a non-EU country on the territory of a given EU Member State is proportional to the number of citizens of that country in the whole EU and to the total population of the EU Member State concerned, so that the expected total number of non-EU citizens will be similar to that which is observed. To give an example, imagine that the 1.5 million Moroccan citizens were distributed among the EU countries simply according to the population of each of these countries. We consider that 8% of the EU population was living in Spain in 2005, which would make the expected number of Moroccan citizens in Spain about 120,000 compared to the observed number of 400,000. Table 7 shows the largest positive *Chi²* differences between observed and expected figures. These positive differences indicate the preference of people with that specific citizenship to live in that specific EU country.

Clearly, Albanese have a preference for Greece, the neighbouring country. For historical reasons, Russian citizens are numerous in Estonia. Turks in Germany follow with Ecuadorians and Colombians in Spain, Algerians in France

Table 8. Distribution of Moroccan and Turkish citizens in all EU Member States

	Morocco	%	Turkey	%
Belgium	81,279	5.34%	39,885	1.71%
Bulgaria	26	0.00%	1,015	0.04%
Czech Republic	143	0.01%	520	0.02%
Denmark	2,902	0.19%	29,956	1.28%
Germany	73,027	4.80%	1,764,318	75.60%
Estonia	1	0.00%	6	0.00%
Greece	526	0.03%	7,881	0.34%
Spain	461,544	30.32%	1,347	0.06%
France	506,305	33.26%	205,589	8.81%
Ireland	161	0.01%	456	0.02%
Italy	294,945	19.38%	11,077	0.47%
Cyprus	11	0.00%	35	0.00%
Latvia	2	0.00%	38	0.00%
Lithuania	1	0.00%	56	0.00%
Luxembourg	252	0.02%	207	0.01%
Hungary	32	0.00%	629	0.03%
Netherlands	91,558	6.02%	100,574	4.31%
Austria	749	0.05%	116,882	5.01%
Poland	64	0.00%	180	0.01%
Portugal	660	0.04%	111	0.00%
Romania	0	0.00%	2,173	0.09%
Slovenia	3	0.00%	31	0.00%
Slovak Republic	11	0.00%	120	0.01%
Finland	621	0.04%	2,359	0.10%
Sweden	1,510	0.10%	12,269	0.53%
United Kingdom	5,797	0.38%	36,093	1.55%
Total	1,522,130	100.00%	2,333,807	100.00%

and citizens from Capo Verde in Portugal. Former-Yugoslavian citizens are more numerous in Germany and in Austria. Moroccans will be found in larger proportions in France, Belgium and the Netherlands, while for Indians, Pakistanis and USA citizens the same will occur in the United Kingdom. In addition, the absolute and proportional distributions of Moroccan and Turkish citizens in the 27 EU Member States is presented in Table 8.

6. Typology of populations with foreign backgrounds

An increasing problem for defining populations with foreign background is linked to the fact that country of citizenship and country of birth are no longer appropriate variables for identifying immigrant populations and their descendents. Accordingly, as expressed by Extra and Gorter (2001: 8), "collecting reliable information about the composition of immigrant groups in EU countries is one of the most challenging tasks facing demographers". The notion of foreign background is very complex and in order to define this concept within a statistical framework, particular objective criteria have to be selected. Each of the following variables separately cannot be sufficient to propose an appropriate typology of the population with foreign background. Such a typology would result from a conjunction of several criteria, keeping in mind that quite often certain information is simply not available and the corresponding variable cannot be used:

– country of citizenship;
– citizenship at birth;
– citizenship of parents at birth;
– citizenship of grandparents and ancestors;
– country of birth;
– country of birth of parents;
– country of birth of grandparents and ancestors;
– ethnic affiliation or attachment to a distinct ethnic group;
– language repertoire with various definitions;
– physical characteristics such as colour of skin or race, as accepted in the US or South Africa.

A typology will never succeed at including all these characteristics together. For a specific country, some variables may be essential or have only little impact. Moreover, being considered as a member of a distinct ethnic group may be accepted in some countries like the United Kingdom while it may be completely unacceptable in other countries like France. In practice, if some of these criteria were to have an important negative impact on the daily lives of the person(s) concerned, their use and the development of an *ad hoc* typology could be really awkward. In these cases, such a typology might be rejected in order to avoid discrimination evolving from such a classification. Finally, if these variables were to be collected through questions in censuses or surveys, self-reported answers might introduce particular biases. In this situation it might even appear impossible to statistically identify populations with foreign background.

Officially, most EU countries prefer to provide and use statistics on citizenship, in spite of several attempts aimed at proposing a more appropriate classification. The use of the country of birth is less common. Within Europe, the Nordic countries and the Netherlands use typologies based on the country of birth including that of the parents. In the United Kingdom and the United States, race and/or ethnicity are commonly used, while in some Central European countries the concept of "ethnic nationality" is preferred. In conclusion, any typology would be specific to the information available in a given country but also to the perception of each of the variables used to build this typology.

As scientific support for policy development and to provide a better insight into the diversity of the population with foreign backgrounds, we have developed such typology for Belgium. Based on the data extracted from the *National Population Register* and the last censuses carried out in 1991 and 2001 the following variables can be obtained:

- current citizenship;
- all changes of citizenship from 1991 onwards;
- citizenship at birth as reported in the 1991 census if the person was counted/registered;
- country of birth;
- year of first immigration into the country as reported in the 1991 census for those living in the country at that time;
- year of first immigration into the country as recorded in the *National Population Register* for those who immigrated since 1991.

The proposed typology does not take into consideration the characteristics of parents. However, it has been possible to identify children who received Belgian citizenship at birth but who have at least one parent with a foreign background. Based on this information it is possible to identify some groups on the basis of a distinction between the following groups:

- persons currently holding Belgian citizenship or not;
- persons holding Belgian citizenship at birth or not;
- foreigners who have been naturalised or not;
- foreigners born abroad who immigrated to Belgium and foreigners born in Belgium;
- immigrated persons according to their age at the time of immigration and their duration of stay in the country.

Table 9 presents a comparison of the population with any kind of foreign background and comparatively the population with a Moroccan background on the same date. A distinction is made between different types of immigrants in terms of age at arrival and duration of stay. Figure 2 shows the evolution of different

Table 9. Typology of population with foreign background developed for Belgium. Comparative figures for population with any foreign background vs. Moroccan background on January 1, 2005 (Source of data: INS, Registre National. Typology and calculations done by GéDAP–UCL)

	All people with foreign background	People with Moroccan background	% All	% Moroccan
Total	2,022,548	299,283	100.0	100.0
Belgian citizenship at birth	451,525	56,448	22.3	18.9
Of whom both parents are of a foreign origin	105,760	35,822	5.2	12.0
Of whom only the father is of foreign origin	196,015	15,481	9.7	5.2
Of whom only the mother is of foreign origin	149,750	5,145	7.4	1.7
No Belgian citizenship at birth	1,571,023	242,835	77.7	81.1
Of whom born in Belgium	505,756	105,004	25.0	35.1
Of whom not naturalised	173,282	16,154	8.6	5.4
Of whom naturalised	332,474	88,850	16.4	29.7
Of whom born abroad and immigrants	1,065,267	137,831	52.7	46.1
Of whom not naturalised	698,128	65,197	34.5	21.8
Immigrated during the past 5 years, aged up to 12	32,504	1,847	1.6	0.6
Immigrated during the past 5 years, aged over 12	212,056	31,482	10.5	10.5
Immigrated more than 5 years ago, aged up to 12	107,726	5,883	5.3	2.0
Immigrated more than 5 years ago, aged over 12	345,842	25,985	17.1	8.7
Of whom naturalised	367,139	72,634	18.2	24.3
Immigrated during the past 5 years, aged up to 12	4,925	566	0.2	0.2
Immigrated during the past 5 years, aged over 12	8,239	2,223	0.4	0.7
Immigrated more than 5 years ago, aged up to 12	129,006	19,510	6.4	6.5
Immigrated more than 5 years ago, aged over 12	224,969	50,335	11.1	16.8

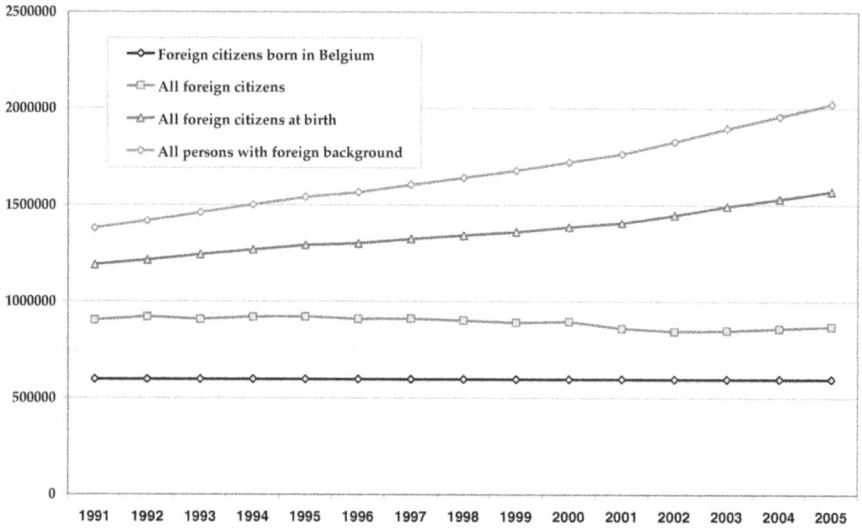

Figure 2. Evolution of different sub-populations with foreign background according to the proposed methodology (Source of data: INS, Registre National. Typology and calculations done by GéDAP–UCL)

sub-groups and makes it possible to follow the population with foreign background in Belgium from 1991 until 2005.

While the number of foreign citizens, both those who are born in Belgium or abroad, is very stable in Belgium, the number of persons not holding Belgian citizenship at birth is increasing. This increase is even larger when we consider all persons with foreign background.

Finally, Figure 3 presents in white the age and gender structure of total population with foreign background and, among them, in grey, the foreign population not holding Belgian citizenship. The differences which are larger for young generations than for the older ones are due to higher naturalisation rates and to the large number of children having a foreign background but having received Belgian citizenship at birth.

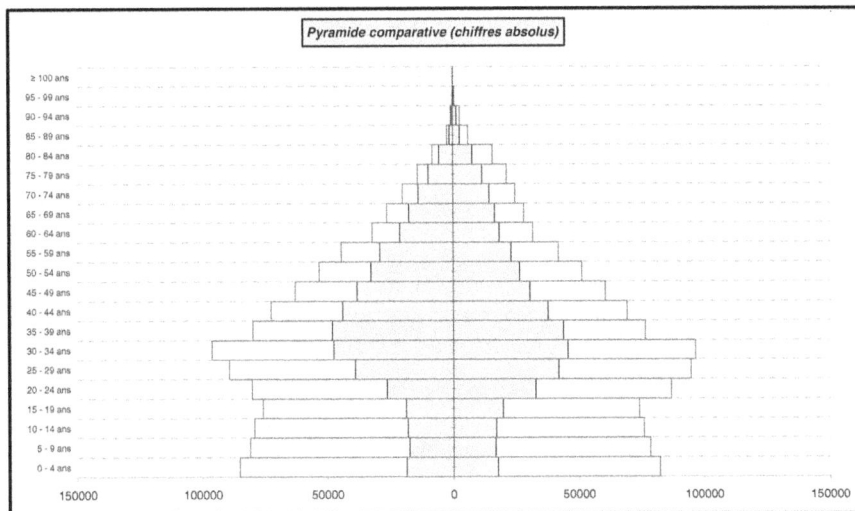

Pyramide comparative (chiffres absolus)

Figure 3. Age and gender structure of the foreign population not holding Belgian citizenship (in grey) and the whole population with any kind of foreign background on January 1, 2005 (Left: males, right: females) (Source of data: INS, Registre National. Typology and calculations done by GéDAP–UCL)

7. Conclusions

As far as migration is concerned, a basic distinction should be made between migration events that occur during a particular period of observation (migration *flows*) and *stocks* of population with foreign background that can be identified and characterised at a given point in time, most commonly at times when censuses are held. Data on migration flows are not always available and if they are, they are often unreliable. Moreover, as long as different definitions keep on being used, it is clear that international migration statistics are not comparable. There is no agreement on how to develop an appropriate typology for populations with foreign backgrounds and most EU countries only consider populations by country of citizenship. Based on this criterion, some analyses have been proposed to characterise how foreigners, both EU citizens and non-EU citizens, are distributed across the EU Member States. In the case of Belgium, a more complex typology has been proposed, based on different variables extracted from administrative population registers and censuses. As yet, only few direct statistical data sources exist that can support research on the link between migration and (home) language use.

References

Eurostat database

> *http://epp.eurostat.ec.europa.eu/portal/page?_pageid=0,1136184,0_*
> *45572595&_dad= portal&_schema=PORTAL*

Extra, G. and D. Gorter (eds.)
2001   *The Other Languages of Europe*. Clevedon: Multilingual Matters.

Kelly, J.
1987   Improving the comparability of international migration statistics: Contributions to the Conference on European Statisticians from 1971 to Date. *International Migration Review* 21: 1017–1037.

Poulain, M.
1999   *Confrontation des statistiques de migration intra-européennes: vers une matrice complète?* Eurostat Working Paper No. 3/1999/E/No. 5. Bruxelles/Luxembourg: Eurostat.

Poulain, M., N. Perrin. and A. Singleton (eds.).
2006   THESIM. *Towards Harmonised European Statistics on Migration*. Louvain-la-Neuve: Presses universitaires de Louvain.

UNECE
2006   *Recommendations for the 2010 census of population and housing* (jointly prepared by the United Nations Economic Commission for Europe and the Statistical Office of the European Communities).

United Nations, Department of Economic and Social Affairs, Statistics Divisions
1998   *Recommendations on Statistics of International Migration*, revision 1, United Nations, Department of Economic and Social Affairs, Statistics Division, N° ST/ESA/STAT/SER.M/REV.1 Pub. Order No. 98.XVII.14.

Section II
Mapping regional languages in Europe

The Welsh language in the United Kingdom: Beyond cartography

Colin Williams

1. Mapping the Welsh language – previous research

The predominant data source for geolinguistic analysis in Wales has been the decennial UK census. Typically analysts have used the census to develop ideas about the spatial representation of Welsh, reflecting either demographic trends or as an expression of a unique marker of sociolinguistic interaction between the Welsh and English languages. Since the early 1950s geographers have used the mapped representation of Welsh as a template upon which they could construct explanatory theories related to cultural change, rural social problems and the shaping of national political consciousness.

1.1. Data

Aggregate data from censuses conducted since 1901 have informed studies describing the spatial and temporal patterns and changes in the Welsh language. Such studies ranged from simple descriptive univariate analyses to sophisticated multivariate analyses and GIS mapping of language in context (e.g., Aitchison and Carter 1994, 1998, 1999a, 2000; Carter and Aitchison 1986; Jones 1999; Williams 1981, 1980, 1987; Pryce and Williams 1988). It is not my intention to report on cartographic developments here, rather I wish to focus on data characteristics.

As reported in Higgs, Williams and Dorling (2004) for the period 1901–1991, there was a constant decrease in the percentage of the population able to speak Welsh, although rates of decline have slowed since 1961 (1961–1971 fall of 17.3%; 1971–1981 6.3% and 1981–1991 1.4% (Aitchison and Carter 1999b)). This has been attributed to a significant increase in the percentage of young people (age 3–15) able to speak Welsh, especially in the southeast of Wales, which contrasts with the fall in the proportions of those over 15 who can speak Welsh. Previous analysis has drawn attention to the contraction and fragmentation of the areas within which the language is dominant (Aitchison and Carter 1999b). Multivariate analysis has been used to describe culture areas, the incidence of distinct Welsh social features and the socio-political contexts which were associated with different political parities, social classes, bilingual education and religious denominations and faiths (Williams 1979). Maps derived from the 1981 Census, as used by Aitchison and Carter (1985), identified clusters of wards where over 70% of the population could speak Welsh, largely in areas of north and west Wales. In other work, Aitchison and Carter (1986) used the Census to compare changes between 1961 and 1981 and found a significant decline in the number of communities with 80% of their respective populations who were Welsh speakers (279 in 1961; 191 in 1971 and 66 in 1981). They also draw attention to the importance of age – until recently Welsh was perceived to be a language of the elderly – and key differences in the trends concerning the ability to speak the language *vis-à-vis* being able to read and write in Welsh. Recent increases in the numbers of younger people speaking the language have been attributed to more pupils being taught through the medium of Welsh. In making such choices parents cite educational and economic benefits in acquiring bilingual skills as they hope their children would benefit from newer opportunities, (especially the media and education sectors) which require knowledge of the language. Despite such growth in numbers there remains a concern over the sustainability of some Welsh-speaking communities and the inward migration of English-speaking people which it is claimed is having a detrimental effect on the language through their impact on employment, housing and education opportunities in the North and West (Cymuned 2002, 2003).

1.2.   Outcomes

The linkages between the use of the language and economic trends, in-migration of non-Welsh speaking populations and local job markets in heartland areas, have formed the focus of studies using statistics from the 1981 and 1991 Census to support a cultural division of labour interpretation (e.g., Aitchison and Carter 1997, 1999; Drinkwater and O'Leary 1997; Williams 1987; Williams and Morris 2000). Many of these concerns were also expressed by those surveyed as part of the *Lifestyles in Rural Wales* project which drew on semi-structured interviews to examine perceived pressures on the Welsh language from in-migration in four study areas (Cloke, Goodwin and Milburn 1998). Aitchison and Carter (2000) have also demonstrated the impact of non-Welsh speaking migrants from other Welsh regions on the vitality of Welsh speakers in traditional heartland areas. Their study highlighted linkages between such trends and economic circumstances and drew attention to the continued out-migration of Welsh speakers from Dyfed and Gwynedd to, for example, the greater Cardiff region, which was associated with increasing job opportunities in the capital. Drinkwater and O'Leary (1997) in a study comparing the relationship between the ability to speak Welsh and unemployment, using data from the *Samples of Anonymised Records* (SARs) from the 1991 Census, suggest that a higher percentage of Welsh speakers had higher qualifications compared to non-Welsh speakers, but that there were regional variations. They also found that individuals with some degree of proficiency in Welsh have a lower chance of being unemployed than non-Welsh speakers, a similar finding to that of Blackaby et al. (2006). However, the analysis presented by Giggs and Pattie (1992) suggests that patterns across Wales are by no means uniform; with, for example, Welsh speakers in South Wales being over-represented in high-status professions as compared to non-Welsh speaking groups born in Wales (the opposite trend was identified for North Wales). Aitchison and Carter (1997) have drawn attention to important social class variations in the language between different counties in Wales, which they suggest confirm the importance of employment opportunities in South-East Wales in particular for those who are bilingual. But they also demonstrate that Welsh speakers in heartland areas are less represented in professional or managerial positions than non-Welsh speakers born outside Wales. The most deep seated concerns and protests relate to the declining numbers of Welsh speakers within the heartland areas and their acute perception that they are loosing control of the local economy and community life, which is both more marginalized and dominated increasingly by affluent English-born in-migrants. It is from such sources that acute scepticism arises regarding the health of the language and the inadequacy of remedial policies employed by different levels of government (Williams 2004).

1.3. Conceptual/methodological problems in collecting data

Several studies have identified the weaknesses of the census as a source with which to monitor detailed trends in the proficiency in, and use of, the Welsh language. Criticisms relate to the ways in which the census has been conducted (and in particular changes in the nature of the language question asked and populations enumerated), the changing geographical boundaries between censuses (which make temporal analysis difficult) and changes in the methods by which census data have been tabulated. Williams (1987) and Williams and Morris (2000) have suggested that the census questions ask respondents for a subjective interpretation of their own competence in the language which does not show how Welsh is being used in the home, workplace and community. Many of these concerns have been echoed by the Welsh Language Board and more widely. The lack of data on the usage of Welsh was recognised in the consultation draft of

The Wales Spatial Plan (Welsh Assembly Government 2003b). The Welsh Assembly Government is committed to providing a more useful set of data on the language with which to monitor the initiatives outlined in *Iaith Pawb,* its broad policy document on creating a bilingual society. Other sources, for example, the Welsh Office Social Survey, undertaken between September and December 1992 (Welsh Office 1995) for a sample of approximately 13,000 households (27,720 individuals), involved more in-depth questions on the use of the language. The survey revealed a higher incidence of Welsh speakers compared to the 1991 Census (21.5% against 18.6%), but its main advantage over the Census was its attempt to gauge ability (albeit still based on self-assessment) and provide a measure of competence in the language. Williams and Morris (2000: 42) provide a detailed comparison of the results from the survey and 1991 Census results, while Jones and Williams (2000) compare such data with current educational and socio-economic trends.

2.   The current situation: An aggregate analysis of the 2001 census

Following a decline during the 20th century the 2001 UK Census of Population recorded a 2% increase in Welsh speakers since 1991. While this is good news for language promoters some doubts have been cast on the utility of the data and that in respect of three significant changes since 1991. The first is that the questions asked in 2001 were slightly different from previous occasions; the second was that rather than register students at their permanent home address the 2001 Census recorded them at their temporary University/College address; the third is that the census in England and Wales did not allow for a Welsh ethnicity or national identity identifier, although it did allow for an Irish one (and the Census in Scotland included Scottish as an ethnic group). A protest campaign against this inconsistency may have led to differential response by Welsh speakers although it seems to have had little, or even a beneficial effect, on overall response (*http://www.statistics.gov.uk/census2001/annexb.asp#byarea*).

2.1.   Conceptual/methodological problems in collecting data

Higgs, Dorling and Williams (2004) have interrogated the census data to assess whether the change in definitions of the language categories limit the ability of researchers to draw any meaningful conclusions from the census figures. Is any degree of optimism warranted given the fact that the central question in the question on the Welsh language was worded differently? How do these results compare to those of other sources of information on the Welsh language? They compared the trends as revealed from preliminary aggregate analyses of the responses to the Welsh language question with those ascertained from other sources, principally the Welsh Local Labour Force Survey which was conducted around the same time.

2.1.1. Unitary Authority level

As with previous census investigations, respondents were asked for a subjective interpretation of their linguistic competence and those of members of their household. Table 1 shows the nature of the question asked in each of the Censuses of Population as well as other sources of information on the Welsh language. For example, in the 2001 Census respondents could tick all the boxes that apply: Understand spoken Welsh, Speak Welsh, Read Welsh, Write Welsh, None of the Above. Respondents could tick one or more of the 5 boxes in any combination. However, the format of the question was different to that asked in the previous census – the question in the 2001 Census was *Can you ...?* compared to *Do you ...?* used in previous censuses. Scholars have highlighted the problems relating to the format of the question included in pre-2001 censuses. Aitchison and Carter (1994: 20) speculate on the implications of the quality of the response to the use of the latter for the 1991 Census question, suggesting that the "question could be interpreted as a request concerning usage rather than fluency". The 1992 Welsh Social Survey may throw some light on the problem. Its question concerning speaking used the same formulation as the 1991 Census, but its formulation of a question concerning reading was different, i.e., it asked *Can you read...* rather than the 1991 Census's *Do you...* The 1991 Census estimated that the percentage who read Welsh was lower than the percentage who spoke Welsh (16.3%, cf. 18.7%). The 1992 Welsh Social Survey on the other hand produced an estimate of the percentage of those able to read Welsh slightly higher than its estimation of the percentage claiming to speak the language (22.5% cf. 21.5%).

Nevertheless it is feasible that the format of the question could have led to a more positive response in 2001. For the first time, the 2001 Census also asked people whether they "understood" Welsh. Aitchison and Carter suggested, in their analysis of the 1991 Census which did not have this question, that if it was to be included then numbers would be higher than those who said they spoke Welsh. Many people who have learnt Welsh in later life can speak it, but find it difficult to understand when spoken by a native Welsh speaker. Despite this, Carter (1991) suggested that the trends should increase in the order write-read-speak-understand. How much of the 2% increase between 1991–2001 in the percentage speaking Welsh could be attributed to the change in the format of the question, however, would be difficult to gauge. Another problem is that

Table 1. Format of the questions on the Welsh language (Census and other sources)

1981 Census	For all persons aged 3 or over (born before 6th April 1978) – Does the person speak Welsh? – If the person speaks Welsh, does he or she also: – Speak English? – Read Welsh? – Write Welsh?
1991 Census	For all persons aged 3 or over (born before 22nd April 1988) – Does the person speak, read or write Welsh? – Speaks Welsh – Reads Welsh – Writes Welsh – Does not speak, read or write Welsh
Welsh Social Survey (1992)	– Cannot speak Welsh and never have – Cannot speak Welsh but could once – Speak only a little Welsh – Speak a fair amount of Welsh – Fluent but never/hardly ever speak it – Fluent but speak only occasionally – Fluent and speak it half the time – Fluent and speak it most of the time
2001 Census	– Can you understand, speak, read or write Welsh? – Understand spoken Welsh – Speak Welsh – Read Welsh – Write Welsh – None of the above
Welsh Labour Force Survey (2002)	Percentage of all persons aged 3 and over – Who can understand spoken Welsh – Who can speak Welsh – Who can read Welsh – Who can write Welsh Percentage of all persons aged 3 and over and born in Wales – Who can understand spoken Welsh – Who can speak Welsh – Who can read Welsh – Who can write Welsh

the Welsh language question is not included in census forms distributed outside Wales and thus the overall figures for Welsh speakers in the UK as a whole are likely to be an under-estimate. Using data from the ONS Longitudinal Study, the Welsh Language Board estimated that in 2001 110,000 residents of England could speak Welsh, with another thousand residents in Scotland and Northern Ireland (Jones 2007).

The first 2001 census results on the Welsh language were reported in March 2003 (National Statistics 2003). The census found that there were 582,400 Welsh speakers aged 3 and over (or 21% of the population) which represented a 2% increase since 1991. The proportion of people in Wales (aged 3 and over) who can speak, read and write Welsh increased from 13.6% to 16.3% (1991–2001). A further 138,000 (5%) said they understood Welsh but did not speak it. In addition, 84,000 people gave a combination of positive responses that was imprecise, making it difficult to work out whether they could understand, speak, read or write Welsh. Encouragingly, the highest percentage of Welsh speakers were among children aged 5 to 15 years, although of more concern, figures included in the Wales Spatial Plan (Welsh Assembly Government 2003b) estimate that only 6% of primary school children speak Welsh at home.

Figure 1 shows the percentages of people aged 3 and over who, based on the census results, can speak Welsh. The overall patterns from previous censuses of 1981 and 1991 are repeated in the 2001 census outcomes with only Anglesey, Gwynedd, Ceredigion and Carmarthenshire having over 50% of their populations who can speak Welsh, although in terms of absolute numbers, Carmarthenshire had the largest numbers of Welsh speakers. The relationship with the percentage of the population born in Wales appears weak, but is important.

There is a strong relationship between change in the percentage born in Wales and the percentage Welsh speaking. Again, population change could account for such trends; Ceredigion, for example, has experienced a 7% decline in the numbers of Welsh speakers and almost a 20% increase in population suggesting non-Welsh speakers are making up the bulk of such migrants. As noted above, college students were enumerated at their term-time university address rather than at their permanent home address and this contributed to the decline in Welsh speakers in and around Bangor, Aberystwyth and Lampeter, each of which have a predominance of monoglot English-speaking students. The relatively low population turnaround, in the Unitary Authorities of South Wales, in former mining and heavy industrial areas, accounts for the large percentages of Welsh-born populations there. Interestingly, these are also the areas, along with the Welsh-speaking heartland areas, where people were more likely to identify themselves as Welsh. In addition, 798,000 (or 28%) of the population aged 3 or over reported one or more skills (including just understanding) in the Welsh lan-

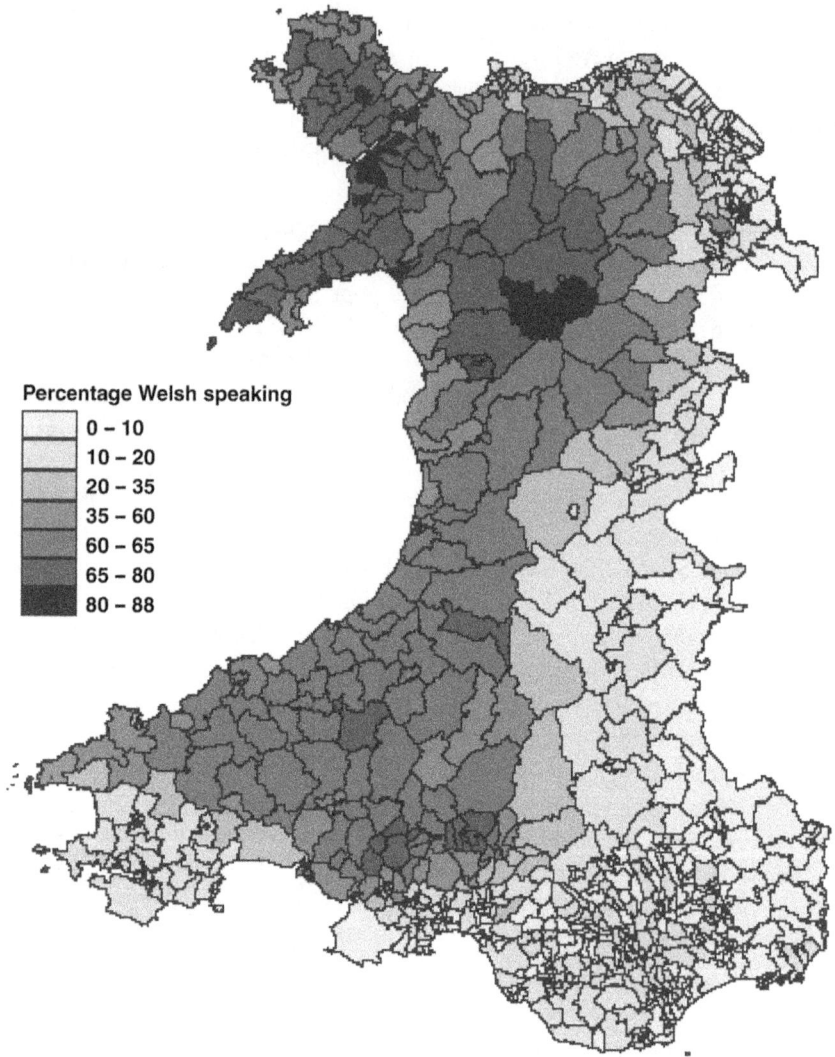

Figure 1. Percentage Welsh speakers for electoral divisions (2001 census)
(Source: Office for National Statistics 2003. Reproduced with permission from Higgs,
Williams and Dorling 2004: 194)

guage with high figures for the unitary authorities of Gwynedd (76%), Anglesey
(70%), Carmarthenshire (64%) and Ceredigion (61%) (ONS 2004).

By 2001 a clear pattern on language skills could be identified with some
661,256 claiming to be able to understand Welsh, 582,368 able to speak it,

567,152 able to read it, 495,519 able to write it and some 659,301 able to speak, read and write. These national figures mask a great deal of unitary authority variation, which is visible in Table 2. The significant issue here though is that the raw numbers enable local language planners to identify clusters of speakers by skill, by local authority and move away perhaps from the aggregate perception that the linguistic vitality of Welsh is to be found mainly in the predominantly Welsh speaking counties of the north and west, merely because they have higher proportions of Welsh speakers. Thus, it is hugely significant for the growth of Welsh-medium education or for the extension of bilingual public services that there are considerable numbers with Welsh language skills in, for example, Caerffili, Newport, or Wrexham.

2.1.2. Electoral division level

Despite signs of national growth, the picture is not entirely promising. At the time of the 1961 Census, there were 279 out of 993 wards in Wales where at least 80% of the population could speak Welsh; by the 1991 census only 32 of these communities remained (National Assembly for Wales Culture and Education Committee 2002). In 1991 there were 82 communities where between 60–70% spoke Welsh, down to 56 by 2001. A similar trend may be observed for communities where over 80% spoke Welsh, i.e., 32 in 1991, down to 20 by 2001. Conversely, while 156 communities were recorded as having between 10–20% in 1991, fully 385 such communities were recorded thus in 2001.This has led commentators, such as Williams (1989: 44), to argue that "instead of talking of a "Welsh-speaking community", it is more appropriate to talk of "Welsh speakers in the community", even within many parts of the heartland areas".

The number of wards where 60–70% of the population speak Welsh has declined from 82 in 1991 to 54 in 2001; from 55 to 41 where 70–80% spoke Welsh and from 32 to 17 where over 80% spoke Welsh (all, within Gwynedd and Anglesey) leading to media concerns that the Welsh Language Act of 1993 and the policies of the National Assembly have failed to halt the decline of Welsh as a living community language (Western Mail 2003). At the other end of the con-tinuum, there was a significant increase in those wards where 10% to 20% of the population could speak Welsh (up from 156 in 1991 to 367 in 2001). These de-velopments represent a continuation of trends identified by Aitchison and Carter (1994) and Williams (1987) which have been attributed to the out-migration of Welsh speaking populations as a result of poor employment or housing oppor-tunities, the in-migration of predominantly monoglot English speakers and a decline in traditional industries which employed a dis-proportionate percentage of Welsh speakers (Aitchison and Carter 1994; WAG 2003).

Table 2. Supplementary table on Welsh language skills. Results from 2001 Census (Unitary authority) (Source: ONS 2003)

All people aged 3 and over	All People ≥ 3 years	Underst. spoken Welsh	Speaks Welsh	Reads Welsh	Writes Welsh	Either speaks, reads or writes Welsh
220 WALES/CYMRU	2,805,701	661,526	582,368	567,152	495,519	659,301
Isle of Anglesey/Sir Ynys Mon	64,679	41,220	38,893	35,510	33,246	39,885
Gwynedd/Gwynedd	112,800	77,966	77,846	72,276	69,264	79,184
Conwy/Conwy	106,316	37,112	31,298	29,085	26,077	33,839
Denbighshire/Sir Ddinbych	90,085	28,146	23,760	22,431	19,858	26,119
Flintshire/Sir y Fflint	143,382	24,630	20,599	20,611	17,687	24,364
Wrexham/Wrecsam	124,024	23,051	18,105	18,386	15,280	21,822
Powys/Powys	122,473	30,754	25,814	24,849	21,428	29,414
Ceredigion/Sir Ceredigion	72,884	39,753	37,918	35,564	32,795	39,424
Pembrokeshire/Sir Benfro	110,183	26,915	23,967	22,006	19,360	26,358
Carmarthenshire/Sir Gaerfyrddin	167,372	93,742	84,196	76,179	67,479	88,946
Swansea/Abertawe	216,226	39,644	28,938	29,434	23,155	35,629
Neath Port Talbot/Castell-nedd Port Talbot	130,305	30,297	23,404	24,204	18,956	29,061
Bridgend/Pen-y-bont ar Ogwr	124,284	17,820	13,397	16,835	12,415	19,449
The Vale of Glamorgan/Bro Morgannwg	115,116	14,795	12,994	13,790	11,632	16,096
Cardiff/Caerdydd	294,208	37,736	32,504	34,060	29,169	39,368
Rhondda; Cynon; Taff/Rhondda; Cynon; Taf	223,924	35,940	27,946	32,838	25,851	37,683
Merthyr Tydfil/Merthyr Tudful	54,115	7,110	5,532	6,241	4,726	7,422
Caerphilly/Caerffili	163,297	19,954	18,237	18,997	16,098	22,611
Blaenau Gwent/Blaenau Gwent	67,795	6,112	6,417	5,820	5,312	7,543
Torfaen/Tor-faen	88,062	8,940	9,780	8,839	8,165	11,041
Monmouthshire/Sir Fynwy	82,351	7,719	7,688	7,191	6,443	8,899
Newport/Casnewydd	131,820	12,170	13,135	12,006	11,123	15,144

2.1.3. Changes since 1991

In terms of changes in the percentages of Welsh speakers by Unitary Authorities, Cardiff has had the largest absolute increase in numbers (up over 14,000), while Torfaen had the largest percentage increase (over 8%). (For details of how census data can be compared over time see Martin, Dorling and Mitchell 2002; and Dorling 1995a, 1995b). Although the trends are not consistent at an aggregate level, there is weak evidence of a link with population change between 1991 and 2001. Further analysis is needed to identify those communities that have experienced increases/declines in non-Welsh speakers/Welsh speakers and more research is needed to compare such trends with population change in order to examine the causes of such changes. At this scale, the unitary authorities that have experienced a decline in the percentage of people speaking Welsh are also those that have experienced significant in-migration since the last census. At the time of the 2001 census 11% of the total population able to speak Welsh were born outside Wales (but whereas 24.7% of the population born in Wales could speak Welsh only 9.0% of those born outside Wales could speak Welsh). An extension of this research would be to identify where such population groups live and to examine their age structure.

Clearly questions of national origin, self-identification, language affiliation and group tensions are complex. The larger question to be examined requires an assessment of the strident claims, made especially by Cymuned (2003), that beneath the simplistic interpretation of census results what is really occurring is the demise of an indigenous ethnic identity. They claim the Welsh language is experiencing a slow death caused by a new and far more effective form of internal colonialism, a re-settlement of the heartland communities by the in-migration of relatively wealthy, generally conservative and unreceptive, English retirement and "new-age" settlers.

3. Welsh Local Labour Force Survey

Balsom (2003) suggests that the Welsh identity question from the 2001 Census is fundamentally flawed and has drawn attention to the potential of using results from a labour force survey conducted around the time of the Census (Office for National Statistics 2002). The aim of this section is to test this claim by comparing the results from the 2001 Census of Population with those of the Welsh Local Labour Force Survey (WLLFS) which, as well as asking if those surveyed in Wales could understand, speak, read or write Welsh, also included questions regarding national identity. The WLLFS was conducted in 2001–2002 and preliminary results were published in November 2002 for the period March 2001–February 2002 (see Table 3).

The results show the variation between unitary authorities for those who speak Welsh (just under 30% of the population of Wales said they spoke Welsh) and those who gave their nationality as Welsh. The ONS Guide to the use of this survey as a comparison to the Census draws attention to the possibility that rates of Welsh speakers, readers and writers are higher in the former because respondents are more likely to respond positively if they have given their national identity as Welsh. While the Census respondents could have ticked the "Other" box and given Welsh as their identity, in the WLLFS a question on national identity immediately preceded the Welsh language question. There are other differences in the nature of the sampling techniques and questions asked which may account for the differences, e.g., 21,000 households were sampled in the WLLFS and the mode of interview may have influenced numbers who said they could speak, read and write Welsh (Haselden 2003).

Results from the WLLFS suggest that just under 30% of the Welsh population (aged 3 and over) reported they could speak Welsh (35% of residents said they could understand spoken Welsh) with the trends in unitary authorities mirroring those in the Census (r-squared = 0.97); with Gwynedd, Anglesey, Carmarthen and Ceredigion having over 50% of respondents who said they spoke Welsh again contrasting with those unitary authorities bordering England which had the lowest proportions. Findings from the WLLFS also suggest that just over 69% of residents claimed Welsh as their national identity, but there is a general spatial correspondence between the census and the WLLFS regarding ideas of national identity. Again, results mirror the census in that people in the South Wales Valleys unitary authorities were more likely to identify themselves as Welsh (e.g., Merthyr Tydfil 86.3%; Blaenau Gwent 85.2%; Rhondda Cynon Taf 84.3%). In contrast, Anglesey and Ceredigion, with one of the highest rates of Welsh speakers, had some of the lowest rates of respondents who identified themselves as Welsh (along with those Unitary Authorities that border England). When non-Welsh born are omitted from the analysis of the national identity question, the relationship with the percentage of Welsh speakers is stronger. Thus although the overall estimates of the percentages able to speak Welsh, as gauged from the WLLFS, are higher than those of the Census, the spatial trends mirror those of the census both for speakers and the relationship with the national identity "question". Clearly a more dis-aggregate analysis is needed to examine such trends in more detail.

In the conclusions to their 1991 atlas of the Welsh language, Aitchison and Carter (1994: 111) drew attention to the difficulties of predicting future patterns given the relative paucity of information and suggested that such problems are

Table 3. Welsh Local Labour Force Survey 2001/2002 (by Unitary Authority) (Source: NOMIS)

Unitary Authority	Population (LFS estimate)	% who gave Welsh as national identity	% born in Wales who gave Welsh as nationality	N aged 3 and over (%) who can speak Welsh (LFS pop.est.)	% of all persons 3 and over born in Wales who can speak Welsh
Anglesey	63,000	60.1	85.3	41,000 (67.2)	87.8
Blaenau Gwent	69,000	85.2	89.0	13,000 (19.0)	19.7
Bridgend	130,000	79.1	89.6	23,000 (18.3)	19.7
Caerphilly	170,000	82.5	88.3	34,000 (21.0)	22.1
Cardiff	325,000	66.5	84.5	70,000 (22.3)	25.9
Carmarthen	166,000	76.0	92.3	87,000 (54.5)	63.9
Ceredigion	72,000	62.2	91.2	43,000 (61.0)	83.7
Conwy	111,000	49.5	82.7	45,000 (42.2)	63.5
Denbighshire	92,000	50.3	85.4	34,000 (38.3)	57.2
Flintshire	147,000	43.3	79.6	38,000 (26.7)	36.7
Gwynedd	113,000	71.3	92.9	87,000 (79.1)	93.9
Merthyr Tydfil	54,000	87.0	92.0	13,000 (25.5)	26.8
Monmouthshire	87,000	54.3	80.7	14,000 (16.4)	20.2
Neath Port Talbot	135,000	82.7	90.7	33,000 (25.0)	26.6
Newport	135,000	69.6	81.8	24,000 (18.0)	20.1
Pembrokeshire	114,000	60.5	83.9	28,000 (25.7)	32.6
Powys	125,000	56.2	85.6	34,000 (28.3)	39.2
Rhondda Cynon Taff	236,000	84.3	89.7	56,000 (24.7)	26.3
Swansea	228,000	73.0	85.7	45,000 (20.4)	22.7
Torfaen	88,000	75.8	85.4	15,000 (17.8)	19.2
Vale of Glamorgan	124,000	69.9	87.0	25,000 (20.8)	22.8
Wrexham	125,000	67.1	86.7	29,000 (23.8)	29.5
Total	2,910,000	69.2	87.0	833,000 (29.6)	34.3

"made more so by the poverty of the population census in terms of language information". Concerns over the lack of a sound statistical base with which to monitor changes over time have been expressed elsewhere (Jones and Williams 2000). Thus a concerted effort was needed to analyse such changes from an official, professional perspective.

4.   Language change between successive censuses

In the past five years, the Welsh Language Board has developed a more robust statistical and data analysis capacity. Its statistician, Hywel Jones, has initiated a wide range of studies so as to provide evidence-based language planning, and the full range of analyses may be obtained from the website (*http://www.bwrdd-yr-iaith.org.uk*). One of these analyses has looked at the consistency of the reporting of an ability to speak Welsh across the 1971 to 2001 Censuses (Jones 2005) (see Table 4). 5.5% of all people were recorded as having a change in their ability to speak Welsh between both the 1971 and 1981 Censuses, and the 1981 and 1991 Censuses. This increased to 7.4% between the 1991 and 2001 Censuses.

The pattern varies noticeably by age group. Whereas for the oldest, over 65 age group, the percentages recorded as changing fell over the same period – from 5.7%, to 5.0%, to 4.4% respectively, percentages for all the other age groups increased. The increases were mostly modest, e.g., from 4.1% to 5.4% for the 35 to 44 year-old age group, apart from the youngest age group. Thus the percentage change of those aged 13 to 24 in 1981 changing their language

Table 4. Percentage recording a change in ability, by censuses matched (Source: Jones 2005)

Censuses matched	Ability to speak Welsh at 1st census of pair	Ability to speak Welsh at 2nd census of pair	
		Can speak Welsh	Cannot speak Welsh
1971–1981	Can speak Welsh	87.2	12.8
	Cannot speak Welsh	3.5	96.5
	Total	21.3	78.7
1981–1991	Can speak Welsh	86.2	13.8
	Cannot speak Welsh	3.6	96.4
	Total	19.6	80.4
1991–2001	Can speak Welsh	83.4	16.6
	Cannot speak Welsh	5.3	94.7
	Total	19.9	80.1

Table 5. Odds ratios, by age group and censuses matched. (source: H. Jones, Census 2001 Welsh Language Board 2003)

Odds on speaking Welsh in 2nd year given Welsh speaking in 1st year ÷ odds on speaking Welsh in 2nd year given not Welsh speaking in 1st year

Age group in 2nd census	1971–1981	1981–1991	1991–2001
13–24	71	49	13[b]
25–34	152[a]	133[a]	107[a]
35–44	306[a]	272[a]	137[b]
45–64	314	332	212
65+	231	283	306[a]

[a]: significantly different, with 95% confidence, from row immediately above
[b]: significantly different, with 95% confidence, from immediately preceding column

was as follows: a) between 1971 and 1981: 7.6%; b) between 1981 and 1991: 9.7%, and c) between 1991 and 2001: 19.7%.

There has been a slight increase overall in the probability that someone who did *not* speak Welsh at one census would be recorded as speaking Welsh in the following census (see Table 5). For someone who did not speak Welsh in 1971 the odds that (s)he would still not speak Welsh in 1981 were 27 to 1, i.e., only 3.5% would speak Welsh in 1981. The situation was very similar in 1981–1991, but by 1991 the odds that a non-Welsh speaker in 1991 would still not speak Welsh in 2001 had fallen by around a third to 18 to 1, i.e., by 2001 5.3% of those not speaking Welsh in 1991 would be recorded as Welsh speaking. Over the three decades since 1971 there has been a slight decrease overall in the probability that someone who spoke Welsh at one census would also be recorded as speaking Welsh in the following census. For someone speaking Welsh in 1971 the odds that (s)he would still speak Welsh in 1981 were 6.8 to 1, i.e., in other words, 12.8% of those who spoke Welsh in 1971 did not by 1981. By 1991, the odds had fallen by a quarter to 5 to 1, i.e., by 2001 16.6% of those speaking Welsh in 1991 would not speak Welsh (Table 5).

Jones has also calculated the odds ratios for 1991–2001 which were significantly different from those of both 1971–1981 and 1981–1991 whereas there was no significant difference between 1971–1981 and 1981–1991. A number of reasons for this can be hypothesised, the most likely of which is the expansion of teaching of Welsh in schools following the reforms of the 1988 Education Act. The figures can be broken down by age. A similar picture emerges of change over the three decades but with the degree of change varying by age group. The 13 to 24 year age group shows increasingly large percentages acquiring a

Welsh-speaking capability. This is the age group that was aged 3 to 14 in the first of the paired censuses and as such is the age group in primary, secondary and possibly further/higher education in the subsequent decade. The odds of a non-Welsh speaker in this youngest age group still not speaking Welsh 10 years later fell from 18 to 1 in 1971–1981 to 13 to 1 in 1981–1991 and to slightly better than 5 to 1 in 1991–2001, i.e., whereas only 5% of the children who could not speak Welsh in 1971 came to speak Welsh by 1981, by the following census the percentage increased to 7%, and by 2001 the percentage was 17%.

The older age groups show higher levels of inter-Census consistency. Some smaller increases have also been seen amongst the older age groups, especially in 2001. The patterns identified between 1971–1981 and 1981–1991 were fairly consistent. The pattern seen between 1991 and 2001 is different, most especially in the youngest age group. Generally, a dropping off in levels of maintenance has occurred since 1971. For the older age groups this has not been dramatic. For example, the odds on a person recorded as speaking Welsh in 1971 being recorded as speaking Welsh in 1981 when in the 65 and over age group were nearly 10 to 1. By 2001 the odds had fallen by about a fifth to 8 to 1. However, the youngest age group has shows a very different pattern. The odds on a person recorded as speaking Welsh in 1971 being recorded as speaking Welsh in 1981 when in the 13 to 24 age group were nearly 4 to 1. By 2001 the odds had fallen by about a third to around 5 to 2. In other words, of 3 to 14 year olds in 1991 who spoke Welsh, only 72% still spoke Welsh by 2001, compared to 80% of 1971s 3 to 14 year olds who still spoke Welsh in 1981.

Of the 30.7% of those aged 13 to 24 in 2001 who said they could speak Welsh at that Census, 42.5% of them had been recorded as not speaking Welsh 10 years earlier. Table 5 indicates significant differences in odds ratios. There were none between 1971–1981 and 1981– 1991 but compared to the latter 1991–2001 showed significant changes for the 13–24 age group. All odds ratios for the 25–34 age group are significantly different to odds ratios for the 13–24 age group.

Analysis of the odds ratios for the two sexes by age group showed that the only significant differences were in the 13–24 age group, for 1981–1991 and in the 25–34 age group for 1991–2001. In each of these cases of significant differences, the odds ratio for males was higher than the odds ratio for females, the percentage of females retaining an ability in Welsh from one census to the next generally being lower than for males, counterbalanced by a higher percentage of those unable to speak Welsh at the earlier census gaining an ability by the second.

From his analysis Jones (2003) concludes that during the 1990s the relative balance of people acquiring an ability in Welsh compared to those losing an ability changed compared to the previous two decades. A change in the balance had been seen in the 1980s in respect of the youngest age group, largely school aged, but in the 1990s a change was seen for most age groups, and affected both sexes.

In 1981, 13.1% of those speaking Welsh had not done so a decade earlier; in 1991 this rose to 14.6%; in 2001 it rose again to 21.7%. The ability to speak Welsh is thus a less established ability for many now counted as Welsh speakers than it was in the past.

Others have suggested alternatives to the use of the census. Both Williams (1989, 2000) and Williams and Morris (2000: 50) demonstrate the potential advantages that may accrue from conducting language use surveys which show how the Welsh language is actually being used in the home, workplace and community in order to gauge "what people actually do with the Welsh which they can speak". Having recognised the merit of this approach, the Welsh Language Board is awaiting the results of surveys it has commissioned on a range of issues such as language reproduction within the family, the sociolinguistic behaviour of young people, the potential for an increased use of Welsh within the economy and the effect of marketing campaigns on the decision of young parents to send their children to Welsh-medium schools.

This section has been concerned with demonstrating the trends that can be gauged from an analysis of aggregate data at the unitary authority level, together with results from previous censuses and with comparing such trends with those from other sources such as the Welsh Local Labour Force survey. Secondly, we have highlighted current gaps in knowledge where the census is less useful to policy-makers charged with investigating such trends. Three outstanding issues remain, namely: 1) If there are future censuses, what additional questions could be asked to provide more diagnostic measures of the evolving nature of the Welsh language? 2) If additional questions are rejected, how could ancillary surveys be used in conjunction with the basic census analysis to provide a more complete picture? 3) Does UK devolution necessarily imply that Wales needs its own national statistical office? If so how might language-related questions be embedded within mainstream socio-economic investigations, so that the reality of usage in all domains, rather than the potential contained within self-ascribed replies, informs policy decisions?

5. Policy applications

Given that there is now a much greater concern with policy development, with capacity building and with relating the fortunes of the Welsh language to other socio-economic indicators, we have moved well beyond cartography and into significant public investment in language planning and the construction of a bilingual society. One of the prime justifications of the devolution agenda was the promotion of a distinct Welsh national identity, of which an important constituent was the unique culture and language of Wales. The Welsh Assembly Government's (WAG) national action plan on the Welsh language, *Iaith Pawb*, was published in February 2003 (Welsh Assembly Government 2003a). This set forward policy initiatives on promoting bilingualism and strengthening the Welsh language, building on the commitments made in the Assembly Government's *A Plan for Wales 2001* (National Assembly for Wales 2001). The broad aim is to create a bilingual Wales and amongst the targets there is a commitment to increase the percentage of people in Wales able to speak Welsh by 5% points from 2001 levels (as gauged from the Census) by 2011 and to arrest the decline in the number of communities where Welsh is spoken by over 70% of the population. As part of the monitoring process, the WAG is committed in *Iaith Pawb* to develop and compile a wider range of statistical indicators on ability levels and usage of the Welsh language. A major proposal is to undertake language use surveys, which it is argued "are more detailed in their level of interrogation than the censuses or other official surveys currently undertaken" (WAG 2003a: 11).

The Welsh Language Board (WLB) has a duty to promote and encourage the use of Welsh in public and voluntary sector organisations and to ensure equal status for the language in society. Recently it has been encouraging bilingualism within the private sector also through its promotional and marketing campaigns (Williams 2007). It has a central role in analysing sociolinguistic and educational trends and in implementing the Assembly Government initiatives. *Iaith Pawb* recognises that the 2001 Census can only provide a broad, historical perspective and that more pertinent and regular surveys need to be undertaken to gauge Welsh language ability levels and usage. The Welsh Language Board in their strategy document for the language for 2000–2005 (WLB 1999: 32) drew attention to the fact that the Census provides "an inexact but irreplaceable measure of language trends", before highlighting their future plans to monitor patterns in more geographical and thematic detail through, for example, specially commissioned surveys of language use which will supplement the continued use of Census findings. Interesting, at times radical, initiatives are being realised in the field of Welsh language planning such as the work of the 23 *Mentrau Iaith* (community enterprise initiatives), *Local Area Language Action Plans*, the TWF project (bilingual family promotion), the statutory *Local Authority and Public Institution Language Plans*, the extension of Welsh-medium educational provision, the increased bilingual character of the professions in Wales, and the marketing of Welsh within the private sector. Until quite recently, most of these initiatives had been launched in the absence of detailed sociolinguistic investigations. The monitoring of such progress has been largely *ad hoc*, fragmented and episodic. The WLB now systematically commissions and analyses a wide range of data sets to inform its initiatives/partnerships with *Mentrau Iaith* (Local Language Enterprise Initiatives) Local Area Action Plans, Youth Programmes, Twf (Family Transfer Programme) and a range of other marketing and sector-specific activities. But all this needs to be set within a national context and there is no adequate national information database within which such initiatives can be calibrated and contextualised *vis-à-vis* other trends in society. But in times of significant investment and political determination to create a bilingual society the inadequacies of the current Census format and its resultant data should not be glossed over, but remedied as part of prudent planning.

One other policy area which is key to the trends noted from our aggregate analysis is education. It is the single most important factor determining the total numbers of young people capable of speaking Welsh. Critically, since the Education Reform Act of 1988, Welsh has become a core subject in the national curriculum of Wales for all children up until the age of 16. This has two broad implications. First, it offers the opportunity to acquire a range of bilingual skills for all Welsh school children wherever they are on the linguistic continuum. Secondly, it helps to mainstream the bilingual policies of the WAG, because now there is a tacit understanding that the language (in theory) belongs to all, not just to a declining minority within the country. The challenge facing language planners is to ensure that those taught Welsh to age 16 continue to have the opportunities to continue speaking the language outside the school environment. A second issue is the significant number of adult Welsh learners who acquire skills in Welsh but who face difficulties integrating within Welsh speaking networks, especially within anglicised areas. This, in turn, points to the need for a more disaggregate analysis as and when the detailed data from the Census and the data sets being collected by the WLB become available.

This need goes beyond Wales to other parts of the UK. The Welsh Language Act, 1993, is a piece of Westminster legislation. The principal statutory instrument to initiate and regulate Welsh medium services is the Language Scheme agreed between public authorities and named Welsh language service providers and the Welsh Language Board. Such language schemes cover all providers regardless of where in the UK they are located. Thus many government departments and public services which operate on behalf of Welsh clients are located across the UK. Specialist agencies also provide a dedicated Welsh language service and range from the *Student Loans Company Limited* (based in Glasgow) to the *British Cattle Movement Service* (based in Workington).

6.   Conclusions

Language issues are directly related to questions of citizenship, education, socialisation and participation, especially in the public sphere. There is tremendous pressure on institutions within Wales, as with the rest of the EU, to simplify and harmonise the range of services offered within a particular suite of languages. Yet the message of this chapter is that even the existing data sets we have are too poor to allow for meaningful services to be planned in relation to other languages and responsibilities. It would be foolhardy in the extreme to reduce expenditure on data collection in the name of fiscal probity and official efficiency, for the issues which such data are meant to inform are increasing rather than decreasing in their complexity. Sound language planning requires robust, consistent evidence; else it is merely rhetoric masquerading as applied knowledge.

Acknowledgements

The ONS (Key Statistics for Local Authorities, 2001 Census) census data used in this chapter are Crown Copyright. I am indebted to my colleague Hywel Jones, for his observations and for providing me with his briefing papers for the Welsh Language Board, and to Prof. G. Higgs (Glamorgan University) and Dr. Dorling (Sheffield University) with whom I co-wrote the 2004 Area paper.

References

Aitchison, J. and H. Carter
   1994   *A Geography of the Welsh Language 1961–1991.* Cardiff: University of Wales Press.
   1997   Language reproduction: reflections on the Welsh example. *Area* 29 (4): 357–366.
   1998   The regeneration of the Welsh language: an analysis. *Contemporary Wales* 11: 167–199.
   1999a   The Welsh language today. In: D. Dunkerley and A. Thompson, (eds.), *Wales Today*, 91–109. Cardiff: University of Wales,
   1999b   Cultural empowerment and language shift in Wales, *Tijdschrift voor Economische en Sociale Geografie* 90 (2): 168–183.
   2000   *Language, Economy and Society: The Changing Fortunes of the Welsh Language in the Twentieth Century.* Cardiff: University of Wales Press.

Ambrose, J. and C.H. Williams
   1991   Language made visible: Representation in geolinguistics. In: C.H. Williams (ed.), *Linguistic Minorities, Society and Territory*, 298–314. Clevedon: Multilingual Matters.

Balsom, D.
  2003   Ticking the Box. *Agenda* Spring 2003, 33–34. Cardiff: Institute of Welsh
            Affairs.

Blackaby D., P. Latreille, P. Murphy, N. O'Leary and P. Sloane
  2006   *The Welsh Language and Labour Market Inactivity.* Report for the Eco-
            nomic Research Unit, Welsh Assembly Government. University of Wales
            Swansea and WELMERC.

Bwrdd yr Iaith Gymraeg Data Sources available at
            http://www.bwrdd-yr-iaith.org.uk/en/index.php

Carter, H.
  1991   The language and the census question. *Planet* 87: 113–115.

Carter, H. and J. Aitchison
  1986   Language areas and language change in Wales, 1961–1981. In : I. Hume
            and W.T.R. Pryce, (eds.), *The Welsh and Their Country*, 1–25. Llandysul:
            Gomer Press.

Cloke, P., M. Goodwin and P. Milbourne
  1998   Cultural change and conflict in rural Wales: competing constructs of iden-
            tity. *Environment and Planning A* 30: 463–480.

Cymuned
  2002   Equality and Justice. Cymuned's response to A Bilingual Future. A Welsh
            Assembly Government Policy Statement and Our Language: Its Future,
            The Policy Review of the Welsh Language by the Culture Committee,
            August 5th 2002, Aberystwyth: Cyhoeddiadau Cymuned.
  2003   *In-migration, yes; Colonisation, no! Colonialism and Anti-colonialism
            in the Bröydd Cymraeg* (Welsh-speaking areas of Wales). Aberystwyth:
            Cyhoeddiadau Cymuned.

Dorling, D.
  1995a   The visualization of local urban change across Britain. *Environment and
            Planning B* 22: 269–290.
  1995b   Visualizing changing social structure from a census. *Environment and
            Planning A* 27 (2): 353–378.

Drinkwater, S.J. and C. O'Leary
  1997   Unemployment in Wales: Does language matter? *Regional Studies* 31 (6):
            583–591.

Giggs, J. and C. Pattie
  1992   Wales as a plural society. *Contemporary Wales* 5: 25–63.

Griffiths, D.
  1992   The political consequences of migration into Wales. *Contemporary Wales*
            5: 64–80.

Haselden, L.
    2003   *Differences in estimates of Welsh Language Skills.* Office for National
            Statistics. (*http://www.statistics.gov.uk/downloads/theme_compendia/fow/
            WelshLanguage.pdf*)

Higgs, G., C.H. Williams and D. Dorling
    2004   Use of the census of population to descern trends in the Welsh language:
            An aggregate analysis. *Area* 36 (2): 187–201.

Jones, H.
    2003   *Census 2001.* Cardiff: Welsh Language Board.
    2005   Ability to speak Welsh in the Censuses of Population: a longitudinal analy-
            sis. *Population Trends Winter 2005 No. 122.* Office for National Statistics:
            Palgrave MacMillan.
    2007   *Estimation of the Number of Welsh Speakers in England.* Cardiff: Welsh
            Language Board *www. bwrdd-yr-iaith.org.uk*

Jones, H. and C.H. Williams
    2000   The statistical basis for Welsh language planning: data, trends, patterns
            and processes. In: C.H.Williams,(ed), *Language Revitalization: Policy
            and Planning in Wales*, 48–82. Cardiff: University of Wales Press.

Jones, R.M.
    1999   Social change in Wales since 1945. In: D. Dunkerley and A. Thompson
            (eds.), *Wales Today*, 11–24 Cardiff: University of Wales Press.

Martin, D., D. Dorling and R. Mitchell
    2002   Linking censuses through time: problems and solutions. *Area* 34 (1): 82–
            91.

National Assembly for Wales
    2001   *Plan for Wales 2001.* Cardiff: NAW.

National Assembly for Wales Culture and Education Committee
    2002   *Our Language: Its Future, The Policy Review of the Welsh Language by the
            Culture Committee and the Education and Lifelong Learning Committee
            of the National Assembly for Wales.* Cardiff: NAW.

National Statistics
    2003   *The 2001 Census of Population: First Results on the Welsh Language SB
            22/2003,* Cardiff: Statistical Directorate, National Assembly for Wales.

Office for National Statistics
    2002   *Annual Local Area Labour Force Survey Section 2: Wales Summary and
            Analysis.* London: TSO.
    2003   *Key Statistics for Local Authorities in Wales.* London: TSO.
    2004   *Census 2001 Report on the Welsh Language.* London: TSO

Pryce, W.T.R. and C.H. Williams
  1988   Sources and methods in the study of language areas: a case study of
           Wales. In: C.H. Williams (ed.), *Language in Geographic Context*, 167–
           237. Clevedon: Multilingual Matters.

Welsh Assembly Government
  2003   *Iaith Pawb: A National Action Plan for a Bilingual Wales,* Cardiff: Welsh
           Assembly Government.

Welsh Language Board
  1999   *The Welsh Language: A Vision and Mission for 2000–2005*, Cardiff: WLB.
  2003   *Number of Welsh Speakers Increases for the First Time for Almost A Cen-
           tury.* Cardiff: WLB, 13th February 2003.

Welsh Office
  1995   *1992 Welsh Social Survey: Report on the Welsh Language*, Cardiff: The
           Welsh Office.

Western Mail
  2003   *Decline in Number of Areas where Majority Speak Welsh*, July 1st 2003.
           Cardiff: Western Mail.

Williams, C.H.
  1979   An ecological and behavioural analysis of ethnolinguistic change in Wales.
           In: H. Giles and B. Saint-Jacques (eds.), *Language and Ethnic Relations.*
           27–55. Oxford: Pergamon.
  1980   Language contact and language change in Wales, 1901–1971: A study in
           historical geolinguistics. *Welsh History Review* 10 (2): 207–238.
  1987   Location and context in Welsh language reproduction. In: G. Williams
           (ed.), The Sociology of Welsh, *International Journal of the Sociology of
           Language*, 66, 61–68.
  1988   An introduction to geolinguistics. In: C.H. Williams (ed.), *Language in
           Geographic Context*, 1-19. Clevedon: Multilingual Matters.
  1989   New domains of the Welsh language. *Contemporary Wales* 3: 41–76.
  1991   Sound language planning is holistic in nature. In: C.H. Williams (ed.),
           Linguistic Minorities, Society and Territory, 315–223. Clevedon: Multi-
           lingual Matters.
  1994   *Called Unto Liberty: On Language and Nationalism*. Clevedon: Multi-
           lingual Matters.
  2002   *The Importance of Holistic Language Planning for the Promotion of
           Minority Languages*. Conference on Creating a Common Structure for
           Promoting Historical Linguistic Minorities within the European Union.
           Finnish Parliament. Helsinki: Folktinget, 11–12, October.
  2004   Iaith Pawb: The doctrine of plenary inclusion. *Contemporary Wales* 17:
           1–21.

2007   Marketing Welsh in an ambivalent context. *Noves SL*, Autumn-Winter, available at *http.www6.gencat.net///llengat/noves/ hm07tardor-hivern*.

2008   *Lingusitic Minorities in Democratic Context*. Basinstoke: Palgrave.

Williams, C.H. (ed.)

1991   *Linguistic Minorities, Society and Territory*. Clevedon: Multilingual Matters.

2000   *Language Revitalization: Policy and Planning in Wales*. Cardiff: University of Wales Press.

2007   *Language and Governance*. Cardiff: University of Wales Press.

Williams, C.H. and I. van der Merve

1996   Mapping the multilingual city: A research agenda for urban geolinguistics. *Journal of Multilingual and Multicultural Development* 17 (1): 49–66.

Williams, G. and D. Morris

2000   *Language Planning and Language Use*. Cardiff: University of Wales Press.

Williams, S.W.

1981   The urban hierarchy, diffusion and the Welsh language: A preliminary analysis. *Cambria* 8 (1): 35–50.

The status of Basque in the Basque country

Jasone Cenoz

1. Introduction

The Basque Country covers an area of approximately 20,742 square kilome-
tres along the Bay of Biscay, north and south of the Pyrenees and comprises
seven provinces. Three of these provinces belong to the French department
Pyrénées Atlantiques (Lapurdi, Nafarroa Beherea and Zuberoa), and four to
two autonomous regions in Spain (the Basque Autonomous Community and
Navarre). This chapter will only focus on the Basque Autonomous Community (henceforward BAC) where approximately two million of the almost three
million inhabitants of the Basque Country live.

Even though the Basques were probably living in the Basque Country since
Palaeolithic times, the oldest historical records are linked to the Romanisation of
the Iberian Peninsula in the second and first centuries BC. The Basque language
was widely spoken all over the Basque Country for many centuries but it was not
used officially or in writing and only isolated sentences and names can be found
in documents written in Navarrese Romance, Occitan and Latin (Zuazo 1995).
The first book in Basque *Lingua Vasconum Primitiae* by Bernard Etxepare was
not published until 1545.

The Basque language has been in contact with Latin and Romance languages
for centuries and it has been influenced by them mainly at the phonological
and lexical levels. For example, intensive contact with its powerful neighbours,
Spanish and French, explains the important influence of these languages on the
Basque phonological system. This contact with Romance languages explains
the important retreat suffered by Basque in the 18th and 19th centuries. The
contact has increased in the 20th century as the result of industrialisation and
the development of communications and the mass media. The Basque provinces
of Gipuzkoa and Bizkaia fought against Franco during the Spanish Civil War
(1936–1939) and many Basques had to be exiled in different countries in Europe and America. Speaking Basque was illegal during Franco's dictatorship
(1939–1975). The "Spanish only" policy during the dictatorship had important

consequences, not only at the institutional and educational levels but also in the private domain.

Another factor that had a very important influence on the decrease of Basque in the 20th century was immigration. The industrialisation of the BAC and Navarre attracted an important number of Spanish speaking immigrants in the 1950s, 1960s and 1970s. It is estimated (Azurmendi and Martínez de Luna 2006: 15) that "about one third of the current population in the BAC is the result of this immigration". These immigrants remained in most cases monolingual in Spanish as they did not have problems to communicate with Basque-Spanish bilingual speakers. Learning Basque is more difficult than learning other languages such as Catalan or Galician because Basque is not an Indo-European language and its morphology and syntax are completely different from Spanish. In contrast to Spanish, Basque is a highly inflected language with sixteen morphological cases and typologically, it has been defined as ergative and agglutinative (Cenoz, in press).

The Spanish Constitution (1978) declared Spanish the nationwide official language and guaranteed the rights of Spanish speakers to use their language but also raised the possibility of recognising other languages as co-official in their own territories. Nowadays, Basque has a co-official status in the BAC and the Northern area of Navarre but not in the Northern Basque Country in France. The differences in legislation have important implications for the resources allocated to the development of Basque and therefore for its maintenance and revival. The use of Basque in education in the BAC can illustrate this point. When the bilingual models were established in 1982, approximately 25% of the students in the BAC attended Basque-medium schools; at present, about 90% of kindergarten/primary school children and 78% of secondary school children have Basque as a language of instruction (Cenoz 2001; Cenoz, forthcoming). This success promoting the minority language in the school context is not reflected in language use in society at large and the Basque language is still a language "at risk".

One of the main challenges is its use in different areas and the development of a standard because Basque has traditionally been used orally and had a very limited use at the institutional level. Apart from the poor writing tradition and the low social prestige of the language, the mountainous terrain of the Basque spreading North and South of the Pyrenees and the administrative division of the country can explain the existence of different Basque dialects. The Academy of the Basque Language (*Euskaltzaindia*), founded in 1918, has played a crucial role in the standardisation of the Basque language at the oral and written levels. The Academy defined a unified standard variety of Basque called *euskara batua* (unified Basque) in the 1960s. This variety is based on the central dialects of

Lapurdi and Gipuzkoa and is nowadays the most widespread variety of Basque; it is generally used in official documents, educational materials, in the teaching of Basque as a second language, the mass media (Basque television, radios and newspapers) and in literature.

Another challenge for the survival of Basque is the use of Basque. Proficiency in the language has increased but many Basque speakers have Spanish as their first language and they feel more comfortable using Spanish than Basque. Moreover, the communicative need to use Basque is low because Basque speakers are also proficient in Spanish and the linguistic distance between Basque and Spanish makes it necessary to switch into Spanish when just one person in a group conversation does not speak Basque. There are important geographical differences in the use of Basque and it is possible to use Basque most of the time in some small towns and villages (mainly in Gipuzkoa) but switching into Spanish is necessary in many situations in the majority of the cities and towns of the Basque Country.

Apart from promoting the learning and use of Basque in education, there are special plans to promote the Basque language in other sectors. The Basque Government has created specific institutions such as HABE for the teaching of Basque to adults or IVAP, the Basque institute of public administration, and has funded a large number of institutions and projects to promote the Basque language. An important effort has also been made by public and private institutions to promote the use of Basque in the media. Nowadays, there are several all-Basque radio stations and others with programs in Basque. The Basque Government finances two television channels, one in Basque and one in Spanish, and there is a Basque newspaper. Other newspapers devote a few pages a week to articles in Basque and there are some magazines and an increasing number of professionally specialised journals written in Basque but with a small circulation. In spite of all these efforts, the use of Basque in daily life and in the mass media is overshadowed by the dominant role of Spanish.

The survival of Basque is also challenged by the new wave of immigration that has arrived in the last five or six years. These new immigrants do not come from Spain but from other countries, mainly South America (Colombia, Ecuador, Argentina), Morocco, Romania or China. The educational data indicate that the number of immigrant students in schools in the BAC was approximately 2,000 between 1995 and 2000 but had raised to 17,165 by the academic year 2006–2007. This is 4.5% of the total number of primary and secondary students. In contrast to pupils born in the Basque Country (including second and third generation Spanish immigrants), most of these immigrant students do not study through the medium of Basque and only have the minimum compulsory number of hours of Basque. Basque classes are also offered to adult immigrants but only a limited number of adults attend them. It is difficult to predict what the impact of immigration will be on the survival of the Basque language but some sectors of the populations are seriously worried about it. In contrast to immigrant languages, Basque is a minority language in its own community, that is, in the only community where it is spoken. Being a minority language, it faces many challenges that can affect its survival.

2.   Rationale and goals of research

Research on the status of Basque in the BAC has focused on different areas. The attempts to reverse language shift after many years of repression have been supported by a strong official language policy. The social movements to promote the knowledge and use of Basque are also very dynamic in the BAC and there is a large number of associations working on different areas. These efforts have had an impact on the vitality of Basque and have triggered research in such areas as the general knowledge and use of Basque, the outcomes of bilingual education, attitudes, and the visibility of the Basque language. These areas will be discussed in sections 2.1–2.4, respectively.

2.1.   General knowledge and use of Basque

One of the main aims of research on the Basque language in the last 20 years has been to provide an accurate picture of the linguistic situation, that is, to get to know the total number of speakers of Basque, their distribution and the use of the language. Information about the knowledge of Basque by the general population is useful for different reasons. It can provide the necessary information to compare the different geographical territories where the Basque language is spoken and it can also provide information for sociolinguistic studies involving variables such a gender, age or size of the municipality. It can also be useful to see the effect of language policy and to forecast the future of the Basque language.

Studies on language use have focused on the use of Basque in the individual's social networks including the family (mother, father, husband-wife, son-daughter, home), the local community (among friends, in shops, with colleagues, in the market and with the priest) and other societal domains: in the bank in the town hall with the children's school teachers and in the health services. So far, three sociolinguistic surveys (1991, 1996, 2001) have been conducted by the Basque Government Department of Culture (Eusko Jaurlaritza 1995, 1997, 2003).

One of the main challenges of the Basque language is its use in everyday life. In order to examine to what extent the Basque language is used, four studies (1989, 1993, 1997, 2001) have focused on street measurements of Basque use. These studies provide a picture of the use of Basque on a specific day all over the BAC (Altuna 2002a). This information is very interesting to see the way the gap between knowledge of Basque and use of Basque is evolving.

2.2. Outcomes of bilingual education

Research in education has focused on the outcomes of bilingual education. The use of Basque as a language of instruction is well established now in kindergarten, primary and secondary education but the use of a minority language as the language of instruction faces many challenges. One of the main problems has been the lack of teachers with enough proficiency in Basque. There have been in-service courses for many teachers and nowadays about 75% of the teachers in public schools are proficient in Basque. Other challenges include the development of teaching materials in Basque and the increasing number of students with Spanish as the first language who attend Basque-medium instruction.

One of the main goals of research on the outcomes of bilingual education has been the measurement of proficiency in Basque and Spanish taking into account the number of hours devoted to each language in each of the models of bilingual education. As using Basque as the language of instruction faces many challenges, another area of interest has been to analyse the outcomes of teaching through the medium of Basque on achievement in other areas of the curriculum such as mathematics or science. Research on the outcomes of bilingual education has resulted in a number of PhD theses and other research studies and evaluations but also in reports commissioned by the Basque Government or municipalities.

Apart from Basque and Spanish, English is becoming increasingly important for Basque citizens as a medium of intra-European and international communication. As in many other areas in Europe, English is considered a third language but in the case of the Basque Country, it is also a foreign language not used in everyday communication. Nowadays most school children start learning English at the age of four, in kindergarten. One of the most important issues in research on the acquisition of English is the effect of bilingualism in Basque and Spanish on English proficiency. Research in this area aims at analysing whether bilingualism has an additive effect on the acquisition of an additional language as related to the advantages associated with bilingualism, such as the development of metalinguistic awareness or some specific strategies.

Another issue is related to the effect of the early introduction of a foreign language in school contexts. Most studies conducted in natural contexts where learners are exposed to the target language through interaction with native speakers confirm the "earlier the better" hypothesis. In these studies (see Singleton and Ryan 2004 for a review) ultimate achievement in the target language is related to age of arrival in the host country. This finding is not confirmed in formal settings in which the target language is only one of the subjects in the curriculum. Research conducted in the BAC in this area compares the acquisition of English by children who have started to learn English at different ages. Research on English in bilingual education has resulted in a number of Ph.D. theses and research articles published locally and internationally (for a review see Cenoz, forthcoming).

2.3.   Attitudes

There are a number of studies on attitudes which have focused on different dimensions. Some studies have measured the attitudes of the general population towards Basque, the Basque Government linguistic policy or the use of two languages in the community. Other studies have focused on the factors affecting attitudes and their relationship with academic achievement in educational contexts. Some other studies take into consideration the increasing influence of English and examine attitudes towards three languages (Basque, Spanish and English). The study of attitudes can be very informative so as to know the way the Basque population in general or students react towards the acquisition and use of the different languages in a community in which linguistic diversity is becoming more important and where the Basque language has a symbolic value as a marker of identity.

The Basque Government has included questions about attitudes in the sociolinguistic surveys. The section of the survey on attitudes focuses on the attitudes towards the Government's language policy and includes questions about assessment of policy to promote the use of Basque, and assessment of the language policy in education and the public sector. These questions give direct feedback to the Government about their general language policy to promote Basque.

Apart from the surveys conducted by the Basque Government, other researchers have carried out studies on other dimensions of attitudes. It is not possible to include all the research conducted on attitudes in this Chapter and we focus on the ones that deal with three languages because they are more representative of linguistic diversity. The studies on attitudes towards Basque, Spanish and English have been conducted in educational contexts.

Cenoz (2002) and Lasagabaster (2001, 2003) analysed attitudes towards learning Basque, Spanish and English and also attitudes towards multilingualism. The first part of their questionnaires is based on Gardner's attitude battery

(1985) and looks at the attitudes towards the three languages separately. The second part focuses on the three languages together and it is based on Baker (1992). Cenoz conducted her study in primary and secondary school and Lasagabaster at the university. Analysing attitudes towards these three languages and multilingualism can give useful information about educational contexts in which several languages are part of the curriculum.

2.4.   Visibility of the Basque language

Another approach to the study of the use of Basque and other languages is to examine the use of different languages in the linguistic landscape (Cenoz and Gorter 2006; Gorter and Cenoz 2007). These studies have focused on the use of Basque, Spanish and English in public and private language signs in different streets. A different way to study the linguistic landscape has been to use questionnaires and to conduct interviews on the way the use of the different languages in language signs is perceived (Gorter and Cenoz 2004). The study of the linguistic landscape provides a very important measure of the visibility of the language and the effect of language policy.

3.   Methods of data collection, data processing and data analysis

Research conducted on Basque has used different methods, different data collection procedures and different analyses. Some studies can be defined as more "institutional" and they tend to provide a description of the situation focusing mainly on the knowledge of Basque or on school achievement. Other studies have been conducted by researchers who have a theoretical model, a theoretical proposal or the results of research on a specific topic conducted in other contexts as a starting point and who try to see if their hypotheses can be confirmed in the Basque context. These studies are usually conducted by researchers and PhD candidates at the university. They usually go beyond the description of the data and in the case of quantitative studies analyse the effect of some variables on the dependent variable. In this section we will look at the methodology used in the four areas already considered.

3.1.   General knowledge and use of Basque

We can make a distinction between the sociolinguistic surveys conducted by the Basque Government and the "Street measurement of Basque use" conducted by the associations EKB and *Sei Elkarte*.

The sociolinguistic surveys on the knowledge and use of Basque by the general population look at the following variables: language proficiency, language use in the family, language use at work and in formal contexts, transmission in the family and attitudes towards language policy. The three surveys have been carried out every five years (1991, 1996, 2001). The data were collected via home interviews using a questionnaire. The sample for the most recent survey was 3,600 participants who were over 15 years of age. The results were projected to the total population of the BAC taking into account the 1996 census and the annual reviews of these data. The results are analysed according to the geographical distribution in the three provinces and in terms of age, gender, type of activity/job and language. The Basque Government Department of Culture has also published sociolinguistic maps of the BAC based on census and survey data. In these maps, the distribution of the Basque-speaking population in all the cities, towns and villages of the Basque Country is presented visually.

The "Street measurement of Basque use" studies use a completely different methodology which is quite original in sociolinguistic studies and we are going to discuss them in more detail. The methodology of this research consists of direct observation of people speaking on the street. The aim is to record the language used by speakers on the street without asking them any questions. Therefore, the data collection is carried out in a completely natural environment and the researcher's presence is hardly noticed by the speakers who do not know that they are providing data for a research study. This methodology has the advantage of not reflecting subjective data reported in questionnaires where subjects may decide to express their wishes or what they think is correct or expected instead of their real linguistic behaviour. In the case of street measurement, the researcher only has to listen to the language spoken and then records the results. As Altuna (2002a) says, this instrument was used after reflecting on the limitations that surveys have. One of the limitations of surveys is the subjectivity of the data and the other is that in situations such as that of Basque the knowledge of the language is not enough for a diagnosis. The "Street measurement of Basque use" does not have these limitations but can give information on the language actually spoken. It shows the number of people who use Basque on a specific date and time in a specific place and not the intention or decision to speak Basque.

Even though this is not measured explicitly, in most cases the conversations on the street are between members of the family, friends or other people and the topics are related to everyday life. In this sense, it is real use of the language in a natural setting. Altuna (2002a) points out that another advantage of this method is that the street is considered to be a neutral space; it has people with different levels of competence, different habits using the language and different ideas. The measurement is made in open places, in streets with lots of people, parks and playgrounds. Closed places (houses, bars, public offices or schools) are left out.

Table 1. Street measurement of Basque use (Source: Altuna 2002a)

N	1989	1993	1997	2001
People	329,860	275,335	254,914	241,708
Towns	47	112	160	173
Size of towns	>10,000 (all)	>5,000 (all) +some smaller	>5,000 (all) + some smaller	>5,000 (all) some smaller
Variables	Age	Age Group size	Age Group size Gender Children	Age Group size Gender Children

The research assistants collect data in one or more streets depending on the size of the town. If the town has less than 15,000 inhabitants then they do one round of the selected area and they do an extra round for every 10,000 inhabitants more. In most cases, the conversation is in one language the moment they are overheard but if the conversation includes a few words in another language only the main language is considered. All those participating in the conversation are considered measured even if they are not talking at the time the research assistants are observing. For example, if there are three people talking and the research assistant who is passing by hears that one of them is using Basque, the three are recorded as Basque users. Approximately 750 research assistants collect data at the same time and on the same two days in which the data collection takes place all over the Basque Country.

There have been four studies of street measurements (1989, 1993, 1997, 2001) and altogether over one million people have been observed. The observations have always taken place in the same month, in November, and every time on two days, a weekday and a Saturday. In addition to recording the language of each speaker, the surveys have looked at other variables. The following variables have been included in the last two surveys: age, gender, presence of children and size of the group. Table 1 shows the number of people, towns and variables included in the four studies.

The "Street measurement of Basque use" studies distinguish four age groups: children (0–14 years old), young people (15–24 years old), adults (25–64 years old) and older people (65+ years old). As the research assistants do not interact with the subjects they estimate which category the people belong to. They also look at the size and gender of the group speaking on the streets, and they note down if children are involved in the conversation, that is, if it is an adult talking to a child or a child talking to an adult or other children. These situations are distinguished from that of a group of adults having a conversation when a child is also present. The idea of looking at children comes from the assumption that Basque is spoken more in the presence of children or to address them. It is common for a couple to speak Spanish between them but Basque to their children even if the parents' first language is Spanish. The strong points of street measurement are the size of the sample and the fact that it is based on direct observation. The results of street measurement studies are useful to be related to the surveys so as to give a better picture of the sociolinguistic situation of the BAC.

3.2.   Outcomes of bilingual education

Research on the outcomes of bilingual education typically compares proficiency in Basque and Spanish in the different educational models. These models have a different distribution of hours for Basque and Spanish, with either Basque or Spanish or both languages as languages of instruction. The research also controls for other variables such as general intelligence, socio-economic background, sociolinguistic context, gender or language use. Most research in this area is quantitative and cross-sectional. Questionnaires and language tests are used to collect the data and statistical analyses are carried out so as to compare the different groups (Etxeberria 1999). Studies on the effect of bilingualism on the acquisition of English as a third language or on the influence of age on the acquisition of English also use questionnaires and proficiency tests and in some cases, they combine cross-sectional and longitudinal designs (Cenoz, forthcoming). These studies also control for other variables (motivation, language use, exposure to the language, etc).

3.3.   Attitudes

Most studies on attitudes are based on questionnaires and interviews. The research methodology used in the section on attitudes in the sociolinguistic surveys conducted by the Basque Government is the same as in the other sections of the surveys. They include specific questions about attitudes towards language policy in the BAC as part of the home interview along with the rest of questions.

The studies on attitudes towards Basque, Spanish, English and multilingualism are based on written questionnaires filled in by students. Cenoz (2002) asked informants to fill out the questionnaires along with other tests of English proficiency and a background questionnaire. The participants were 81 primary and secondary school students divided into three groups: 4th year of primary, 2nd year of secondary and 5th year of secondary. All subjects were from the same school and they all had Basque as the language of instruction. They all studied Spanish and English as school subjects. Lasagabaster (2001) collected data from 113 university students specialising in language studies and in his 2003 study he collected data from 1087 university students with different specialisations. Both Cenoz (2002) and Lasagabaster (2001, 2003) used questionnaires to measure attitudes towards the three languages, attitudes towards multilingualism and to get background information about the knowledge and use of the different languages.

3.4. Visibility of the Basque language

The studies of linguistic landscapes use different methodological approaches (Barni 2006; Gorter and Cenoz 2007). The direct measurement of languages signs on the streets is based on digital pictures of all the signs on the streets which are later analysed according to different categories such as public/private, number of languages on the sign, the languages on the sign, first language on the sign, etc. (Cenoz and Gorter 2006). Then the data are analysed using the SPSS program so as to obtain the different percentages on the use of the languages. This methodology has some problems related to the unit of analysis because either each individual sign or each establishment can be taken as the unit of analysis. In some cases it is also difficult to decide how to classify the name of the establishment. In spite of these problems the method can give an idea of the relative weight of the different languages in a given street or area. The studies on the perception of the linguistic landscape use questionnaires and interviews where the idea is to ask the participants which languages are used in the linguistic landscape and which languages are used more than others (Gorter and Cenoz 2004).

4. Outcomes

4.1. General knowledge and use of Basque

According to the most recent sociolinguistic survey conducted by the Basque Government (Eusko Jaurlaritza 2003), 29.4% of the population in the BAC is bilingual (Basque-Spanish), and 11.4% is passive bilingual, i.e., they can understand Basque but have limited production skills. Monolinguals in Spanish are 59.2% of the population. Therefore, Basque is a minority language within its own territory and with very few exceptions, speaking Basque equals being bilingual in Basque and Spanish. Table 2 gives the percentages of speakers corresponding to the surveys conducted in 1991, 1996 and 2001.

Table 2. Language competence in the Basque Autonomous Community (percentages)
(Source: Eusko Jaurlaritza 2003)

Language competence	1991	1996	2001
Bilingual (Basque-Spanish)	24.1	27.7	29.4
Passive bilingual (Basque-Spanish)	8.5	15.8	11.4
Monolingual (Spanish)	67.4	56.5	59.2

The data indicate that there is an increase in the percentage of bilinguals but monolinguals in Spanish are still the majority of the population. According to the same survey, the proportion of people who are proficient in Basque has increased in the three BAC provinces and in 2001 there were approximately 110,000 bilinguals more than in 1991, mainly because of the educational system. The number of Basque speakers has risen from 419,200 to 530,900 since 1991. The main increase has taken place in the 16–24 age group that has gone up from 25% of Basque speakers in 1991 to 48% in 2001.

Many of the new bilinguals are speakers of Basque as a second language who have learned Basque at school. In most cases, second language users do not speak Basque at home but sometimes they speak Basque with their friends. Bilinguals in Basque and Spanish have been further divided into three categories, i.e., "Basque-dominant bilinguals" (28.2% of the bilinguals), "balanced bilinguals" (26.8% of the bilinguals) and "Spanish-dominant" bilinguals (45% of the bilinguals). Almost half of the speakers of Basque find it easier to use Spanish and Basque and according to the survey data this percentage is increasing.

The survey data indicate that there is a slight increase in the use of Basque. The use changes according to the number of speakers in the individual's social networks, the sociolinguistic area and the age group. Family transmission is one of the most crucial aspects of reversing language shift (Fishman 1991; Azurmendi et al. 2001) and it is still weak in the Basque context. According to the survey data, 76.1% have Spanish as the first language, 18.8% Basque and 5.1% both Basque and Spanish. When both parents speak Basque, there has been clear progress in Basque language transmission; this holds even in those cases in which only one parent speaks Basque.

According to the survey the two main factors influencing the use of Basque are the density of Basque speakers in the social networks and the fluency in Basque and Spanish. The former is closely linked to the sociolinguistic area and the latter to being a speaker of Basque as a first language. Other factors such as age or the attitude towards supporting Basque have some influence on the use of Basque but they are not as important. Basque is still a language with

Table 3. Use of Basque on the streets (percentages) (Source: Altuna 2002b)

Provinces	1989	1993	1997	2001
Gipuzkoa	23.3	25.5	29.2	29.9
Bizkaia	8.1	9.1	9.7	11.0
Araba	3.9	3.9	3.8	3.3
Basque Country	10.8	12.0	13.0	13.5

a very limited number of speakers; the total number of active bilinguals who use more Basque than Spanish or as much Basque as Spanish is estimated to be 291,500, which is only 18.6% of the population of the BAC. There are also 251,600 bilinguals who speak Basque but less than Spanish, which is 16.9% of the population. The majority of the population (64.4%) only uses Spanish in all contexts.

The surveys also provide information about the distribution of the Basque-speaking population and show that there are important differences in the three provinces: Gipuzkoa has 48% of bilinguals (9.5% passive bilinguals), Bizkaia 22.4% of bilinguals (12.6% passive bilinguals) and Alava only 13.4% of bilinguals (11.1% passive bilinguals).

The "Street measurement of Basque use" studies (Altuna 2002b) have reported a slight increase in the use of Basque in two of the three Basque provinces (Gipuzkoa and Bizkaia) but not in Araba. The general figure for the whole of the Basque Country (including Navarre and the North Basque Country in France) has increased from 10.8% in 1989 to 13.5% in 2001 (see Table 3).

It has also been observed that the increase in the use of Basque has taken place mainly in towns between 25,000 and 100,000 inhabitants but that there has been a decrease in towns with less than 5,000 inhabitants. When the data on language use are compared to those on the knowledge of Basque it can be observed that the increase in the use of Basque has taken place in towns in which the number of speakers does not reach 50%. This slight increase in the use of Basque has taken place in the towns with most Spanish speakers.

4.2. Outcomes of bilingual education

A large number of studies have focused on the outcomes of bilingual programs; some have been conducted by the Basque Government Institute of Education and Research in Education and others by university researchers (Etxeberria 1999 and Cenoz, forthcoming). The evaluations have focused mainly on proficiency in Basque and Spanish and academic achievement.

Proficiency in Basque

The results of the studies indicate that there are significant differences in Basque proficiency when the three models are compared. Students with Basque as the language of instruction are the ones with the highest proficiency in Basque followed by students who have both Basque and Spanish as the language of instruction. The lowest level of proficiency in Basque corresponds to students who have Spanish as the language of instruction and only study Basque as a subject for a few hours a week.

Proficiency in Spanish

The results indicate that there are no significant differences related to the language of instruction. Even students who have Basque as the language of instruction and only study Spanish for 4–5 hours a week achieve very high levels of proficiency in Spanish. It seems likely that since Spanish is the majority language in the BAC, opportunities for extensive exposure to it outside school compensate for reduced exposure to it in school.

Academic achievement

Evaluations of achievement in mathematics and the natural and social sciences indicate that so far there are no significant differences between students in different models.

Proficiency in English

Research findings on the acquisition of English as a third language in the BAC indicate that the use of Basque as the language of instruction and higher levels of bilingualism are positively related with higher levels of proficiency in English (Cenoz and Valencia 1994; Lasagabaster 2000; Sagasta, 2003). These results could be explained as related to higher levels of metalinguistic awareness associated with bilingualism and more highly developed learning strategies associated with L3 acquisition. The studies on the age factor in the acquisition of a third language in the school context indicate that an early introduction of English as a third language does not necessary imply higher proficiency in this language (Cenoz, forthcoming). The limited amount of exposure to English in the Basque educational context is a possible explanation for these results which have also been reported in Catalonia (Muñoz 2006).

4.3.   Attitudes

The results of the attitudes section of the most recent sociolinguistic survey (2001) indicate that attitudes towards the Government's policy for the promotion of Basque have not changed as compared to previous surveys. In general terms, the majority of the population in the BAC supports this policy. Tables 4 and 5 show percentages corresponding to the survey questions on the Government's policy to promote the use of Basque and the policy in education and the public sector. As expected, the most favourable attitudes towards the promotion of Basque can be found in those areas of the BAC with a higher percentage of Basque speakers.

The results of the studies in which attitudes towards Basque, Spanish and English have been measured confirm that attitudes towards Basque and towards learning Basque are positive. Cenoz (2002) found that students had more positive attitudes towards Basque than towards Spanish and English. She also found that younger students had more positive attitudes towards the three languages than older students but that positive attitudes towards English did not imply better scores in the English tests. Lasagabaster (2001) found that students with Basque as the first language had more positive attitudes towards Basque than other students but less positive attitudes towards English and multilingualism. Lasagabaster (2003) reported that the level of proficiency is closely associated with positive attitudes, mainly in the case of the minority language. He also

Table 4. Support for the Government's promotion of the use of Basque (percentages) (Source: Eusko Jaurlaritza 2003)

	1991	1996	2001
Agree and completely agree	52.1	47.3	50.3
Indifferent	29.5	37.2	33.6
Against and completely against	18.3	15.4	16.1

Table 5. Basque Government policy in education and the public sector (percentages) (Source: Eusko Jaurlaritza 2003)

	Education	Public sector
Appropriate	63	52
Not enough to support Basque	8	11
Too much is done	5	7
Indifferent	24	30

found that the sociolinguistic context of the students has an influence on their attitudes.

4.4.   Visibility of the Basque language

The study of the linguistic landscape (Cenoz and Gorter 2006), conducted on one of the main shopping streets in Donostia-San Sebastián, shows that Basque on its own or in combination with other languages appeared in over 50% of the signs. Spanish is by far the most dominant language and it appears in 82% of the signs. English appears in 28% of the signs. There are also differences between official and private signs. More Basque is used in official signs but English is only used in private signs. Cenoz and Gorter (2006) conducted a comparison of these results to those of the main shopping street in the Frisian city of Ljouwert-Leeuwarden. They found a positive effect of a strong language policy to protect the minority language in the case of Basque as compared to Frisian. While Basque appeared in over 50% of the signs, Frisian only appeared in 5% of the signs even though the percentage of speakers who are fluent in Frisian is higher than those fluent in Basque. In another study, Gorter and Cenoz (2004) found that speakers in the Basque Country have a stronger preference for bilingual/multilingual signs than speakers in Friesland.

5.   Conclusions and discussion

Research conducted in the Basque Country on different aspects of the vitality of Basque indicates that the strong language policy to promote the Basque language in the BAC has stopped the decrease of Basque but that its knowledge and use is quite limited in everyday life, with the exception of education.

The situation of Basque is related to the specific context of the Basque language and it is the result of a variety of social, historical and economic factors. The fact that it is a language "at risk" is related to its long contact with more powerful languages and the centralised Spanish and French policy in the 19th and 20th centuries. The most critical stage for the Basque language came after the Spanish Civil War (1936–1939) during Franco's dictatorship (1939–1975). At the end of this period there were important political changes and strong social movements to support Basque. This explains that nowadays Basque is one of the minority languages in Europe with very strong institutional and social support. This situation together with other linguistic, cultural and social factors make the situation of Basque different from that of other minority languages. However, research conducted in the Basque country can contribute to research on linguistic diversity in Europe and can also benefit from the research conducted in other

European contexts with regional minority (RM) and immigrant minority (IM) languages.

As Extra and Gorter (2001) say, RM and IM languages have a lot in common because of their minority status which implies processes of language maintenance and language shift towards the majority language. The interaction between researchers of these languages and the study of their research methodologies can certainly improve our knowledge of these processes. According to Extra and Gorter (2001), RM and IM languages also share their role as marker of identity. This is certainly true in the case of Basque which is a salient marker of Basque identity but it is also true in the case of majority languages. For example, the important budget allocated by the European Union to interpretation for the "majority" languages is an indication of this role; there is no agreement to use somebody else's language as the language of communication.

There are some important differences between RM and IM languages which have to be taken into consideration when comparing different contexts. One of them has to do with the definition and identification of population groups. In the Introduction to this Volume, Barni and Extra discuss four different criteria to identify different groups, i.e., nationality, birth country, self-categorisation and home language. In the case of RM languages only the last two of these criteria could be considered but the main problem of applying these criteria is that, at least in the case of Basque, it would be very difficult to identify a population group. It is possible to give figures or percentages for self-categorisation (feeling Basque, Spanish or both) or home language (Basque, Spanish or both) but the problem is the concept of population group. It is difficult to draw a clear line between the "Spanish" group and the "Basque" group because they are completely mixed in many situations. Compare the following examples:

– *Family A*
  A family with Basque-speaking grandparents, Spanish speaking parents and children who have learned Basque at school but do not use it with their Spanish speaking parents. They all have Basque names and some feel only Basque and others both Basque and Spanish.

– *Family B*
  The two parents are Spanish-speaking and they interact in Spanish but are proficient in Basque and only use Basque with the children. At school, the children have Basque as the language of instruction. They have Spanish names because the grandparents immigrated from Spain in the 1960s but they feel more Basque than Spanish.

It is certainly difficult to apply the concept of population groups to situations like these, which are extremely common in the Basque Country and probably more common in the case of RM than in the case of IM languages. Another important difference between RM and IM languages is the vitality of the language in its more general sense of being alive or "at risk". Following the UNESCO Declaration (2002) that compares cultural diversity to biodiversity, languages such as Basque, Frisian or Welsh are the rare species that need special measures to be protected, as it is the case with the blue whale, the Tristan Albatross or the *Hibiscus Insularis*. On the other hand, many of the IM languages such as Mandarin, Turkish or Arabic are spoken by millions of people and are not "at risk". At the same time, these IM languages are minority languages which also contribute to the cultural diversity of Europe and should be protected but important differences in language policy and in the allocation of economic resources for the protection of the two types of languages can be expected.

The research methodology used in the Basque Country includes different measures and confirms what Barni (2006) discusses about the need for triangulation in order to get a more accurate picture of the situation. The combination of language surveys with studies of language use on the street, studies on the outcomes of bilingual education, studies on the visibility of Basque and studies on attitudes can contribute to get a better picture of the important changes that have taken place in the Basque Country and of its current sociolinguistic situation. Both RM and IM languages are in a dynamic situation and face new challenges all the time. Basque research reflects one of the main challenges of Basque the use of the language in everyday life and has developed an interesting research methodology to analyse this use. This "Street measurement of Basque use" could also be adapted to other contexts. Another challenge for Basque is the impact of IM languages on the knowledge and use of Basque. This is another important point that can be discussed in different European contexts. It is certainly necessary to share the information from different RM and IM contexts and to develop methodologies for mapping and measuring diversity in the European context.

References

Altuna, O.
    2002a   Erabileraren kale neurketa. Ibilbidea eta metodologia. *Bat Soziolinguistika Aldizkaria* 43: 25–35.
    2002b   Erabileraren IV kale neurketa. Emaitzen azterketa. *Bat Soziolinguistika Aldizkaria* 43: 37–48.

Azurmendi, M.J., E. Bachoc and F. Zabaleta
    2001   Reversing language shift: the case of Basque. In: J.A. Fishman (ed.), *Can Threatened Languages Be Saved?*, 234–260. Clevedon: Multilingual Matters.

Azurmendi, M.J. and I. Martínez de Luna
    2006   Introduction. In: M.J. Azurmendi and I. Martínez de Luna (eds.), *The Case of Basque: Past, Present and Future*, 13–18. Andoain: Soziolinguistika Klusterra.

Barni, M.
    2006   *From Statistical to Geolinguistic Data: Mapping and Measuring Linguistic Diversity.* (*www.feem.it/Feem/Pub/Publications/WPapers/default.htm*)

Baker, C.
    1992   *Attitudes and Language.* Clevedon: Multilingual Matters.

Cenoz, J.
    2001   Basque in Spain and France. In: G. Extra and D. Gorter (eds.), *The Other Languages of Europe*, 45–57. Clevedon: Multilingual Matters.
    2002   Three languages in contact: language attitudes in the Basque Country. In: D. Lasagabaster and J. Sierra (eds.), *Language Awareness in the Foreign Language Classroom*, 37–60. Bilbao: University of the Basque Country.
    in press The Basque language Baskisch. In: U. Ammon and H. Haarmann (eds.), *Wieser Enzyklopädie der Sprachen Westereuropas*. Klagenfurt: Wieser.
    forthc.   *Towards Multilingual Education: Basque Educational Research in International Perspective.* Clevedon: Multilingual Matters

Cenoz, J. and D. Gorter
    2006   Linguistic landscape and minority languages. *The International Journal of Multilingualism* 3: 67–80.

Cenoz, J. and J. Valencia
    1994   Additive trilingualism: evidence from the Basque Country. *Applied Psycholinguistics* 15: 157–209.

Etxeberria, F.
    1999   *Bilingüismo y Educación en el País del Euskara.* Donostia: Erein

Eusko Jaurlaritza
    1995   *Euskararen Jarraipena. La Continuidad del Euskera. La Continuité de la Langue Basque* (Volume I). Vitoria-Gasteiz.
    1997   *Euskararen Jarraipena. La Continuidad del Euskera. La Continuité de la Langue Basque* (Volume II). Vitoria-Gasteiz.
    2003   *Euskararen Jarraipena. La Continuidad del Euskera. La Continuité de la Langue Basque* (Volume III). Vitoria-Gasteiz.

Extra, G. and D. Gorter
2001   Comparative perspectives on regional and immigrant minority languages in multicultural Europe. In: G. Extra and D. Gorter (eds.), *The Other Languages of Europe*, 1–41. Clevedon: Multilingual Matters.

Extra, G. and K. Yağmur
2004   Demographic perspectives. In: G. Extra and K. Yağmur (eds.), *Urban Multilingualism in Europe*, 25–72. Clevedon: Multilingual Matters.

Fishman, J.
1991   *Reversing Language Shift: Theoretical and Empirical Foundations of Assistance to Threatened Languages*. Philadelphia: Multilingual Matters.

Gardner, R.
1985   *Social Psychology and Second Language Learning*. London: Arnold.

Gorter, D. and J. Cenoz
2004   *Linguistic Landscapes and L2 Learners in Multilingual Contexts*. Paper at EUROSLA 14 (European Second Language Association Conference), 8–11 September 2004, San Sebastian/Donostia, Basque Country, Spain.
2007   Knowledge about language and linguistic landscape. In: J. Cenoz and N.H. Hornberger (eds.), *Encyclopedia of Language and Education* Volume 6: Knowledge about language, 343–355. Berlin: Springer

Lasagabaster, D.
2000   Three languages and three linguistic models in the Basque Educational System. In: J. Cenoz and U. Jessner (eds.), *English in Europe: The Acquisition of a Third Language*, 179–197. Clevedon: Multilingual Matters.
2001   University students' attitudes towards English as an L3. In: J. Cenoz, B. Hufeisen and U. Jessner (eds.), *Looking Beyond Second Language Acquisition*, 43–50. Tübingen: Stauffenburg.
2003   *Trilingüismo en la Enseñanza: Actitudes hacia la Lengua Minoritaria, la Mayoritaria y la Extranjera*. Lleida: Milenio.

Muñoz, C. (ed.)
2006   *Age and the Rate of Foreign Language Learning*. Clevedon: Multilingual Matters.

Sagasta, Mª P.
2003   Acquiring writing skills in a third language: The positive effects of bilingualism. *International Journal of Bilingualism* 7: 27–42.

Singleton, D. and L. Ryan
2004   *Language Acquisition: the Age Factor*. Clevedon: Multilingual Matters.

UNESCO
2002   Unesco Universal Declaration on Language Diversity.
        http://www.unesco.org/education/imld_2002/unversal_decla.shtml

Zuazo, K.
1995   The Basque Country and the Basque Language: An overview of the ex-
        ternal history of the Basque language. In: J. Ignacio Hualde, J. Lakarra
        and L. Trask (eds.), *Towards a History of the Basque Language*, 5–30.
        Philadelphia: John Benjamins.

Language surveys on Frisian in the Netherlands

Durk Gorter

1. Introduction

This chapter focuses on language survey research at a macro-level. In some European cases, for instance in Friesland and in Ireland, language surveys have been replicated at regular time intervals over a period of more than thirty years or longer. The first survey in Friesland was carried out in 1967 and the first in Ireland in 1973 (CILAR 1975). In recent years, several surveys have been conducted in most minority language communities across the European Union (henceforward EU). The Euromosaic study in particular (1996, 2004) included a number of survey studies of minority language groups that had not been carried out before.

Language surveys can give us representative data about a language group, about the language competence of its members, and about the use of languages across generations and in different sectors of society. The aim of this chapter is to point to some of the advantages, problems, possibilities and limitations of conducting sociological language surveys among minority language groups based upon the experiences in Friesland, The Netherlands.

Section 2 opens with a description of the background of the Frisian language. The next section contains a description and analysis of the major Frisian sociolinguistic surveys since the 1960s. The section deals with survey research as a way to map the linguistic diversity of the region of Friesland. Section 3.1 deals with a number of general characteristics of surveys in a minority language context. In section 3.2, their goals and rationale are given. Section 3.3 deals with the method of survey research emphasizing aspects related to the multilingual context. In section 3.4, some of the major outcomes are presented. In the final section 4, conclusions about current and future research into the mapping of linguistic diversity in a multilingual province such as Friesland are outlined.

2.   Background to the Frisian language: history, migration and dialects

2.1.   History

Somewhere between 500 and 700 AD North Sea Germanic (also called *Ingweonic*) evolved into separate languages, Frisian being one of them (Bremmer 1997: 69–70). Historically, Frisian is most closely related to English and both languages are part of the North-Sea Germanic branch of the larger West Germanic language group. As a result of language contact over several centuries, the development of Frisian was influenced most strongly by Dutch.

In the early Middle Ages, Frisian was spoken not only in the present province of Friesland (*Fryslân*) but over a much larger area in a narrow strip along the coast of what are now the Dutch provinces of Zuid-Holland, Noord-Holland and Groningen and also in the adjoining area of East Friesland (*Ostfriesland*) in the north-west of Germany up to the river *Weser*. Over the ages, Frisian gradually disappeared from these areas (Niebaum 2001).

The change from Latin to the vernacular implied that Frisian was widely used in writing during the 14th and 15th centuries. In 1498, Friesland got new rulers; during the 16th and 17th centuries the area became gradually incorporated into the Republic of the Netherlands. During the 16th century, Frisian texts became scarcer and the language gradually disappeared from the more densely populated towns and retreated to the countryside (Vries 1997). In the same period, a new variety arose in the towns through intensive contact with (early) Dutch in administration and in trade. It is designated as *town-Frisian*, but linguistically it is regarded as a dialect of Dutch (Jonkman 1993; Van Bree 1994).

During the 17th and 18th centuries, Frisian scarcely functioned as a written language at all. A movement to revive Frisian began in the early 19th century (Zondag 1993). Only in the 20th century did the Frisian language regain a modest position in government, education and the media (Gorter 2001a).

2.2.   Migration

It can be estimated that up until the 1950s over 90% of households in the rural areas spoke Frisian, while it was spoken in less than 20% of households in the towns (Boelens and Van der Veen 1956). The majority in some towns spoke town-Frisian. Migration has changed this pattern, although Frisian still has its strongest base in the countryside. Changes in intergenerational language transmission and mixed-language marriages led to fewer children with Frisian as their mother tongue.

Friesland experienced an emigration surplus over almost the whole of the 19th and 20th centuries. In most years the negative balance of migration was in the order of 2,000 to 5,000 people. Two periods stand out. Towards the end of the 19th century (1880–1899) and right after World War II (1946–1955), the surplus reached a level of over 10,000 people per year. It was only in the period between 1971 and 1980 that Friesland experienced an influx of immigrants, with an average of around 5,000 newcomers. The growth in the population is due mainly to a birth surplus and longer life expectancy (from a total of 176,000 inhabitants in 1815 through 340,000 in 1900 to 643,000 in 2007).

Since World War II, industrialisation and technological changes in agriculture have had an enormous impact in the countryside. Population growth has become concentrated in a limited number of larger towns with a linguistically heterogeneous population. In addition, improvements in transport, the development of mass-tourism and new forms of telecommunication have led to more frequent contact with Dutch and with other languages, English in particular. The whole population has undergone a process of mental urbanisation.

The provincial borders of Friesland roughly coincide with the linguistic borders of the area in which Frisian is spoken. It is only in a small part of the neighbouring province of Groningen, where the language border crosses the administrative border, that a few thousand speakers of Frisian are found outside the province of Friesland (Gorter, Jansma and Jelsma 1991).

2.3. Dialectal varieties

The Frisian-speaking community is basically homogeneous and the main dialectal varieties are mutually intelligible; peripheral dialects may present more difficulties. Traditionally, the Frisian language is divided into three broad regional dialects: Clay Frisian (*Klaaifrysk*), Woodlands Frisian (*Wâldfrysk*) and South-West Corner Frisian (*Súdwesthoeksk*) (Hof 1933; Van der Veen 2001). The standard variety of Frisian evolved gradually during the 19th and 20th centuries.

More peripheral dialects of Frisian are in use by the inhabitants of the small town of Hindeloopen (*Hylpen*) and the Wadden Islands of Schiermonnikoog (*Skiermûntseach*) and Terschelling (*Skylge*). They cannot be understood without effort. The dialects are hardly transmitted to the next generation.

Town-Frisian is spoken in the towns of Leeuwarden, Bolsward, Dokkum, Franeker, Harlingen, Sneek and Stavoren. As a mixture of Dutch and Frisian it can be readily understood by speakers of both languages. The municipality *It Bilt* is a polder where since the 16th century so-called *Biltsk* is spoken; this is also a Dutch-Frisian mixture.

In the south-eastern part of Friesland, in the municipalities of *Ooststellingwerf* and *Weststellingwerf*, a Saxon dialect is spoken (Wouda 2003). All these dialects have a hard time surviving and they are spoken less and less with every new generation.

It should finally be pointed out that (West-) Frisian bears a strong linguistic resemblance to the Sater Frisian and North Frisian languages of Germany. Because of their separate historical development and great geographical distance, the three languages are quite different from each other today and cannot be treated as one minority language.

The language situation in Friesland involves more than just the bilingualism of Frisian and Dutch and their dialects. The number of languages in daily life has increased substantially over the last few years due to immigration and globalisation. This can be demonstrated by the changes in the provincial capital of Leeuwarden, where over 50 different languages are spoken at home today by primary school children (Van der Avoird et al. 1999). English is among the most important of these home languages. The importance of English is also reflected in the linguistic landscape (the public display of languages) where English and Dutch are most prominent and Frisian only takes up a minor place (Cenoz and Gorter 2006).

3.   Sociolinguistic surveys

3.1.   Characteristics of a survey in a minority language context

Carrying out a survey project may seem a relatively straightforward exercise, which is not all that difficult to carry out if the right resources in terms of staff, finance and time are available. In a superficial sense this is completely true, as the basic ingredients can easily be listed and are well known in our society today. Surveys with standardised questionnaires have become one of the most widely used research instruments over the past few decades. This type of survey is not only used for scientific studies, but also and quite widely for market research and public opinion polling. The only reason for doing such surveys sometimes seems to be to create news for the mass media. Table 1 gives an overview of the various stages that can be distinguished in carrying out a survey.

Although such a list of steps seems simple and straightforward, each stage is in fact characterised by a multitude of problems and several detailed methodological studies have been done on each of the stages separately. One can find a plethora of handbooks dealing with designing and executing survey research in general (Alreck and Settle 1985; Babbie 1973; Bradburn and Sudman 1980; Miller 1991), and several specialised books on, e.g., questionnaire design, sampling methods or statistical techniques of data analysis. However, there is only a rather limited number of publications on the technical and methodological pe-

Table 1. Stages and activities in carrying out a survey project

Stage	Activities
1	Formulation of objectives
2	Formulation of research questions
3	Determination of variables
4	Design of questionnaire
5	Definition of sampling frame
6	Data collection
7	Data analysis
8	Reporting and dissemination

culiarities of surveys where language, multilingualism or minority languages is the focus of research. Lieberson already pointed out this lack of studies in 1980, but not much has changed in the 25 years that have passed since then. When handbooks or specialised studies on survey methodology are examined, one finds little or nothing relating to the issues of language or multilingualism. The only issues that do get some attention are values in cross-cultural studies (Peng, Nisbett and Wong 1997) or the translation of questionnaires in international studies or studies that involve different language groups (e.g., Behling and Law 2000). In short, the study of how language functions as a social phenomenon is a rather specialised type of survey research. Each of the stages mentioned in Table 1 has some peculiarities in the context of a language survey among a minority language group.

(1) The *objective* of a language survey can be to take stock of the situation and of the development of a minority language *vis-à-vis* a majority language in one particular language community. Another objective can be to measure the degree of language maintenance or language vitality among one or more minority language groups. Various additional objectives might be testing a theory or a theoretical proposition, providing a detailed description to underpin a language policy, or comparing different communities.

(2) The *research questions* depend on the objectives of the survey and have been paraphrased in a classic sociolinguistic study as the broader issue of "who is speaking what language to whom, when and why?" (Fishman 1965).

(3) The research questions have to be transformed into measurable *variables*. As concept-indicators they will help to answer the research questions. Table 2 gives an idea of the concept-indicators that were used to draft questionnaires in studies of four different European minority languages, i.e., Basque, Frisian, Irish and Welsh. These variables were operationalised in a questionnaire with mainly closed, multiple-choice type questions.

Table 2. Concept-indicators (ELSN 1996)

Concepts	Variables
Language competence	Speaking Understanding Reading Writing
Language use	Family Interpersonal relations Neighbourhood Work Public environment Media
Language attitudes	Group identity Language and identity Reasons for language learning Education policies Media policies Language policies in public sector

(4) Once the variables have been determined, they in turn have to be operationalised into a *questionnaire*. The formulation of questions, based on concept-indicators, is among the most important steps in any survey project. In total, the four questionnaires in the *European Language Survey Network* contained over one thousand discrete questionnaire items on a wide variety of topics, not counting socio-demographic background questions on, e.g., age, marital status, place of residence, education, or socio-economic status. When dealing with survey studies in a bilingual community there are additional problems, such as which language to use for the questions: only one (if so, which one?), both languages (or even three)? Questionnaires need to be developed in more than one language and should be reliable, complete, accurate, and culturally appropriate.

(5) As far as the *sampling frame* is concerned, most people would agree that the sample has to be representative. But a researcher may forget to answer questions like "representative of what, or how?" Will the sample include only speakers of the minority language, for instance, because the group is only a small proportion of the total population, or are all inhabitants of a certain area interviewed? The criterion of randomness is important in a sample, but few people are able to decide whether a two-stage cluster sample is best used to fulfil that criterion rather than a stratified sample. For regional minority language communities, the issue of borders may also come up: is the sample to be drawn

from the population of the administrative area or from the linguistic area (the two areas in most cases do not fully overlap)? All these questions are important for the outcomes to be obtained and have to be answered before data collection can start.

(6) In terms of *data collection*, there are many other, but all of them related issues. A decision has to be made whether the interviews are to be carried out through surface mail, by telephone, by means of face-to-face interviews, or through the Internet. If carried out through interviews, another important issue is the language to be used during the interview. This choice may be quite complicated when dealing with a minority language (with low prestige and/or not likely to be used in formal situations). A related issue concerns the proficiency of the interviewers to carry out interviews: are they sufficiently skilled to carry them out in two (or more) languages?

(7) Many general techniques for *data analysis* are well known, such as frequency counts, cross-tabulation, analysis of variance, correlation, factor analysis, multiple regression or structural modelling. These are usually independent of issues of multilingualism.

(8) Finally, writing up the *report* and disseminating the results may seem quite straightforward, but again one is faced with many questions, such as the language to choose or the target audience to write for.

3.2.   Rationale and goals of research

Large-scale surveys on language competence, language use and language attitudes were conducted three times in the province of Friesland in the Netherlands, and a fourth time is planned for 2008. In the meantime, a large number of similar smaller surveys of one town, of an institution or a school population were carried out, some of them using a different technique, such as telephone interviews or an Internet panel.

The first population survey in Friesland was held in 1967. It was carried out and reported on by Pietersen (1969). This survey was repeated and extended substantially in 1980, as reported by Gorter et al. (1984, 1988). Again in 1994, a similar large-scale survey was carried out and published by Gorter and Jonkman (1995). A fourth survey is to take place in 2008. These four surveys will be dealt with in this section.

The rationale for these surveys is a mixture of scientific, language-political and practical motives. The basic objective of these overall population surveys is to obtain insight into the social and geographical distribution of the language varieties spoken in the province: Frisian, Dutch, several non-Frisian dialects and "other" languages. Over a period of several decades longitudinal data have become available because these surveys are partially replicated. This makes it possible to search for the dynamics in the relative social positions of each language variety.

In the introduction to the first survey, Pietersen (1969: 7–8) describes the reason for his survey as the need for data on reading habits and reading preferences in Friesland. His aim is also clear from the structure of the questionnaire. It is only in the second half that questions are asked on language proficiency and language use and on people's opinions of Frisian. This first survey can be called pioneering work. Pietersen (1969: 8) was right when he remarked that "so far there has been very little sociolinguistic research on the topic of bilingualism". Today no one would dare to state the same.

Once the effects of the study by Pietersen had worn off after a few years, the initiative was taken to repeat the study. This was perceived as all the more pressing because from 1971, for the first time in history, the province of Friesland had a surplus of immigrants. Many people were convinced that language relationships had changed profoundly. In 1975, a plan was launched to repeat the survey. In the publication of the second survey the goal is described as follows (translated from Gorter et al. 1984: 1):

> Our research is first of all aimed at the description of multilingualism in Friesland. We will describe according to a number of important themes:
>
> – the geographic spread of the language groups
> – the social stratification of the language groups
> – the transmission of the languages, in particular within the family
> – the proficiency in the languages, in particular in Frisian
> – the opinions about the Frisian language and the identification with the Frisian language group
> – the use of the languages, in particular of Frisian, in a number of important domains of daily life: work, neighbourhood, school, public life and in associations
> – the position of Frisian, the attitude towards Frisian and the role of Frisian speakers in particular in the arena of the school, the church, the media, and politics; buying and reading of Frisian books and magazines will be dealt with as well

The third survey refers to the two previous surveys and repeats "the goal (is) to obtain good insight into the proportions of the language varieties spoken there: Frisian, Dutch and several non-Frisian dialects". With this third survey, a longitudinal corpus of sociolinguistic data became available covering more than a quarter of a century. Looking for systematic trends also became a goal (Gorter and Jonkman 1995; Jonkman 1999). The third survey also refers explicitly to the importance of international comparison in a European context. The researchers took part in the *European Language Survey Network* where knowledge and experience were exchanged with researchers from the Basque Country, Ireland and Wales, Catalonia and Galicia. The fourth survey in 2008 will again have to provide a basic description of the dynamics in language relationships.

3.3. Methods of data collection

Methodological differences and similarities between the first three projects appear in the domains of (a) the problem definition, (b) the questionnaire, (c) the sample, and (d) the language used in the interviews (see also Gorter et al 1984: 280–283; Gorter and Jonkman 1995). The relationship between the three projects can best be referred to as one of partial replication. Replication of a survey means that a project builds on a former one in terms of its design, for instance, and the way the questions are formulated. At the same time, new elements were added and others were removed.

The problem definitions are only partly the same. In the first project, the emphasis was on reading habits, and the sociolinguistic questions on language proficiency, use and attitudes were "taken along", which gives the project a somewhat dual character (Pietersen 1969: 7–8). In *Taal yn Fryslân*, the well-known question "Who speaks what language to whom and when?" is taken as the point of departure (Gorter et al. 1984: 3). The questionnaire only contains language-related questions. The third survey takes the same WWWW-question as its point of departure, but also takes a second survey on board, which concerns issues of religion and convictions.

The questionnaire in all three projects has about the same length. But the contents diverge through different emphases in the problem definitions. Also the order of comparable questions differs. Moreover, Pietersen used rather broad questions on language use. Thus, in one single question he asked "When you go to a physician, a notary, a minister/pastor, a chief/managing director, which language do you usually speak?" In the second and third projects, such questions were split up into a series of separate questions. Questions on language transmission are conspicuously absent in Pietersen, while in the later studies a series of questions are asked about children's language background and language use. Changes in the patterns of intergenerational language transmission can thus only be established on the basis of the last two surveys.

A conspicuous difference is that the language-related questions in the first questionnaire are introduced cautiously. The intention was to "prevent too emotional reactions (...) Therefore in the questionnaire (...) always an approach was sought that would not meet with resistance" (Pietersen 1969: 51). In retrospect, the researchers of the second survey project found this approach too cautious. The second survey was introduced to the respondents as a study of the use of and the attitude towards the languages in Friesland. A similar approach was chosen in the third survey, which was introduced as a study about language and convictions. As far as language proficiency, language use and language attitudes are concerned, the aim was to repeat as much as possible. All in all, there are 67 questions, including background variables, in the first and the second surveys which are more or less the same (Gorter et al. 1984: 321–323) and some 40 questions are repeated in all three surveys.

The samples of the projects differ in size and in design. In 1967, there were 800 respondents in the sample, against 1,126 in 1980 and 1,368 in 1994. Thus there are some differences in size, but these are relatively small. More important is the difference in sampling design. Pietersen (1969) has a two-stage sample, which is very common when a sample is drawn from the Netherlands as a whole. He first draws municipalities, 11 out of 44 in Friesland, and after that in every municipality the same number of addresses. In a technical sense, there is nothing against this sample design. One can, however, have one's doubts whether the practical reasons for such a design in the Netherlands with (then) over 900 municipalities are equally applicable when dealing with only 44 municipalities. In 1980, it was decided to have a single-stage sample design in terms of drawing from all Frisian municipalities a number of respondents depending on the size of the population. An advantage is the optimal geographic spread, which is especially important where regional dialects are concerned.

An important difference between the three samples is the percentage of non-responses. In the case of Pietersen it is not certain how high this was, as replacements were used (in order to obtain the targeted sample of 800 respondents). In any case, the percentage of non-response was very low, probably less than 5%. At that time, a survey was an exceptional event in society in general. There are even anecdotes of people dressing up in their Sunday clothes because the interviewer had selected them for an interview. When the second large-scale survey took place, people had become used to surveys and some had got tired of them. Non-response was then 19%, still relatively low compared to many surveys in the Netherlands. In the 1990s, people were flooded by all manner of surveys, especially by commercial telephone surveys. Quite a few people "just did not feel like taking part in surveys" and could not be persuaded to participate, as a result of which the percentage of non-response rose to 30%, still quite low compared to other surveys, the average general non-response rate having risen to over 50%.

The language of the interviews and thus of the questionnaires is one of the most striking differences between the first two surveys. Pietersen (1969: 50–119)

Table 3. Overview of the four language surveys in Friesland

Survey	Fieldwork	N questions	N inform.	Publ. in
Pietersen	Spring 1967	76 (224 items)	800	1969
Gorter, Jelsma, Van der Plank and De Vos	Autumn 1980	138 (311 items)	1,126	1984
Gorter and Jonkman	Spring 1994	80 (172 items)	1,368	1995
Gorter et al.	Spring 2008	>100	>1,000	2009

defends the use of Dutch only in his interviews. In the second and third surveys, interviews were conducted both in Frisian and Dutch. The idea was to get as close as possible to the daily language behaviour of the respondents. The solution was to let the respondent choose the language of the interview. All interviewers (with few exceptions) were bilingual and they were specially instructed at this point. At the initial contact with a respondent, they had to choose the language that they would also choose as a stranger in a similar situation. In other words, the everyday knowledge of the interviewers was used. An advantage of this system of language choice is that it yields some "hard" facts about language behaviour. It could now be said that at least 62% of the inhabitants of Friesland (over a period of 12 years) were able to conduct an interview in Frisian. The percentage was almost the same 13 years later when it was 63%. This issue of language choice in interviews constitutes a general theme for research methods of sociolinguistics and sociology on which little has been published.

An important consideration is, of course, what effect the differences between the three projects have had on the results. When the points mentioned above are taken into consideration, the outcomes of the three projects are most certainly comparable. The results show that on average the changes in the outcomes are not very big.

In order to study further similarities and differences, the third Frisian survey can be compared to three other surveys in three other regional minority language communities, i.e., those carried out in Basque Country, Ireland and Wales, which took place around the same time. It was to be expected that the total number of (countable) questions among the four surveys would differ. It should be born in mind that in some cases only parts of the questionnaire had to be answered by all respondents. The results of this analysis are given in Table 4 for two questions, i.e., on language use and language attitudes.

From Table 4, it can be deduced that the Frisian questionnaire was the shortest and the one in Wales the longest, although the differences are not very big. The

Table 4. Questionnaires in Basque Country, Friesland, Ireland and Wales: questions on language use and attitudes (Aizpurua 1995; Gorter 1997; Ó Riagáin and Ó Gliasáin 1994; Williams and Morris 2000)

Survey	N questions	% questions on language use	% questions on attitudes
Basque country	246	25	14
Friesland	233	18	31
Ireland	267	13	46
Wales	317	42	7

Welsh list contained by far the most questions on language use and relatively few questions on language attitudes. By contrast, the Irish questionnaire was more concerned with attitudes than any of the others. This in part reflects a difference in theoretical approach and the importance attached to attitudes. Moreover, in Wales only speakers of Welsh were involved and a major aim of this survey was to trace language habits. In Ireland, where only a very small proportion of the total population uses Irish extensively on a daily basis, language attitudes play a more important role. It fits in the pattern where the first major survey in Ireland was conducted in 1973 by the *Committee on Irish Language Attitudes Research* (CILAR 1975; Ó Riagáin and Ó Gliasáin 1994).

However, these differences in the number and distribution of questions do not tell us anything at all about the complexity of the questions or how difficult they may be for respondents to answer. It is obvious that a battery-type series of questions that only require straightforward answers in terms of "yes" or "no" (or "don't know") is much easier than a complicated sorting task where respondents have to select their most preferred answer from five different alternatives. Moreover, it should be noted that the Welsh questionnaire was used to set an example for another series of language surveys (each N = 300) in different regions in the EU, conducted as part of the Euromosaic study (Euromosaic 1996).

One of the central theoretical considerations in the type of survey dealt with here relates to the variable of *language competence.* If one wants to measure proficiency in the minority language (and sometimes also the dominant language), what then are the dimensions that have to be measured and how does one include one or more questions on competence in a self-report questionnaire? In particular, what degrees of competence does one distinguish? As all four surveys include one or more questions on competence, a detailed comparison for this specific item can be made, the results of which are given in Table 5.

Table 5. Utilised scales for questions on language competence

Basque	Frisian	Irish	Welsh
1 well	1 very easily 2 good	6 native speaker ability	1 very good
2 quite well	3 fairly well	5 most conversations 4 parts of conversations	2 quite good
3 a little 4 only a few words	4 with difficulty	3 few simple sentences 2 the odd word	3 some
5 nothing	5 not at all	1 none	4 none

The issue of language competence is quite basic for all four surveys concerned. The four surveys differ in using 4, 5 or 6 different levels of language competence in the minority language. Also, there is a difference in the wording employed to indicate the different levels the respondents can choose from. Incorporating these differences into one table leads to the onclusion that there is a fair degree of overlap between the independently developed scales. Thus, researchers seem to agree at least to some extent on what it means to have full command of a language. On the other hand, direct comparison of the results would be quite difficult because of the different wording used to indicate the same or almost the same level of proficiency. Also, some of the subtleties in the wording may have been lost in the translation into English.

One further issue should be mentioned. If one is first and foremost interested in the social status of the minority language, does one also ask about the respondent's competence in the dominant language? In the case of Irish and Frisian, this was not done, as it was deemed unnecessary or superfluous. However, in both the Basque and the Welsh surveys, respondents were also asked about their level of competence in the dominant language (Spanish and English, respectively).

3.4.   Major outcomes of survey research

The basic percentages of the surveys on language proficiency in Frisian are quoted very often. This gives us an indication of the scientific and social relevance of the outcomes. The publication of Pietersen (1969) had a great impact because it was perceived as the first factual evidence ever. His most important language variables are the degree of proficiency in Frisian, the use of Frisian in a limited number of domains, and the attitude towards Frisian. The Frisian language situation could now be captured in "hard facts" which put an end to many personal impressions. Outsiders who doubted the extent of the use of Frisian could be told that 71% of the inhabitants of Friesland use Frisian at home. They

Table 6. Major outcomes of the second survey (in %): geographic and social stratification (Gorter et al. 1984)

First language	Frisian	Dutch	Dialects	N informants
Average	54	31	13	1126
Geographic stratification				
Capital Leeuwarden	28	45	22	145
Major towns	47	38	14	255
Countryside	70	23	5	584
Dialect areas	28	40	32	142
Social stratification				
Higher professions	24	62	14	29
Middle professions	57	40	10	189
Lower professions	49	33	18	198
Workers	69	17	15	164

were also confronted with the outcome that 96% could understand Frisian, 83% could speak, 65% could read, and 11% could write the language. The results of the second survey could never have had the same impact as the first. Both publications present a description of the language situation. Broadly speaking, the description provides a series of percentages for certain language variables for the population. The second project has the same language variables as the first, but they are worked out in more detail. Further extensions concern the description of the Frisian language situation in terms of its geographic spread (a "language map"), the variation according to language background in different social strata, and additional attention for domains like the school, the media and politics. In Table 6, some results of the project *Taal yn Fryslân* are given on geographic and social spread according to the first language learned.

On average, just over half of the population have Frisian as their first language. There are important geographic differences. On average, the provincial capital of Leeuwarden and the traditional dialect-speaking areas have far fewer Frisian speakers. The countryside continues to be the basis of Frisian, although there too, one third of the respondents do not have Frisian as their first language. The stratification by profession shows that Dutch is over-represented in the higher professions.

The third survey in the mid-1990s was expected to confirm the common anticipation in Friesland that the use of Frisian had decreased sharply. The results of the survey were awaited eagerly. But to the surprise of many people, the third survey did not show that the use of Frisian was diminishing. On the surface, little had changed in the position of the Frisian language over a period of 25 years.

Table 7. Home language findings in four successive surveys (in %)

	1967	1980	1994	2003
Frisian	71	56	55	50
Dutch	13	33	34	40
Dialects/other	16	11	10	10
N informants	800	1,125	1,368	390

The basic percentages of people who have the ability to understand (94%), speak (74%), read (67%) or write (17%) Frisian remained more or less the same. Those four percentages only changed a little between the first sociolinguistic survey of 1967 and the third of 1994. Gorter and Jonkman (1995: 55) concluded that the results of their survey, in terms of language ability, usage in intimate and more public settings, and language attitudes, point to a relatively stable situation for the Frisian language. However, they also point to underlying dynamics. There is a gradual decline of the Frisian language, which can be illustrated by the variable of home language. The proportions for "language usually spoken at home" are shown in the Table 7.

The overall trend is that the use of Frisian is decreasing and that of Dutch is increasing. In 1967, 71% of the population usually spoke Frisian at home and today that has fallen to 50%. Dutch is clearly on the increase from 13% in 1967 to 34% in 1994 and (probably) 40% in 2003.

There is some evidence that part of the decline of Frisian is caused by differences in the sampling frameworks. The 1967 sample did not include some of the regions in the province that are historically considered to be non-Frisian speaking. The decline in an adjusted sample would be 7% instead of 10%. Thus, there is an over-representation of the rural areas in the Pietersen sample.

As can be noticed, the differences between 1980 and 1994 are small. This is related to the wave of migration that was experienced in the 1970s, when large numbers of non-Frisian speakers came to work and live in Friesland. The most important reason for this is the labour market. The 2003 survey was based on a relatively small sample and carried out by a commercial firm through telephone interviews that focused on the proficiency in, the use of and attitudes towards Frisian.

There is something paradoxical about the language situation. There is stability for the minority language Frisian in terms of proficiency, but at the same time there is an increase in the presence of the dominant language Dutch as a home language and in other domains. Fewer and fewer members of the younger generations are acquiring Frisian as their first language at home. Large-scale studies

among primary and secondary school children carried out in 2000 found that
the percentages for Frisian as the mother tongue were around 45% (Van Ruijven
2005: 77; Van der Bij and Valk 2005: 138). A second reason is that bilingual
speakers have learned to speak and use Dutch with more ease, but at the same
time have not "unlearned" their Frisian. The average for the whole population
(in 1994) was that 60% could speak Frisian with more ease than Dutch; among
primary school children in 2000 the percentage of those who reported greater
fluency in Frisian than in Dutch was 45%.

An interesting survey was carried out in 2004 by a commercial firm TNS-
NIPO at the request of the Frisian Broadcasting Corporation. Two special groups
were studied: parents of young children (under 12 years of age, N = 208) and
prospective parents (persons under 35 who have no children yet, N = 195)
(Foekema 2004). On average, the respondents compared well with the results
of former surveys. The percentages for language proficiency (understanding,
speaking, reading and writing), for instance, were compatible. This study showed
that the problem of non-transmission of Frisian was not a very recent phenomenon and was already in evidence among these (potential) parents: 30% of
the parents born in Friesland were raised in Dutch and 12% in town-Frisian.
The large group that was born outside Friesland (30% of the sample) was raised
almost completely in Dutch. As soon as one of the partners is non-Frisian speaking, the language of the family is almost always Dutch. Mixed marriages and
immigration are the determining explanatory factors. Thus, it is not a lack of
transmission from the generation of the parents to that of the children: when
both parents speak Frisian, they will almost always also do so with their children. Still, the outcomes were shocking to policy makers because they showed
that only 30% of the future generation would be raised in Frisian.

Of course these figures tell us little about the actual use that is made of
the language outside the home. In the successive surveys, many questions were
asked about language use. They show an uneven pattern over language domains.
Just over 50% of the population habitually uses Frisian in the domains of family,
work and village. Frisian holds a relatively strong position there. In the more
formal domains of education, the media, public administration and law, the use
of Frisian has made some inroads in the last few decades, but overall is still
fairly limited (see Gorter 2001; Gorter and Jonkman 1995; Jonkman 2000).

4. Conclusion and discussion

Survey research has contributed to the development and evaluation of language
policy in various ways. The three large-scale surveys in Friesland that were
carried out over a period of almost 30 years, were well received by academic

researchers, journalists, policy makers, language activists and interested citizens. They became well known in the community and were widely quoted in the research literature. There is evidence that the outcomes of the surveys have influenced certain policy decisions, sometimes directly. The sociolinguistic surveys in Friesland thus far have been almost exclusively oriented towards descriptive goals. But even when description is the goal, there can be substantial differences in how descriptions are made. In the social sciences, there is some agreement on what a technically well-conducted survey is, but there is much less agreement on what an adequate description of a social phenomenon is. Similarly, within the sociology of language, there is no agreement on what dimensions have to be included in an adequate description of a language situation.

Repeated measures using the same questions make the goal of measuring change possible, even if only little change would actually be found. Similar surveys were carried out at different times and thus created opportunities for comparison and for establishing developments over time. However, it is probably not a good strategy to replicate studies completely. It is better to aim at partial replication. This is the relationship between the projects discussed in this Chapter. At another level, the study of the Frisian language situation may contribute to the comparative analysis of European language minorities.

Language surveys can aim at the investigation of a policy problem, or simply try to provide a description of a language situation. Surveys can also have the explicit purpose of testing theory. Usually such clear-cut distinctions cannot be made. Many surveys of the descriptive type are undertaken within a conceptual framework, but practical limitations of time and staff or the requirements of a contracting party leave theoretical statements implicit rather than explicitly stated. Ideally, theoretical and empirical research interact continuously, as in any social survey.

The overall format of a sociological survey on language is determined to a large extent by the specific social and political context. Practical considerations lead to substantial differences between surveys, which makes it more difficult to compare across communities (Euromosaic 1996). The contexts of the languages studied differ enormously in their sociolinguistic characteristics, even when all are so-called *unique* European minority languages.

A language survey as a quantitative technique has its inherent limitations because data rely on self-report of respondents and because random sampling always implies a degree of statistical uncertainty due to chance. The technique cannot be used in all circumstances or for all problems. Other techniques can be more appropriate, such as ethnographies based upon participant observation or open-ended, in-depth interviewing. A problem of the latter techniques is that they are time-consuming and expensive in operation and often used only in limited social or geographic contexts. A combination of different techniques to study the same phenomenon, an approach called *triangulation*, is even better. Surveys can be used to provide a context for qualitative research techniques, where these, in turn, are being used to deepen and extend the scope of survey research.

A research ideal would be to collect Europe-wide comparable data on minority language communities, while at the same time meeting local requirements of the uniqueness of each local context. It is not expected that such language surveys would be identical. In the *European Language Survey Research Network*, a core module of questions has been developed for inclusion in future surveys of regional minority language groups. It provides a basis for comparison and at the same time also allows ample space for adequate coverage of issues specific to particular language communities. Thus, the aims of a European-wide collection of comparable data about minority languages and the sensitivity to meet local requirements are compatible. In an ideal situation, this whole endeavour would be combined with approaches in which quantitative and qualitative research methods are triangulated.

References

Aizpurua, X.
   1995   *Euskararen jarraipena* (La continuidad del Euskera/La continuité de la langue basque). Vitoria-Gasteiz : Eusko Jaurlaritza.

Alreck, P.L. and R.B. Settle
   1985   *The Survey Research Handbook*. Homewood, Illinois: Irwin Press.

Babbie, E.R.
   1973   *Survey Research Methods*. Belmont: Wadsworth.

Behling, O. and Law, K.S.
   2000   *Translating Questionnaires and Other Research Instruments: Problems and Solutions*. London: Sage.

Bij, J. van der and R.W. Valk
   2005   *Fries in het Voortgezet Onderwijs: een Echternachse Processie*. Leeuwarden: Fryske Akademy.

Boelens, K. and J. van der Veen
   1956   *De Taal van het Schoolkind in Friesland*. Leeuwarden: Fryske Akademy.

Bradburn, N.M. and S. Sudman
   1980   *Improving Interview Method and Questionnaire Design*. San Francisco: Jossey Bass.

Bree, C. van
 1994 The development of the so-called Town-Frisian. In: P. Bakker and M. Mous (eds.), *Mixed languages*, 69–82. Amsterdam: Ifott.

Bremmer, R.H.
 1997 Het ontstaan van het Fries en het Hollands. In: P.H. Breuker and A.Janse, (red.), *Negen eeuwen Friesland-Holland (Geschiedenis van een haat-liefde verhouding)*, 67–76. Zutphen: Fryske Akademy/Walburg Pers.

Cenoz, J. and D. Gorter
 2006 The linguistic landscape and minority languages. *International Journal of Multilingualism* 3 (1): 67–80.

CILAR
 1975 *Committee on Irish Language Attitudes Research – Final report*. Dublin: The Government Stationary Office.

ELSN
 1996 *European Language Survey Network. A Comparative Analysis of Four Language Surveys (Ireland, Friesland, Wales & the Basque Country)*. Dublin: ITE.

Euromosaic
 1996 *Euromosaic: The Production and Reproduction of the Minority Language Groups of the EU*. Luxembourg: Office for Official Publications of the European Communities.
 2004 Euromosaic III (*http://ec.europa.eu/education/policies/lang/languages/langmin/euromosaic/index_en.html*)

Fishman, J.A.
 1965 "Who speaks what language to whom and when". *La Linguistique* 1: 67–88.

Foekema, H.
 2004 *Overdracht van de Friese Taal*. Amsterdam: TNS-NIPO.

Gorter, D.
 1997 Social surveys of minority language communities. In: B. Synak and T. Wicherkiewicz (eds.), *Language Minorities and Minority Languages in the Changing Europe*, 59–76. Gdansk: Wydawnictwo Uniwersytetu Gdanskiego.
 2001 A Frisian update of reversing language shift. In: J.A. Fishman (ed.), *Can Threatened Languages be Saved? Reversing Language Shift: A 21st Century Perspective*, 215–233. Clevedon: Multilingual Matters.

Gorter, D., G.H. Jelsma, P.H. van der Plank and K. de Vos
 1984 *Taal yn Fryslân (Undersyk nei taalgedrach en taalhâlding yn Fryslân)*. Ljouwert: Fryske Akademy.

1988   *Language in Friesland (English summary of "Taal yn Fryslân", a survey of language use and language attitudes in Friesland, The Netherlands).* Ljouwert: Fryske Akademy.

Gorter, D., L.G. Jansma and G.H. Jelsma
1991   *Taal yn it Grinsgebiet.* Ljouwert: Fryske Akademy.

Gorter, D. and R.J. Jonkman
1995   *Taal yn Fryslân: Op e nij Besjoen.* Ljouwert: Fryske Akademy.

Hof, J.J.
1933   *Friesche dialectgeographie.* 's-Gravenhage: Nijhoff.

Jonkman, R.J.
1993   *It Leewarders (In taalsosjologysk ûndersyk nei it Stedsk yn ferhâlding ta it Nederlânsk en it Frysk yn Ljouwert).* Ljouwert: Fryske Akademy.
1999   Wikselwurking tusken stêd en lân: fierdergeande taalheterogenisearring yn Fryslân. *It Beaken* 61 (3/4): 185–215.

Lieberson, S.
1980   Procedures for improving sociolinguistic surveys of language mainte-nance and language shift. *International Journal of the Sociology of Lan-guage* 25: 11–27.

Miller, D.C.
1991   *Handbook of Research Design and Social Measurement* (5th ed.). New-bury Park: Sage Publications.

Ó Riagáin, P. and M. Ó Gliasáin
1994   *National Survey on Languages 1993: Preliminary Report.* Dublin: In-stitiúid Teangeolaíochta Éireann.

Peng, K., R.E. Nisbett and N.Y.C. Wong
1997   Validity problems comparing values across cultures and possible solu-tions. *Psychological Methods* 2 (4): 329–244.

Pietersen, L.
1969   *De Friezen en hun Taal.* Drachten: Laverman.

Ruijven, B. van
2005   *Onderwijseffectiviteit in Fryslân.* Ljouwert: Fryske Akademy.

Van der Avoird, T. et al.
1999   *Meertaligheid in Leeuwarden: De Status van Allochtone Talen Thuis en op School.* Tilburg/Utrecht: Babylon/Sardes, 23–76.

Vries, O.
1997   From Old Frisian to Dutch: the elimination of Frisian as a written language in the sixteenth century. In: B. Synak and T. Wicherkiewicz (eds.), *Lan-guage Minorities and Minority Languages*, 239–244. Gdansk: Wydaw-nictwo Uniwersytetu Gdanskiego.

Williams, G. and D. Morris
   2000   *Language Planning and Language Use (Welsh in a Global Age).* Cardiff:
            University of Wales Press.

Wouda, W.
   2003   Op 'e grins fan ferskate talen: geografysk ûndersyk nei taalgrinzen en taal-
            gebieten fan it Frysk yn 'e gemeente Eaststellingwerf. *De Pompeblêdden*
            74 (4): 70–72.

Zondag, K.
   1993   The very beginning of the Frisian movement. *International Journal of the
            Sociology of Language* 100/101: 193–201.

Section III
Mapping immigrant languages in Europe

Mapping immigrant minority languages in multicultural cities[1]

Guus Extra and Kutlay Yağmur

1. Rationale and goals of the study

Given the overwhelming focus on mainstream second language acquisition by immigrant minority (henceforward IM) groups, there is much less evidence on the status and use of IM languages across European nation-states. In contrast to regional minority (henceforward RM) languages, IM languages have no established status in terms of period and area of residence. Obviously, typological differences between IM languages across EU nation-states do exist, e.g., in terms of the status of IM languages as EU languages or non-EU languages, or as languages of former colonies. Taken from the latter perspective, e.g., Indian languages are prominent in the United Kingdom, Arabic languages in France, Congolese languages in Belgium, and Surinamese languages in the Netherlands.

Tosi (1984) offers an early case study on Italian as an IM language in England. Most studies of IM languages in Europe have focused on a spectrum of IM languages at the level of one particular multilingual city (Kroon 1990; Baker and Eversley 2000), one particular nation-state (LMP 1985, Alladina and Edwards 1991; Extra and Verhoeven 1993a; Extra and De Ruiter 2001; Caubet, Chaker and Sibille 2002; Extra et al. 2002), or one particular IM language at the nation-state or European level (Tilmatine 1997 and Obdeijn and De Ruiter 1998 on Arabic in Europe, or Jørgensen 2003 on Turkish in Europe). A number of studies have taken both a cross-national and a cross-linguistic perspective on the status and use of IM languages in Europe (e.g., Husén and Opper 1983; Jaspaert and Kroon 1991; Extra and Verhoeven 1993b, 1998; Extra and Gorter 2001). Churchill (1986) has offered an early cross-national perspective on the education of IM children in the OECD countries, whereas Reid and Reich (1992) have carried out a cross-national evaluative study of 15 pilot projects on the education of IM children supported by the European Commission.

```
┌─────────────────────────────────────────────────────────────────────┐
│                                                                       │
│      Dominant Germanic        Mixed form        Dominant Romance      │
│                                                                       │
│                                                                       │
│   Swedish     German     Dutch          French            Spanish     │
│                                                                       │
│                                                                       │
│   Göteborg   Hamburg   The Hague   Brussels   Lyon          Madrid    │
│                                                                       │
└─────────────────────────────────────────────────────────────────────┘
```

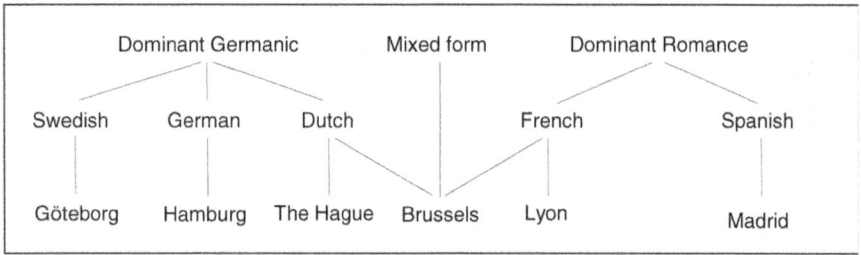

Figure 1. Outline of the Multilingual Cities Project (MCP)

Here, we present the rationale, methodology, and kernel outcomes of the *Multilingual Cities Project* (henceforward MCP), a co-ordinated multiple survey study in six major multicultural cities in different EU nation-states. The project was carried out under the auspices of the *European Cultural Foundation*, established in Amsterdam, and it was coordinated by a research team of *Babylon, Centre for Studies of the Multicultural Society*, at Tilburg University in the Netherlands, in cooperation with universities and educational authorities in all participating cities. The aims of the MCP were to gather, analyse, and compare multiple data on the status of IM languages at home and at school, taken from cross-national and cross-linguistics perspectives. In the participating cities, ranging from Northern to Southern Europe, Germanic or Romance languages have a dominant status in public life. Figure 1 gives an outline of the project.

The criteria for selecting a city to participate in this multinational study were that it should be prototypical for a multicultural environment with a great variety of IM groups, and that it should offer a university-based research facility that would be able to handle the local data gathering and local data analysis, and the final reporting of the local results. Given the increasing role of municipalities as educational authorities in all partner cities, the project was carried out in close cooperation between researchers at local universities and local educational authorities. In each partner city, this cooperation proved to be of essential value. In sum, the rationale for collecting, analysing and comparing multiple home language data on multicultural school populations derives from four different perspectives:

- taken from a *demographic* perspective, home language data play a crucial role in the definition and identification of multicultural school populations;
- taken from a *sociolinguistic* perspective, home language data offer valuable insights into both the distribution and vitality of home languages across

different population groups, and thus raise the public awareness of multilingualism;

- taken from an *educational* perspective, home language data are indispensable tools for educational planning and policies;
- taken from an *economic* perspective, home language data offer latent resources that can be built upon and developed in terms of economic chances.

Local reports about the participating cities have been made available for *Göteborg* (Nygren-Junkin and Extra 2003), *Hamburg* (Fürstenau, Gogolin and Yağmur 2003), *The Hague* (Extra, Aarts, Van der Avoird, Broeder and Yağmur 2001), *Brussels* (Verlot, Delrue, Extra and Yağmur 2003), *Lyon* (Akinci, De Ruiter and Sanagustin 2004), and *Madrid* (Broeder and Mijares 2003). For the final cross-national report we refer to Extra and Yağmur (2004).

2. Method of research

2.1. Design of the questionnaire

Except in some countries like Great Britain, Sweden or Switzerland, there is no European tradition of collecting home language statistics on multicultural (school) population groups. In fact, collecting home language data in some countries is even in conflict with present language legislation. This holds in particular for Belgium, where traditional language borders have been allocated and legalised in terms of Dutch, French or German.

Our method of carrying out home language surveys amongst primary school children in each of the six participating cities has profited from experiences in non-European English-dominant immigration countries with nationwide population surveys in which commonly single questions on home language use were asked. In contrast to such questionnaires, our survey was based on multiple rather than single questions on home language use and on cross-nationally equivalent questions. In doing this, we aimed at describing and comparing multiple language profiles of major IM communities in each of the cities under consideration.

The questionnaire for data collection was designed after ample study and evaluation of language-related questions in nationwide or large-scale population research in a variety of countries with a longer history of migration and minorisation processes. The design of the questionnaire also derived from extensive empirical experiences gained in carrying out municipal home language surveys amongst pupils in both primary and secondary schools in the Netherlands (Broeder and Extra 1995; 1998 and Extra et al. 2001; 2002).

A number of conditions for the design of the questionnaire needed to be met. The first prerequisite was that the questionnaire should be appropriate for all children and should include a built-in screening question for distinguishing between children in whose homes only the mainstream language is used and children in whose homes one or more other languages next to or instead of this language are used. In the latter case, a home language profile had to be specified.

The second prerequisite of the questionnaire was that it should be both short and powerful. It should be short in order to minimise the time needed by teachers and children to answer it during school hours, and it should be powerful in that it should have an optimal and transparent set of questions which should be answered by all children individually, if needed – in particular with younger children – in cooperation with the teacher, after an explanation of the goals and design of the questionnaire in class. The survey consisted of 20 questions which were made available to schools in a double-sided printed format.

The third prerequisite of the questionnaire was that the answers given by the children should be controlled, scanned, interpreted, and verified as automatically as possible, given the large size of the resulting database. In order to fulfil this demand, both hardware and software conditions had to be met.

Table 1 gives an outline of the questionnaire. An English version is made available in the Appendix.

In compliance with privacy legislation in different nation-states, the resulting database contains language data at the levels of districts, schools, and grades only; no data have been processed that can be traced back to individuals. The answers to questions 9–12 make it possible to compare the status of birth country data and home language data as demographic criteria. The countries and languages explicitly mentioned in questions 9–12 were determined on the basis of the most recent municipal statistics about IM children at primary schools. Thus,

Table 1. Outline of the MCP questionnaire

Questions	Focus
1–3	Personal information (name, age, gender)
4–8	School information (city, district, name, type, grade)
9–11	Birth country of the pupil, father and mother
12	Selective screening question (Are any other languages than X ever used in your home?
	If yes, complete all the questions; if no, continue with questions 18–20)
13–17	Language repertoire, language proficiency, language choice, language dominance, and language preference
18–20	Languages learnt at/outside school and demanded from school

the list of prespecified languages for, e.g., Hamburg was quite different from the one used in Madrid. The selective screening question 12 (see also Appendix) was aimed at a maximal scope from three different perspectives, i.e., by the passive construction *are used* instead of *do you use*, by the modal adverb *ever*, and by asking for *use* instead of one of the four language skills. The language profile, specified by questions 13–17, consists of the following dimensions:

– language repertoire: the number and type of (co-)occurring home languages next to or instead of the mainstream language;
– language proficiency: the extent to which the pupil can understand/speak/read/write the home language;
– language choice: the extent to which the home language is commonly spoken with the mother, father, younger and older brothers/sisters, and best friends;
– language dominance: the extent to which the home language is spoken best;
– language preference: the extent to which the home language is preferably spoken.

Taken together, the four dimensions of language proficiency, choice, dominance, and preference result in a language vitality index (see Section 4). On the basis of questions 18–20, a school language profile can be specified. This profile provides information about the available language education in and outside school, as well as the expressed interest in learning other languages. The agreed-upon questionnaire was translated into equivalent versions in Dutch, French, German, Spanish, and Swedish. These versions were tested in at least one primary school in each partner city. On the basis of the suggestions of local educational authorities and researchers, the phrasing and wording of the questionnaires were further adapted. All six cities had the same questions, but one additional question on "nationality" was added to the German questionnaire. This question was not included in any of the other cities.

2.2.   Data collection

The local questionnaires were printed in multiple copies. Due to the requirements of automatic processing, it was essential that printed rather than photocopied questionnaires were used. Uniformity, both in terms of content and form, was a prerequisite for data processing. Local educational authorities sent out letters of permission to schools and/or parents so that their children could participate in the survey. In each city, the printed questionnaires were distributed to school directors. Both for classroom teachers and for data collection assistants, a manual in the local language was prepared to facilitate interaction with the pupils.

The completed questionnaires were delivered by the schools to the researchers at the participating universities. After checks of the total set of questionnaires per school had been made, all delivered questionnaires were sent to Tilburg University in the Netherlands for data processing.

2.3.   Data processing

Data processing was centrally done in Tilburg by *Babylon* researchers. Given the large size of the database, an automatic processing technique based on specially developed software (*Teleform*) and available hardware was developed and utilised. By means of these tools about 5000 forms could be scanned per day. Because some questionnaire items were filled-out in handwriting, additional verification of these items had to be done using character recognition software; in this way, around 4000 forms could be processed per day. After scanning and verification had been completed, the database for each city was analysed by using the SPSS program. Table 2 gives an overview of the resulting database, derived from the reports of primary school children in an age range of 4–12 years (only in The Hague were data also collected at secondary schools). The total cross-national sample consists of more than 160,000 pupils.

In order to carry out systematic analyses on the data set, a SPSS syntax file which was developed step-by-step was used in the preparation stage. In the analysis stage, another SPSS syntax file was used in order to achieve uniformity of the findings. The last stage of data processing was transmitting the outcomes of the analyses in a readable format. Given the fact that the research results should be presented in the same format in all six participating cities in the

Table 2. Overview of the MCP database

City	Total of schools	Total of schools in the survey	Total of pupils in schools	Total of pupils in the survey	Age range of pupils
Brussels	117[a]	110[a]	11,500	10,300	6–12
Göteborg	170	122	36,100	21,300	6–12
Hamburg	231 public	218 public	54,900	46,000	6–11
	17 catholic	14 catholic			
Lyon	173[b]	42[b]	60,000	11,650	6–11
Madrid	708 public	133 public	202,000	30,000	5–12
	411 catholic	21 catholic	99,000		
The Hague	142 primary	109 primary	41,170	27,900	4–12
	30 secondary	26 secondary	19,000	13,700	12–17

([a] Dutch medium schools only; [b] Reseau d'Education Prioritaire only)

project, a cross-nationally uniform format was set up. In presenting the results, *Excel Worksheets* and *Microsoft Graphics* within *Word for Windows* were used. Both the worksheets and the templates for figures within *Microsoft Graphics* were predefined. In this way, a uniform format for all the tables and figures could be achieved, which then needed to be interpreted.

3.   Distribution of languages across cities

The local language surveys amongst primary school children have delivered a wealth of yet unknown cross-national evidence on the distribution and vitality of IM languages at home. Apart from selecting one or more of the prespecified languages in each of the local surveys, pupils could also opt for self-references to other home languages by filling-out in hand-writing the boxes provided for this objective (see Appendix).

The resulting database consists of a huge variety of self-references (types) and their frequencies of mentioning (tokens). In most cases, the pupils referred to entities that could be (re)traced as existing languages. In this context, the regularly updated database of *The Ethnologue* (*www.sil.org/ethnologue*; Grimes 1996) on languages of the world proved to be very helpful. In cases of doubt or lacking information, other resources were used, such as Comrie et al. (2003), Campbell (2000), Dalby (1999/2000), Giacalone Ramat and Ramat (1998), and Crystal (1997). Apart from self-references to known and unknown languages, the pupils also made references to countries that could not reasonably be traced back to languages or to other/unknown categories. In general, however, the resolution level of the language question in the survey was very high, and relatively few references could not be traced back to languages. Table 3 gives a cross-national overview of the data under consideration.

Table 3. References made by pupils in terms of types and tokens (x = not specified)

Municipality	Reference to languages		Reference to countries		Other/unknown references	
	Types	Tokens	Types	Tokens	Types	Tokens
Göteborg	75	7,598	8	40	10	20
Hamburg	90	16,639	12	229	10	92
The Hague	88	23,435	13	788	17	24
Brussels	54	12,737	9	186	7	11
Lyon	66	6,106	17	130	—	—
Madrid	56	2,619	x	x	x	x

Based on the overview of types and tokens of (re)traced home languages, the distribution of these home languages was specified in a ranked order of decreasing frequency. A common phenomenon, familiar in type/token studies of word frequencies, in all participating cities was that few languages (types) were referred to often (tokens), and that many languages (types) were referred to rarely (tokens). Therefore, the most frequently mentioned home languages represent a very high proportion of the total number of occurrences/tokens in all cities.

Apart from Madrid, late-comer amongst our focal cities in respect of immigration, the proportion of primary school children in whose homes other languages were used next to or instead of the mainstream language ranged between one third and more than a half. The total number of languages other than Swedish/German/Dutch (The Hague/Brussels)/French/ Spanish ranged per city between 50 and 90. The figures were 36% of the total student population in Göteborg, 35% in Hamburg, 49% in The Hague, 82% in Brussels, 54% in Lyon, and 10% in Madrid.

The outcomes of the local surveys were aggregated in one cross-national database. On the basis of the number of references made to home languages, the top 20 of the most frequently mentioned languages in each city were identified. Forty-nine languages were in the group of the top 20 list in the six cities. Out of these 49 languages, 19 languages were represented in 3–6 cities and 30 languages in only 1–2 cities. There were also unique references in the top 20 per city; most of these languages were either languages of neighbouring countries, languages of former colonies, or RM languages. For purposes of cross-national and cross-linguistic analyses, 20 of the most frequently mentioned languages in these cities were chosen.

Two criteria were used to select these 20 languages from the list of 49 languages. Each language should be represented by at least three cities, and each city should be represented in the cross-national database by at least 30 pupils in the age range of 6–11 years. Our focus on this age range was motivated by comparability considerations: This range was represented in the local databases of all participating cities (see Table 2). Romani/Sinte was included in the cross-national analyses because of its special status in our list of 20 languages as a language without territorial status. Two languages had an exceptional status: English "invaded" the local databases as a language of international prestige, and Romani/Sinte was solidly represented in Hamburg and Göteborg only. The concept of language group was based on the pupils' answers to the question whether and, if so, which other languages were used at home instead of or next to the mainstream language (see Appendix, question 13). On the basis of their

Table 4. Overview of the numbers of pupils (6–11 years) per reported language and city

Reported languages	Gö	Ha	tH	Br	Ly	Ma	Coverage
English	1,039	1,077	950	676	426	359	6
Arabic	768	464	1,391	1,608	2,789	662	6
Portuguese	88	360	88	77	259	202	6
Italian	51	192	92	361	255	43	6
Turkish	385	4,948	2,535	606	468	1	5
Spanish	328	431	288	389	353	–	5
German	148	–	156	119	91	45	5
French	118	17	185	7,327	–	157	5
Chinese	184	7	180	22	37	160	4
Kurdish	468	197	273	11	36	4	4
Albanian	186	410	5	107	62	3	4
Polish	163	1,729	16	33	3	100	4
Russian	70	1,652	14	32	11	37	4
Berber	4	–	1,334	214	145	37	4
Serbian/Croatian/Bosnian	795	460	46	29	26	6	3
Vietnamese	55	153	14	14	91	–	3
Somali	315	–	135	–	49	–	3
Urdu/Pakistani	27	238	294	32	1	3	3
Armenian	8	82	5	47	41	1	3
Romani/Sinte	51	219	6	8	3	1	2

answer patterns, pupils may belong to more than one language group. Table 4 gives an overview of the resulting database.

As shown in Table 4, eight languages were represented in 5–6 cities, while eleven languages were represented in 3–4 cities. With respect to French, Brussels offers a special case, given the public and private status of both French and Dutch in this city (Verlot et al. 2003). There is a remarkable municipal distribution of two pairs of languages which are often in competition in their source countries, i.e., Turkish and Kurdish in Turkey, and Arabic and Berber in Northern African countries (in particular, Morocco). Only in Göteborg was Kurdish more strongly represented than Turkish, and only in The Hague were Berber and Arabic represented in balance. In our database, Kurdish hardly emerged in Brussels and Madrid. The same holds for Berber in Göteborg and Hamburg.

4. Specification of language profiles and language vitality

For all language groups mentioned in Table 4, pseudo-longitudinal and intergenerational profiles were specified and visually represented in graphs and tables. For all language groups, three age groups and three generations were distinguished. The age groups consisted of children aged 6/7, 8/9 and 10/11 years old. The three generations were operationalised as follows:

- G1: pupil + father + mother born abroad;
- G2: pupil born in country of residence, father *and/or* mother born abroad;
- G3: pupil + father + mother born in country of residence.

The pseudo-longitudinal profiles consisted of age-specific information on: *proficiency* in the minority language in terms of language understanding, speaking, reading and writing; *choice* of the minority language in interaction with the mother, father, younger and older siblings, and best friends; *dominance* in the minority *vs.* mainstream language; *preference* for the minority *vs.* mainstream language.

In addition, age-specific and generation-specific information was provided on language vitality. The final aim was the construction of a language vitality index (henceforward LVI), based on the outcomes of the four dimensions presented above. Since Giles et al. (1977) introduced the concept of ethnolinguistic vitality, the focus has been on its extralinguistic determinants rather than its empirical operationalisation. Determinants have been proposed in terms of lists of factors, clustered in status factors, demographic factors, and institutional support factors, e.g. by Giles et al. (1977), or in additional factors such as cultural (dis)similarity, e.g., by Appel and Muysken (1987: 32–38).

The proposed lists of factors suffer from various shortcomings that cannot be solved easily: the lists of factors are neither exhaustive nor mutually exclusive; different factors contribute in different ways to (lack of) vitality and may even neutralise each other; some of these factors are personal characteristics (e.g., age, gender, or educational level), whereas other factors are group characteristics (e.g., group size or group spread); moreover, a distinction has been proposed and found between the objective status of these factors and their subjective perception by minority and/or majority groups (Bourhis et al. 1981, Van der Avoird 2001); finally, no quantitative weighing has been suggested for the proposed (clusters of) factors, which makes the establishment of a language vitality index and the verification of empirical outcomes unfeasible.

For a comprehensive overview of the origins of the concept "language vitality" and its theoretical and empirical development over time since Weinreich

(1953), we refer to Achterberg (2005: 23–100), in the context of a case study on Slavonic languages in Germany. In the present research project, we took a different approach by focusing on the empirical operationalisation of language vitality rather than on its extralinguistic determinants. This operationalisation was derived from the following four reported dimensions:

– language proficiency: the extent to which the minority language under consideration is *understood;*
– language choice: the extent to which this language is commonly spoken at home *with the mother*;
– language dominance: the extent to which this language is spoken *best;*
– language preference: the extent to which it is *preferably* spoken.

The focus of the chosen dimensions was on oral skills at home and not on literacy in order to give IM languages a fair chance of emerging in societal contexts in which the acquisition of literacy is rarely promoted, whether at home or at school (see also section 8). Moreover, earlier analyses have shown that the four selected dimensions are highly correlated and lead to reliable scores (Extra et al. 2002: 129). The operationalisation of the first and second dimension (language proficiency and language choice) was aimed at a maximal scope for tracing language vitality. Language understanding is generally the least demanding of the four language skills involved, and the mother acts generally as the major gatekeeper for intergenerational language transmission (Clyne 2003).

In the analyses, the four above-mentioned language dimensions were compared as proportional scores, i.e., the mean proportion of pupils per language group that indicated a positive response to the relevant questions. The LVI is, in turn, the mean value of these four proportional scores. This LVI is by definition a value-driven index, in the sense that the *chosen* dimensions with the *chosen* operationalisations are *equally* weighted. The establishment of such an index makes it feasible to carry out cross-linguistic and cross-national comparisons of large databases in wich equal criteria for such comparisons are used.

In this context, it should be mentioned that, from a conceptual point of view, the chosen dimensions are more closely related than in many other large-scale attempts to operationalise multiple human properties in terms of an index. An interesting case in point is the widely used *Human Development Index* (HDI), proposed by the United Nations in its annual UNDP reports. The HDI measures the overall achievements in a particular country in three basic dimensions of human development, i.e., life expectancy, educational achievement, and income per capita. For each of these dimensions, an index based on multiple values has been created. The ultimate HDI is based on the average of the three indices mentioned. In this case also, the chosen dimensions with the chosen operational-isations are equally weighted (for details see UNDP 2002).

On the basis of the established LVI in our project, LVI scores have been calculated per age group and per generation, for each language group. On the basis of this categorisation, intergenerational shift can be estimated. In all cases, the total population of age groups was always larger than the total population of generations. This discrepancy is the result of a predictably larger number of missing values (i.e., non-responses) for generation than for age. In the former case, references have to be made to the countries of birth of the pupil, the father, and the mother; in the latter case, reference has to be made only to the age of the pupil. Language vitality indices for age and generation were calculated only if at least 5 children were represented in a particular group. Given the possible non-responses of children to any of the questions, all figures and tables were presented and interpreted in proportional values. In Table 5, we demonstrate the provided cross-national and pseudolongitudinal information on the Turkish language group (see Table 4 for the absence of data on Madrid).

Table 5. Turkish language group: cross-national numbers of pupils and LVI per age group and per generation

	Age groups							
	Population				Vitality			
Cities	6/7	8/9	10/11	Total	6/7	8/9	10/11	Mean
Göteborg	124	115	146	385	69	67	66	67
Hamburg	1,384	2,381	1,183	4,948	66	62	65	64
The Hague	833	853	849	2,535	75	68	65	69
Brussels	225	213	168	606	73	75	71	73
Lyon	146	176	146	468	65	63	68	65
Total / Mean	2,712	3,738	2,492	8,942	70	67	67	68

	Generations							
	Population				Vitality			
Cities	G1	G2	G3	Total	G1	G2	G3	Mean
Göteborg	51	308	10	369	67	68	43	59
Hamburg	627	3,676	205	4,508	69	64	49	61
The Hague	539	1,842	46	2,427	73	68	62	68
Brussels	75	417	42	534	74	74	70	73
Lyon	78	308	24	410	70	64	65	66
Total / Mean	1,370	6,551	327	8,248	71	68	58	65

Pseudolongitudinal profile of the Turkish language group

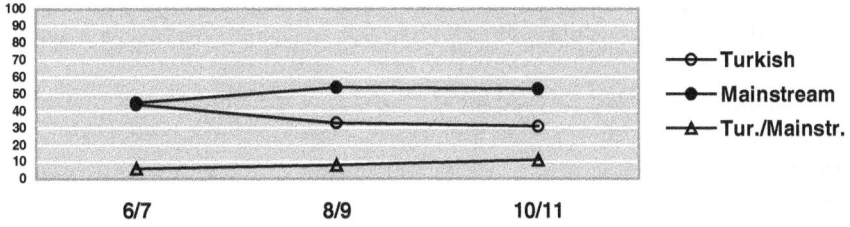

Figure 2a. Language proficiency in Turkish

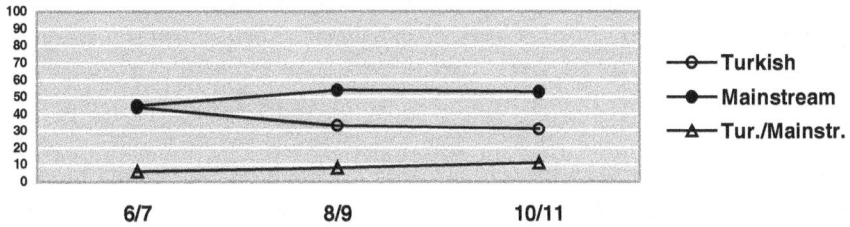

Figure 2b. Language choice for Turkish

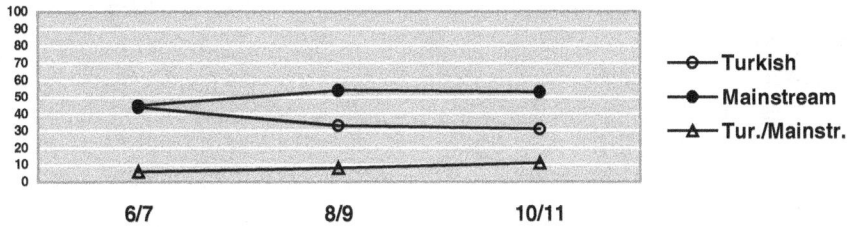

Figure 2c. Language dominance of Turkish and/or mainstream language

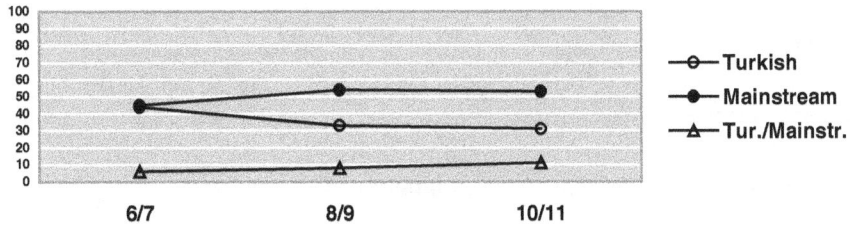

Figure 2d. Language preference for Turkish and/or mainstream language

Language proficiency (Fig. 2a). For all age groups, reported understanding (96–97%) and speaking skills (94%) in Turkish are higher than reported reading (38–80%) and writing skills (33–73%), but the differences narrow as children get older.

Language choice (Fig. 2b). At home, 77-82% of the children reported commonly speaking Turkish with their mothers, 70–76% with their fathers, 38–43% with their younger siblings, 27–36% with their older siblings, and 30–36% with their best friends.

Language dominance (Fig. 2c). The reported dominance of Turkish decreases as children get older (44%, 33%, and 31%, respectively). The reported dominance of the mainstream language increases across age groups (45%, 54%, and 53%, respectively). A slight increase in balanced bilingualism was reported across age groups (6–11%).

Language preference (Fig. 2d). Similar to dominance, the reported preference for Turkish decreases as children get older (43%, 35%, and 30%, respectively). In a complementary pattern, an increasing preference for the mainstream language was reported across age groups (44%, 50%, and 50%, respectively). No preference was reported by an increasing 7–12% of all children.

Language vitality across age groups and generations (Table 5). The Turkish language group is the largest group in the overall research population (except for Madrid). Turkish is spoken in the homes of 8,942 children across the age groups in 5 cities. A great majority of the Turkish-speaking pupils was traced in Hamburg and The Hague, followed by Brussels, Lyon, and Göteborg. In terms of intergenerational differences, first-generation children born abroad reported the highest language vitality (71%), followed by second- and third-generation children (68–58%). In Brussels, there is almost no difference between the 3 generations. Turkish has the highest vitality in Brussels (73%) for all age groups, and the average vitality of Turkish for all cities in the given age groups is 68%.

Languages other than Turkish. Next to Turkish, a number of other languages were reported as home languages. French (381), Kurdish (375), English (133), Arabic (96), German (29), Albanian (17), and Spanish (17) were the major languages reported.

5.   Cross-linguistic perspectives on language vitality

In this section, we present a cumulative language vitality index (LVI) for all 20 language groups on the basis of the obtained proportional scores for language proficiency (understanding), language choice (with mother), language dominance, and language preference. As mentioned before, the LVI is based on the mean value of the obtained scores for each of the four language dimensions

Table 6. Language vitality per language group and age group (in %, LVI in cumulative (%)

Language group	Total pupils	6/7 years	8/9 years	10/11 years	Average
Romani/Sinte	270	76	71	64	70
Urdu/Pakistani	564	65	70	69	68
Turkish	8,942	70	67	67	68
Armenian	170	64	59	65	63
Russian	1,791	66	58	57	60
Serbian/Croatian/Bosnian	1,285	60	58	59	59
Albanian	765	63	56	58	59
Vietnamese	299	57	60	58	58
Chinese	561	56	58	60	58
Arabic	7,682	59	58	58	58
Polish	1,925	57	59	53	56
Somali	499	58	54	53	55
Portuguese	1,074	54	54	54	54
Berber	1,730	51	54	51	52
Kurdish	974	54	47	51	51
Spanish	1,789	47	49	47	48
French	7,787	47	40	44	44
Italian	994	39	40	39	39
English	4,527	37	33	39	36
German	559	35	31	32	33

referred to. Table 6 gives a cross-linguistic and pseudolongitudinal overview of the LVI per language group and age group. LVI calculations have only been made if at least 5 children were represented in a particular age group and generation.

Considering its non-territorial status, it is not surprising that Romani/Sinte emerged with the highest language vitality. English and German ended up in bottom positions given the fact that they often had a higher status at school than at home. When the average scores of the youngest and oldest age groups were compared, 11 language groups showed the highest scores for the former and 5 language groups for the latter. The largest interval between the scores emerged for Romani/Sinte.

Strong maintenance of language vitality across the youngest and oldest age groups, with intervals of −1/0/+1 only, emerged for 8 out of the 20 language groups.

A different cross-linguistic and pseudolongitudinal perspective is provided in Table 7, in terms of generations. Table 7 reveals significant differences between language groups in the distribution of pupils across different generations. In most language groups, second-generation pupils were most-represented and

Table 7. Inter-generational distribution (in %) and inter-generational language vitality (LVI in cumulative %) per language group

Language group	Total pupils	Inter-generational distribution			Inter-generational language vitality		
		G1	G 2	G3	G1	G2	G3
Albanian	675	39	56	5	72	51	34
Arabic	7,002	21	73	6	64	57	35
Armenian	153	49	42	9	69	55	—
Berber	1,656	20	78	2	59	50	45
Chinese	523	22	74	4	72	59	—
English	4,045	16	42	41	43	41	28
French	7,090	7	45	48	55	43	30
German	506	18	45	38	43	35	22
Italian	916	12	60	28	49	43	29
Kurdish	900	50	49	2	61	43	33
Polish	1,837	14	82	4	73	59	31
Portuguese	1,004	27	66	8	63	52	33
Romani/Sinte	231	35	41	23	76	66	65
Russian	1,616	81	16	3	64	—	—
Serbian/Croatian/Bosnian	1,191	38	58	4	71	50	—
Somali	464	38	58	5	70	50	—
Spanish	1,570	18	61	21	63	47	30
Turkish	8,248	17	79	4	71	68	58
Urdu/Pakistani	534	25	72	3	70	67	—
Vietnamese	270	12	85	3	60	57	—

third-generation pupils least. Remarkable exceptions to this rule were Armenian and in particular Russian, with mainly first-generation pupils.

Third-generation pupils were relatively well represented (>20%) for English, French, German, Italian, Romani/Sinte, and Spanish. In conformity with expectations, Table 7 shows a stronger decrease of language vitality across generations than Table 6 shows across age groups.

All language groups show more or less decreasing language vitality across generations. The strongest inter-generational shift between G1 and G3 emerged for Polish (42%), Albanian (38%), Spanish (33%), and Portuguese (30%), whereas the strongest inter-generational maintenance of language vitality occurred for Romani/ Sinte and Turkish.

The top position for language vitality of Romani/Sinte across age groups in Table 6, and its relatively strong maintenance across generations in Table 7, were also observed in earlier and similar research in the Netherlands (Broeder and Extra 1998: 70). The high vitality of Romani/Sinte was also confirmed by other studies on this language community (Acton and Mundy 1999; Kyuchukov 2002). One reason why language vitality is a core value for the Roma across Europe is the absence of source country references as alternative markers of identity – in contrast to almost all other language groups presented in Tables 6 and 7.

6. Conclusions

The findings of the *Multilingual Cities Project* have delivered a wealth of hidden evidence on the distribution and vitality of IM languages at home across European cities and nation-states. Apart from Madrid, late-comer amongst our focal cities in respect of immigration, the proportion of primary school children in whose homes other languages were used next to or instead of the mainstream language ranged per city between one third and more than a half. The total number of traced "other" languages ranged per city between 50 and 90; the common pattern was that a limited set of languages were often referred to by the children and that many languages were referred to only a few times.

The findings show that making use of more than one language is a way of life for an increasing number of children across Europe. Mainstream and non-mainstream languages should not be conceived in terms of competition. Rather, the data show that these languages are used as alternatives, depending on such factors as type of context and interlocutor. The data also reveal that the use of other languages at home does not occur at the cost of competence in the mainstream language. Many children who addressed their parents in another language reported to be dominant in the mainstream language.

Among the major 20 non-national languages in the participating cities, 10 languages are of European origin and 10 languages stem from abroad. These findings clearly show that the traditional concept of language diversity in Europe should be reconsidered and extended. The outcomes of the local language surveys also demonstrate the high status of English among primary school pupils across Europe. Its intrusion in the children's homes is apparent from the position of English in the top 5 of languages referred to by the children in all of the cities (Table 4). This outcome cannot be explained as an effect of migration and minorisation only. The children's reference to English also derives from the status of English as the international language of power and prestige. English has invaded the repertoire of all of the national languages under consideration. Moreover, children have access to English through a variety of media, and English is commonly taught in particular grades at primary schools.

In addition, children in all participating cities expressed a desire to learn a variety of languages that are not taught at school. The results of the local language surveys also show that children who took part in instruction in particular non-mainstream languages at school reported higher levels of literacy in these languages than children who did not take part in such instruction. Both the reported reading and writing proficiency profited strongly from language instruction. The differences between participants and non-participants in language instruction were significant for both forms of literacy skills and for all the 20 language groups under consideration. In this domain in particular, the added value of language instruction for language development is clear. Owing to the monolingual *habitus* (Gogolin 1994) of primary schooling across Europe, there is an increasing mismatch between language practices at home and at school. The findings on multilingualism at home and those on language needs and language instruction reported by the children should be taken into account by national and local educational authorities in any type of language policy.

Appendix: English version of the language survey questionnaire

Anchorage points
Software and processing of the filled-out questionnaires are discussed in Extra and Yağmur (2004: 116–118). The bottom-line texts on the first and second page of the questionnaire function as anchorage points for data base recognition before the process of data scanning can start.

Questions 9/10/11
C 1 = country of residence (*in casu* Sweden, Germany, the Netherlands, Belgium, France or Spain).
C 2–20 = alphabetical list of countries most frequently represented in a particular city (in casu Göteborg, Hamburg, The Hague, Brussels, Lyon or Madrid, respectively), derived from local municipal statistics.

Questions 12/13
xxx = mainstream language of country of residence (*in casu* Swedish, German, Dutch, French or Spanish, respectively).

Questions 13–20
L 1 = mainstream language of country of residence.
L 2–20 = alphabetical list of languages most frequently represented in a particular city, derived from assumptions on countries 2–20.

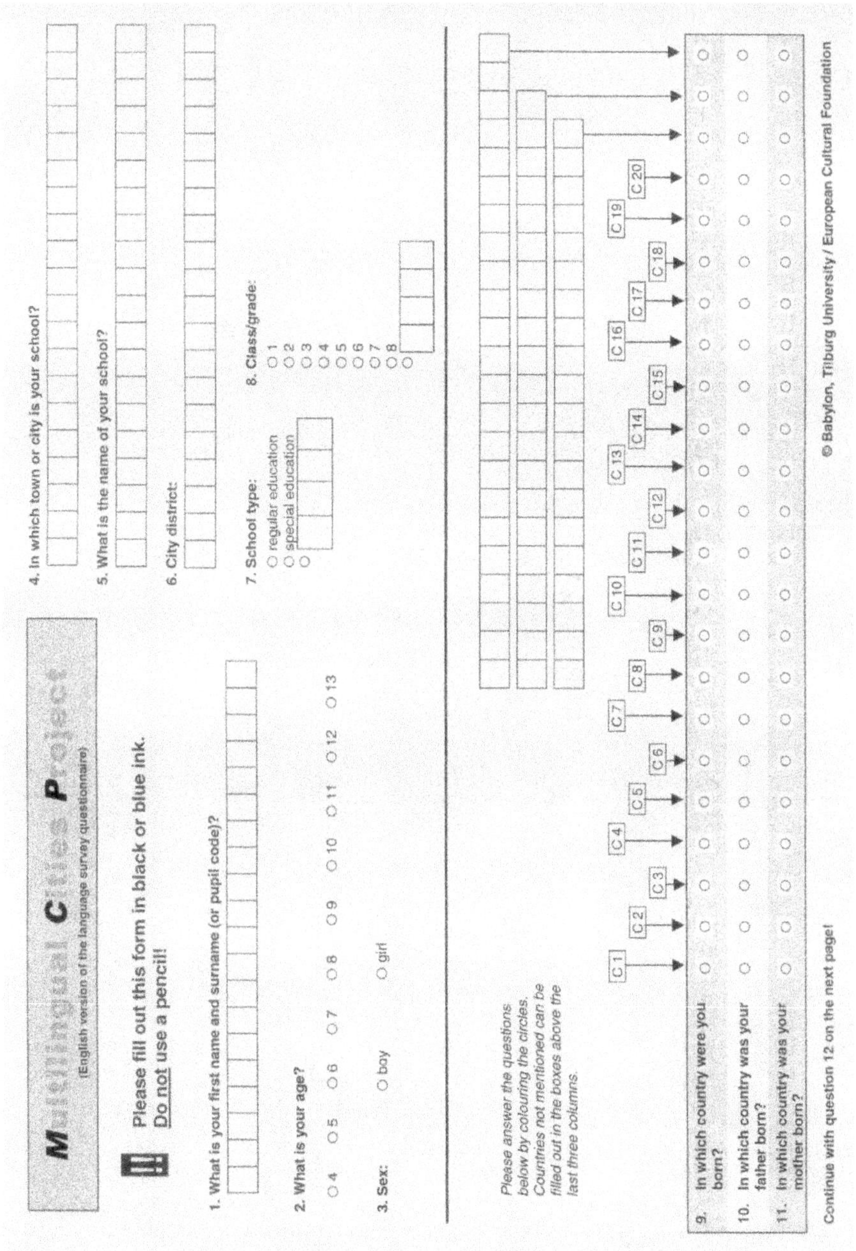

Multilingual Cities Project
(English version of the language survey questionnaire)

Please fill out this form in black or blue ink.
Do not use a pencil!

1. What is your first name and surname (or pupil code)?

2. What is your age?
   O 4   O 5   O 6   O 7   O 8   O 9   O 10   O 11   O 12   O 13

3. Sex: O boy   O girl

Please answer the questions below by colouring the circles. Countries not mentioned can be filled out in the boxes above the last three columns.

4. In which town or city is your school?

5. What is the name of your school?

6. City district:

7. School type:
   O regular education
   O special education
   O

8. Class/grade:
   O 1
   O 2
   O 3
   O 4
   O 5
   O 6
   O 7
   O 8
   O

9. In which country were you born?

10. In which country was your father born?

11. In which country was your mother born?

Continue with question 12 on the next page!

C1 C2 C3 C4 C5 C6 C7 C8 C9 C10 C11 C12 C13 C14 C15 C16 C17 C18 C19 C20

© Babylon, Tilburg University / European Cultural Foundation

Figure 3. Survey Questionnaire

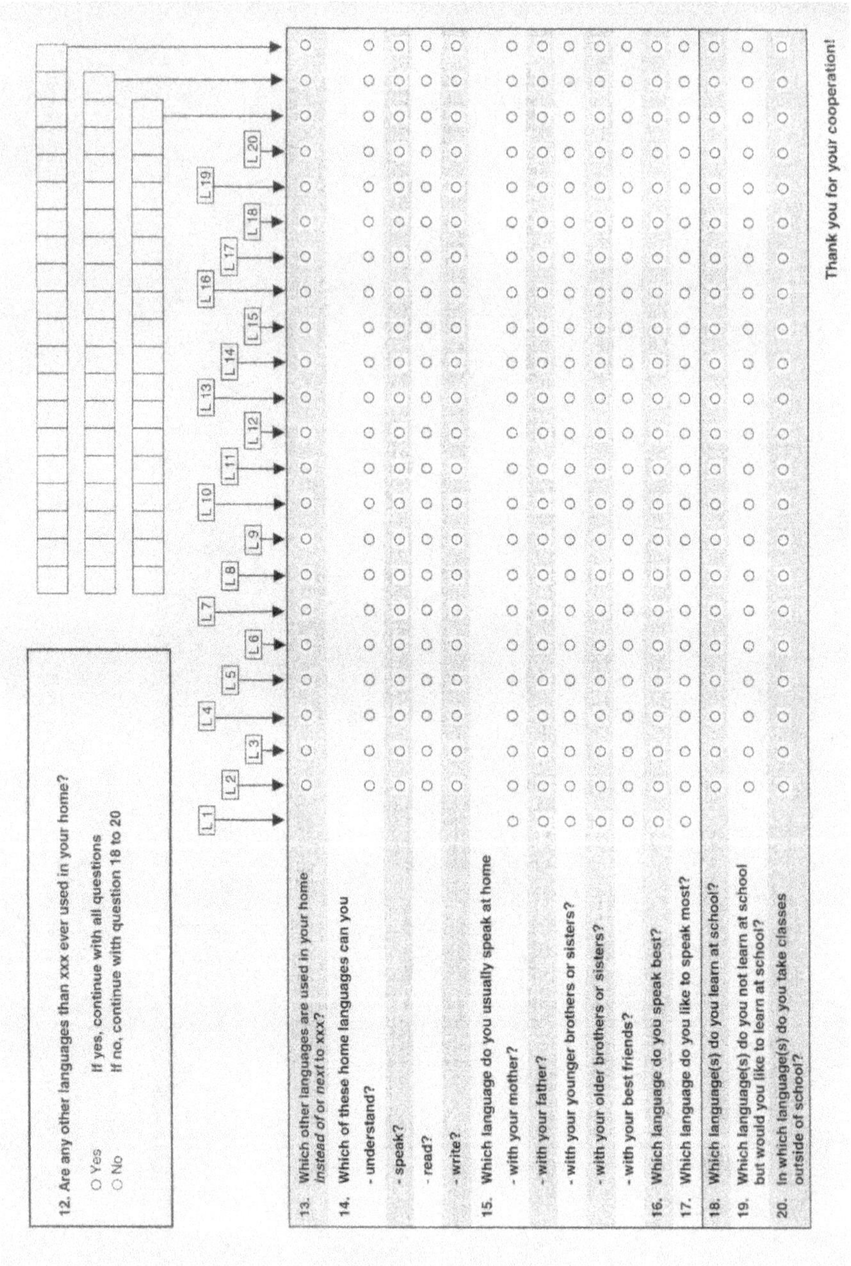

12. Are any other languages than xxx ever used in your home?

   O Yes   If yes, continue with all questions
   O No   If no, continue with question 18 to 20

13. Which other languages are used in your home *instead of or next to xxx?*

14. Which of these home languages can you
   - understand?
   - speak?
   - read?
   - write?

15. Which language do you usually speak at home
   - with your mother?
   - with your father?
   - with your younger brothers or sisters?
   - with your older brothers or sisters?
   - with your best friends?

16. Which language do you speak best?

17. Which language do you like to speak most?

18. Which language(s) do you learn at school?

19. Which language(s) do you not learn at school but would you like to learn at school?

20. In which language(s) do you take classes outside of school?

L 1 L 2 L 3 L 4 L 5 L 6 L 7 L 8 L 9 L 10 L 11 L 12 L 13 L 14 L 15 L 16 L 17 L 18 L 19 L 20

Thank you for your cooperation!

Figure 4. (cont.)

Note

1   This is and adapted and extended version of an earlier text in *International Journal of the Sociology of Language* 175/176 (2005): 17–40.

References

Achterberg, J.
   2005   *Zur Vitalität slavischer Idiome in Deutschland. Eine empirische Studie zum Sprachverhalten slavophoner Immigranten.* München: Verlag Otto Sagner.

Acton, T. & G. Mundy (eds.)
   1999   *Romani Culture and Gypsy Identity.* Hatfield: University of Hertfordshire Press.

Akinci, M-A., J.J. de Ruiter and F. Sanagustin
   2004   *Le Plurilinguisme à Lyon. Le Statut des Langues à la Maison et à l'École.* Paris: L'Harmattan.

Alladina, S.
   1993   South Asian languages in Britain. In: G. Extra and L. Verhoeven (eds.), *Immigrant Languages in Europe*, 55–65. Clevedon: Multilingual Matters.

Alladina, S. and V. Edwards (eds.)
   1991   *Multilingualism in the British Isles* (Vol. 1: The older mother tongues and Europe; Vol. 2: Africa, the Middle East and Asia). London: Longman.

Appel, R. and P. Muysken
   1987   *Language Contact and Bilingualism.* London: Edward Arnold.

Baker, P. and J. Eversley (eds.)
   2000   *Multilingual Capital. The Languages of London's Schoolchildren and their Relevance to Economic, Social and Educational Policies.* London: Battlebridge Publications.

Bourhis, R., H. Giles and D. Rosenthal
   1981   Notes on the construction of a 'Subjective Vitality Questionnaire' for ethnolinguistic groups. *Journal of Multilingual and Multicultural Development* 2: 145–155.

Broeder, P. and G. Extra
   1995   *Minderheidsgroepen en Minderheidstalen.* Den Haag: VNG.
   1998   *Language, Ethnicity and Education. Case Studies on Immigrant Minority Groups and Immigrant Minority Languages.* Clevedon: Multilingual Matters.

160   *Guus Extra and Kutlay Yağmur*

Broeder, P. and L. Mijares
2003   *Plurilingüismo en Madrid. Las Lenguas de los Alumnos de Origin Inmigrante en Primaria.* Madrid: Centro de Investigación y Documentación Educativa.

Campbell,. G.
2000   *Compendium of the World's Languages* (Volume 1 & 2). London: Routledge.

Caubet, D., S. Chaker and J. Sibille (eds.)
2002   *Codification des Langues de France.* Paris: l'Harmattan.

Churchill, S.
1986   *The Education of Linguistic and Cultural Minorities in the OECD Countries.* Clevedon: Multilingual Matters.

Clyne, M.
2003   *Dynamics of Language Contact.* Cambridge University Press.

Comrie, B., S. Matthews and M. Polinsky
2003   *The Atlas of Languages.* Revised Edition. London: Eurospan Group.

Crystal, D.
1997   *The Cambridge Encyclopedia of Language.* Cambridge: Cambridge University Press.

Dalby, D.
1999/2000   *The Linguasphere Register of the World's Languages and Speech Communities* (Volume 1 & 2). Wales-Hebron: Linguasphere Press.

Extra, G., R. Aarts, T. van der Avoird, P. Broeder and K. Yağmur
2001   *Meertaligheid in Den Haag. De Status van Allochtone Talen Thuis en op School.* Amsterdam: European Cultural Foundation.
2002   *De Andere Talen van Nederland: Thuis en op School.* Muiderberg: Coutinho.

Extra, G. and D. Gorter (eds.)
2001   *The Other Languages of Europe. Demographic, Sociolinguistic and Educational Perspectives.* Clevedon: Multilingual Matters.

Extra, G. and J.J. de Ruiter (eds.)
2001   *Babylon aan de Noordzee. Nieuwe Talen in Nederland.* Amsterdam: Bulaaq.

Extra, G. and L. Verhoeven (eds.)
1993a   *Community Languages in the Netherlands.* Amsterdam: Swets and Zeitlinger.
1993b   *Immigrant Languages in Europe.* Clevedon: Multilingual Matters.
1998   *Bilingualism and Migration.* Berlin/New York: Mouton De Gruyter.

Extra, G. and K. Yağmur (eds.)
2004   *Urban Multilingualism in Europe: Immigrant Minority Languages at Home and School.* Clevedon: Multilingual Matters.

Fürstenau, S., I. Gogolin and K. Yaðmur (Hrsg.)
2003   *Mehrsprachigkeit in Hamburg. Ergebnisse einer Sprachenerhebung an den Grundschulen in Hamburg.* Münster/New York: Waxmann.

Giacalone Ramat, A. and P. Ramat
1998   *The Indo-European Languages.* London: Routledge.

Giles, H., R. Bourhis and D. Taylor
1977   Towards a theory of language in ethnic group relations. In: H. Giles (ed.), *Language, Ethnicity, and Intergroup Relations,* 307–348. London: Academic Press.

Gogolin, I.
1994   *Der Monolinguale Habitus der Multilingualen Schule.* Münster: Waxmann.

Grimes, B. (ed.)
1996   *Ethnologue. Languages of the world* (13th Edition). Dallas: Summer Institute of Linguistics (*www.sil.org/ethnologue*).

Husén, T. and S. Opper (eds.)
1983   *Multicultural and Multilingual Education in Immigrant Countries.* Oxford: Pergamon Press.

Jaspaert, K. and S. Kroon (eds.)
1991   *Ethnic Minority Languages and Education.* Amsterdam/Lisse: Swets and Zeitlinger.

Jørgensen, J. (ed.)
2003   *Turkish Speakers in North Western Europe.* Clevedon: Multilingual Matters.

Kroon, S.
1990   *Opportunities and Constraints of Community Language Teaching.* Münster/New York: Waxmann.

Kyuchukov, H. (ed.)
2002   *New Aspects of Roma Children Education.* Sofia: Ictus.

Linguistic Minorities Project
1985   *The Other Languages of England.* London: Routledge and Kegan.

Nygren-Junkin, L. and G. Extra
2003   *Multilingualism in Göteborg. The Status of Immigrant Minority Languages at Home and at School.* Amsterdam: European Cultural Foundation.

Obdeijn, H. and J.J. de Ruiter (eds.)
 1998   *Le Maroc au Coeur de l'Europe. L'Enseignement de la Langue et Culture d'Origine (ELCO) aux Éleves marocains dans cinq Pays Europeens.* Tilburg: Tilburg University Press, Syntax Datura.

Reid, E. and H. Reich
 1992   *Breaking the Boundaries. Migrant Workers' Children in the EC.* Clevedon: Multilingual Matters.

Tilmatine, M. (ed.)
 1997   *Enseignment des Langues d'Origine et Immigration Nord-Africaine en Europe: Langue Maternelle ou Langue d'Etat?* Paris: Inalco/Cedrea-Crb.

Tosi, A.
 1984   *Immigration and bilingual education. A case study of movement of population, language change and education within the EEC.* Oxford: Pergamon Press.

UNDP
 2002   *www.hdr.undp.org/reports/global/2002/en/pdf/backone.pdf*

Van der Avoird, T.
 2001   *Determining language vitality. The language use of Hindu communities in the Netherlands and the United Kingdom.* Dissertation, Tilburg University.

Verlot, M., K. Delrue, G. Extra and K. Yağmur
 2003   *Meertaligheid in Brussel. De Status van Allochtone Talen Thuis en op School.* Amsterdam: European Cultural Foundation.

Weinreich, U.
 1953   *Languages in contact. Findings and problems.* The Hague: Mouton.

Immigrant languages and languages of France[1]

Dominique Caubet

1. Introduction

The prestige of the French language is a well-known phenomenon and France has a strong tendency to see itself as monolingual. This prestige can take on unreasonable proportions, to the point that the linguist Pierre Encrevé talks of a true *religion de la langue* (*Libération,* May 11, 2002), which dates back to 1870 and not to the French revolution, as is often thought:

> It is time to finally "secularise" the language question. For a century, after the an-nexation of Alsace, being at is was German speaking, a linguistic ideology spread in France, particularly through schools, making francophone monolingualism a quasi-State religion for the Republic: French was to be not only the unique lan-guage of the State and the common language of all French people – which is undoubtedly positive – but the only language of each and every French person. The other historical languages of France were presented as a menace to the unity and indivisibility of the Republic. (translated version)

Another permanent issue in France is the prohibition, by law and by public opinion, to ask people about or to label them according to criteria that might be used to discriminate against them. The French Republic which is referred to as "indivisible", recognises all citizens as being equal, "without any distinction of origin, race or religion". As a result, there are no official statistics in France relating to ethnicity, race or religion, for instance.

This chapter tries to track down figures on language practices in Metropoli-tan France according to statistics published after the last national census of 1999, conducted by INSEE (*Institut National de la Statistique et des Études Économiques*) and INED (*Institut National d'Études Démographiques*). INED was allowed to add a question on language practices to the *enquête famille* (family survey), traditionally associated with the census since 1954 and based in 1999 on an unusually large sample (380,000 people; Héran, Filhon, and De-prez 2002; Clanché 2002). This survey, traditionally focused on the evolution of family structures and language practices, was a complete novelty. Until then, only pilot questionnaires had been administered regionally for much smaller samples.

The results of the family survey were published in 2002 (Héran, Filhon, and Deprez 2002) but the complete results on a regional basis were still being printed at the time of writing. Some regional issues of INSEE bulletins have published short articles with partial figures (Blot, Eloy, and Rouault 2004; Burricand and Filhon 2003; Duée 2002; Deguillaume and Amrane 2002; Le Boëtté 2003). I will go into more details on the outcomes for Arabic, a language for which I have personal data on a group of over 10,000 students that I collected while correcting an optional test for the French *Baccalauréat* (1995–1999). First, I will discuss the delicate question of ethnic statistics in France, a matter of debate in 2006–2007, and after that I will consider the status of the *Langues de France* and refer to the published results of the 1999 family survey on immigrant languages.

François Héran, the director of INED, had to find proper arguments to include the question on language practice in the 1999 family survey. The debate was still open in 2006–2007, when the MRAP (*Mouvement contre le racisme et pour l'amitié entre les peuples*) and other associations expressed their fear of *fichage ethnique* (ethnic labeling)[2] after INED was granted permission to do a survey for the Ministry of Education on the ethnic origin of children.

One must bear in mind that Law n° 78–17, January 6, 1978 (*Loi relative à l'informatique, aux fichiers et aux libertés*, modified on August 6, 2004), on the use of statistics and registration is clear and prohibits collection or use of personal data that might show, directly or undirectly, people's racial or ehtnic origins, their political, philosophical or religious persuasions, their trade-union affiliations, or provide information about their health or their sexual life. The law prohibits any study that will bring to the fore information about racial or ethnic origin and political or religious affiliations of anyone living in France. The only way this can be circumvented is to obtain special dispensation for each particular study, arguing that it is in the public interest, that all information gathered will be kept anonymous or that express consent of the persons involved has been obtained. The CNIL (*Commission nationale de l'informatique et des libertés*) protects this freedom and its decision on (dis)approval has to be published in *Le Journal Officiel*, after a time-consuming procedure.

In January 2007, the debate on ethnic statistics became extremely vivid. A conference on this theme was organised by the government in Paris on October 19, 2006, at the *Centre d'Analyse Stratégique*.[3] For the first time since the CNIL was created in 1978, public hearings were held by the CNIL.[4] The question was how to measure cultural diversity, who would be the people to do it, for what purpose and by what means? The method of using family names was not permitted and first names could only be used at certain occasions with large samples, provided anonymity would be guaranteed. In April 2006, the CNIL refused to allow a survey ordered by the CRIF (*Conseil Représentatif des Institutions Juives de France*), to be carried out by SOFRES (a private organisation specialised in polling and opinion surveys) where the sample was to be chosen from supposedly Jewish patronyms from the telephone book.[5] However, the CNIL did allow the 2006 INED survey for the Ministry of Education, aimed at checking the level of integration of "second generations[6]" in Europe whose parents originated from Morocco or Turkey. The aim was a sample of 250 persons born in France, from at least one parent born in Morocco or Turkey, both parents born in Morocco or Turkey and both parents born in France. In fact, the study was meant to examine family characteristics, education and training, employment, cultural practices, place of residence, social relations and political participation, distribution of tasks within the household, education of children, religion and religious practices, discrimination, construction of identity, earnings and sexual life.[7] INED was granted dispensation on the basis of the study being a matter of public interest, and was exceptionally allowed to select Moroccan and Turkish patronyms[8] in order to create the sample.

François Héran, director of INED, reacted to various objections against this permission in an article in *Le Monde, Statistiques ethniques, c'est possible,*[9] and in the January 2007 public hearing by the CNIL, where he argued in favour of an opening guaranteed by the size of the sample and the anonymisation of the data.

The site of *Ligue des Droits de l'Homme* in Toulon[10] sums up the chronology of particular questions asked in French national statistics. In 1871, a question was introduced on nationality, but religion was crossed out; in 1962, foreigners and immigrants who had aquired the French nationality were asked about their former nationality; in 1991, a new category called *immigrés*[11] was introduced by the *Haut Conseil à l'Intégration* (HCI), which combines data on nationality of birth and country of birth. In the 1999 family survey, there was a question on the country of birth of both parents. In 2008, the new survey by INSEE and INED *Trajectoires et origines* is to gather information on people's origins, on their self-declared ethnic belonging and on discriminatory factors with respect to colour, accent or eating habits, for instance.

2. The 1999 family survey on language practices

The idea for a survey on language practices in France dates back to Victor Duruy in 1863, when he was Minister of Education (Héran 2002); partial regional results (Occitany, Britanny, Corsica) indicated that 75% of the children in those regions could not speak French at the time. The family survey of 1999 was seen as a last chance of getting an overview of language practices in France during the 20th century. Before 1999, family surveys were only addressed to women between 18 and 65 years old; in 1999, the survey also included men and very old people in order to get an idea of what existed a generation ago in terms of language practices. The analysis of the linguistic part of the survey was funded by DGLFLF (*Délégation Générale à la Langue Française et aux Langues de France*).

An exploratory survey led by François Héran in 1992[12] (Héran 1993, 2004) ensured that the family survey would not give too much space to languages other than French and would focus in particular on regional languages (Blanchet et al. 2005). It concluded that the linguistic unification of French was more or less a fact and stressed the "overwhelming domination" of French because only 16% of the informants declared that they usually spoke a language other than French. It indicated Arabic as the first other language spoken in France (estimated at less than 2%), Portuguese came second (1%), Alsacian third (0.6%), preceding Turkish (0.4%) and Spanish (0.2%).

The way the questions were phrased in 1999 was designed in such a way that it favoured French (Blanchet et al. 2005). The sample was exceptionally large (380,000 people) and some regions were over-represented on purpose (Flandres, Alsace, Moselle, Corsica, Pays Catalan, Pays Basque and Britanny; Burricand 2003); the figures were then extended to the national level and discussed with linguists (particularly Christine Deprez; Héran, Filhon, and Deprez 2002). The figures revealed officially in February 2002 came as a surprise, especially the outcomes on immigrant languages, Arabic in particular.

2.1.   Results of the family survey

To the question *What language(s), dialect(s) or "patois" did your parents usually speak to you around the age of 5?*, 26% of the adults living in Metropolitan France, i.e., 11.5 million people, answered it was a language other than French; 6/10 associated with French (whereas the 1992 survey had given 16% for usual transmission; Héran 1993; Héran, Filhon, and Deprez 2002). The results can be read as follows: "usually" corresponds to "usual transmission" while "and also" corresponds to "occasional transmission".

Half of these 11.5 million people indicated that they were spoken to in regional languages (1 adult out of 7 = 5.5 million) and the other half in immigrant languages, learned before or after immigration to France (1 adult out of 7 = 5.5 million). This survey did not include people under the age of 18, as a result of which the outcome only gives a partial overview. 6,700 names of languages appeared in the answers, which were reduced to 400 actual languages according to the classification of SIL (Summer Institute of Linguistics), out of which 10 languages represented 2/3 of the answers. The clear tendency is that the languages transmitted by both parents (mother and father) and usually spoken are most certainly languages of recent immigration. For example, Arabic and Portuguese appear in this category more commonly than Spanish or Italian. Only 8% of the whole population did not speak French at all at home.

Arabic comes first for common use; 940,000 adults living in Metropolitan France remember that their parents spoke Arabic first to them in their childhood (age of 5), while only 230,000 adults mention occasional transmission usually associated with French (Héran, Filhon, and Deprez 2002). The 1992 survey had only estimated a total of 439,000 people who had received Arabic from their parents. This represents between half and 1/3 of the 1999 results, which yielded between 930,000 and 1,185,500 people for usual transmission, to which between 230,000 and 389,000 people should be added for occasional transmission.

Regional languages, by contrast, were mostly transmitted occasionally and together with French, and most often by one parent, except for Alsacian which comes second with 660,000 people for usual transmission and 240,000 for occasional transmission. Occitan has 610,000 people for usual transmission and 1,060,000 for occasional transmission; *langues d'oïl* have 570,000 and 850,000 people, respectively.

If priority is given to usual transmission, Arabic comes first (940,000 + 230,000 occasional = 1,170,000; Héran, Filhon, and Deprez 2002), before Alsacian (660,000 + 240,000 occasional = 900,000). If we combine usual and occasional transmission, Occitan with 1,060,000 occasional and 610,000 usual takes first place (1,670,000), followed by *langues d'oïl* (570,000 usual + 850,000 occasional = 1,420,000), before Arabic as the first immigrant language. Portuguese is the second immigrant language, with 580,000 people usually, plus 100,000 occasionally (= 680,000).

The figures for transmission of regional languages in Metropolitan France range from five languages under 200,000 (120,000 for *Flamand occidental*, 130,000 for *Basque*, 150,000 for *Francique*, 180,000 for *Catalan*, 190,000 for *Corsican*), two languages under 300,000 (230,000 for *Franco-provençal* and 290,000 for the various *Creoles*) to *Alsacian* (900,000) and the two large families, *langues d'oïl* (1,400,000) and *Occitan* (1,800,000).

Before 1930, one out of four adults usually spoke a regional language with his/her parents, whereas it was only one out of ten in the 1950s and one out of twenty in the 1970s, with the exception of Corsica and Alsace. The tendency for regional languages is to be spoken mostly by people in the countryside and born before 1940.

2.1.1.   Retransmission

When it comes to the question of whether these adults have transmitted to their own children the languages they received from their parents, the figures collapse drastically. 26% of the total population (11.5 million) had received a language other than French from their parents, but only 9% (4 million) declared to have transmitted this language to their own children; the average for transmission is 35%. Arabic is transmitted by 45%, in 10th position behind English, Turkish, Chinese languages, Serbian/Croatian, and languages of South East Asia (e.g., Vietnamese, Cambodian (see Figure 2 in Héran, Filhon, and Deprez 2002). Regional languages have even lower figures for retransmission; only *Alsacian* and *Basque* are above the national average (with 67% and 61%, respectively). For *Corsican* it is about average, for *Catalan* it is 30%, for *langues d'oïl* 28%, for *langues d'occ* 13% and for *Breton* 11%. For immigrant languages, it holds that the more recent the immigration is, the higher is the figure for retransmission.

2.1.2.   Comments on the survey

The survey needs some extra comment with respect to the method used in the phrasing of the questions, the composition of the sample, the rectifications and the variation in the figures. It should not be forgotten that it is the first survey of its kind in France and that the macro-quantitative tendencies do hold, although some languages have probably been tuned down.

First of all, the study is based on voluntary declarations and some languages are sometimes not considered worth mentioning by their own speakers, even though the phrasing of the question tried to include as many languages as possible, using the formulation *langues, dialectes ou "patois"*. This can be very significant in diglossic situations as we find them in many parts of France (Blanchet et al. 2005), particularly when the questionnaire is especially about this issue. Moreover, the figures only concern the population over the age of 18, leaving out important figures for certain languages, in particular recent immigrant languages. Thirdly, the way the questions were phrased in order to detect usual *vs.* occasional transmission may seem surprising. Blanchet et al. (2005) recall the three questions aimed at measuring language practice (translated in English here):

> 19. In which language, dialect or "patois" did your parents usually speak to you when you were a child around the age of five?
>
> Your father or the man who raised you
> 1. usually spoke to you in...
> 2. and also in ...

Your mother or the woman who raised you
1. usually spoke to you in...
2. and also in ...
Examples: Alsacian, Basque, Breton, Catalan, Corsican, Creole, Flemmish, Gallo, Occitan, Picard, Platt, Provençal, Arabic, Spanish, Kabyle, Portuguese, Sign Language.
- For French, simply note "F"
- In the case of a dialect or a "patois", clearly state its region (Picardie, Béarn, Rouergue, Moselle ...)
- For foreign languages, do not mention the nationality but the language. Example: do not mention Algerian, Moroccan, Senegalese, but Arabic, Kabyle, Wolof etc ...

20. In which language, dialect or "patois" did you speak to your young children when they were five (or do you speak to them now if they are younger)?
    1. you spoke to them usually in ...
    2. and also in ...

21. And now, do you speak with relatives (parents, friends, colleagues, business people...) in languages other than French?
    Yes or no?
    If yes, in which languages?
    1. ...
    2. ...

The questions are not phrased in a neutral way; they are leading questions, aimed at receiving desired answers, particularly with respect to the names given to languages. Why ask people to say *Arabic* and not *Moroccan Arabic*, for instance, and thus deprive us of interesting data (proportion of Moroccan, Algerian and Tunisian Arabic). Why, on the other hand, ask informants to write *kabyle* and not *Berber*, if the tendency for Arabic is towards generalisation?

The naming of languages is anything but void of ideology, in particular in the case of Arabic. The people who designed the questionnaire acted as if Arabic is one language and, above all, were not interested in important details, since the Algerian, Moroccan and Tunisian massive immigrations occurred at different periods. Héran (1993) explained that most Algerian fathers and mothers arrived in France in 1964 and 1972 respectively, most Tunisian fathers and mothers in 1972 and 1977 respectively, and most Moroccan fathers and mothers in 1972 and 1978 respectively. He added that this affected the non-transmission of the language to young children, with rates of 65%, 60% and 30% in 1992 for Algerian, Tunisian and Moroccan Arabic, respectively. Another issue is: What does speaking a language, *parler une langue*, imply? In the mind of the interviewees, it most probably meant to be fluent in or to have mastered the language, which means that partial knowledge will be disregarded and that people will not mention languages they have only a limited command of. Moreover, the sample purposely chose to put forward certain regions and within these regions urban centres, leaving out rural areas.

One has to be very cautious in the phrasing of the results as well. For example, two different figures are given for Arabic in the article on *Ile de France* (Burricand and Filhon 2003). The title of the paragraph is *L'arabe, langue d'usage familial la plus fréquente* and reads as follows: "Among the 480,000 adults living in *Ile de France* whose parents spoke Arabic, 67% declare having transmitted this language to their own children. (...) After English, Arabic and Portuguese are the most frequently spoken languages in the region with 330,000 and 270,000 adult speakers respectively". This would imply, although it is not mentioned explicitly, that only 68.8 % of the people who received Arabic from their parents speak it nowadays (330,000/480,000); but it would also mean that nearly all of them declared passing it on to their children (67% of 480,000 declared transmission, i.e., 321,600), which is not very probable. Where is the flaw?

What is more worrying is that the figures tend to fluctuate a little; the synthesis and the figures published in 2002 (Héran, Filhon, and Deprez 2002; Clanché 2002) mention "940,000 adults living in Metropolitan France who remember that their parents mostly spoke to them in Arabic in their early childhood, against only 230,000 adults who mention occasional transmission, usually associated with French. The same applies to Portuguese: 580,000 adults received it usually, against 100,000 occasionally." Other sources issued from the same 1999 family survey report higher figures.

For the number of adults who received Arabic from their parents, the survey gives 1,446,800 (3.3% of the total adult population); for those who currently speak Arabic, 1,147,000 (2.6%); and for those who transmitted Arabic to their children, whether they received it from their parents or not, 665,600 (1.5%). Among those to whom the parents spoke Arabic, 1,021,900 speak it currently (70.6%). Another table gives the number of adults having received Arabic at the age of 5, associated with another language 861,500, usually: 1,185,500, occasionally: 389,000, which would produce a total of 1,574,000 people. How does this correspond with the figures published in Héran, Filhon, and Deprez (2002), where the given usual transmission is 940,000, instead of 1,185,500; and the occasional is 230,000 instead of 389,000? In total, there are at least 404,500 people missing among the adults who received Arabic from their parents in the official figures.

The figures for Berber also seem very low compared to Chaker (2003: 5).[13] For the number of adults who received Berber from their parents, the unpublished sources give 305,400 (0.69% of the adult population); for those who currently speak Berber, they give 196,000 (0.45 % of the adult population); and for those who transmitted it to their children, whether they received it from their parents or not, 105,500 (0.24 % of the adult population). Another table gives the number of adults having received Berber at the age of 5 usually (225,200) and occasionally (110,000), associated with another language 223,200 (among which 158,400 with French, and 65,00 with a language other than French). Berber-speaking immigrants from Algeria, Morocco and even Tunisia were the first ones to come to France, as early as at the end of the 19th century. The strength of their presence in Metropolitan France is even more noticeable than for their fellow Arabophones. They came in great numbers with their families in the 1960s and 1970s, so an explanation has to be found for these very low figures. Are they due to the diglossic situation or to the composition of the sample?

2.2.   "Langues *en* France, Langues *de* France"

The 1999 survey focused upon regional, foreign and immigrant languages. Simultaneously (April 1999), some of these languages were promoted to *Langues de France* when France intended to ratify the Council of Europe *Charter for regional or minority languages*. On that occasion, some immigrant languages were treated differently and acquired a new status. To prepare its ratification, the then Prime Minister Lionel Jospin asked a linguist to write a report on the *Languages of France*. A totally new situation was created when Cerquiglini (1999) established an impressive list of 75 languages other than French and brought up the new concept of "non-territorial languages", where he listed five languages, i.e., *berbère, arabe dialectal, arménien occitental, yiddish* and *romani*.

For it to be recognised as a *Langue de France*, the language must have been spoken and transmitted for several generations by French citizens: if that is the case it is no longer considered as an immigrant language, but as a *Langue de France* together with the historical regional languages. The condition for a language to be recognised in Cerquiglini's report was that it must not to have any official status in another state (Chinese, Wolof, Spanish, Portuguese or Polish were thus not eligible). This means that *arabe maghrébin* and Berber were considered as languages of French citizens. They now officially belong to the Republic's patrimony and should be protected. This recognition was not just a political decision, but took into account the depth of the historical relation (colonial at first) between France and Northern Africa (Caubet 2001a, 2004a; Chaker 2004).

Unfortunately, no direct measure followed this recognition by the leading French institutions. The Council's Charter was signed by France on May 7, 1999, but it was never ratified because President Jacques Chirac at times of political cohabitation seized the *Conseil Constitutionnel*, which decided that the spirit of the Charter was against the French constitution, and stopped the ratification process.

3. The case of Arabic and Berber in France

Until 1999, there have been no large-scale quantitative studies in France on the prominence of languages other than French. The 1999 family survey yielded important figures. It is worth comparing them with previous estimates and with what we experienced when the *Institut National des Langues et Civilisations Orientales* (INALCO) had to organise an optional test in *arabe dialectal* for the French *baccalauréat* (1995–1999). We will try to present a picture of the situation at the end of the 20th century, because the 1999 census, the 1999 family survey and the last year for Maghrebi Arabic at the *baccalauréat* present unique data for the year 1999.

3.1. Low estimates for people of Northern African origin

Since France introduced the notion of *immigrés*, i.e., persons born abroad from foreign parents, people remain *immigrés* all their lives, whether they have acquired French nationality or not. There are figures on the number of foreigners and *immigrés* by nationality of origin. However, this does not include the children born in France, since acquisition of the French nationality is not automatic and has to be requested at the age of 13, 16 or 18.

A low estimate is that there are 3 million people in France originating from the Maghreb. This was confirmed in 2003 by the *Secrétaire d'état aux Affaires Étrangères*. Renaud Muselier presented some extremely interesting figures in his address to a conference at the University of Austin:[14] "There are four to five million Muslims in France, which is almost 10% of the total population. Muslims in France come from no fewer than 123 countries, although more than 70% hail from Algeria, Morocco and Tunisia". 70% of 4 to 5 million people represents between 2.8 and 3.5 million people originating from these three countries.

In the absence of statistics on religious affiliation, another source quoted in a report by the *Haut Conseil à l'Intégration* (2000)[15] confirms the figure. Alain Boyer (*Secrétaire Général de la Région Auvergne*) gives an estimate of 2,900,000 Muslims from Northern African origin (1,550,000 from Algeria, 1,000,000 from Morocco and 350,000 from Tunisia), to which 300,000 Jews from Northern

Table 1. Number of *immigrés* born in the Maghreb (INSEE, 1999 national census)

Country of birth	Total	French by naturalisation	Foreigners
Algeria	575,740	156,856 (27.2%)	418,884
Morocco	521,059	133,405 (25.6%)	387,654
Tunisia	201,700	80,987 (40.2%)	120,713

Africa should be added. The source for the latter figure is the survey directed by Erik Cohen in January 2002 using the patronym method, consulting 1,132 heads of family for the *Fonds social juif unifié*,[16] estimating there are some 500,000 Jews in France, among whom 70% are sephardic Jews and 300,000 come from Northern Africa (24% are ashkenazy and only 12% of the youngsters); 56% of the Jews live in *Ile de France* and the rest mostly in Marseille, Nice (PACA), Lyon (Rhône-Alpes) and Strasbourg (Alsace).

We also know that in 1999 (year of both the census and the family survey), there were 1,298,273 *immigrés* born in the Maghreb, i.e., naturalised or still foreigners (see Table 1).

All French people of Northern African origin born in France since the 1970s or under French colonisation before 1962 (who may have recovered their nationality of birth) are probably still missing from these figures.

3.1.1. Arabophones or Berberophones?

Once the number of people of Northern African origin is established (which is not the case yet), one would still have to be able to distinguish between the Arabophones and the Berberophones, keeping in mind that a great proportion of Berberophones also speak (and sometimes transmit) Arabic. Berberophones from Algeria and Morocco are over-represented in immigration in France and those from the Rif in Morocco, even more so in the North of Europe (Belgium, The Netherlands, and Germany). This is why the figures for Berber in the 1999 family survey seem extremely low. It is puzzling because in France some sources give 40% Berberophones for Algerian immigrants, 50% for Moroccans and no more than 1.5% for Tunisians (Chaker 1997, 2004).

3.2. The optional test at the French *baccalauréat*

Another source of information, coming directly from INALCO, is the optional test of *langues ne faisant pas l'objet d'un enseignement* (non-taught languages) at the French *baccalauréat*. INALCO was formally asked by the Ministry of Education to organise this optional test when it took a written form in 1994–1995[17] (Caubet 1999).

3.3.   The suppression of arabe dialectal

In 1999, the year of the recognition of Maghrebi Arabic as a *Langue de France*, the Ministry of Education decided to cross out *arabe dialectal* from the list of 28 possible languages, while all other languages, among them the other *Langue de France*, Berber, remained. There was a long fight to try to restore this, but *arabe dialectal*, which counted 9,886 candidates (76.6% for non-taught languages and 1.95% for candidates at the *baccalauréat* nationally) paid for its success, which obviously did not earn sympathy in some circles.

It later became known that this suppression was initiated by the *Inspection Générale d'arabe*, which may seem surprising. The reason for this curious attitude probably lies in the fact that Arabic has very few students in secondary education (about 6,000 for the seven years of secondary education) and the high figures of *arabe dialectal* (9,886 candidates) were a challenge to them; but it is also caused by the fact that INALCO was officially in charge of the test and they probably also felt they were losing control. The final suppression, however, was a political decision taken by the Minister of Education, Jack Lang (*Bulletin Officiel de l'Éducation Nationale 1 Feb. 2001, Note de service*). On this debate and long but lost fight, see Caubet (2001a, 2001b, 2002a, 2003, 2004a, 2004b, 2004c).

3.3.1.   Figures

Effectively, *arabe littéral* (the official French name in *Education Nationale* for reference to Standard Arabic) only had 1,772 candidates plus 895 as an option (2,667) at the level of the *baccalauréat*. In the seven years of public and private secondary schooling in France in 1999, it had 5,893 students (*collège*: 2,101; *Lycée*: 3,605; *professionnel*: 187; see *Midad* n.11, *Direction de la programmation et du développement – Ministère de l'éducation nationale*: http://crdp.ac paris.fr/d_ librairie/res/ Midad_ no11.pdf). Table 2 gives more detailed information.

It is interesting to note that the two languages chosen as *Langue de France*, i.e., Maghrebi Arabic and Berber, represented 11,637 candidates and 90.15% of the total for this test, and 2.3% of all *baccalauréat* candidates nationally. The strength of their presence in France is established on a solid quantitative basis. The figures presented result from our personal work and from fieldwork,[18] which has been going on for more than ten years for Berber and lasted five years for Maghrebi Arabic (1995–1999).

Until recently, we only had the figures for students who had registered for the exam that were presented in previous publications. It is now possible to trace the number of people who actually took the exam (*http://www.educationnationale.*

Table 2. Number of candidates for *baccalauréat* 1999 – Optional test for *Langues ne faisant pas l'objet d'un enseignement* (non-taught languages) (figures collected by Caubet and Chaker)

1999	Number of candidates	
Total 29 languages	12,908	
Total arabe dialectal		
(maghrébin + oriental)	10,111	(78.3% total of 29 languages)
Arabe maghrébin	9,886	(76.6% total of 29 languages)
Algérien	3,191	(32.3% arabe maghrébin)
Marocain	4,817	(48.7% arabe maghrébin)
Tunisien	1,878	(19% arabe maghrébin)
Arabe oriental	225	(1.7% total of 29 languages)
Syro-libano-palestinien	160	(71.1% arabe oriental)
Egyptien	65	(28.9% arabe oriental)
Total berbère	1,751	(13.6% total of 29 languages)
Chleuh	531	(30% berbère)
Rifain	341	(20% berbère)
Kabyle	879	(50% berbère)
Languages of the Maghreb	11,637	(90.2% total of 29 languages)
Arabe maghrébin + berbère		
Total 27 other languages	1,046	(8.1% total of 29 languages)

com/edu_diplomes_bac.html), which yields an outcome that is more compatible with our figures, corresponding to the number of papers marked.

With such high absolute figures it is interesting to produce a map of the repartition of candidates by *académie* (which is the unit for *Education nationale*), see Map 1.[19] It also gives the proportion of students who chose Moroccan, Algerian or Tunisian Arabic. Unfortunately, the way the questions were asked in the 1999 family survey does not allow for this important distinction.

The *académies* can be grouped into regions, resulting in Map 2, which can later be compared with the figures provided by INED for cross-references (Map 5). Map 2 presents the absolute figures of the candidates by region; when necessary, the *académies* have been grouped[20] to present the figures by region. We have chosen to leave out the distinction by country of origin in order to allow for a more striking comparison with the INED survey in Maps 5 and 6.

Tentatively, with much lower figures, a regional map can also be drawn for Berber. Map 3 gives the figures for 1999, our year of reference (compare Map 1). However, the figures have gone up to 2073 candidates in 2006 and the proportions of the various components have changed since *rifain* was introduced in

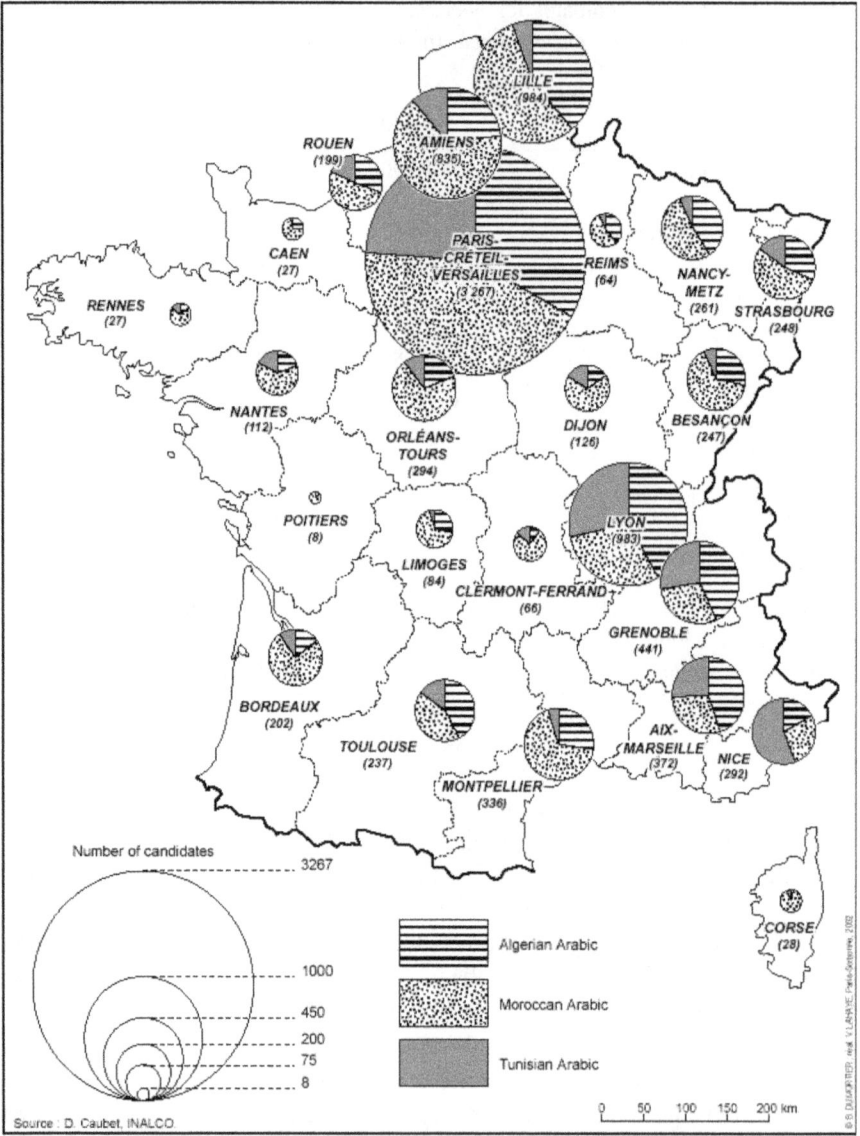

Map 1. Candidates for Maghrebi Arabic by *académie* (*baccalauréat* 1999)

1999, with nearly twice as many people originating from Morocco (*chleuh +
rifain* = 1385) compared to Algeria (*kabyles* = 688).

Berber can still be taken as an optional subject at the *baccalauréat*, contrary
to Maghrebi Arabic, but it is concentrated in certain regions and half of the

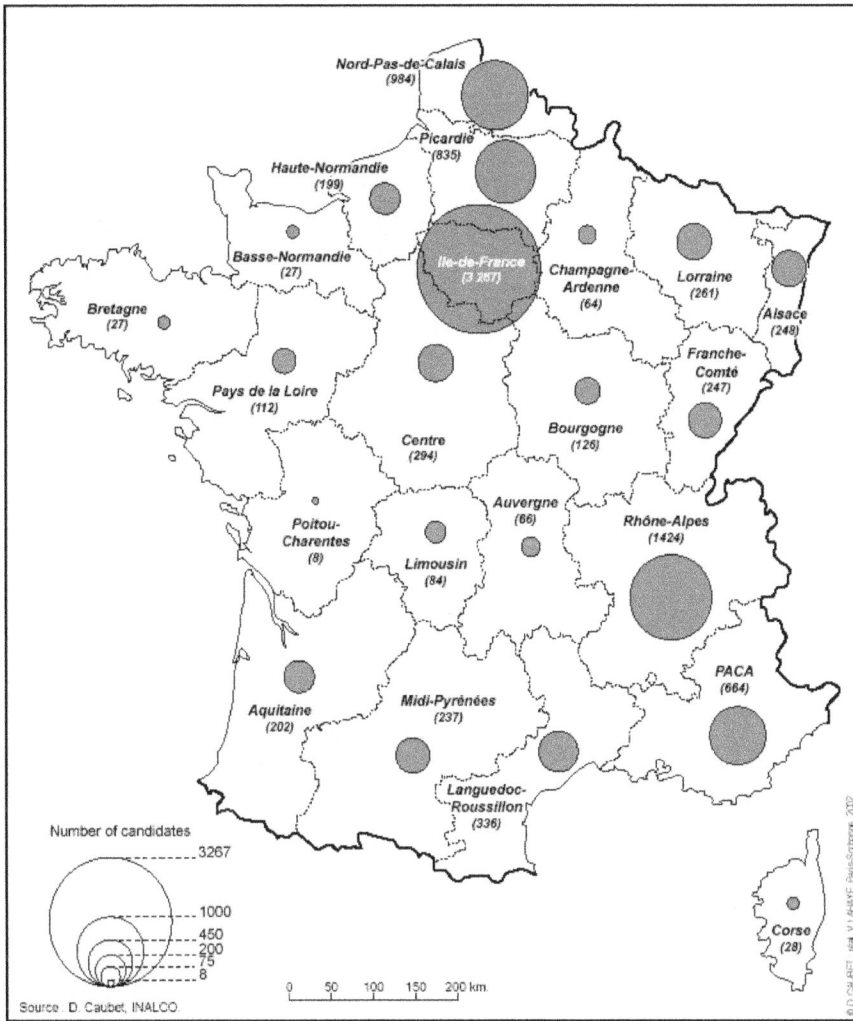

Map 2. Candidates for Maghrebi Arabic by region (*baccalauréat* 1999)

regions have no candidates or only very few (11 out of 22 regions have 0 to 13 candidates), in the west and mid-east of the country (Map 4).

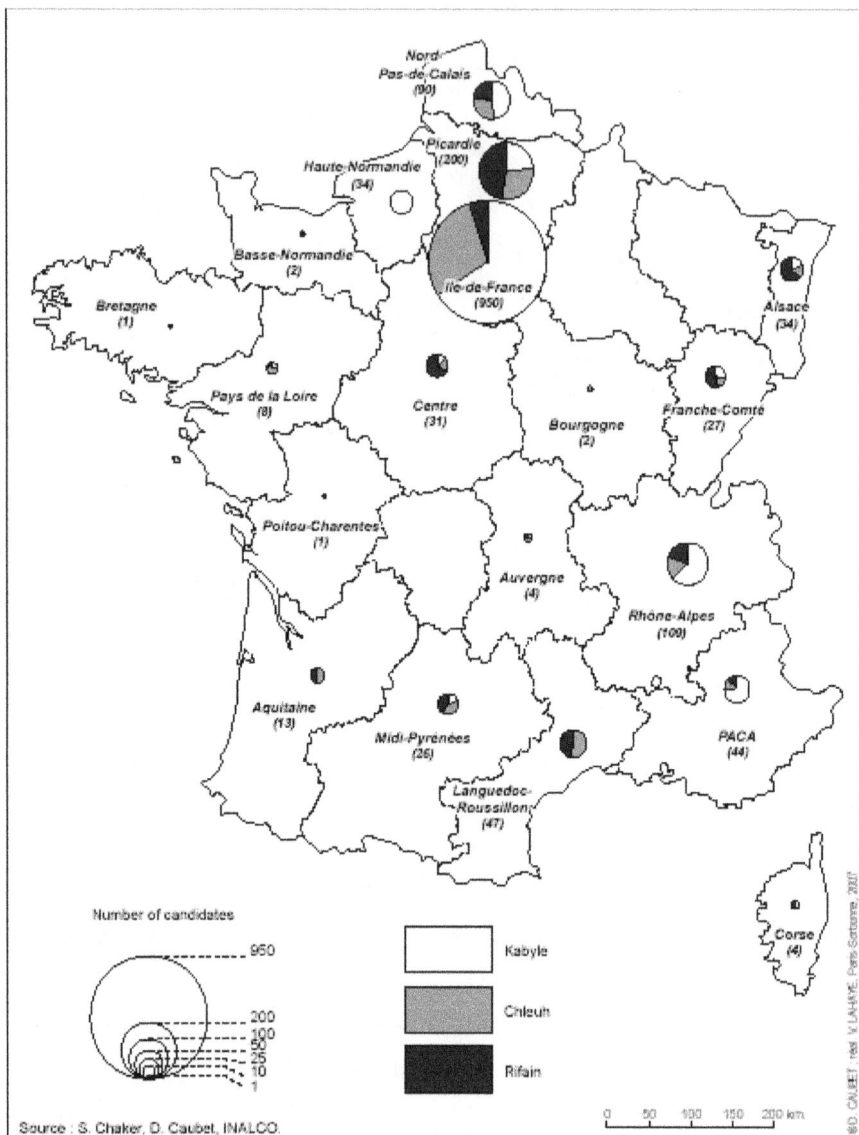

Map 3. Candidates for Berber by region (*baccalauréat* 1999)

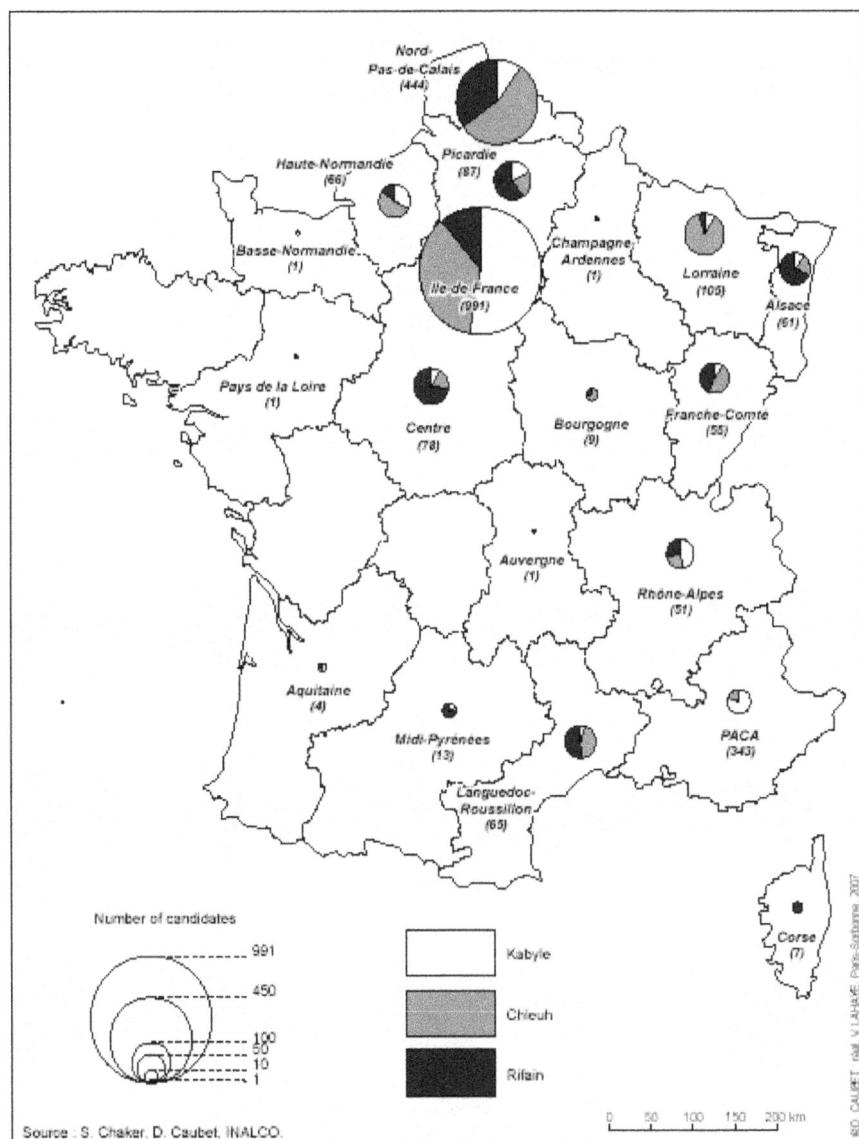

Map showing candidates for Berber by region. Labels by region:

Nord-Pas-de-Calais (444)
Haute-Normandie (66)
Picardie (87)
Basse-Normandie (1)
Île-de-France (991)
Champagne-Ardennes (1)
Lorraine (105)
Alsace (61)
Pays de la Loire (1)
Centre (78)
Bourgogne (9)
Franche-Comté (55)
Auvergne (1)
Rhône-Alpes (51)
Aquitaine (4)
Midi-Pyrénées (13)
Languedoc-Roussillon (65)
PACA (343)
Corse (7)

Number of candidates
991
450
100
50
10
1

Kabyle
Chleuh
Rifain

0   50   100   150   200 km

Source : S. Chaker, D. Caubet, INALCO.

©D. CAUBET, réal V.LAHAYE, Paris-Sorbonne 2007

Map 4. Candidates for Berber by region (*baccalauréat* 2006)

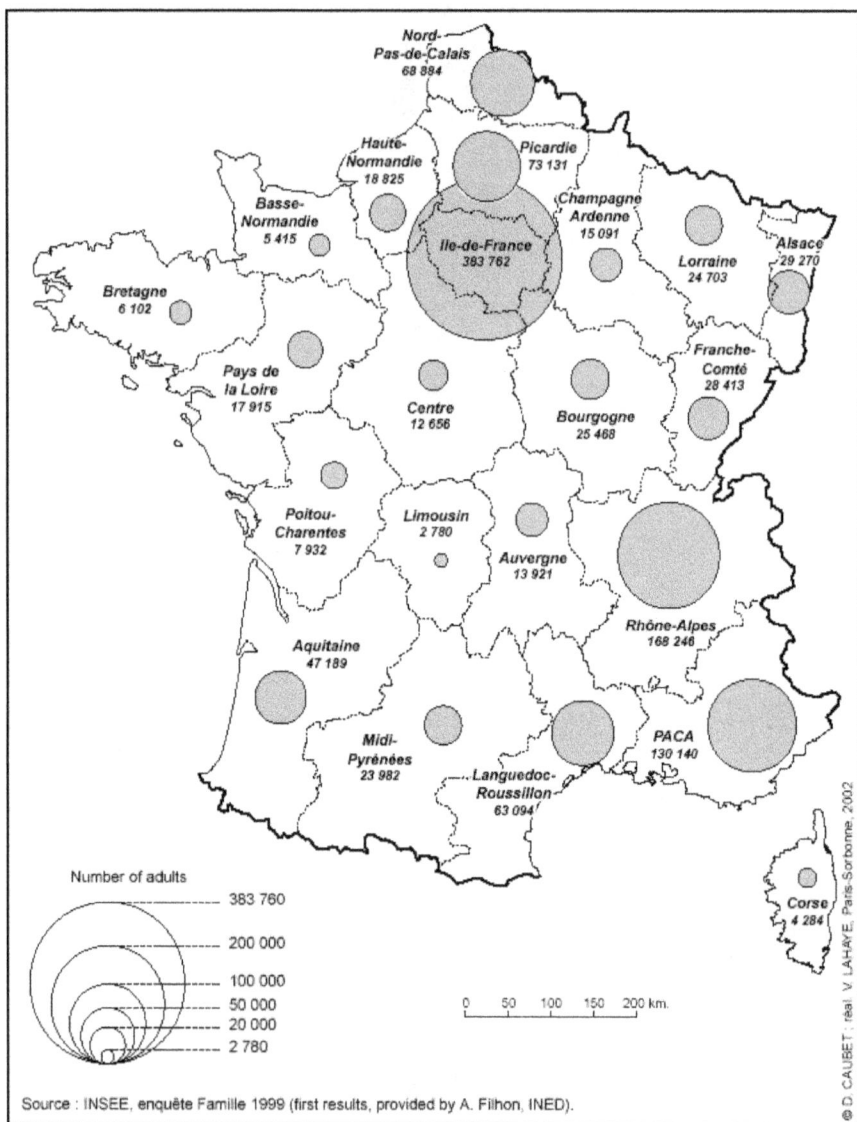

Nord-
Pas-de-Calais
68 894

Haute-
Normandie
18 825

Picardie
73 131

Basse-
Normandie
5 415

Champagne
Ardenne
15 091

Ile-de-France
383 762

Lorraine
24 703

Alsace
29 270

Bretagne
6 102

Pays de
la Loire
17 915

Centre
12 656

Bourgogne
25 468

Franche-
Comté
28 413

Poitou-
Charentes
7 932

Limousin
2 780

Auvergne
13 921

Rhône-Alpes
168 246

Aquitaine
47 189

Midi-
Pyrénées
23 982

Languedoc-
Roussillon
63 094

PACA
130 140

Corse
4 284

Number of adults

383 760

200 000

100 000
50 000
20 000
2 780

0   50   100   150   200 km.

© D. CAUBET : réal. V. LAHAYE, Paris-Sorbonne. 2002

Source : INSEE, enquête Famille 1999 (first results, provided by A. Filhon, INED).

Map 5. Adults having received Arabic from at least one parent (1999)

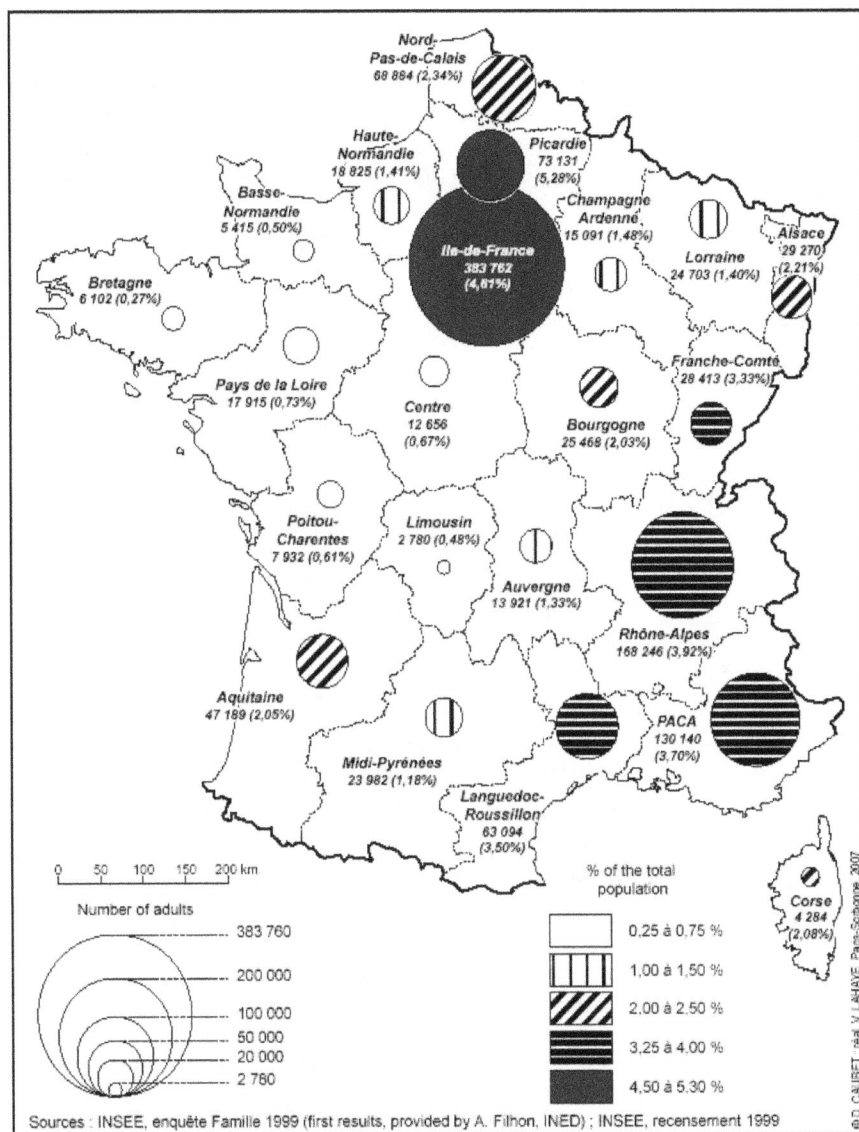

Map 6. Adults having received Arabic from at least one parent: % of the population over 18 by region ("enquête famille 1999")

3.4.   Mapping the regional presence of Arabic in France

In 2002, I had the opportunity to obtain some unpublished provisional figures from Alexandra Filhon (who was still working on her thesis at INED, Filhon 2004); I have not been able to get the final figures since. In absolute figures, we know that 23,000 adults out of the 380,000 family survey questionnaires (1999) declared that Arabic had been passed on to them by one or both parents, usually or occasionally. The figures that were given to me are the results of provisional calculations on the estimated absolute figures by region. The similarity of the repartition between the INED and *baccalauréat* figures was striking when we consider the figures by region.

3.4.1.   *INED and baccalauréat, a closer comparison*

The *baccalauréat* is an exam taken theoretically at the age of 18. Our figures concern the 506,377 candidates who actually took the exam for *baccalauréat général et technologique* in 1999 (Table 3). There were 643,161 registered candidates, but only 620,007 took the exam, 486,575 of whom passed with an official success rate of 78.3%. If we compare the *baccalauréat* data and the family survey data, the regions where the figures are higher turn out to coincide (compare Maps 1 and 5).

The great tendencies converge and the top twelve regions almost come in the same order for both sources (over 20,000 INED adults and over 200 *baccalauréat* candidates): *Ile de France*, Rhône-Alpes, PACA, Nord-Pas-de-Calais and Picardie (which come 4th and 5th instead of the other way round), Languedoc-Roussillon, with the exception of Aquitaine (with 47,189 INED adults and only 202 *baccalauréat* candidates), Lorraine, Franche-Comté, Alsace, Midi-Pyrénées, with the exception of Centre where there are only 12,656 INED adults and 294 *baccalauréat* candidates (see Figures 1 and 2). The twelve regions correspond to a total of 1,050,527 adults having received Arabic out

Table 3.   Baccalauréat 1999 optional test. Candidates in languages of the Maghreb (figures collected by Caubet and Chaker)

1999	Total baccalauréat	Total arabe maghrébin	Total Maghreb (arabe maghrébin) + berbère)
Bac général	330,067	4,663 (1.41%)	
Bac technologique	176,310	5,174 (2.93%)	
Total	506,377	9,886 (1.95%)	9,886 + 1,751 = 11,637 (2.3%)

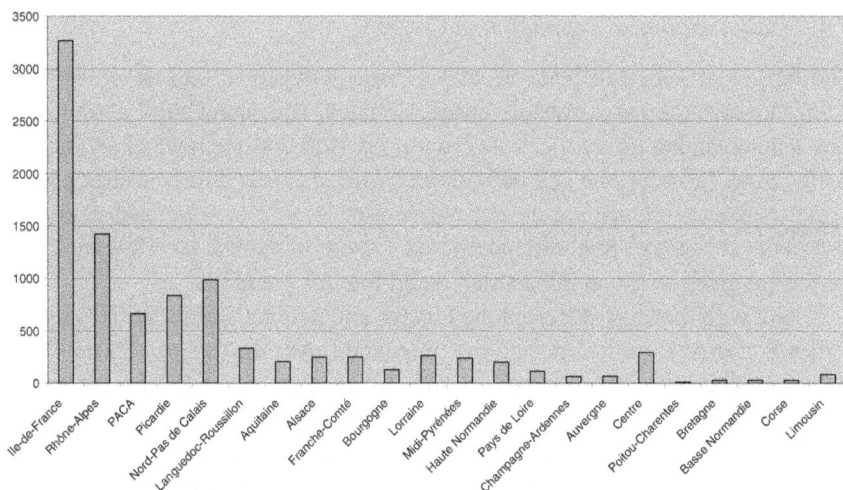

Figure 1. Candidates in Maghrebi Arabic (baccalauréat – 1999)

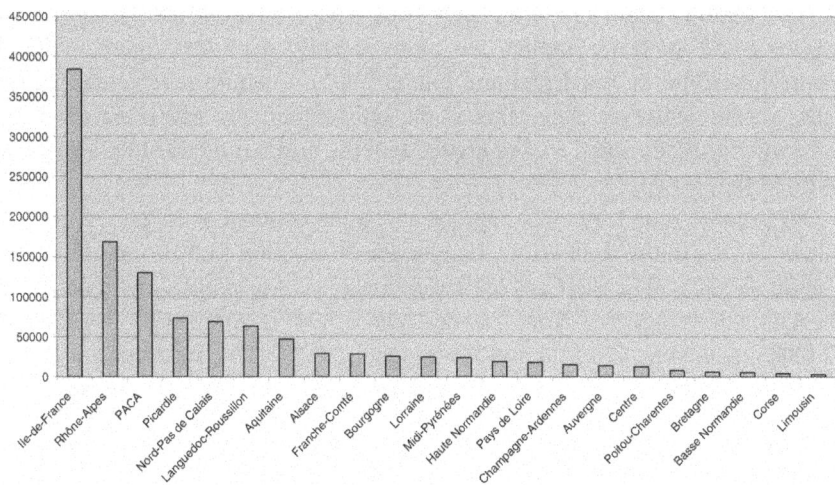

Figure 2. Adults having received Maghrebi Arabic as a child (by region – 1999)

of 1,171,205 adults, i.e., 89.7%. For the *baccalauréat*, they represent 8,705 out of 9,886 candidates, i.e., 88%. The population of Northern African origin is obviously concentrated in the centre, north and east of France and in the urban centres; see Blanchet et al. (2005) for Provence and Marseille.

3.4.2. *Proportions of population per region*

The figures provided in 2002 by Filhon were provisional and as we gathered from the start, they are probably underestimated. Burricand and Filhon (2003) give a much higher figure for *Ile de France*, i.e., 480,000 and not 383,762 as seen on the map: "Among the 480,000 adults living in *Ile de France* whose parents spoke Arabic, 67% declare having transmitted Arabic to their own children". But in the absence of final official figures, I chose to publish the 1999 figures as they were given to me in 2002 (Map 5 and Figures 1 and 2).

Then, with the help of Véronique Lahaye and Brigitte Dumortier (from Paris IV-La Sorbonne), we had to find the population over the age of 18 in 1999, in order to obtain the rates by region. The choice made by INED for the family survey (adults over the age of 18) is not the common partition chosen by statistics and INSEE (often opting for over or under 15). The population over 18 in 1999 was 44,950,689 and the number of people who received Arabic according to the provisional figures given by INED in 2002 was 1,171,203, which gives a national rate of 2.60%; the unpublished sources gave 1,446,800 and the rate would then be 3.28%.

Two regions come first with high rates, i.e., Picardie (5.28 %) and *Ile de France* (4.61%). If we applied the more recently published figure to *Ile de France* (480,000 in Burricand and Filhon 2003), it would receive the highest rate: 5.76%. However, since this is the only region for which we have this information, Maps 5 and 6 were drawn with the original figures to preserve the unity of the source.

Next come four very close regions above the national average, i.e., Rhône-Alpes (3.92%), PACA (3.70%), Languedoc-Roussillon (3.50%) and Franche-Comté (3.33%). The next set of five regions are one point down and below the national average, i.e., Nord-Pas-de-Calais (2.34%), Alsace (2.21%), Corsica (2.08%), Aquitaine (2.05%) and Bourgogne (2.03%). The next eleven regions are below 1.50%, i.e., five over 1% and six below 1%, as can be derived from Map 6.

4.   Languages offered in the French educational system

On paper, France offers a wide choice of languages that can be learned at school but in practice it is not always easy to find a *Collège* or *Lycée* where the language of one's choice is taught. An evaluation of the system was published in a critical report by six *inspecteurs généraux de l'Education nationale* (Gaillard et al. 2005).

4.1.   Primary education (five levels from age 6–11)

Theoretically, there is a choice of 6 languages other than French for which all children receive initial instruction: from *cycle 3* during the last 3 years, or even from *cycle 2* during the last year of kindergarden and first two years of primary schooling. But what is referred to in the above-mentioned report as *demande sociale*, based on parental choice, the vast majority tend to opt for English at primary school (79.70% in 2003–2004, against 15.2% for German, 2.5% for Spanish, 1% for both Italian and Portuguese, and 0.16% for Arabic for which there are only few classes in France).

Since the 1970s a special frame has been set for ELCO (*Enseignement des Langues et Cultures d'Origine*), apart from public primary education, which at the time aimed at allowing foreign-born children to re-integrate easily at any time in the school system of their countries of origin. The teaching is taken care of by teachers handpicked and paid by these countries of origin (see Obdeijn and De Ruiter 1998; Caubet 1997; Chaker 1997). A few comments should be made on ELCO. There is an obvious misunderstanding with respect to the term *langue d'origine*; the language taught in the case of children from the Maghreb is not the language of origin (Maghrebi Arabic or Berber), but the official language, Standard Arabic. Another issue is the fact that the teaching is restricted to a particular community, as a result of which only children originating from the Maghreb can learn Arabic within the ELCO framework, and not all French pupils.

During the last three decades, the figures for ELCO have gone down dramatically because the links with the countries of origin are not very tight, and because the children want to be like all other kids and learn English at primary school. They also want to have their Wednesday afternoons and Saturdays off, to be free like their French friends, instead of having to go to ELCO classes.

In the official reports, one finds labels such as *Arabe (marocain)*, *Arabe (algérien)* but this does not refer to the language taught but to the nationality of the teachers. They actually teach Standard Arabic. In 1999,[21] there were 31,465 students learning Standard Arabic but labelled according to the nationality of the teachers: *Arabe algérien* (7,816), *Arabe marocain* (20,159), *Arabe tunisien* (3,494), i.e., 56.8% of all ELCO classes which also included *Espagnol* (1,529), *Italien* (4,944), *Portugais* (6,976), *Turc* (10,313) and *Ex-Yougoslavie* (157).

4.2.   Secondary education (seven levels from age 12–18)

The situation is complicated and the offer is wide and varied: 19 foreign languages (LVE, *langue vivante étrangère*) and 9 regional languages, to which should be added a list of 28 "non-taught" languages which can be chosen as electives, for *épreuves facultatives* (optional). *Arabe dialectal* was an option until 1999 when it was crossed from the list; it represented 76.6% of the candidates. The Gaillard report (2005: 17) states that secondary education offers 64 foreign or regional living languages and ancient languages which can be either taught and chosen as a subject at exams, the *baccalauréat* in particular. Theoretically, one can choose to start learning a language at 3 levels: LV1 at level 1 of *Collège* (*6ème*, age of 12), LV2 at level 3 (*4ème*, age 14); and finally LV3 at level 5 (*2nde*, level 1 of *Lycée*=Gymnasium, age 16). For the latter option, there are many other competing options.

The list of languages that can be learned at the *Collège* (LV1 or LV2) contains 11 languages, i.e., *allemand, anglais, arabe, chinois, espagnol, grec ancien, hébreu, italien, latin, portugais, russe* plus 9 *langues régionales*, i.e., *basque, breton, catalan, corse, langues régionales d'Alsace, langues régionales mosellanes, langues mélanésiennes, occitan-langue d'occ, tahitien*. At the *Lycée*, 8 foreign languages can be added as LV3, i.e., *polonais, danois, grec moderne, japonais, néerlandais, suédois, turc, vietnamien*. This comes to a total of 28 languages. All of these languages can be chosen at *baccalauréat* for *épreuves obligatoires* (compulsory), to which 5 non-taught languages can be added, i.e., *arménien, cambodgien, finnois, norvégien, persan*, which adds up to a total of 33 languages.

4.2.1.   Massive choice for English and Spanish

Although the choice is vast (Gaillard et al. 2005), the complexity of the system, the contradictory factors and the rivalry between languages, the wide range of alternative options lead to a situation where the vast majority of the parents, notwithstanding the wide variety of choices, opt for English and Spanish. For 2004–2005, the numbers reported for English (LV1, LV2 and LV3) account for 62.1% of all students (4.5 million), Spanish scores 24.1% (1.7 million), German 9.9% (726,000), Italian 2.8% (200,000), regional languages 0.42% (31,000), and Arabic comes in 8th position with 0.09%. Here again, there is a problem in the figures, because Arabic is said to have 6,876 students, when it only had 6,250 for secondary education in Metropolitan France; and Chinese is counted as only 5,856, when according to other sources it had 9,328 in 2004 (*http://www.radio86.fr/culture/831/enseignement-du-chinois-en-france-le-grand-bond-en-avant*).

4.2.2.   Different evolutions for Arabic and Chinese

Among the *langues à faible diffusion* (i.e., languages with few students), Chinese is the exception with a recent and impressive increase. It has acquired a positive social image and the approach to teaching is very progressive and pragmatic, compared to the rigid conceptions governing the teaching of Arabic, which result from the ideology of considering Arabic as one language. It creates an embarrassing situation where people who are completely fluent in their own language, e.g., Moroccan Arabic or Algerian Arabic, are considered as "not knowing Arabic" because they cannot read and write Standard Arabic. It is worth mentioning that, according to UNESCO, the level of illiteracy is estimated at about 40% in the Arab countries, which gives us an idea of the number of people who cannot read or write.

With such preconceived ideas, the figures speak for themselves (Gaillard et al. 2005): Chinese was in 9th place for the number of students in 2004–2005 in secondary education, behind Russian, Portuguese and Arabic; in 2006–2007, Chinese reached 5th position, behind Italian, with 16,000 students. "Contrary to preconceived ideas, this progression is not due to the increase of the Chinese-speaking population in France, since 90% of the students of Chinese in secondary education have French as a mother tongue", explains the *Inspecteur Général*, Joël Bellassen, a former colleague from INALCO. Chinese had 190 teachers and 12,628 students in 2005, i.e., 1,200 in 12 primary schools and 9,543 in 194 secondary schools.[22]

By comparison, Arabic has had about 6,000 students in secondary education since 1994. In 2004–2005 it had 224 teachers in 242 secondary schools, according to *Midad* no. 25, the magazine published under the direction of Brigitte Tahhan, *Inspectrice Pégagogique régionale* of Arabic. But in January 2006, according to AFP,[23] *Inspecteur Général* Bruno Levallois was quoted as mentioning 182 teachers in 220 schools: a difference of 22 schools and 60 teachers. Getting the proper figures is a constant problem with *Education Nationale*.

During the years 1999–2003, student recruitment for Arabic was very high because the then Ministers Claude Allègre and Jack Lang had decided to promote Arabic by increasing the number of teachers. They raised the number of posts for the *concours* from eight or nine every year (which was a lot as it was for a subject where many teachers already did not teach their legal number of hours) to 20, 25, 24 and 25 posts respectively from 2000 to 2003; 94 teachers (+10 for *Lycées professionnels* = 104) were recruited in four years, i.e., an increase of 66% (there were 158 teachers in 1999; *Midad* no. 10).

The result is that many teachers of Arabic, all of whom are fully paid, either teach only part of their legal hours, do not teach at all or are posted elsewhere in various administrative positions.[24] The Gaillard report (2005: 42) mentions an equivalent in hours of 75 teaching posts and 41.4% of the teaching potential left unused for Arabic. The situation for Chinese is the opposite; there are not nearly enough teachers to meet the demand.

4.2.3. *Different approaches for Arabic and Chinese*

The approach to Chinese is very practical, the focus being on trying to get the children to learn the language as fast as possible orally and leaving aside Chinese writing in the initiual stages.[25] With Arabic, on the other hand, teachers have only been trained to teach Standard Arabic, and stress is put on the writing, which is seen as the basic knowledge to acquire. This implies that the advantage the students of Maghrebi origin should have by being able to speak Moroccan or Algerian Arabic is sometimes even seen as a handicap towards learning Standard Arabic, the "proper" language.

For Chinese, student recruitment is aimed at underprivileged groups in society rather than the prestigious *Lycées* and at non-Asian students (see *http://www. education.gouv.fr/lettre_information/lettre_flash/lettre_flash_16.htm*). For Arabic, the vast majority of students are of Northern African origin for LV1 and LV2, and the *Inspecteur Général* seems unhappy about their social background:[26] "Arabic classes have always been heterogeneous; children of rural origin sit next to children of more urban origin who are good arabophones". On the other hand, he complains that not enough children with Arabic backgrounds learn the language at school: "Assimilation had a devastating effect on Arabic. (...) the idea that integration must be done against the identity of origin still persists". The combination of a generally negative image of the Maghreb in the public opinion and a rigid approach to teaching Arabic lead to a blocked situation within the national context of education.

5. Conclusions

Some French leading institutions, in particular the Ministry of Foreign Affairs (which follows the policies of the Arab countries) and the Ministry of Education, refuse to recognise or pay tribute to the actual languages and cultural contributions of an increasingly large proportion of the population of France, i.e., the immigrants from Northern Africa and their descendants. They prefer to consider Arabic as a foreign language and to comply with the official policies of the "countries of origin". The Ministry of Culture is the only leading institution to give Maghrebi Arabic proper recognition as a *Langue de France* and to regularly associate so-called "non-territorial" languages and "regional" languages. Something more subtle is to be seen in civil society, i.e., the steadily rising recognition of *arabe maghrébin* and the indisputable place it has gained in the French cultural and social scene (Caubet 2004d, 2007).

Notes

1. With special thanks to Brigitte Dumortier, Professor at the Department of Geography (Paris IV) for her help and to Véronique Lahaye for preparing the maps in this Chapter.
2. *http://tempsreel.nouvelobs.com/actualites/20060904.OBS0455/?idfx=RSS_notr.* MRAP worried that "the ethnic interpretation might replace a social analysis and present the danger to radicalise certain data".
3. See *www.strategie.gouv.fr/IMG/pdf/actesstatistiquesethniques101106.pdf.*
4. For the first time since it was created in 1978, the CNIL organised public auditions open to the press presided over by Alex Turk, member of the Senate, on the measurement of diversity between January 18 and 25, 2007, at the Senate; among whom Azouz Begag, *Ministre pour la promotion de l'égalité des chances*, Louis Schweitzer, *Président de la HALDE (Haute Autorité de Lutte contre les Discriminations et pour l'Egalité)* and François Héran, *Directeur Général de l'INED*.
   See *http://www.senat.fr/evenement/cnil/cnil_auditions.html.*
5. *http://www.cnil.fr/index.php?id=1990&news[uid]=339&cHash=312ed92d4f.* But it had allowed another study on French Jews on the basis of patronyms in 2002.
6. A euphemism commonly used to refer to children of migrant parents born in France.
7. *http://www.legifrance.gouv.fr/WAspad/UnTexteDeJorf?numjo=CNIX0609534X;* In *J.O.* n° 204 du 3 septembre 2006, texte n° 39; or *http://www.cnil.fr/index.php?id=2061&news[uid]=369&cHash=d1edef22d7.*
8. It is not always easy to distinguish between Moroccan and Algerian patronyms.
9. *http://www.lemonde.fr/web/article/0,1-0@2-3232,36-812990,0.html*
10. *http://www.ldh-toulon.net/spip.php?article1659*
11. In translation, the definition is as follows: "A person born abroad with a foreign nationality and residing in France. In France, an individual will always remain an immigrant. Even if he has become French through naturalisation, (s)he still belongs to the immigrant population. It is the country of birth and not the nationality that defines the state of an immigrant".
12. This was part of the survey *Efforts d'éducation des familles*, led by INSEE and INED in 1992, covering Metropolitan France. The sample consisted of 5,300 couples who had children between 2 and 25 years of age.
13. See Chaker (2003: 5), where he gives an estimate of 1,500,000 speakers including children.
14. *Language and (Im)migration in France, Latin America, and the United States: Sociolinguistic Perspectives*, September 25-26, 2003, Conference at the University of Texas at Austin sponsored by the France-UT Institute for Interdisciplinary Studies (see Chaker 2004 and Caubet 2004a).
15. *Haut Conseil à l'Intégration*, November 2000, see p. 26: *http://lesrapports.ladocumentationfrancaise.fr/BRP/014000017/0000.pdf*
16. *Fonds social juif unifié*; it does not say anything about the dispensation by the CNIL (see 2.). See an article in *Le Monde* (November 2, 2002) quoted in: *http://www.mafhoum.com/press4/121S23.htm.*

[17] Since Maghrebi Arabic does not have any official orthography, we provided the test both in Arabic and Latin script.

[18] Salem Chaker is Professor of Berber (INALCO) and Director of LACNAD (*Langues et Cultures du Nord de l'Afrique et de la Diaspora*), which consists of three teams : CRB (*Centre de Recherche Berbère*), CREAM (*Centre de Recherche et d'Etude sur l'arabe maghrébin*, under the direction of Dominique Caubet) and LCJMMO (*Langues et Cultures Juives du Maghreb et de la Méditerranée Occidentale*).

[19] All maps were drawn in 2002 and 2007 by Véronique Lahaye from the UFR *de géographie et aménagement* and are the result of long-term collaboration with Brigitte Dumortier, *Maître de Conférences* at the UFR. I am very thankful to both of them.

[20] For example, the *académies* Aix-Marseille plus Nice correspond to region PACA, Grenoble plus Lyon to Rhône-Alpes.

[21] These figures come from a report about ELCO at the National Assembly in 2004; the names are reproduced as they were presented; see *http://www.assemblee-nationale.fr/ 12/rapports/r1618.asp*

[22] It had 2,500 students in 1995; see *http://www.radio86.fr/culture/831/enseignement-du-chinois-en-france-le-grand-bond-en-avant* and *http://www.education.gouv.fr/ lettre_information/lettre_flash/lettre_flash_16.htm*

[23] At *Expolangues*, January 19, 2006, Paris (AFP), see *http://www.aloufok.net/article.php3?id_article=2789*

[24] See the report by *Cour des Comptes*, January 2005: *http://www.ccomptes.fr/cour-des-comptes/publications/rapports/enquete-personnels-educ-nat/rapport.pdf*

[25] In *Libération*, 13 september 2004, p. 16.

[26] In *Libération*, 13 september 2004, p. 16.

References

Blot, D., J.-M. Eloy and T. Rouault
    2004   La richesse linguistique du nord de la France. *INSEE Picardie* 125.

Blanchet, P., L.-J. Calvet, D. Hillereau and E. Wilczyk
    2005   Le volet linguistique du recensement français de 1999. Résultats et analyse appliquée à la Provence plurilingue et au provençal. *Marges Linguistiques*, 10, *http://www.marges-linguistiques.com*.

Burricand C. and A. Filhon
    2003   Transmission et pratiques des langues étrangères en Ile de France. *INSEE Ile de France à la Page* 226, *http://www.insee.fr/fr/insee_regions/idf/rfc/ docs/alapage226.pdf*.

Caubet, D.
    1997   L'épreuve d'arabe dialectal au Bac: passage à l'écrit - Bilan comparatif des sessions 1996 et 1995. In: M. Tilmatine (ed.), *Enseignement des Langues d'Origine et Immigration nord-africaine en Europe: Langue maternelle*

ou Langue d'Etat?, 163–172. Document pédagogique Erasmus, INALCO/CEDREA-CRB.

1999   Arabe maghrébin: passage à l'écrit et institutions. In: L. Danon-Boileau and M.-A. Morel (eds.), *Parole orale/Parole écrite: Formes et Théories*, 235–244 (Faits de Langue, 13).

2001a   Maghrebine Arabic in France. In: G. Extra and D. Gorter (eds.), *The Other Languages of Europe: Demographic, Sociolinguistic, and Educational Perspectives*, 261–277. Clevedon: Multilingual Matters.

2001b   L'arabe dialectal en France. In: *Arabofrancophonie, Les Cahiers de la Francophonie n° 10*. Paris: L'Harmattan, 199–212.

2003   La reconnaissance de l'arabe "dialectal" en France : un parcours sinueux. In: J. Lentin and A. Lonnet (eds.), *Mélanges David Cohen, Etudes sur le Langage, les Langues, les Dialectes, les Littératures* (offertes par ses élèves, ses collègues, ses amis, présentées à l'occasion de son quatre-vingtième anniversaire), 135–148. Paris: Maisonneuve et Larose.

2004a   About the transmission of Maghrebi Arabic in France. In: *Language and (Im)migration in France, Latin America, and the United States: Sociolinguistic Perspectives*, September 25–26 2003, Conference at the University of Texas at Austin, France-UT Institute for Interdisciplinary Studies, *http://www.utexas.edu/cola/insts/france-ut/archives/Fall2003/ConfLangImmigration/caubet.pdf*

2004b   Enseigner l'arabe maghrébin, langue de France? *Cahiers d'Études Pédagogiques* 423: 52–54.

2004c   L'arabe maghrébin-*darja,* langue de France. *La Célibataire* 8: 139–145.

2004d   La *darja,* langue de culture en France. *Hommes et Migrations, Les Langues de France* 1252: 34–44.

2007   Langues et musiques de France depuis les années 80. In: C. Alén Garabato and H. Boyer (eds.), *Les Langues de France au XXIe Siècle: Vitalité socioliguistique et Dynamiques culturelles*, 51–75. Paris: L'Harmattan

Cerquiglini, B.
1999   *Les Langues de la France*. Rapport aux ministres de l'Education nationale et de la Culture, *http://www.dglf.culture.gouv.fr*gu

Cerquiglini, B. (ed.)
2003   *Les Langues de France*. Paris: PUF.

Chaker, S.
1997   La langue berbère en France, situation actuelle et perspectives de développement. In: M. Tilmatine (ed.), *Enseignement des langues d'origine et immigration nord-africaine en Europe: Langue maternelle ou langue d'Etat?*, 15–30, document pédagogique Erasmus, INALCO/CEDREA-CRB.

2004   Berber, a "long-forgotten" language of France. In: *Language and (Im)migration in France, Latin America, and the United States: Sociolinguistic*

Perspectives, September 25–26 2003, Conference at the University of Texas at Austin, France-UT Institute for Interdisciplinary Studies. *http:// www.utexas.edu/cola/insts/france-ut/archives/Fall2003/ ConfLangImmigration/chaker_ english.pdf*

Clanché, F.
2002   Langues régionales, langues étrangères: de l'héritage à la pratique. *INSEE Première* 830. Paris: Insee.

Deguillaume, C. and E. Amrane
2002   Langues parlées en Aquitaine: la pratique héritée. *Le quatre pages Insee Aquitaine* 110.

Duée, M.
2002   L'alsacien, 2ème langue régionale de France. *Chiffres pour l'Alsace* 12.

Filhon, A.
2004   Transmission familiale des langues arabes et berbère en France. Langues, cultures et identités des migrants nord-africains et de leurs enfants. Thèse de doctorat en sociologie non publiée. Université de Versailles Saint-Quentin-en-Yvelines.

Gaillard, G., P. Charvet, Y. Bottin, G. Saurat, L. Dutriez and J.-P. Pittoors
2005   *Pilotage et Cohérence de la carte des langues*. Rapport à Monsieur le Ministre de l'éducation nationale, de l'enseignement supérieur et de la recherche, n° 2005-019, La Documentation française, *http://lesrapports.ladocumentationfrancaise.fr/BRP/054000373/0000.pdf*

HCI (Haut Conseil à l'Intégration)
2000   *L'Islam dans la République*. La Documentation française, *http://lesrapports.ladocumentationfrancaise.fr/BRP/014000017/0000.pdf*

Héran, F.
1993   L'unification linguistique de la France. *Population et Sociétés* 285. Paris: INED.
2002   Les langues et la statistique publique. Des comptages du Second Empire au volet linguistique de l'enquête Famille. *Ville-Ecole-Intégration Enjeux* 130: 51–76.
2004   Une approche quantitative de l'intégration linguistique en France. *Hommes et Migrations* 1252.
2006   Statistiques ethniques, c'est possible. *Le Monde* 14 sept. 2006; see *http://www.lemonde.fr/web/article/0,1-0@2-3232,36-812990,0.html*

Héran, F., A. Filhon and C. Deprez
2002   La dynamique des langues en France au fil du XXe siècle. *Population et Sociétés* 376. Paris: INED.

Le Boëtté, I.
    2003   Langue bretonne et autres langues : pratique et transmission. *Octant* 92,
              janvier 2003, INSEE Bretagne.

MIDAD (Magazine d'information et de documentation sur l'arabe et sa didactique),
CRDP, Paris, see *http://crdp.ac-paris.fr/index.htm?url=d_librairie/production-CRDP.htm*

Obdeijn, H. and J.-J. de Ruiter (eds.)
    1998   *Le Maroc au Cœur de l'Europe, l'Enseignement de la Langue et Cul-
              ture d'origine (ELCO) aux Élèves marocains dans cinq Pays européens.*
              Tilburg: Syntax Datura.

Mapping immigrant languages in Switzerland

Georges Lüdi

1. Introduction

The stereotype that Switzerland is quadrilingual and basks in peaceful linguistic harmony is misleading and needs to be corrected in four respects.

Firstly, the Federal Constitution mentions four national languages (German, French, Italian and Romansch), the first three of which also have the status of official languages, but there is abolutely no equilibrium between them: German is clearly dominant, French and Italian are minority languages, but in no way endangered; and Romansch is struggling for survival. The proportions of the national languages have changed slightly in the last decades (see Table 1). The figures for Italian reflect the different migratory waves, with peaks at the beginning of the 20th century and between the late 1950s and the late 1970s. The number of German speaking Swiss has been declining since World War II, while French has began to climb again in the last twenty years. The situation of Romansch is deteriorating steadily.

Secondly, the territoriality principle that allows or rather constrains the use of only one of the official languages in each of the three large language regions of the country, with the exception of a few overlap areas such as Bienne, Fribourg and the federal capital Berne, leads to a quite uneven distribution of the speakers of the national languages. Juridically, Switzerland is thus a mosaic made up of

Table 1. Swiss population according to main languages (= "the language in which you think and that you master best" [only one answer permitted]), in % (Source: Swiss Federal Census 1950–2000. Swiss Federal Statistical Office)

	1950	1960	1970	1980	1990	2000
German	72.1	69.4	64.9	65.0	63.6	63.7
French	20.3	18.9	18.1	18.4	19.2	20.4
Italian	5.9	9.5	11.9	9.8	7.6	6.5
Rhaeto-Romance	1.0	0.9	0.8	0.8	0.6	0.5
Other languages	0.7	1.4	4.3	6.0	8.9	9.0

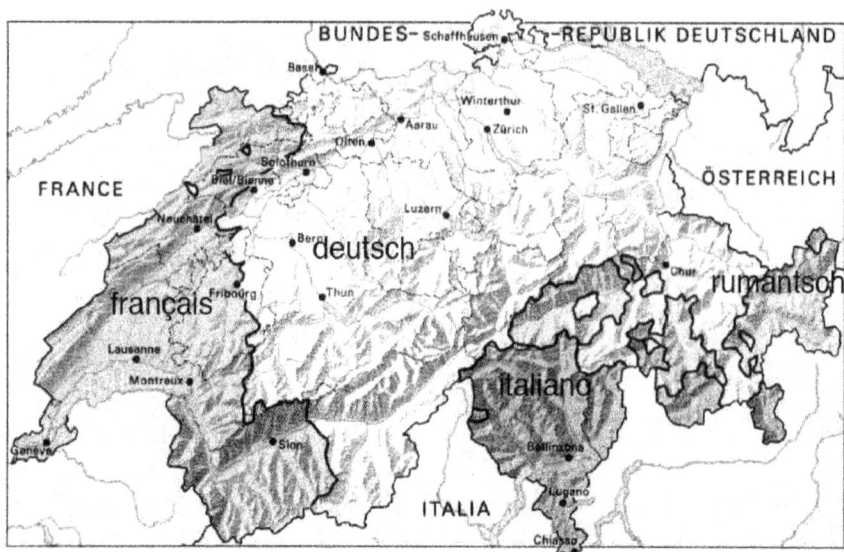

Figure 1. Resident population in Switzerland, by most spoken national languages and municipalities in % (Source: Swiss federal census 2000. Swiss Federal Statistical Office)

four largely monolingual regions in which the other national languages enjoy more or less the same status as, say, Spanish or English. The linguistic map presented in Figure 1 shows the territories where each national language is dominant.

Thirdly, German-speaking Switzerland provides the stage for a diglossic situation between standard German (often called High German or written German) and Swiss German, the functional distribution of which can be called roughly "medial".

Last but not least, as in all the industrial nation-states of Western Europe, there are other sizeable linguistic minorities, in addition to the national languages. After having been a country of emigration for centuries, Switzerland has become a country of immigration. In 2005, 20.7% of the permanent resident population were foreigners (OFS 2006: 12). This has a clear impact on the linguistic landscape. Since the second half of the 20th century, an increasing number of new linguistic minorities have settled in Switzerland (see Table 1).

In other words, Switzerland is developing steadily from a quadrilingual to a multilingual country, despite the fact that, as allowed by the European Charter for Regional or Minority Languages (Council of Europe 1992), the "new minorities" have no official recognition. The most important languages of immigration in

Table 2. Distribution of the 14 most important non-national languages of the Swiss population, 2000. (Source: Swiss Federal census 2000. Swiss Federal Statistical Office)

	in %	in absolute figures
Serbian/Croatian	1.4	103,350
Albanian	1.3	94,937
Portuguese	1.2	89,527
Spanish	1.1	77,506
English	1.0	73,425
Turkish	0.6	44,523
Tamil	0.3	21,816
Arabic	0.2	14,345
Dutch	0.2	11,840
Russian	0.1	9,003
Chinese	0.1	8,279
Thai	0.1	7,569
Kurdish	0.1	7,531
Macedonian	0.1	6,415

2000 (in absolute figures and in percentage of the whole resident population) are presented in Table 2.

These figures include foreigners (i.e., residents of other nationalities than Swiss) and nationals speaking these languages, the latter having acquired Swiss nationality by birth, marriage or naturalisation. An immigrant may thus be a foreigner or a Swiss and speak a language of immigration or a national language of Switzerland. As mentioned above, in spite of the official quadrilingualism, Switzerland is, juridically, a mosaic made up of largely monolingual regions in which the other national languages enjoy more or less the same status as the languages of immigration (thus, their speakers are *alloglots*, i.e., speakers of a language other than the local official language) as most immigrants. Nevertheless, Swiss society, especially in the urban areas, is more and more polyglot.

We will investigate how Switzerland deals with this increasing linguistic diversity. Firstly, we ask for the distribution of the different languages at a demographic level. The question is where the alloglots live, whether persons with the same linguistic background remain closely together in the same villages or suburbs of the cities and form *alloglot islands* where the respective language would have a majority or at least constitute a strong minority, or whether the clustering of languages follows different patterns (for example economic ones). We work secondly at the educational and political level by investigating the ways in which immigrants, and especially alloglots, are linguistically and socially integrated in the respective language region, whether they acquire the host language and how their bilingualism evolves. In doing this, we try to "measure" their degree of integration. Thirdly, we analyse the complex dynamics of communicative encounters between persons from different linguistic backgrounds at the micro level of daily verbal interaction, whether they live in the same linguistic region or communicate across the language borders, in order to analyse the ways in which members of a polyglossic society take mutual profit from all the languages they know by exploiting all the resources that are at their disposal. We consider, in other words, plurilingual repertoires as shared resources of the interacting partners that are mobilised in common in function of the situation. This leads us to analyse the ways multilingual forms of communication are valorised by the agents and to revise stereotypes about "mixed" forms of language use.

2. Methods of data collection, data processing and data analysis

The analytical framework designed to meet these objectives was developed during the last couple of years, negotiated and elaborated with other Swiss colleagues, and is now part of the DYLAN project (Berthoud et al. 2005). It seeks to provide a conceptual basis that meshes with the epistemological and methodological requirements of the various approaches brought to bear on the questions. In particular, it must allow for the examination of the use of language resources, which are structured themselves by their use in specific contexts. Analytical constructs should therefore address multilingual repertoires at the symbolic and discursive levels, as well as at the level of the practical use of these repertoires in a number of given contexts, along with the consequences of such use. These requirements generate an analytical framework made up of four dimensions between which interrelations may be observed. These dimensions are:

– Actual language practices as directly observed and photocopied (written production) or audio- or videotaped (oral production);
– Representations of multilingualism and linguistic diversity as captured through discourse (including questionnaires), since discourse can be seen as the trace of representations of individuals and groups;
– The language policies of states or other public bodies and the language strategies of private-sector companies;
– The linguistic context or language environment in which agents operate.

Methodologically, we proceed by triangulation, using various tools:

- Our main statistical instrument is the Federal census. Since 1990, the language data of the census are particularly rich. Indeed, people had to indicate not only their main or dominant language as defined above (one choice only), but also the languages used at home and at work (several choices possible, including dialectal varieties of the national languages). This generates a wealth of data and allows cross-calculations like main language by language at home or at work. Unfortunately, languages of immigration could not be specified, but only chosen as "other". For detailed results, see Lüdi et al. (1997, 2005);
- In addition, we exploit the Cantonal registers. They commonly only include information about citizenship, and nothing about languages. For a citizen of Cameroon, for example, we do not know whether her or his dominant language is English, French or an African language, and how many languages (s)he speaks;
- For the Canton of Basle-City, we also draw upon school statistics that mention the dominant language spoken by the pupils (as indicated by their parents) by school type and suburb.
- Language use at work was the focus of a survey organised by the University of Applied Sciences in Solothurn (Andres et al. 2005);
- These data are completed by a set of political documents, i.e., decisions in matters of language policy at school (EDK 1998, 2004, *Erziehungsdepartement Basel-Stadt* 2003), on integration of foreigners (*Bundesgesetz über die Ausländerinnen und Ausländer* 2005; *Sicherheitsdepartement Basel-Stadt* 2006) and articles from newspapers on questions about languages, migration and integration;
- An important part of our qualitative database consists of semi-directed interviews and language biographies. For instance, we ask our informants to draw their social networks indicating which language(s) they use at each point of the network; they establish lists of all the languages they have learnt, giving details about the learning context and the degree of competence achieved on the basis of the *European Language Portfolio* (*http://www.coe.int/T/DG4/ Portfolio/*).

All these data are discursive. In other words, they reflect the representations of agents about their and others' language competences and language use, not the real use itself. For whatever reasons, a Kurdish father might indicate Turkish as the dominant language of his son, who in reality speaks Kurdish at home and – better – German at school.

- In order to gain access to real language practices, we make tape and video recordings of verbal interactions in different contexts and collect authentic texts written at home and at work;
- A new instrument is the collection of written texts in the public space along with the principles of the so-called *linguistic landscape* (e.g., Landry and Bourhis 1997; Gorter 2006).

Here we only present a small sample of these data, but always keep in mind that the elements analysed form part of a whole. Further, we try to relate data and findings at all four cornerstones of our framework. Roughly speaking, we combine a quantitative approach based on statistical data with more qualitative considerations taken from discourse analysis and the linguistic analysis of authentic oral and written language use.

3.   Results

Four particular topics exemplify the type of results gathered in our research.

3.1.   Integration

One of the most important points on the Swiss political agenda concerning immigrants deals with their linguistic integration. The new law on foreign nationals (*Bundesgesetz über die Ausländerinnen und Ausländer*), promulgated by the Swiss Parliament on 16 September 2005, accepted in a referendum a year later by Swiss voters, and entered into force on 1 January 2008, contains several articles asking for competences in the local language (German text translated in English):

> Art. 4 Integration
> 4. It is necessary for foreigners to be familiar with the social situation and the way of life in Switzerland and in particular to learn a national language.

> Art. 23 Permit of residence
> 2. In addition, the granting of residence permits is dependent on the anticipation that professional and social adaptability, language competences and age will make a sustainable integration into the Swiss labour market and society likely.

> Art. 34 Permit of settlement
> 4. This can be granted on the base of successful integration, in particular if the person concerned has a good command of a national language (. . .)

Art. 54 Consideration of integration in decision taking
1. The granting of a permit of residence or short stay can be submitted to the condition of attending a language or integration course (...)

Our initial hypothesis is that the vicinity of language of origin and host language facilitates linguistic integration. We can observe that immigrants speaking Portuguese and Spanish show a preference for the French speaking part of the country, as is shown in Map 1.

Does this mean that speakers of related languages are more willing to learn the local language? The tool we have used for measuring linguistic integration is the use of the local language (dialectal and/or standard variety, exclusively or together with other languages; as mentioned above, because of the labelling of the question – there were boxes for the national languages, English and "other languages" – there is no way to identify the languages of immigration in this questionnaire) by persons indicating a language of immigration as their dominant language. The integration is particularly important when the use of the local language penetrates the family. For the most numerous groups of alloglots, the results for 2000 are depicted in Figure 2.

The results show that for all languages of origin, the Italian and French speaking areas integrate better than the German one, but that the difference is much more important for Spanish and Portuguese. This confirms the relatedness hypothesis, but as an added factor only. The influence of the Swiss German diglossia between Standard German and German dialects is certainly also important because immigrants must indeed learn two local language varieties in the German region. The tight social control among language minorities could also help to explain the ranking.

A second hypothesis concerns the duration of the immigration. Indeed, the duration of immigration at the group and individual level can be shown to be a strong factor favouring integration. For the first factor, we compare in Table 3 the figures for those groups that were already numerous in 1990. Most values are higher in 2000 than in 1990, with the remarkable exception of English in the German and French region.

The second effect is visible from the values attained by those alloglots who have acquired Swiss nationality. They are significantly higher than for foreigners and reached for example between 53.8% (Albanian) and 83.3% (Portuguese) in the Italian-speaking part of the country in 2000. There is also a most evident impact of the country of birth on the values for the local language as the main language of foreigners, as is clear from Figure 3.

One can conclude that those immigrant foreigners who were born in Switzerland or came to Switzerland as small children integrate fairly well linguistically.

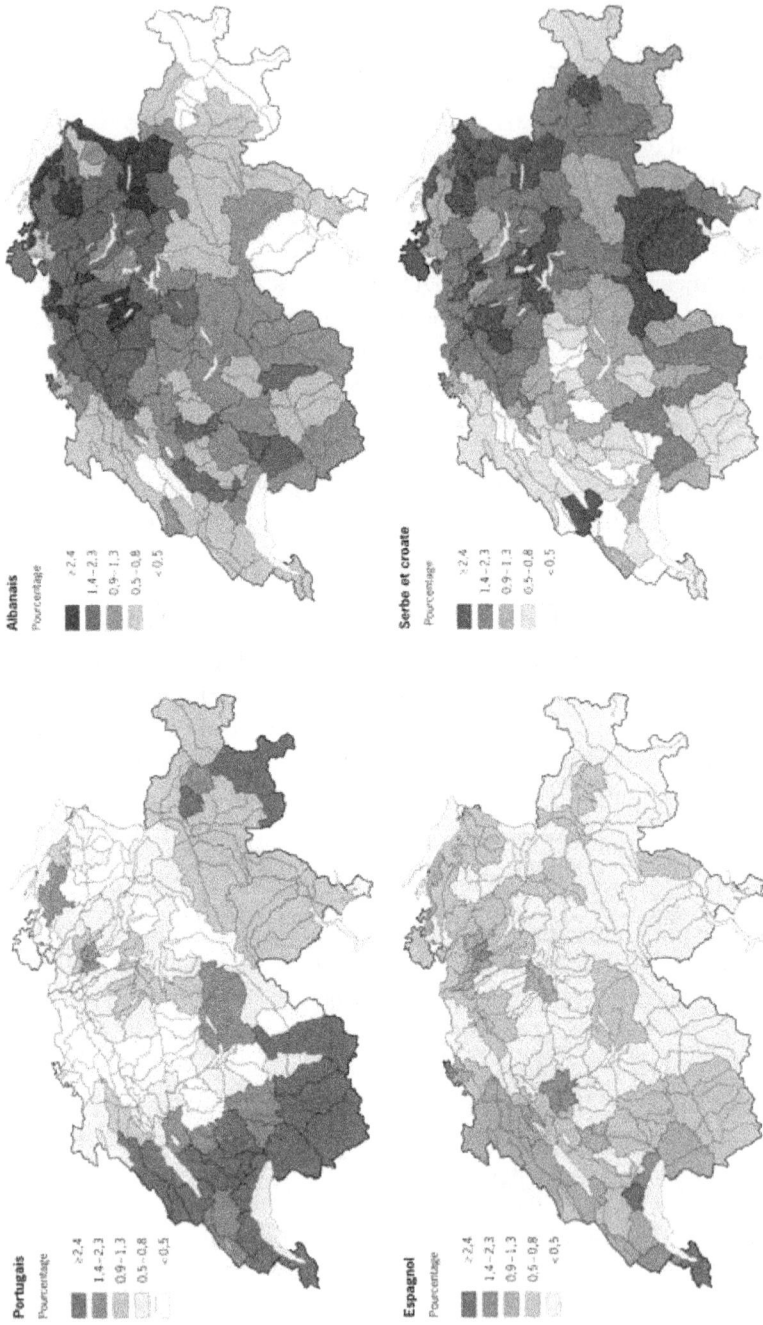

Albanais
Pourcentage
≥ 2,4
1,4 - 2,3
0,9 - 1,3
0,5 - 0,8
< 0,5

Serbe et croate
Pourcentage
≥ 2,4
1,4 - 2,3
0,9 - 1,3
0,5 - 0,8
< 0,5

Portugais
Pourcentage
≥ 2,4
1,4 - 2,3
0,9 - 1,3
0,5 - 0,8
< 0,5

Espagnol
Pourcentage
≥ 2,4
1,4 - 2,3
0,9 - 1,3
0,5 - 0,8
< 0,5

Map 1. Resident population in Switzerland, non-national languages, in %, 2000. (Source: Swiss Federal Census 2000. Swiss Federal Statistical Office)

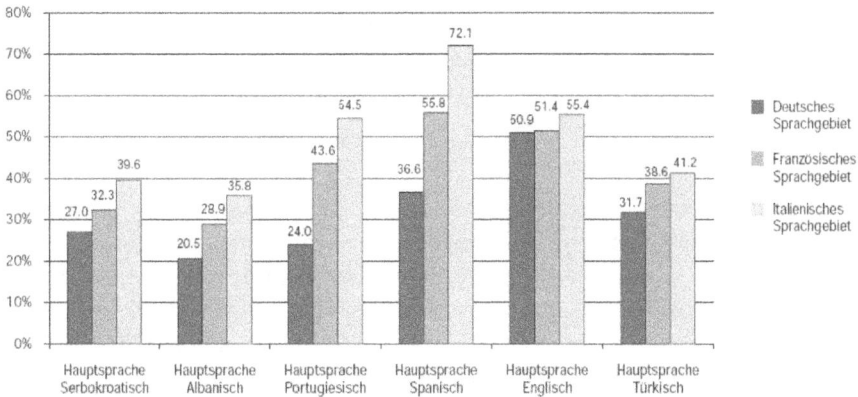

Figure 2. Local language as part of the family repertoire for speakers of the six most frequently mentioned languages of immigration, by language region. (Source: Swiss Federal census 2000; Lüdi et al. 2005)

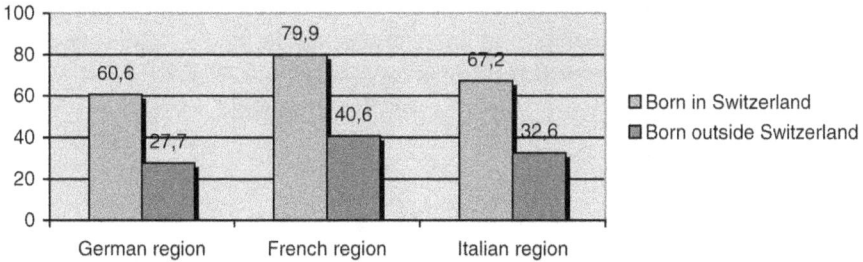

Figure 3. Local language as main language of foreigners by country of birth and language region, 2000 (Source: Swiss Federal census 2000)

Table 3. Integration of the local language into the family repertoire of speakers of the four languages of immigration which ranked among the most important ones in 1990 and 2000, by language region, in % (Source: Swiss Federal census 2000)

	Spanish		Portuguese		Turkish		English	
Language region	1990	2000	1990	2000	1990	2000	1990	2000
German	25.4	36.6	18.7	24.0	28.8	31.7	58.8	50.9
French	47.1	55.8	36.0	43.6	38.5	38.6	53.3	51.4
Italian	54.7	72.1	40.8	54.5	35.2	41.2	45.4	55.4

This is mainly an effect of schooling, but might also be explained by measures like the obligation to speak the local language in youth centres and, more generally, by the fact that the local language is the only official means of communication with the local administration and the dominant language at work (97.9% for German, 98% for French and 98.6% for Italian in the respective language regions).

3.2.   Distribution

A question of related political importance concerns the distribution of alloglots and foreigners, respectively. We have seen an overall tendency of foreigners of the same origin to favour the same regions. However, this is not the case at the micro level, as can be illustrated by the city of Basle which shows one of the highest concentrations of foreigners in the country, i.e., almost 30% (varying from 16.3% in the upper middle-class Bruderholz to 50.7% and 52.2% in the rather lower-class Klybeck and Rosental, respectively).

A close comparison of the distribution by suburbs shows that members of the same social groups, but of different language background, live together in the same suburbs. Their reason for grouping is thus social, not linguistic.

This picture is confirmed if we look at the school statistics containing information about the first language ("mother tongue") of the pupils. After four years of primary school and three years of lower secondary school, pupils continue at two different levels: pre-professional or vocational school (WBS) of two years

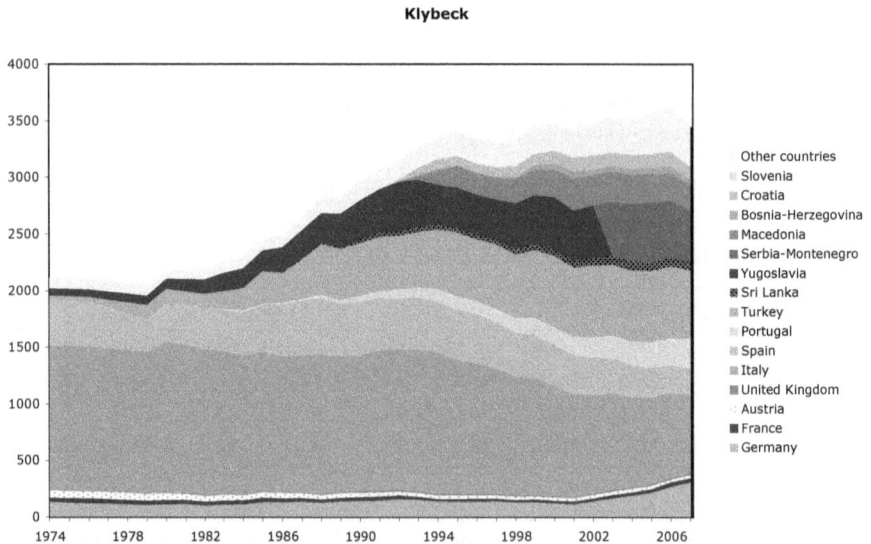

Figure 4a. Composition of foreigners by nationality in three suburbs of Basel, 2005 (Source: Basel-City, cantonal statistics)

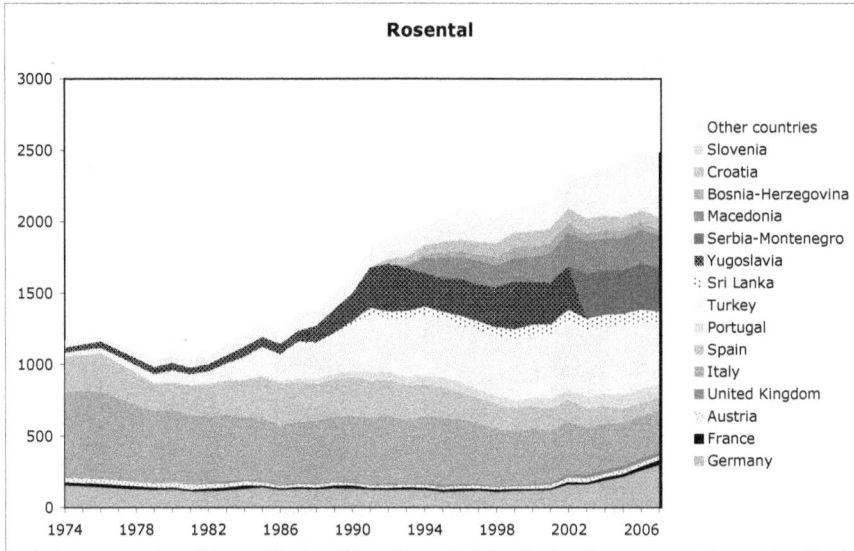

Figure 4b. (cont.)

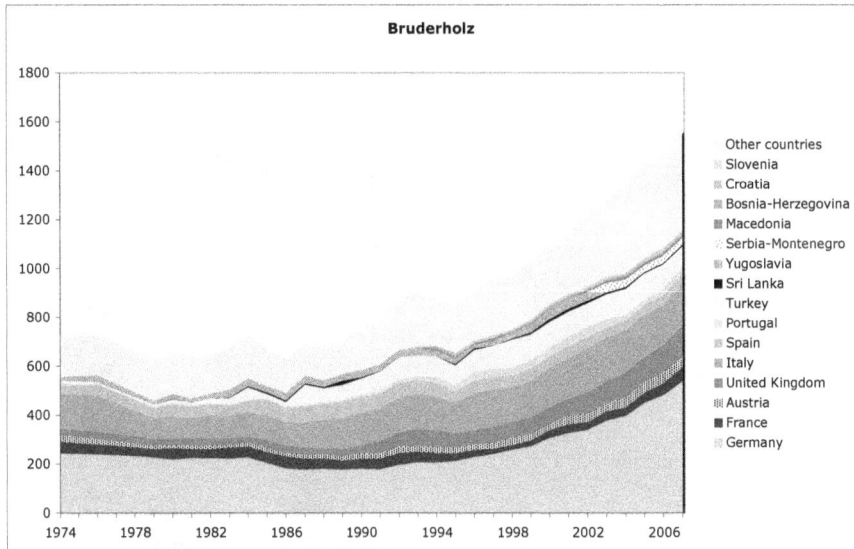

Figure 4c. (cont.)

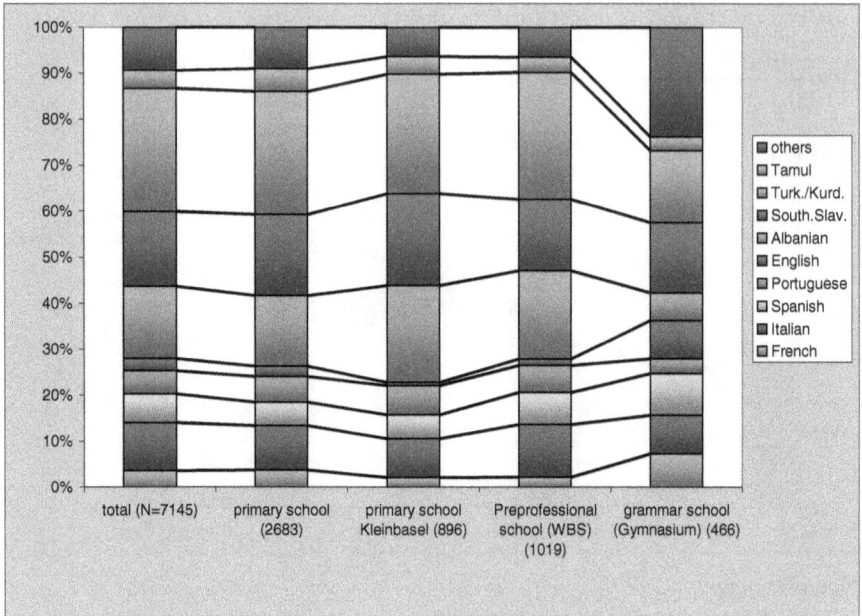

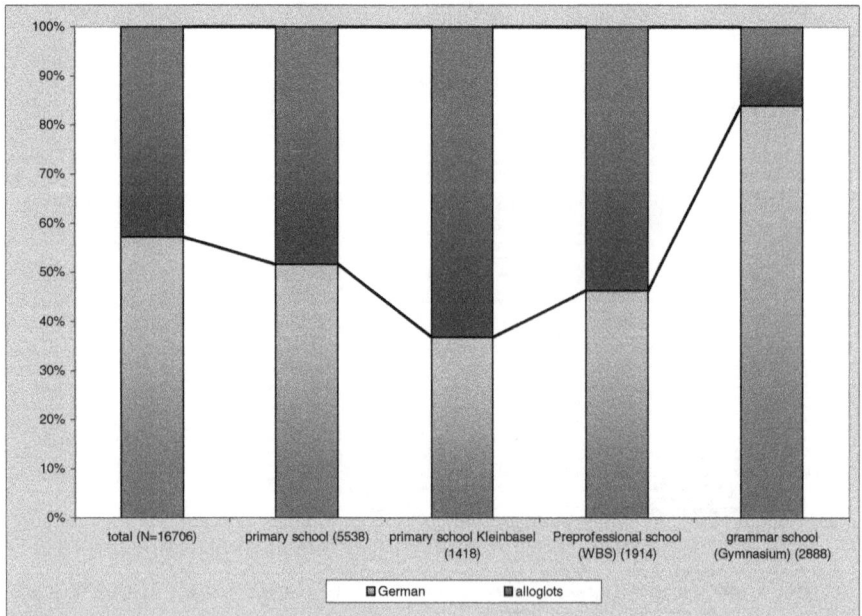

Figure 5. Proportion of first language of foreign pupils by school type in Basel, 2005 (Source: Basel-City, cantonal school statistics)

or grammar school (Gymnasium) of five years. Generally speaking, the proportion of alloglots is higher than the mean (about 42%) in primary schools of the popular suburbs of Kleinbasel (over 60%) and much higher in lower-qualified pre-professional schools (about 55%) than in grammar schools (less than 20%).

The social effect shows up even more strongly when we look at the distribution of languages of origin by school type. The languages that are better represented in grammar schools are typically those of so-called "affluent" immigrants like English, French and others (e.g., Dutch and Japanese), whilst the languages of working-class immigrants like Turkish/Kurdish and Albanian dominate in pre-professional schools.

3.3.   Language policy at school

Due to Swiss federalism, the cantons bear the primary responsibility for education in Switzerland. Together with their communes, they bear the major share of expenditure on education (90%). The main coordinating body is the Swiss Conference of Cantonal Ministers of Education (EDK), an assembly of the 26 cantonal ministers who are responsible for education, training, culture and sport. The Federal Government has very few competences in this area, except for higher education.

The *Basler Gesamtsprachenkonzept* (ED BS 2003), i.e., the language policy plan for the canton of Basle-City, is an example of good practice with respect to language problems of immigrant children:

> All children acquire a high oral and written competence in Standard German. In addition, they get a functional competence in a second national language as well as in English. They must have the opportunity to elaborate the use of their language of origin and to learn an additional national language and other foreign languages. (*http://www.edubs.ch/die_schulen/projekte/archiv/gesamtsprachenkonzept/pdf/ gsk_reflexionsgruppe.pdf*)

The main focus is on the acquisition of the host language. But the educational authorities recognise the importance of the language of origin for the integration (which is not equated with assimilation) of immigrant children. Furthermore, the immigrant children should have the same opportunities as Swiss-born children to broaden their repertoires in the direction of functional plurilingualism, within the realms of an integrated language pedagogy and without augmenting the total strain, because proficiency in various languages becomes increasingly important as a basic professional qualification on the labour market. These measures are in line with the *Holistic Language Policy Plan* commissioned by the EDK. The plan was presented in 1998 (*http://www.romsem.unibas.ch/sprachenkonzept*)

and has become the basis of subsequent political decisions, the most decisive one in March 2004 (EDK 1998, 2004).

3.4.   Multilingual speech

There is an important body of research on language choice in polyglot societies, be it listener-oriented, by domains or based on factorial analysis (Fishman 1967; Grosjean 1982: 135sq.). Generally speaking, multilingual speakers exploit their repertoire in order to press the maximum gain out of their language choice. In contradiction to dominant monolingual representations of communication, representing that a speaker has to decide for him- or herself on one specific language after perhaps a short period of "exploratory language choice" (Myers Scotton 1993), in reality, in many cases, language choice is highly unstable, very dynamic and permanently renegotiated among the participants, as tape recordings of actual talk in interaction show (Lüdi and Py 2003). Multilingual competences are considered here as linguistic resources available to members of a community for different purposes. The totality of these resources constitutes the linguistic repertoire of a person or a community and may include different languages, dialects, registers, styles and routines. The interactionist interpretation of repertoire underlying this approach is grounded on a contextualised and collective conception of activities and human cognition, and focuses on the central role that practical communication and, therefore, social action play in their formatting. According to this concept, multilingual repertoires are configured in the course of practical activities that are linked with specific socio-cultural contexts and with particular forms of action, interaction and inter-subjectivity. This leads to various forms of multilingual speech as a response to specific communicative needs.

This can be illustrated with the case of *Italoschwyz* in Zürich. Originating from Italy, continuous migration movements have reached the larger cities in the German part of Switzerland over the last century. When immigrant workers first arrived, they intended to return to their country of origin after some time. Socio-political measures supporting the reunion of families and macro-economic developments in both countries motivated many Italians to stay in Switzerland. This led to a growing Italian-Swiss community raising their children in Switzerland. A typical form of code switching has been observed among these second generation adolescents, correlated to their bilingual identity as well as the discovery of their own cultural roots. Franceschini (1998: 59) reported the following typical example:

(A) *perché meinsch che se tu ti mangi Emmentaler o se tu ti mangi una fontina isch au en*
because, do you mean, that when you eat Emmentaler cheese or when you eat a Fontina there is also a

Unterschied, oder? schlussändlich è sempre dentro lì però il gusto isch andersch.
difference isn't it? finally it is always in there but the taste is different

(B) *è vero!*
that's true

Forms of bilingual speech have also been adopted by first generation Italians, who commonly have a lower competence in the host language. For this reason, their switches show different patterns and are in general limited to insertion of discourse markers like *joo* [yeah], *oder* [isn't it] and *meinsch* [you mean] (Franceschini 1998: 56).

In recent years, similar forms of talk have been analysed for other groups of immigrants from, e.g., Turkey, Portugal, and former Yugoslavia. They match a phenomenon which can be observed in the semiosphere of Swiss cities at the level of what Landry and Bourhis (1997) call the "linguistic landscape", i.e., the language of public road signs, advertising billboards, street names, place names, commercial shop signs, and public signs on government buildings. In Basel, in accordance with the territoriality principle, all official signs are in German. The polyglossia shows up in advertising billboards, commercial shops and private inscriptions. As can be expected, German – the main language of more than 70% of the population – is still clearly dominant, but there are many signs in English, French, Italian, Russian and, depending on the suburb in the city, Turkish, Serbian, Croatian and other languages of immigration.

In many cases, the signs are multilingual. But translation of the same message in one or more other languages is quite rare. And even then, there are unequivalences, as in the case of a Chinese restaurant which says in English *Closed*, and paraphrases this message in Chinese by a much more polite invitation like *Please, dear customer, come back another time*, as can be seen in Figure 6. The poster for a driving school makes a clever use of Turkish (*Sürücü Kursu*), Swiss German (*Fahrschuel*), the official sign for aspirant drivers (L) and the first name of the owner (*Ali*).

Very frequently, the signs use a combination of messages in different languages. In the illustrated example of English and German, the use of German might acknowledge the fact that most Swiss clients do not really understand English. A recent survey, published on the website *Spiegel Online*, showed that an overwhelming majority of the German public radically misunderstood English-only slogans like *Life by Gorgeous*, translated by some informants as *Live in Georgia*, or *Feel the difference* translated as *Like no other* (*http://www.spiegel.de/ wirtschaft/ 0,1518,450681,00.html*).

4. Discussion and conclusions

Our results illustrate different dimensions of a modern polyglossic society. Unfortunately, the views of a majority of people on multilingualism are still troubled by homoglossic ideologies, pretending that all speakers of a language belong to the same "nation", that each "nation" should have its own state and that all inhabitants of this state should speak the same language. This leads to the political claim that immigrants should assimilate linguistically and culturally, or leave. The minimal consequence is the belief that there are "natural" inequalities among the languages or language varieties spoken within a particular territory, only one being "legitimate". The result is a lack of balance of power between indigenous people and immigrants. Indeed, as Fairclough (2001) argues, language and power are intimately related. Language indexes and reinforces the power relationships of a society and naturalises them. Language is a tool in the creation and recreation of power.

Being competent in the host language means having the capacity to perceive, name and resolve the problems of daily life, acquire new knowledge and participate in decision-making processes and in the construction of social reality. On the other hand, someone who does not speak the host language bears the risk of using other means (including physical violence) to achieve their ends, failure at school, the impossibility of gaining appropriate professional training and being excluded, marginalised, or jobless. It is not by accident that the *gestus* of commanding and punishing with restricted verbal means, the use of forms of communication that are asymmetric and distorted, oriented towards domination, are frequently reported for immigrants (Beilhardt et al. 1979). The claim for learning German in Basle as it is formulated in the *Gesamtsprachenkonzept* quoted before is justified from this perspective.

The value on the linguistic market place of most immigrant languages (except English) is quite reduced; none reaches more than a few percentage points as a language spoken at work (Andres et al. 2005) and this only by the lower socioprofessional categories. However, Grin (2004) considers, after a pilot study on the value of languages of immigration on the linguistic market place, that it is also necessary to take into account their symbolic value. In fact, the partial focus on the acquisition of the host language hides the traumatic consequences

Figure 6. Examples of commercial signs in the linguistic landscape of the city of Basle

the loss of the language and culture of origin can entail. The German writer of Turkish origin, Birol Denizeri, uses to good effect the strong metaphor of hands tearing away the face of a young girl speaking the host language German:

> Dann fing sie [sc. Saniye] an, sich zu integrieren. Sie sprach inzwischen sehr gut Deutsch und fragte sich oft, ob man es merke, dass sie eine Ausländerin ist. (...) Ihre Alpträume häuften sich. Sie sah immer wieder Hände, die ihr Gesicht abrissen. ("Das verlorene Gesicht", in: *In zwei Sprachen leben,* Deutscher Taschenbuchverlag, 1983, 16–18)

Berthelier (1988: 112) insists on the negative aftermath of educational systems neglecting totally the language of origin:

> Le problème, pour ces enfants, est donc celui d'une déprivation de la langue (et, à travers elle, de la culture) maternelle liée à son exclusion totale de l'appareil pédagogique (...).

Accordingly, the Basle *Integrationskonzept* (integration plan) claims for a change of paradigm from a deficit-based to a potential-based approach. It considers that the existing potential, i.e., the knowledge, experiences and competences of immigrants, constitute the basis for political measures. Integration is understood as a common task for both the city and the country at large. All members of society, both locals and immigrants, are called upon to participate in the process. The policy of integration should thus entail a conscious and respectful relation to difference. Superficial attribution of problems to culture or ethnicity, which in fact have social or structural reasons, should be avoided, and gender-specific aspects should not be ignored or neutralised (*Sicherheitsdepartement des Kantons Basel-Stadt* 2006). Away from the focus on the national language only, which means destabilising the alloglots' identity, this means a process of empowerment of immigrants in polyglossic settings in the sense the notion has been defined for historical minorities. As De Mejía and Tejada (2003: 42) say:

> Empowerment is the process through which the participants in the (...) process become conscious of their capacities, potential, knowledge and experiences (...) so that they can assume responsibilities in the development of autonomy and full participation in decision-making (...) in the light of the changes and new advances in national educational policies.

On the linguistic side, this means revising stereotypes about "mixed" forms of speech and revalorising multilingual forms of communication. On the one hand, they match the idea of plurilingual repertoires as shared resources that the interacting partners mobilise in function of the situation, i.e., an optimal exploitation of all communicative means of which plurilinguals dispose. On the other hand, mixed forms of speech are strong markers of plural identities.

Le Page et al. (1985), Grosjean (1985), Lüdi et al. (1994) and many others show evidence of the fact that immigrants do not add different identities one to another – and, even less, exchange one identity for another – but they integrate different dimensions into a multiple identity system. In an article entitled *Ural Tufan*, a journalist born in the Canton of Aargau (*Freiamt*), with roots in Turkey and living and working for decades in Basle, calls himself a *best-of-program* of all these cultural backgrounds, each part being a necessary part of his personality (translated version):

> (...) As a "secondo" (= member of the so-called second generation of immi-grants), I own various hats, i.e., I lead a double or even a fourfold live. (...) I am an Argovian from the *Freiamt* with Turkish roots who created himself a new home in Basel. Maybe I am also a Basler with roots in the *Freiamt* whose parents exchanged Istanbul with Switzerland forty years ago. Only one thing is sure: I am in a way a "best-of-program" of all these cultural backgrounds. One who knows that there is always one hat that suits. If I had to restrict my life to my being Turkish or to my socialisation in Wohlen (*Freiamt*), I would not be complete. (*Basler Zeitung*; 13.09.2006; S. 18 second@schweiz)

In summary, individual plurilingualism and social multilingualism are an im-portant capital that immigrants as well as the host countries should maintain and expand. It is time that political and educational decision-makers took this task seriously.

References

Andres, M. et al.
   2005   *Fremdsprachen in Schweizer Betrieben.* Solothurn: Fachhochschule Nord-westschweiz Solothurn.

Beilhardt, K., O. Kübler, and D. Steinbach
   1975   *Formen des Gesprächs im Drama: ein Kurs im Deutschunterricht auf der Oberstufe.* Stuttgart: Klett.

Berthelier, R.
   1988   Adaptation sociale, adaptation scolaire. In: A. Yahyaoui (dir. 1988), *Trou-bles du Langage et de la Filiation chez le Maghrebin de la Deuxième Génération*, 101–118. Grenoble: La Pensée Sauvage.

Berthoud, A.-C., F. Grin, and G. Lüdi
   2005   *La Gestion de la Diversité Linguistique dans des Contextes Professionnels et Institutionnels.* Lausanne: Projekteingabe an die EU.

Bundesversammlung der Schweizerischen Eidgenossenschaft
   2005   Bundesgesetz über die Ausländerinnen und Ausländer.

Council of Europe
   1992   *European Charter for Regional or Minority Languages.* Strasbourg: Council of Europe, Treaty Office (entry into force 1/3/1998).

De Mejía, A.-M. and H. Tejada
   2003   Bilingual curriculum construction and empowerment in Colombia. *International Journal of Bilingual Education and Bilingualism* 6 (1): 37–51.

EDK
   1998   *Welche Sprachen sollen die Schülerinnen und Schüler der Schweiz während der obligatorischen Schulzeit lernen?* Bericht einer von der Kommission für Allgemeine Bildung eingesetzten Expertengruppe "Gesamtsprachenkonzept" an die Schweizerische Konferenz der Kantonalen Erziehungsdirektoren (EDK), 15. Juli 1998 (*http://www.romsem.unibas.ch/sprachenkonzept*).
   2004   *Sprachenunterricht in der obligatorischen Schule: Strategie der EDK und Arbeitsplan für die gesamtschweizerische Koordination.* Beschluss der Plenarversammlung der EDK vom 25. März 2004 (*http://www.edk.ch/d/EDK/Geschaefte/framesets/mainAktivit_d.html*).

Erziehungsdepartement des Kantons Basel-Stadt
   2003   *Gesamtsprachenkonzept für die Schulen Basel-Stadt.* Bericht der Reflexionsgruppe. März 2003 (auch: *http://www.edubs.ch/die_schulen/projekte/archiv/gesamtsprachenkonzept/pdf/gsk_reflexionsgruppe.pdf*)

Fairclough, N.
   2001   *Language and Power.* 2nd revised edition. London: Longman.

Fishman, J.
   1967   Bilingualism with and without diglossia; diglossia with and without bilingualism. *Journal of Social Issues* 23 (2): 29–38.

Franceschini, R.
   1998   Code Switching and the notion of code in linguistics: Proposals for a dual focus model. In: P. Auer (ed.), *Code-switching in Conversation*, 51–72. London: Routledge.

Gorter, D. (ed.)
   2006   Linguistic landscape: A new approach to multilingualism. *Interational Journal of Multilingualism* 3 (1).

Grin, F.
   2004   Sur la rentabilité des langues de l'immigration. *Babylonia 2004/1: D'autres Langues en Suisse.*

Grosjean, F.
   1982   *Life with Two Languages: An introduction to bilingualism.* Cambridge, MA: Harvard University Press.

Landry, R. and R.Y. Bourhis
  1997   Linguistic landscape and ethno-linguistic vitality: An empirical study. *Journal of Language and Social Psychology* 16: 23–49.

Le Page, R. and A. Tabouret-Keller
  1985   *Acts of Identity*. Cambridge: Cambridge University Press.

Lüdi, G.
  2006   Multilingual repertoires and the consequences for linguistic theory. In: K. Bührig & J.D. ten Thije (eds.), *Beyond Misunderstanding. Linguistic Analyses of Intercultural Communication,* 11–42. Amsterdam: John Benjamins,

Lüdi, G., B. Py et al.
  1994   *Fremdsprachig im eigenen Land. Wenn Binnenwanderer in der Schweiz das Sprachgebiet wechseln und wie sie darüber reden.* Basel: Helbing und Lichtenhahn.

Lüdi G. and B. Py
  2003   *Etre bilingue*. 3e éd. revue. Berne/Francfort-s. Main/New York: Lang.

Lüdi, G., I. Werlen, and R. Franceschini et al.
  1997   *Le Paysage Linguistique de la Suisse*. Berne: Office Fédéral de Statistique (Statistique de la Suisse. Recensement fédéral de la population 1990).

Lüdi, G. and I. Werlen et al.
  2005   *Le Paysage Linguistique en Suisse*. Neuchâtel: Office Fédéral de Statistique (Statistique de la Suisse. Recensement fédéral de la population 2000).

OFS (ed.)
  2006   *La Population étrangère en Suisse*. Neuchâtel: Office Fédéral de la Statistique (Statistique de la Suisse).

Sicherheitsdepartement des Kantons Basel-Stadt
  2006   *Integration Basel (http://www.welcome-to-basel.bs.ch)*.

Mapping immigrant languages in Italy

Monica Barni

1. Introduction

This chapter aims to describe one of the lines of research established at the Centre of Excellence for Research *Permanent Linguistic Observatory of the Italian Language among Foreigners and of Immigrant Languages in Italy*. The role of the centre, instituted by MIUR – the Ministry of Education, University and Research – at the University for Foreigners in Siena, is to constantly monitor groups of users of Italian as a foreign language and their motivations for learning the language, and to keep track of the dynamics influencing the position of Italian on the language market (Calvet 2002) or, if you like, within the new global linguistic order (Maurais 2003). Here we define one of the lines of research underway at the Centre, *Immigrant languages in Italy,* which seeks to monitor the trends bestirring the linguistic space of Italian in contact with the languages that have entered Italy through migratory events[1].

Statistical and sociological research shows that since the mid-1970s the number of migrants entering Italy has continued to grow, and now stands at around 3,700,000 people, i.e., 6 % of the overall population (Caritas 2007). Migration is certainly a social phenomenon in which language acts as a catalyst, shaping forms of identity and providing a focal point for the reformulation of identities. In this sense, the linguistic issue assumes a central position because it encompasses the issues surrounding learning the language of the host communities in order to survive and integrate socially and professionally; and because contact with new languages and cultures brings to the fore the individual cultural and linguistic identity of all the communities within a given area. This is the line of research *Immigrant languages in Italy* focuses on. The issue of language in immigration is also considered from the point of view of the immigrant languages and how they interrelate with their new linguistic context.

By focusing on how migrant group languages enter into the Italian linguistic space, and on the effects this has on that linguistic space, our aim is to analyse the data collected with respect to these processes to verify the hypothesis that these languages may constitute a factor that restores space and vitality to

Italy's longstanding plurilingualism, rejuvenating it by adding new elements of plurilingualism (Bagna, Barni and Vedovelli 2007). We thus need to understand the conditions that make interaction possible between this new plurilingualism and the pre-existing linguistic make-up on a local and national scale, in all its different structural permutations in terms of socio-cultural characteristics. For this reason, the results of the research are pertinent to a number of linguistic disciplines (sociolinguistics, linguistic ecology, language teaching). The data on immigrant languages are analysed according to their effects and possible interpretations and not solely in terms of quantitative and qualitative data. The relationship with the physical territory is thus not only one of support or surroundings, a simple panorama in which the immigrant languages can be seen, but is itself a factor in the construction of the significance of these languages. The Italian linguistic space, for historical reasons, by its intrinsic nature, and through its own contact dynamics, thus assumes the role of amplifier, and is not simply a host to traces of immigrant languages.

If we consider the spin-off of this type of research, i.e., a systematic study to identify the presence and vitality of immigrant languages, it constitutes a necessary cognitive tool for linguistic policy, and also for the planning of direct social intervention for immigrants by the institutions responsible for handling contacts. Several sectors come to mind, such as schools to improve the knowledge of the pupils' linguistic background and to plan activities aimed at maintaining their L1, or health service, justice and businesses, for a more effective handling of communications.

First of all, we need to give at least a brief description of the Italian context. In recent years, we have witnessed a major turning point: the generalised diffusion of a commonly shared spoken Italian as a language used by the vast majority of Italian society. This phenomenon, which has been driven by a range of forces ever since the unification of Italy (De Mauro 1963), has profoundly altered the idiomatic and cultural identity of this country. The drive towards the diffusion of consistent forms of Italian in everyday use, particularly spoken, has triggered a progressive trend towards the creation of shared modules, and at the same time has reduced Italy's traditional linguistic variety (De Mauro et al. 1993; De Mauro 1994). The diffusion of a shared language has in fact led to an increasing regression in the use of dialects, the presence and vitality of which have traditionally been a distinguishing feature of the Italian language repertoire. Although dialects still undeniably retain considerable force, we are witnessing an unavoidable decrease in their use, albeit in a variety of ways, dependent on, e.g., social class, age group, level of education or geographical area. The same process has affected the languages of Italy's historical minority groups. Over all, our national linguistic identity is still marked by the coexistence of a vast range of idioms, varieties and registers. Nonetheless, the Italian-speaking camp is in constant and increasing expansion, and the trend towards linguistic unification seems ever clearer.

The leading role of the various Italian institutions in governing cultural and linguistic processes is evident: the education policies of the unified state regarding the *questione della lingua* lead to action centred exclusively on the Italian language, considered as the national and official language, with marginal attention for the other longstanding and new components of the national linguistic repertoire. The institutional language policy, aimed at the adoption of a common tool for mutual comprehension, was also supported by social drives from below, the broadening of the base of interaction and communication networks. This can be defined as "a general right to self-expression, which manifests itself in the search for neutral idiomatic tools for communicating with people of different languages and dialects, or the social aspiration to ownership of the national language, perceived as the centuries-old prerogative of the upper classes" (Bagna, Barni and Vedovelli 2007: 336). This is the composite situation into which the immigrant languages have entered, at a time when Italianisation was gradually spreading, and the dynamics of collective and individual variation in language use were changing in form and structure.

2. Rationale and goals of research

In the field of migration research, theoretical and applied linguistic studies have analysed the primary need of migrants, which is to learn the language of the new community in which they live (Giacalone Ramat 2003). Thus these studies have focused on the informal and formal processes of learning Italian as L2 (again in this case, giving only marginal consideration to other language input that migrants necessarily come into contact with, such as dialect forms, for instance). However, there is an increasing necessity to add a further perspective, to ask what is to be the destiny of the languages of origin of the migrants when they enter into the new collective linguistic space, and what effects this will have.

The object of our research is to analyse the conditions that make interaction possible between this new plurilingualism and the pre-existing linguistic make-up on a local and national scale, in a variety of ways in terms of socio-cultural characteristics. This analysis must succeed in identifying factors that may allow for the maintenance of the migrants' languages, the types and networks of language use, the factors exerting pressure on the local linguistic space and those facilitating change in different directions: the maintenance or loss of new languages, the formation of new varieties through contact and linguistic assimilation to differing degrees depending on generation and cultural back-ground. In Bagna, Barni and Vedovelli (2007), within the complexity of the subject in question, often somewhat concealed and elusive, we have nonetheless identified some factors that need to be considered: the tension between unifica-tion/homogenisation and diversification; the levels of interaction on the linguis-tic dimension; the concept of migrant languages and immigrant languages.

2.1. The tension between unification/homogenisation and diversification

In the interaction between the two distinct drives towards unification/homogen-isation and diversification, we should first of all consider the pressure that Italian society (and its expressive/communicative space) exerts on groups of migrants and on new languages. We also need to identify and evaluate the drives towards Italianisation experienced by migrants, for whom the need for mutual compre-hension with natives has both instrumental value (learning Italian for interactive survival) and symbolic value, as a way to gain a sign of social prestige and a tool for the right to full self-expression and thus to the idea of full citizenship. In this process, linguistic unification is favoured by schools, where children and adults, if included in literacy classes, experience and share the mastery of Italian. At the other end, the degree of acceptance of the immigrant languages within the school context, i.e., the immigrant languages' symbolic value in the motivation to maintain one's identity of origin, has direct implications for their actual maintenance in terms of competence and use. The outcome of the tension between linguistic unification and diversification also depends on the migrants' motivation to conserve their identity, individually and as a group, which may be linked to a variety of factors, such as the possibility of defining a precise migratory plan, including intentions regarding the length of stay in Italy, and religious factors.

2.2. The levels of interaction on the linguistic dimension

Since interaction between native Italians and immigrants has become an every-day phenomenon, involving a very broad range of contexts of social exchange, there is a very high level of conditioning of native usage by immigrant usage. On the level of language use, where the interaction between the new plurilingual-ism and the pre-existing linguistic make-up is focused on mainly, the interaction between native Italians and immigrants speaking other languages gives rise to mechanisms of role and function selection, influenced by a broad range of fac-tors, from the imagery of the languages brought by the speakers to their attitudes and to the intentions underlying the interaction. The natives, by assuming atti-tudes of cooperation or intentions to create barriers, even to the extent of forms of communicative racism, show systematic linguistic behaviours that appear marked relative to those commonly seen in interactions with other native speakers. They may speak more slowly, choose morpho-syntactic and lexical forms considered easier for foreigners, use strategies for mutual comprehension and facilitation or, in contrast, they may make communicative choices that have the opposite effect. Behavioural modalities that facilitate or hinder communication with foreigners do not necessarily and mechanically have effects on linguistic structure, nor do the interlinguistic forms produced in the process of acquiring Italian necessarily and mechanically become part of the linguistic structure or become perceived by native Italians as acceptable and usable. Nonetheless, the change in interactive behaviour between natives and foreign immigrants may constitute one of the conditions for change in linguistic form, according to how systematic it is and the extent to which it is broadly shared within the community.

2.3. The concept of migrant languages and immigrant languages

In order to understand the nature and the effects of the interaction between new plurilingualism and local linguistic repertoire, we use the classification proposed by Bagna, Machetti and Vedovelli (2003), which distinguishes the concept of migrant languagefrom that of immigrant language. We refer first of all to the capacity for and the level of rootedness of the immigrant group within a local community in terms of, e.g., numeric ratios, level of integration, migratory mobility, autonomous vitality of the migrant group or pressure from the community.

Migrant languages are languages passing through, used by migrant groups who drift around the social territory, non-cohesive and in relatively small numbers; for this reason these languages are unable to put down roots and leave traces of their presence in the linguistic contact constellation of the host community, or succeed in doing so only sporadically. *Immigrant languages*, on the other hand, are those of numerically larger and stable groups, with intentions of putting down roots within a local community; languages that are used systematically by the immigrant group and that are able to leave their mark in the linguistic contact make-up with the host community. Only the latter can hope to become a part of the new plurilingualism of the Italian peninsula and, given that they are in a more stable and lasting situation of contact with the other language varieties present in the area, they are in a position to affect its communicative and linguistic space.

Thus we can clearly perceive the need to evaluate the condition of migrant or immigrant languages within a given community. This evaluation becomes even more necessary if we consider that foreign immigration in Italy shows an extremely high degree of polycentrism, involving a sweeping variety of countries and languages of origin, further diversified according to the location of settlement. Following the initial phases of high mobility, migratory flows have increasingly assumed clearly defined characteristics in terms of areas of arrival, fields of professional inclusion, and mobility dynamics. Family members joining immigrants and the schooling of their children have contributed further to strengthening the rootedness of migrants within local communities. Statistical data on immigration in Italy (Caritas 2007) confirm year after year that there is a strong drive to take roots. What still remains to be evaluated, in regards to the communicative characteristics of the various groups within their specific local communities, is the linguistic result of this rootedness: the degree of adherence to their language of origin; their ability to exhibit socially the language use of their homeland; the strength of negotiation at a social and institutional level (especially in schools) regarding the integration and acceptance of the language of origin within the local community; and the level of cultural, social and also linguistic cohesion of this community.

3. Goals of research

The aim of our research is to reconstruct the forces of interaction in the contact between the immigrant languages and the Italian linguistic space by describing, from a range of points of observation, the traces of change and measuring the new use of alloglot languages in relation to the typical dynamics of the phenomenon. This model must thus be capable of taking into account factors concerning the languages of the migrant groups, investigating the level of maintenance or loss in the language use of their speakers, to differing degrees according to generation, types and networks of use, their capacity to exert pressure on the local linguistic repertoire and the creation of new forms deriving from contact and linguistic assimilation; but also the attitudes and behaviour both of the local community, in terms of the pressure it exerts on migrant groups and on new languages, and of the migrants themselves towards Italian, a language that is necessary for mutual comprehension and a symbolic tool for integration.

The complexity of the research topic led the Centre of Excellence to construct a methodological model based on a multidimensional approach, whose main features are theoretical and methodological innovation on the one hand, and on the other, its attentiveness and readiness to capture the changes in the current linguistic situation in Italy. The Centre's research integrates different subject areas (IT, geography and statistics as well as linguistics) that work together to produce an integrated analytical perspective on a complex subject, and it uses innovative elicitation tools. The objective of our research is to detect the presence and visibility of languages within this territory, to make it "speak" in its various manifestations, in order to analyse the conditions and ways in which one or more languages become (or can become) visible within a space to which they do not traditionally belong, and how, through contact, their languages and cultures are recreated.

4.   Research methods and research tools

In order to identify the conditions for relations between languages and thus between cultures and their respective members, both social data (numbers and sedentariness of migrants) and linguistic data (presence and visibility of languages, attitudes of speakers and maintenance of languages) are required. The underlying idea is to obtain a large set of data from which, for the same point or for several points or a sequence of points in a given location a comprehensive portrayal of the linguistic space can be derived. This kind of mapping entails constant monitoring of sociolinguistic dynamics, and thus needs to rely on methods suitable for acquiring wide-scale quality data, using "triangulated" data collection, i.e., including the use of instrumentation that is groundbreaking in its heuristic potential and economy of resources required for its use. By linking the "triangulated data", the mapping enables us to portray the new profiles of the linguistic contact constellations in the various migratory contexts, e.g., large urban areas and specific zones within them, and small and medium-sized centres and isolated areas. To this end, the Centre of Excellence has invested in IT equipment and geographic mapping gear. The most important of these is the *Sociolinguistic Data Collection Mobile Laboratory*, the first mobile apparatus equipped for carrying out field research in the linguistic sector. This camper van is equipped for collecting linguistic data directly on the ground (Figure 1).

The Mobile Laboratory is highly functional because it enables researchers to acquire a mass of data far greater than anything that could be done through normal linguistic data collection procedures. Indeed, with the Mobile Laboratory, researchers can go directly to the places in question and handle all operations for collecting and analysing data in complete autonomy.

The observation parameters we adopted for monitoring linguistic changes within a given territory concern the presence of speakers of immigrant languages, their demographic weight and their location (areas of residence, neighbourhoods), their statements with respect to language use, attitudes and skills, and the behaviour and attitudes of natives; the presence, visibility and actual use of the languages in social interaction contexts. The degree of penetration of the languages in the area is thus measured in terms of:

Figure 1. Mobile Laboratory

- presence of the languages;
- declared vitality;
- visibility/interaction/use.

For each of these three observation parameters a different data-collection model was designed. These are *Toscane Favelle* (*TF*), *Monterotondo-Mentana* (*MM*) and *Esquilino* (*ES*), respectively, named after the places of reference where they were first applied and tried. Each of the three models entails geolinguistic mapping of the area: potential (from nationality to language) in the first model, perceived or self-declared (by the contact actors) in the second model, and actual usage (based on direct observation) in the third model. When compared, the mappings produced by the three data collection models enable us to draw the different linguistic contact scenarios that can take place in the various migratory contexts, and to identify the parameters and factors that can combine to affect their configuration.

The first investigation model – *Toscane Favelle* (*TF*) – aims to give a graphic representation of the languages present, the number of speakers, and their level of aggregation within an area, using thematic maps and statistical data on the nationality of foreigners, and transforming them into data regarding the languages present within the area. The input data are statistical data on the presence of foreigners, regarding nationality, numbers and sedentariness, all easily obtained from public institutions. Using existing classifications regarding the languages spoken in the immigrants' countries of origin (Grimes 2000; Katzner 2002), these data can be transformed into data on the languages potentially present in that given territory. It is also possible to represent languages in graphic form as geolinguistic maps (Baker and Eversley 2000). Using this procedure, the demographic weight of a community is revealed, in terms of both quantity and quality (numerousness, sedentariness and aggregation) and, when considered from a linguistic point of view, it becomes a prerequisite for the language spoken by that community to be considered an immigrant language. Only if it bears demographic weight in a given territory can a community hope to bear sociolinguistic weight too (Bagna, Barni and Siebetcheu 2004). This is a relatively simple procedure to use to gain an initial, if not well-defined, idea of the potential degree of plurilingualism within a given area. Its results could be useful to local authorities, schools, etc., in planning linguistic policy in the area. However, since a group's demolinguistic weight within an area is a necessary but not a sufficient requirement for the maintenance and vitality of their language, this model alone is not able to explain the complex dynamics of linguistic contact described above.

The second model of analysis – *Monterotondo-Mentana (MM)* – is more complex to apply, but it offers a more precise description of the local situation. It involves the use of traditional techniques, such as questionnaires or audio/video-recorded interview protocols, in order to collect data on the speakers' self-declarations about use and contact with languages, in various social contexts (family, public, school, work), and on attitudes and perceptions towards them, both those of Italians and those of foreigners (Bagna and Barni 2005b; Bagna and Pallassini 2006). This approach blends the procedures and the processing of results seen in the models of Baker and Eversley (2000) and the *Multilingual Cities Project* (Extra and Yağmur 2004; see also this Volume). The questionnaires can be administered to whole classes in schools. The model proved to be functional not only for immigrant languages, but also for more general data collection on the linguistic habits and expectations of large numbers of school pupils of Italian origin (Bagna and Barni 2005b). The results are significant and substantial in terms of quantity, but their quality also offers a reading of the micro and macro language use of the people involved. Quantitative data on the languages present and used can be represented in map form, and it is also possible to obtain qualitative data on linguistic practices in different situations and contexts, and thus on the degree of maintenance and vitality of a language (Extra and Yağmur 2004). However, this model is based exclusively on self-declarations of interviewees, and not on the real and thus documented use of languages in contexts of interaction.

The third model – *Esquilino (ES)* – aims to survey the presence and use of languages in contexts of social interaction (Bagna and Barni 2005a). This model combines three different dimensions:

- the *static* visibility and vitality of languages, i.e., in texts in public communication;
- the *interactive* visibility and vitality of languages, i.e., in language use in interactive exchanges between speakers;
- the *aggregate* visibility and vitality of languages, i.e., in language use in particular places of social contact.

The structure of the ARC-GIS geographic software used and customised *ad hoc* enables data to be processed in more than one dimension, using *dots*, *lines* and *polygons* on the map to give a more precise and suitable representation of the linguistic data. The data-collection tools used (digital cameras and video cameras, hand-held computers) record the forms of contact (written texts or interactions) and the ways in which these are structured according to the type of territory in question. All the data collected are georeferenced. In practice, the data are not linked simply to the place of collection using a general classification (city, neighbourhood, school, etc.), but to a precise location or section of a territory, identified by geographical coordinates. In this way, each portion of the area is linked only with the data gathered within that space, and vice versa: a permanent connection is created between the data and the territory to which they belong. Georeferencing also means that data can be analysed both *synchronically* and *diachronically*: synchronically in that it allows us to compare different portions of data and territory surveyed in a single survey campaign; diachronically because data gathered in a single geographical location on different occasions some time apart can be superimposed in order to create maps that highlight the changes in the linguistic repertoire within that territory.

The static visibility and vitality of languages is measured by observing the traces of presence of the immigrant languages within the social communication space. Photographs are taken of all the written traces that contribute to form the so-called "linguistic landscape" (Landry and Bourhis 1997): work-related and personal public announcements, posters and publicity, business cards, shop signs, information boards, menus, writings on vehicles, etc. The conformation of the linguistic landscape is assumed to be a contributing factor in describing the language use characteristic of a given territory: "the linguistic landscape may act as the most observable and immediate index of the relative power and status of the linguistic communities inhabiting a given territory" (Landry and Bourhis 1997: 29). Underlying the above statement are the informative and symbolic functions that the linguistic make-up and its conformation can perform in multi-ethnic and thus multilingual areas (Landry and Bourhis 1997: 25–29; Ben-Rafael et al. 2004). The informative function of the linguistic landscape is determined by its capacity to signal the presence of a specific language community within its territory, to represent the sociolinguistic composition of the linguistic groups present, and to indicate the languages that may be used there. The symbolic function of the linguistic landscape relates to the fact that language is the most important dimension of ethnic identity: the presence and visibility of a language thus indicates a positive attitude on the part of ethno-linguistic groups towards their identity of origin. Furthermore, as regards this function, the linguistic landscape can also be linked to the concept of "ethno-linguistic vitality" (Giles 1977): the use of a language for social communication is a sign of its level of vitality, and therefore represents one of the factors contributing to its maintenance. Barker and Giles (2002) highlighted the fact that the conformation of the linguistic landscape also contributes to modifying native attitudes towards other communities present within a given territory: a greater degree of plurilingualism within the social communication space corresponds to less hostile native attitudes.

All the texts photographed in the linguistic landscape are georeferenced according to their location within the area and catalogued on hand-held computers containing special geographic and data archiving software. They are then entered into a database and analysed. Using this procedure, vast quantities of data can be collected and stored, and thematic maps can be produced[2]. As shown in Figure 2, each text is classified according to various other parameters: the *type of text* (signs, menus, leaflets, posters, publicity, announcements, regulations, etc.); the *position* (outside or inside a commercial establishment); the *location* (central or peripheral urban area, industrial, craft industry or commercial area, rural area, etc.); the *domain* of use (private, public, educational, work-related); the *context* (catering, hospitality, health, public administration, public services, education, the workplace, etc.); the *place* (bar, coffee bar, restaurant etc.).

A second sheet in the database is also prepared (Figure 3) for each photo giving a macro- and micro-linguistic analysis of the text contained in it, i.e., from the identification of the languages present to the linguistic analysis of the occurrence observed.

It is also possible to perform a combined analysis of different parameters, referring to the macro- or microanalysis of the text. In fact, each individual field of the geodatabase is indexed, and can thus be selected as a base point from

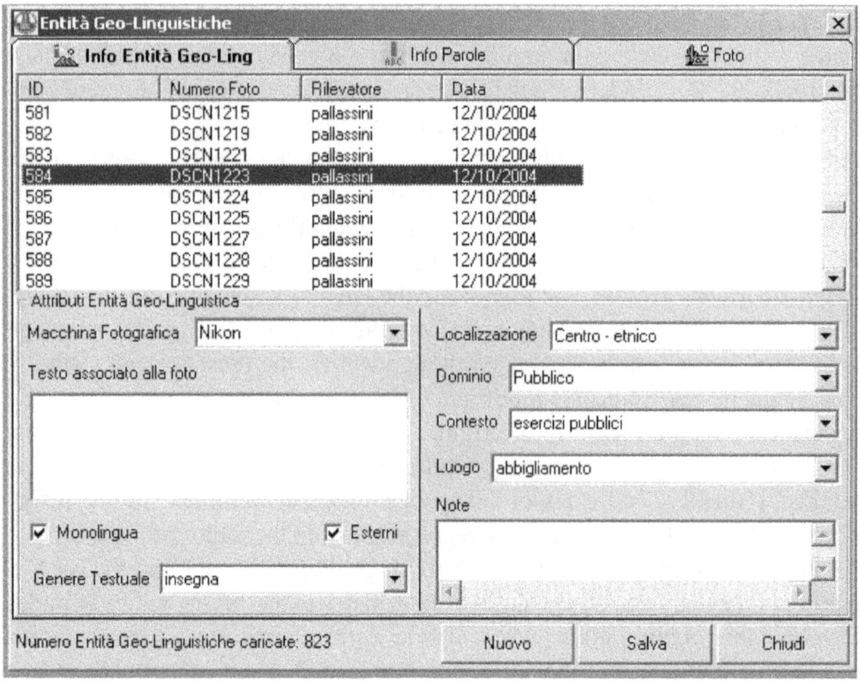

Figure 2. Geodatabase 2000 sheet

which to approach and interpret the data, including its graphic representation, in that different geolinguistic maps can be created according to the theme selected (e.g., maps on the languages present, or on languages and genres of text, etc.).

The second investigative dimension, regarding the visibility of groups and the vitality of languages in interaction, entails the recording of interactions involving contact subjects during communicative events. Here what is being observed is actual language use in different communication contexts (in the street, on the bus, at the bar, etc.) between speakers of the same language or of different languages: the linguistic repertoire may range from the language of origin to Italian or other languages used as *lingua franca*, in order to observe the ways and types of linguistic contact, code mixing or switching.

The third investigative dimension, which seeks to highlight the visibility of groups and the aggregate vitality of languages, is used for research in environments closed by physical boundaries or other factors (schools, marketplaces, apartment blocks, slums, circumscribed areas within a neighbourhood or city, etc.). In this third dimension, the focus of the investigation is the place in which different language repertoires can be seen, in that the researcher records the way

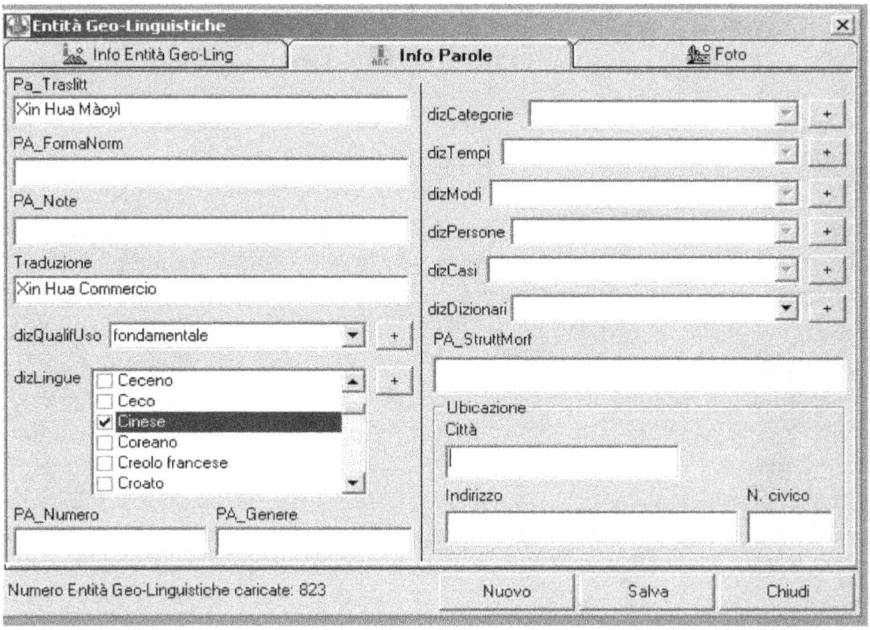

Figure 3. Geodatabase 2000 sheet 2

in which the same communicative event in the same location (e.g., buying goods at a market stall) changes as the actors involved in the interaction change.

5. Some case studies

We will give a brief illustration of data collection and mapping performed in various parts of Italy using the models and methodologies described above.

5.1. Siena and its province

The city of Siena provides us with a special case within the Italian linguistic space. Here people speak the Tuscan variety, which was selected as the national language and which was at the centre of the *questione della lingua* (language debate). In people's minds, Siena is one of the cities where the "purest" Italian is spoken, and a city that has always been considered monolingual. The research carried out in the city sought to critically highlight the fact that its linguistic make-up is undergoing profound change, partly due to the drive from immigrant languages. Despite the fact that there is not a strong presence of migrant groups in Siena, the investigation using the *Toscane Favelle* model brought to light at least 25 languages spoken by groups settled within the area (Bagna, Barni and Siebetcheu 2004). These languages, which are distributed in a differentiated way around the province, are part of the changing structure of its linguistic make-up.

If we then analyse the urban linguistic landscape, we can see that plurilingual texts are more and more prominently visible, not only in the international languages widely used to communicate with the many tourists that visit the city, but also in the languages of migrant groups. The greatest concentration of different languages is to be found in a specific area of the city in its historical centre. This is not an ethnic neighbourhood (immigrants in Siena do not generally live in the city centre), but it is the street where most sources of information are to be found: two universities (one of which is the University for Foreigners), a library, two newsagents, some Internet cafes, and a public aid association. Alongside these establishments, foreign shops have proliferated and with them written communications. Only in this part of the city is the battle to bring in the new being fought, the frontier to language contact being opened.

5.2.   Monterotondo and Mentana

The research carried out in schools in Monterotondo and Mentana, two municipalities just outside Rome, showed various attitudes, perceptions and positions regarding languages on the part of children of Italian origin and those of foreign origin (Bagna and Barni 2005b; Bagna and Pallassini 2006). The destiny of the immigrant languages present within the territory is by no means identical. For example, even allowing for differences in number, Romanian, the language of the numerically largest group in the area, shows greater visibility and strength than Albanian (the language of the second largest group), both because it is used more often in contexts of daily interaction, and because its presence is strongly felt in the preferences and desires of its speakers. Albanian, on the other hand, does not show the same strength in its maintenance, or in the minds of its speakers. These data were confirmed in interviews with the parents of informants from the schools: the Romanians expressed a strong desire to ensure that their children maintained their language of origin. A generally closed attitude was also observed towards immigrant languages and plurilingualism on the part of Italians, gradually growing stronger as we observed pupils from higher grades within the schools. The most common tendency is towards monolingualism, as witnessed by the highly marked presence of Italian among the preferred and desired languages and the preponderance of English due to pressure from the school and the home environment.

In the same area, we held a photographic campaign to observe language traces in the urban linguistic landscape. In the two towns and their territories we took just 50 photos, a very low number considering the high percentage of settled groups of immigrants living there. In shop signs, advertisements, messages, etc., few traces remain of their languages, concentrated almost exclusively in places institutionally designated as meeting places for immigrants (public and private associations, parish churches, call centres, support centres, etc.) or in public offices, meant to facilitate mutual understanding and access to services. In most cases, these signs are not produced by the immigrant community themselves but by the local institutions who translate their public communications. Translation, not only into the languages of international communication, but also into the languages of the immigrant communities with the strongest presence within the area, is required by current legislation on immigration (Law n°. 189/2002). These are referred to as "top-down" signs, because they are produced "from above", by institutions (Ben-Rafael et al. 2004). During data collection on the ground, photographs were taken of posters containing announcements from the local municipal administration and written in other languages as well as in Italian; also observed were large billboards of Italian companies written in Romanian only, to promote services to this sector of the population, considered as real clients (Bagna and Barni 2005b).

5.3.   The city of Rome

The city of Rome was another place where our models of surveying were applied. Of all Italian cities, Rome offers perhaps the best representation of the paradigm of the Italian linguistic make-up. Indeed, in its role as capital of Italy and as a large city, Rome has on the one hand always been marked by the coexistence and juxtaposition of ethnically different groups, and is thus a long-standing centre of multilingual contact dynamics, a laboratory for the reorganisation of expressive language use. On the other hand, it has always performed a dual role as a driving force for the standardisation processes of the Italian language community (De Mauro 1963).

Our analysis was carried out in Esquilino, the city's most multi-ethnic neighbourhood, a place of residence for immigrants (Comune di Roma 2005), but also the location of most of the city's foreign-run businesses. For a preliminary analysis of the plurilingualism potentially present in the neighbourhood, we transformed the demographic data into linguistic data. The total number of all the languages spoken in all the countries of origin of the immigrants yields a result of 1,581 languages potentially present within the *Municipio I* area: this figure obviously refers to the languages theoretically possible. Taking into consideration only the official languages of the first 20 countries, we obtain a total of 29 languages. The top languages potentially present are Bengali, Philippine (Tagalog), English and Chinese.

We then surveyed the languages used in the texts of social communications within the neighbourhood, with the aim of establishing which of them are visible in the linguistic landscape (Bagna, Barni and Vedovelli 2007). Photographs were taken of all the texts written in foreign languages, be they monolingual or multilingual, and also of texts in Italian or contact Italian, used by immigrants of different first-language backgrounds, where the context was clearly not Italian, such as signs on shops run by immigrants, or where the goods on display were not typical of the local market. Occurrences in Italian (or contact Italian) were classified where present in multilingual texts. Traces of 24 languages were found in the Esquilino neighbourhood. Apart from Italian and contact Italian, the other languages found are presented in Table 1. In terms of quantity, the range goes from languages with a vast number of occurrences to languages that appear just once.

In terms of quality, we used three parameters to analyse the languages: *presence* (the number of times a language occurs in signs, posters, etc.), *dominance* within a multilingual text (the number of times a language is prevalent/dominant within a text relative to the other languages present), and *autonomy* (monolingual texts, signs, posters). Analysis based on these three parameters (see Table 1 and Figure 4) shows that Italian is present in the largest number of texts (500) and that Chinese is the most strongly represented other language in the linguistic landscape of Esquilino: as well as being seen in as many as 483 texts, it also comes first in terms of dominance (in bilingual Chinese-Italian texts, Chinese is prevalent) and autonomy (the number of texts written in Chinese only is significantly greater). Amongst the other languages, the most frequently present are English, in 277 texts, and Bengali, in 119 texts. Italian acts as *lingua franca*, transmitting the content of texts written in other languages. The local language is selected for use between language communities, so that all speakers can understand the content of the text, and, in contexts such as shops, as a means to attract people from beyond the bounds of the individual language community, thus embracing other communities, including the local community.

It is interesting to observe that the vast majority of cases of plurilingual texts or texts in languages other than Italian are not texts produced by public bodies or associations (top-down) but by individuals (bottom-up).

As can be gathered from Figure 4, it is also interesting to analyse the way in which languages are distributed across the territory. Chinese, clearly the predominant language, tends to cluster in specific areas, leaving no space for other languages. The widely-used international languages (French, English, Spanish,

Table 1. Languages in l'Esquilino in terms of presence, dominance and autonomy

Presence			Dominance			Autonomy		
Language	N	%	Language	N	%	Language	N	%
Italian	500	31.09	Chinese	312	36.75	Chinese	197	66.56
Chinese	483	30.03	Bengali	71	8.36	English	33	11.15
English	277	17.22	Italian	67	7.90	Bengali	15	5.07
Bengali	119	7.41	English	55	6.48	Italian	15	5.07
Sinhalese	32	2.00	Sinhalese	29	3.41	Russian	9	3.04
Spanish	31	1.92	Russian	13	1.53	Contact Italian*	6	2.00
Hindi	24	1.50	Spanish	12	1.41	Punjabi	5	1.69
French	20	1.25	Contact Italian*	10	1.17	Sinhalese	5	1.69
Russian	19	1.19	Korean	6	0.70	Spanish	3	1.01
Arabic	18	1.11	Albanian	5	0.59	Arabic	2	0.68
Contact Italian*	13	0.81	Arabic	5	0.59	Korean	2	0.68
Romanian	13	0.81	Punjabi	5	0.59	Albanian	1	0.34
German	12	0.74	Hindi	3	0.35	Japanese	1	0.34
Punjabi	11	0.69	Romanian	3	0.35	Hindi	1	0.34
Korean	10	0.62	Japanese	2	0.23	German	1	0.34
Japanese	10	0.62	German	2	0.23			
Albanian	5	0.31	French	1	0.12			
Tagalog	4	0.25	Tagalog	1	0.12			
Turkish	2	0.13	Ukrainian	1	0.12			
Farsi	1	0.06	No dominance	246	29.00			
Polish	1	0.06						
Portuguese	1	0.06						
Ukrainian	1	0.06						
Urdu	1	0.06						
Total	1608	100.00	Total	849	100.00	Total	296	100.00

* Contact Italian, used by immigrants of different first-language background

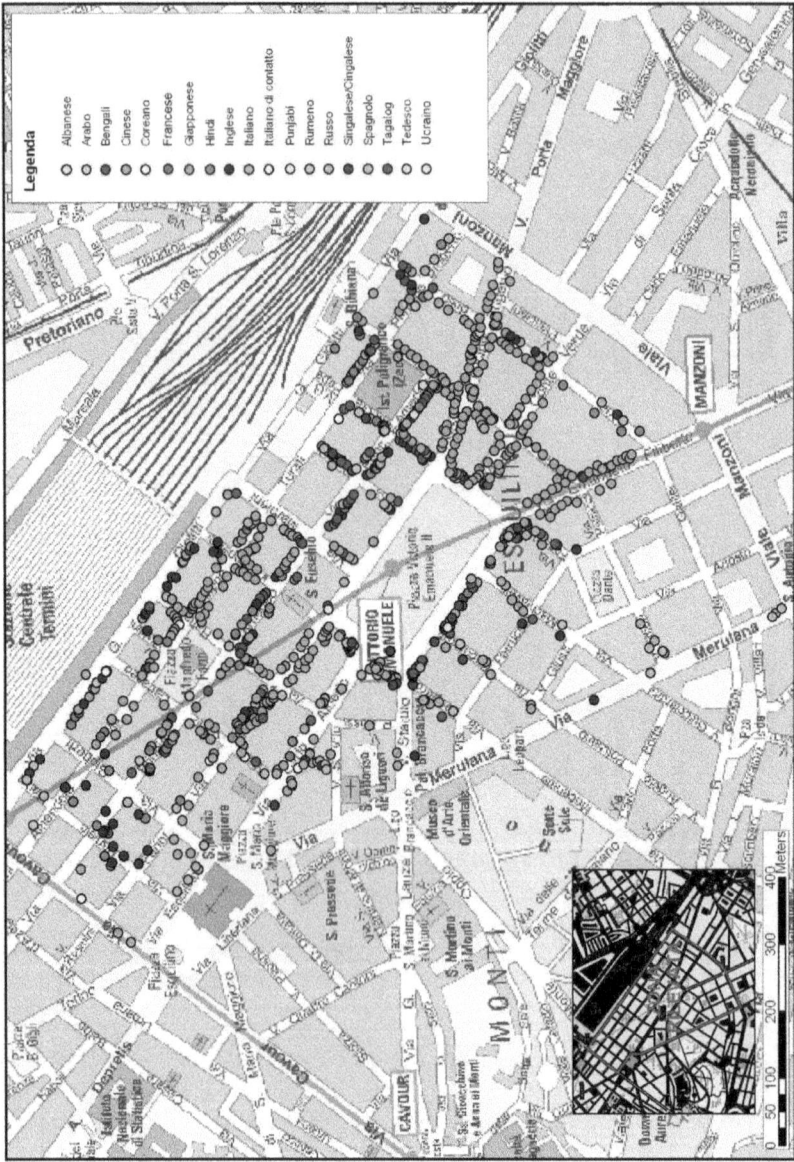

Figure 4. Languages in l'Esquilino in terms of dominance

German) are found more around the fringe areas of the neighbourhood and near the historical monuments most frequently visited by tourists. In the central square of the neighbourhood, a meeting place for Italians and foreigners alike, and the location of the underground station, all the languages can be seen in the urban linguistic landscape. The same is true around Rome's central station, another place of arrivals, departures, meetings and exchanges.

An even more significant factor is the way in which languages are interwoven in use, even within a single text. Indeed, we counted 90 different attested ways of combining languages in a communicative occurrence. There are texts written in a single language, texts in two languages, and texts containing as many as 8 different languages. The communicative potential and semiotic value of monolingual and multilingual usage are completely different. The different uses do not serve only to select, and, if monolingual, to restrict the users of a given message, representing the closed attitude of the language community towards others. They can also highlight the symbolic value of using a specific language, the presence of a community that continues to use its own language to communicate and, consequently, the strength of this language, as well as the closure of the community towards local usage or, by contrast, the openness towards contact both with the local language, giving rise to interlinguistic varieties, as can be seen in Italian as *lingua franca*, and with other immigrant languages. To identify these usage relations we sorted the combination modes between the languages found at 15 different levels (plus a level 0). From level 1 – exclusive use of the immigrant language (242 texts out of 851) – to various levels of coexistence of Italian with one immigrant language (207 texts), or of Italian, an immigrant language and other *linguae francae* (103 texts). In our analysis of levels, alongside multilingualism, we also considered the degree of openness, i.e., the level of comprehensibility of the message for groups of potentially interested readers within the urban communicative space surveyed.

Level 1 refers to so-called *immigrant language monolingualism*: the only language used is an immigrant language. This is a selective choice on the part of the person issuing the message, intended to favour specific sectors of the public/speakers/clients, consisting of those who can understand and interact in a particular immigrant language. This choice also indicates the presence of a strong, close-knit language community, with closed language use. Level 1 is a category with a strong presence within the urban space in Rome: the immigrant languages, which represent a numerical minority relative to Italian, adopt a strategy of exhibited monolingualism.

At *Level 4 (Immigrant language + Italian)*, Italian can be used both to translate the text from the immigrant language and to provide other information. The two languages account for varying proportions of the text, and also perform

Table 2. Levels of language use

Level	Description	N occurrences
0	No written words present	2
1	Immigrant language	242
2	Immigrant language + other immigrant language(s)	2
3	Immigrant language + Italian (addresses/place names)	94
4	Immigrant language + Italian	207
5	Immigrant language + Italian + other immigrant language(s)	1
6	English	33
7	Immigrant language + English	65
8	Immigrant language + English + other languages	4
9	Immigrant language + English + Italian	103
10	Immigrant language + English + Italian + other languages	17
11	English + Italian	39
12	English + Italian + other languages	14
13	Contact Italian	6
14	Contact Italian + immigrant language	7
15	Italian	15
	Total	851

different functions. Italian is often used to indicate the subject matter of the text, using key words for the world of migrant life, such as *residence permit, demonstration.*

Levels 5, 9, 10 and *12* may be considered as those of *full multilingualism.* Openness is shown by the presence of an immigrant language which is the distinguishing feature of the text examined and by the presence of other languages that allow the text to be used by an Italian-speaking public (or people with some competence in Italian) and/or a general public competent in English and other languages.

Finally, *Level 15 – Italian* shows total *assimilation* and *adherence* to the language of the host country, with acceptance of all its rules of usage. The choice of Italian may be interpreted as an openness towards the audience considered to be linguistically dominant in the area, even in a typically ethnic district. It also shows the choice to accept a new language into one's own linguistic domain, penalising one's language of origin (at least in terms of visibility).

The possible models of language use combinations observed in Esquilino can also be represented graphically in a Cartesian plane, with *linguistic openness* on the y-axis and the *presence of two or more languages* on the x-axis (see Figure 5).

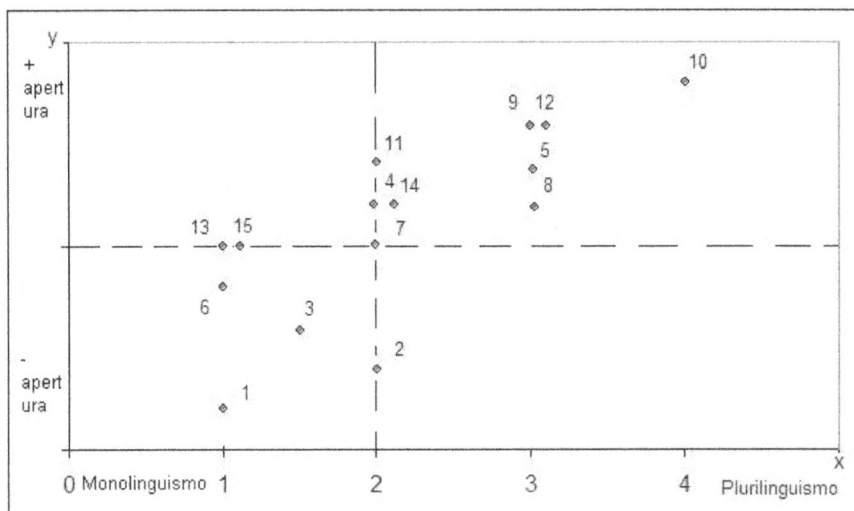

Figure 5. Openness and multilingualism in language use

In Figure 5, the different combination levels observed are placed according to the intersection of these two parameters, so as to illustrate the tension between openness towards various groups of immigrants/speakers/readers of the texts through the use of more than one language, and the actual presence of combinations of two or more languages as a sign of the area's multilingualism. In the resulting graph, we can see that Esquilino's linguistic space, as well as featuring a variety of usage patterns, can be described as substantially open and multilingual. Most of the levels (levels 7, 4, 14, 11, 8, 5, 12, 9 and 10) are positioned in the upper right-hand quadrant of the Cartesian plane, which contains the data for maximal multilingualism and maximum openness. Only three levels are placed in the lower left-hand quadrant, denoting monolingualism and minimal openness (levels 1, 3 and 6).

If we combine this data on quality with data on quantity, referring to the number of texts observed for each level, and again represent them graphically on a Cartesian plane (see Figure 6), we see that not only most levels but also most texts tend to be placed in the quadrant for maximum multilingualism/maximum openness. This quadrant counts a total of 457 texts, with the constant presence of at least one immigrant language. In the quadrant for monolingualism/minimal openness, 277 texts were counted, most of which were in one of the immigrant languages. These data provide an index of visibility for the immigrant group's language, but also of closed attitude, i.e., a low message accessibility index.

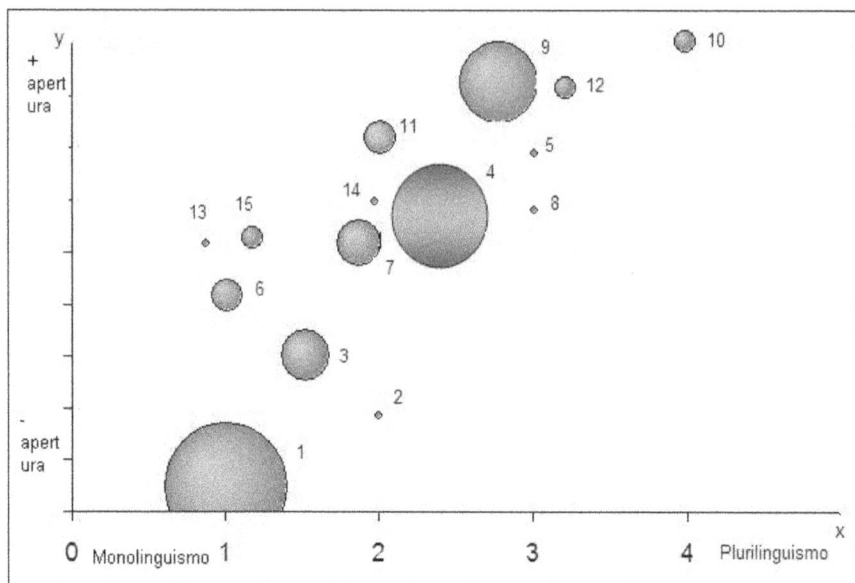

Figure 6. Degree of multilingualism and openness and number of occurrences at the levels observed

6.   Conclusions

The application of the different investigative models in the various cities and towns has shown that the mapping and measuring of linguistic diversity is an operation that must take into account various factors, including the different socio-cultural characteristics that make interaction possible between the new plurilingualism and the pre-existing linguistic make-up on a local and national scale. The interweaving of these factors will determine the conditions for the maintenance of immigrant languages, the types and networks of usage, their capacity to exert pressure on the local linguistic space, the creation of new forms deriving from contact between languages or linguistic assimilation to its various degrees. The different dynamics of contact between languages will reshape the Italian linguistic space in different ways according to the geographical, social and economic characteristics of the area where the contact takes place, and according to the groups in contact. All these factors, which manifest themselves tangibly in the attitudes and behaviours of natives and non-natives, have a profound effect on the dynamics of relationships and communication.

As the data from the various studies show, the outcomes of contact vary dramatically according to the size of the town or city. In most cases, with the exception of historical centres (which attract a lot of tourists and thus show evident signs of plurilingualism), small centres show greater openness in terms of social exchanges and availability of and access to services. Top-down plurilingual communication commands more space and visibility. In contrast, in the same places we observed greater pressure from the locals upon the new languages and, as a consequence, the choice by immigrant groups and individuals not to exhibit the use of their languages in public spaces. In these territories the visibility of different languages is minimal, despite the relative size of the groups present. Due to the characteristics mentioned, in small and medium-sized towns the level of rootedness of immigrant languages seems to be expressed in terms of linguistic vitality within private spaces, and it does not always show visibility characteristics. Large cities, in contrast, are perceived by their very nature as places of transit, passed through by various groups and flows of immigrants, and also as places where some groups have settled. Ethnic neighbourhoods have developed in the large cities (including their historical centres, e.g., in Rome, Genoa, Turin and Palermo), and a stratification of immigrants has taken place that we could define as time-based, based on the different flows and the overlaying of flows.

The dynamics that develop in this way provide a clearer illustration of the close link between the social dimension (different groups of different source countries) and the linguistic and territorial dimension of immigrants (presence of commercial activities, meeting places, homes), conditions of contact and of the reshaping of the linguistic space. The data gathered in Rome highlight how a large city, a place open to contact, offers the possibility for languages to manifest and combine themselves in a vast range of usage. The texts seen in the social communication space in Esquilino show quite a complex and varied urban linguistic landscape: monolingual choices, seen in the use of a single immigrant language or of Italian alone, open up to innumerable possibilities for interweaving with other languages, increasing the degree of plurilingualism and openness in language use. The various modes of combination between languages seen in social communication in this large city appear to be an element capable of preserving the balance between assimilation to Italian and the publicly displayed maintenance of one's own linguistic and cultural identity.

Notes

[1]   The line of research on immigrant languages at the Centre of Excellence is directed by Massimo Vedovelli, with contribution from Monica Barni, Carla Bagna, Sabrina Machetti, Alessandro Pallassini, Francesca Gallina, Anna Bandini and Livia Bazu, as well as the participation of students from the three-year degree specialisation and PhD courses at the University for Foreigners in Siena.

[2] In technical terms, each time a text containing an immigrant language is identified, it is photographed. The use of hand-held computers equipped with a GIS Mobile application (ArcPad 6.x) suitably customised (using an Applet), and a GPS receiver (Jacket GPS or Bluetooth), means the researcher can locate each linguistic occurrence geographically; should the GPS receiver be unable to identify the researcher's position, he/she can use a georeferenced raster map of the territory, which is a useful support for the correct identification of the text location. The texts are classified using the *MapGeoLing 1.0.0,* structured in a PALM version, for an initial textual analysis on the ground, and in a PC version for PC for later, more thorough analysis. The data required for initial classification are linked with the texts observed (and their geographical position) and acquired in shapefile format before being uploaded using personalised check-in/check-out procedures (developed with ArcObjects) to a Personal GeoDataBase which serves as the main data repository. The entire program was created in collaboration with Dr. Paolo Chiricozzi of *Etruria Telematica.*

References

Bagna, C. and M. Barni
    2005a   Dai dati statistici ai dati geolinguistici. Per una mappatura del nuovo plurilinguismo. *SILTA* XXXIV (2): 329–355.
    2005b   Spazi e lingue condivise. Il contatto fra l'italiano e le lingue degli immigrati: percezioni, dichiarazioni d'uso e usi reali. Il caso di Monterotondo e Mentana. In: C. Guardiano, E. Calaresu, C. Robustelli and A. Carli (eds.), *Lingue, Istituzioni, Territori,* 223–251. Roma: Bulzoni.

Bagna, C., M. Barni and R. Siebetcheu
    2004   *Toscane favelle. Lingue Immigrate nella Provincia di Siena.* Perugia: Guerra.

Bagna, C., M. Barni and M. Vedovelli
    2007   Lingue immigrante in contatto con lo spazio linguistico italiano: il caso di Roma. *SILTA* XXXVI (2): 333–364.

Bagna, C., S. Machetti and M. Vedovelli
    2003   Italiano e lingue immigrate: verso un plurilinguismo consapevole o verso varietà di contatto? In: A. Valentini, P. Mulinelli, P. Cuzzolin and G. Bernini (eds.), *Ecologia Linguistica,* 201–222. Roma: Bulzoni.

Bagna, C. and A. Pallassini
    2006   Nativi e non-nativi a confronto: tra percezione dell'italiano e mediazione linguistico-culturale. In: E. Banfi, L. Gavioli, M. Vedovelli and C. Guardiano (eds.), *I Problemi e i Fenomeni di Mediazione Linguistica e Interculturale,* 197–219. Perugia: Guerra.

Baker, P. and J. Eversley
   2000   *Multilingual Capital. The Languages of London's Schoolchildren and their Relevance to Economic, Social and Educational Policies*. London: Battlebridge Publications.

Barker, V. and H. Giles
   2002   Who supports the English-only movement?: Evidence for misconceptions about Latino group vitality. *Journal of Multilingual and Multicultural Development* 23 (2): 353–370.

Ben-Rafael, E., E. Shohamy, M. Hasan Amara and N. Trumper-Hecht
   2004   *Linguistic Landscape and Multiculturalism: A Jewish-Arab Comparative Study*. Tel Aviv: Tami Steinmetz Center for Peace Research Tel Aviv University.

Calvet, L.-J.
   2002   *Le Marché aux Langues*. Paris: Plon.

Caritas
   2007   *Immigrazione. Dossier Statistico 2007*. Roma: Idos.

Comune di Roma
   2005   *I Numeri di Roma*. Roma: Ufficio Statistico del Comune di Roma.

De Mauro, T.
   1963   *Storia Linguistica dell'Italia Unita*. Roma/Bari: Laterza.

De Mauro, T., F. Mancini, M. Vedovelli and M. Voghera
   1993   *Lessico di Frequenza dell'Italiano Parlato*. Milano: Etaslibri – IBM.

De Mauro, T. (ed.)
   1994   *Come Parlano gli Italiani*. Firenze: La Nuova Italia.

Extra, G. and K. Yağmur (eds.)
   2004   *Urban Multilingualism in Europe. Immigrant Minority Languages at Home and School*. Clevedon: Multilingual Matters.

Giacalone Ramat, A. (ed.)
   2003   *Verso l'Italiano*. Roma: Carocci.

Giles, H. (ed.)
   1977   *Language, Ethnicity and Intergroup Relations*. London: Academic Press.

Grimes, B. (ed.)
   2000   *Ethnologue: Languages of the World*. Dallas: SIL International.

Katzner, K.
   2002   *The Languages of the World*. London/New York: Routledge.

Landry, R. and R.Y. Bourhis
    1997   Linguistic landscape and ethnolinguistic vitality: an empirical study. *Journal of Language and Social Psychology* 16 (1): 24–49.
Maurais, J.
    2003   Towards a new linguistic world order. In: J. Maurais and M.A. Morris (eds.), *Languages in a Globalising World,* 13–36. Cambridge: Cambridge University Press.

Section IV
Mapping linguistic diversity abroad

Mapping linguistic diversity in an emigration and immigration context: Case studies on Turkey and Austria

Katharina Brizić and Kutlay Yağmur

1. Introduction

In this chapter, we will present the issues and challenges involved in mapping linguistic diversity in Turkey and its resulting effects in a particular European immigration context, i.e., Austria. Documenting linguistic diversity in Turkey is difficult because of the limited availability of academic resources and the non-availability of up-to-date information on language groups. Even though Turkey has taken steps to change its language policy to comply with European Union (henceforward EU) conditions, there is still a lack of academic research on minority issues. First, demographic data on Turkey are presented. Various aspects of linguistic diversity and educational practice are examined in line with the most recent developments. Moving away from the emigration context, the European immigration context is presented, with special consideration of the Austrian situation in an explorative qualitative study. Some theoretical and methodological challenges of language mapping in migration research are unveiled by pointing out the specificity of the Turkish context.

2. Demolinguistic characteristics of Turkey

Most Western European countries have large numbers of immigrants coming from Turkey, because of which Turkey is known to be an emigration country. However, Turkey is also a historical immigration country, the details of which will be presented in section 2.1, followed by the scope of language diversity in Turkey in section 2.2.

2.1.   The emigration context

Being at the crossroads of Europe and Asia, historically, Turkey has been a country of constant emigration and immigration. Starting from the early 1960s and well into the 1970s, large numbers of Turkish citizens migrated to Western European countries, particularly to Germany. This emigration continued into recent times through family reunification schemes and the asylum track. What most people do not know is that Turkey has long been a country of immigration and asylum itself. From 1923 to 1997, more than 1.6 million people immigrated to Turkey, mostly from Balkan countries. More recently, Turkey has also experienced a mass influx of almost half a million Kurdish refugees from Iraq in 1988, and 1991. There were also large-scale influxes of Albanians, Bosnians, Pomaks, and Turks from the Balkans in 1989, 1992–1995, and 1999. Historically, the Turkish Ottoman Empire has been known to be a multilingual and multinational society. Cultural and linguistic diversity is a well-known phenomenon for Turkish people. Arabs, Armenians, Greeks, Jewish people and others all lived for the last thousand years together on Turkish territory. The Ottoman Empire was also well known for its pluralistic policies towards minorities. They always provided shelter for people who fled persecution, e.g., 100,000 Sephardim Jews fleeing the Spanish Inquisition in 1492. The Russian defeat of the Circassians in 1864 led to an estimated one million refugees fleeing to the Ottoman Empire. Turkey has also become a country of asylum. Around 110,000 Jews from German-occupied Europe made Turkey their country of first asylum (Kirisci 2003); most of them were resettled in Palestine and later in Israel. Recently, Turkey has also become known as a country of transit to EU nation-states for irregular migrants from Asian countries such as Afghanistan, Bangladesh, Iraq, Iran, and Pakistan (Kirisci 2003). Due to future European immigration prospects, irregular immigrants from neighbouring countries such as Armenia, Azerbeijan, Georgia, Iran, Moldova, Ukraine, Russia and the Central Asian republics come in large numbers to Turkey; figures ranging from 150 thousand to one million are cited in different sources. Because there is no systematic registration, exact figures are unknown. Moreover, a different form of migration from EU nation-states to Turkey is on the rise. Around 120 thousand EU citizens took up residence in Turkey so far. Given past and recent patterns of immigration, as well as indigenous minorities on Turkish territory, Turkey is linguistically a diverse society. However, this diversity is not visible in national statistics. Officially, Turkish is the only national language that can be used in education, with the exception of some European modern foreign languages.

2.2. Statistical data

For a thorough understanding of Turkish language policy and the current socio-linguistic situation in Turkey, we refer to Yağmur (2001) and Lewis (1999). In today's Turkey, there are many different groups who speak a language other than Turkish. The numbers come basically from three main different sources (Andrews 1989; Dündar 1999; Grimes 1996). Andrews (1989) shows that not only religious conviction but also religious denomination is crucial in understanding the complex Turkish setting. When we closely examine language maintenance and marriage patterns of persons from different language groups, intergroup marriages are quite common provided that both persons belong to the same religious denomination. An ethnic Sunni-Kurd can marry a Sunni-Turk, but a Sunni-Kurd cannot easily marry an Alevi-Kurd because of strict religious sanctions (like the religious restrictions imposed on the marriages between Protestants and Catholics in the past). In other words, not ethnicity but religious denomination of the person to be married is the most decisive factor. Tribal organisation is another prevailing force that affects intergroup relations and in-group norms. *Turkomans* and *Yörüks* (both are nomadic Turks) in Anatolia are good examples. In some cases, language groups maintain their group identity because of a sense of exile or expulsion from their homeland. The immigrants from Crimea, Russian Altays, or the Circassians are good examples. As a matter of fact, various factors of language, religion (denomination), organisation, occupation, exile, and material culture (sometimes in isolation or in combination) make-up group characteristics and group identity. As pointed out by Andrews (1989), multiple ethnicity is an inherent characteristic of Turkey. The Ottomans were able to achieve unity in spite of this diversity through Islam and through semi-autonomous bodies of religious minorities, but the prevailing present-day Turkish policy aims at forming "one nation-one language" through the principle of *linguistic unitarianism*, as practiced in France (see also Caubet, this Volume).

The only available database on the speakers of various languages in Turkey is the national census. The history of censuses goes back to the Ottoman Empire in Turkey. The first two censuses were taken in the periods of 1326–1360 and 1360–1389 for the purpose of gathering information about the farming land and the population that worked on the land. Until the 19th century, censuses were carried out every thirty years with the purpose of identifying cultivated areas and the population associated with the land so that an estimation of revenues could be made. The first comprehensive census during the Ottoman period took place in 1844. In this census, all people, both male and female, were registered. In 1891, the first Central Statistics Bureau was established, and activities of this institution were defined by legislation. This system continued until the beginning of the Republican period.

In the Republican period, the first census was done in 1927 for the purpose of documenting the characteristics of all people residing in the country. This census is considered to be the first statistically reliable and comprehensive census in Turkish history. In this census, age, gender, marital status, education, languages spoken, religion, and occupation of the population were documented. The results were made public. The second census was carried out in 1935. Afterwards, a census has been taken every five years. Beginning with the 1927 census, there were questions on the first and second language spoken at home and on religious conviction. Until 1965, the findings on first and second language spoken at home and religion were published, but the findings on these data were not made public between 1965–1985. From the 1985 census on, questions on language and religion were completely excluded from the list of census questions.

On the basis of the information obtained in the 1965 census (cf. Dündar 1999), Andrews (1989) and Grimes (1996), the estimated number and distribution of language groups in Turkey are presented. Because the available data are inconsistent in different sources, figures from three different sources are presented here. In the 1965 census, 34 languages were reported to be spoken in Turkey. According to Grimes (1996), this number is 42. Details are presented in Table 1.

Some notes on Table 1: *Gagauz Turks* commonly practice Christianity. *Bulgarian Turks*: According to Mango (cited in Andrews 1989: 93), between 1923 and 1980, 488,000 Turks from Bulgaria either immigrated or were deported to Turkey. Balim (1996: 103) reports that around 300,000 Turks were expelled to Turkey in 1989. There are still 1.5 million ethnic Turks in Bulgaria. The number in Table 1 for *Bulgarian-Pomak* excludes ethnic Turks. For *Tatar*, the number given is an approximation for all Tatar speakers in all countries. The exact number of Tatar speakers in Turkey is unknown (Grimes 1996). *Zaza* is commonly confused with Kurmanji (Kurdish) but Zaza and Kurdish are not mutually comprehensible (Andrews 1989: 122).

2.3.   Patterns of language variation

2.3.1.   Turkic Languages

Grimes (1996) reports that Turkish is spoken by the largest group of people, estimated at about 90% of the total population. Turkish is the official language of Turkey. It is an agglutinative language and belongs to the Altaic group of Turkic languages. The Turkic group includes languages like Altay, Azerbaijani, Bashkurt, Kazakh, Kirghiz, Tatar, Turkmen, Uyghur, Uzbek, and Yakut. The ma-

Table 1. Distribution of languages and estimated number of speakers per language in the Republic of Turkey (*no information available).

Language	Dündar (1999) based on 1965 census	Andrews (1989)	Grimes (1996)
Abaza (Abazintsy)	12,399	*	10,000
Abkhaz (Abxazo)	*	*	35,000
Adyghe (Circassian / Cherkes)	106,960	1,100,000	1,000,000
Albanian, Tosk	53,520	53,520	65,000
Arabic (North Mesopotamian)	533,264	569,058	400,000
Armenian	55,354	69,526	70,000
Avar (Daghistan)	*	5,223	*
Gagauz Turkish	*	*	327,000
Balkar and Karaçay	*	3,917	*
Bulgarian (Pomak)	57,372	101,328	270,000
Chechen & Ingush	*	8,998	8,000
Crimean Tatar	*	*	300,000
Domari (Romani)	*	*	20,000
Estonian	*	300	*
Georgian	79,234	83,306	91,000
Greek (Christians)	127,037	10,000	4,000
Greek (Muslims)	*	4,535	*
Hebrew	13,491	25,000	*
Hemshinli	*	44,000	*
Hertevin	*	*	300
Kaldani (East Syrians / Asuri)	*	7,000	*
Kabardian	*	*	202,000
Karapapah	68,000	106,000	*
Kazak	*	5000	600
Kirghiz	*	1,137	1,137
Kumyk	*	1,703	*
Kurmanji (Northern Kurdic)	2,817,313	6,200,000	6,500,000
Ladino (Judaeo-Spanish)	*	7,226	20,000
Laz	81,165	115,000	92,000
Molokans (Russians)	*	1,600	*
Osetin (Ossete)	8,943	8,943	588,000
Polish	*	501	*
Romani (Kiptice / Gypsy)	4,656	10,633	40,000
Serbo-Croatian (Bosnian)	57,209		61,000
Sudanese	*	5,000	*
Syriac (Assyrians / Arameans)	*	40,000	*
Tatar	12,302	*	*
Turkish (Anatolian Turkish)	28,289,680	28,289,680	46,278,000
Turkmen	*	*	925
Turoyo	*	*	3,000
Uyghur	*	700	500
Uzbek	*	5,051	1981
Zaza	*	2,000,000	1,000,000

jority of Turks practice Sunni-Islam, and endogamy is very strong among them. As opposed to Sunni-Turks, most Alevi-Turks support the Turkish Republic's modernisation and westernisation principles.

Group identity of Turks is primarily based on language and nationality (Turkishness), and partly on religion. According to the official discourse, anyone who lives within the borders of Turkey is a Turk, irrespective of his or her ethnic, linguistic or religious background. In this reasoning, citizenship is taken to be the unifying factor between people of diverse linguistic and religious backgrounds. Even though other Turkic-speaking groups were categorised differently in the 1965 census, all Turkic speaking populations are generally treated as Turkish but their languages are not always mutually comprehensible. Most of these groups assimilated into the mainstream society much faster than other groups but they still speak their own language varieties (for details of their numbers, see Table 1).

2.3.2. Kurdic languages

Kurdic languages are spoken by a large group of people in Turkey. Kurmanji, Sorani, Gorani, Behdini, Herki, Kurdi, Shikaki, Surchi (and also various dialects such as Guwii, Hakkâri, Jezine, Urfi, Bâyazidi, Qochani, Birjandi, Alburz, Sanjâri, Judikâni) belong to the Kurdic language group (Grimes 1996). Zaza is mostly associated with Kurdish but it is a different language. The main Kurdic language spoken in Turkey is *Kurmanji*, which is a branch of the Iranic languages, with extensive Arabic and Turkish loans. Due to the long-standing language contact between Kurmanji and Turkish, there are many loan words in Kurmanji, which is why some Turkish scholars mistakenly claimed that Kurdish is originally a Turkic language. The total number of Kurmanji speakers in Turkey is highly controversial because of the political concerns of all parties involved. If we take Grimes (1996) as the most representative and well-documented source, the total number of Kurmanji speakers in Turkey is about 6,500,000. Because of Turkish-medium instruction in schools, Turkish is the dominant language among most Kurdish speakers but in rural areas and among less educated people, Kurdish is more dominant. One can also hear Kurdish spoken in major cities such as Istanbul, Ankara, and Izmir. Although Kurdish is not taught in schools, a number of cultural centres for the development of Kurdic languages and cultures have recently been established.

Just as in the case of Turkish speakers, religious denomination carries more weight than ethnicity for Kurdish speakers. Group identity is formed primarily by religion, then by language and tribal organisation (Andrews 1989). Especially among Alevi-Kurds, intergroup marriages with other Alevi-Turks and

Alevi-Zazas are more frequent than with Sunni-Kurds. Also for Kurdic people, endogamy is based on religious denomination and not on ethnicity.

2.3.3. *Zaza*

Like Kurmanji and Gorani, Zaza is also an Iranic language. Zaza and Kurdic languages are not mutually comprehensible (Andrews 1989). Different from Kurdic people, Zaza identity is effectively based firstly on language, and then on religion. There are two main groups of Zaza's based on religious denomination, i.e., Sunni and Alevi. The total population of Zaza speakers is estimated at 2 million. Zaza is mostly spoken in east and southeast Anatolia.

2.3.4. *Arabic*

Arabic speaking people belong to one of the largest language minority groups in Turkey. They mostly live in the southeast of Turkey, in the provinces of Mardin, Urfa, Siirt, Hatay, and Adana. There are smaller groups in the provinces of Muş, Bitlis, Diyarbakır, and Gaziantep. The prominence of the Arabic language differs from region to region. In Mardin and Hatay, local people speak Arabic dominantly but in towns like Siirt, Konya-Ereğli, Tarsus and Adana, it is replaced by Turkish.

2.3.5. *Immigrant languages from the Balkans*

After the First World War, a number of Islamic groups from Balkan countries were exchanged with Christian populations living on Turkish territory. Greeks, Bulgarian Pomaks, Bosnians, Croatians, Serbians, and Romanians are some of them. There are only rough estimations of their figures vary from source to source. According to Mango (1981) (cited in Andrews 1989), between 1923 and 1980, 488,000 Bulgarian immigrants settled in Turkey. Also 303,000 inhabitants of former Yugoslavia and 122,000 of Romania settled in Turkey in the given period. These groups have not always assimilated to the mainstream society and they are still identified as *muhacir* or *göçmen* (both meaning immigrants) by local people. In some rural areas, local people avoid contact with these "immigrants". Different physical characteristics of these groups also differentiate them from the majority. Nevertheless, being from the same religious background, intergroup marriages between these immigrant groups and local populations have been increasing, especially in the urban areas. Another major group from the Balkan are the Albanians. Most of them are fully Turkicised, and they speak mostly Turkish. Intergroup marriages between mainstream community members and Albanians are very common.

2.3.6.   Immigrant languages from the Caucasus

Like the immigrants from the Balkans, many language groups from the Caucasus were either expelled, fled away or immigrated to Turkey. Almost all language groups from the Caucasus share a common history of expulsion from their lawful lands to Turkey. All of these *Circassian, Chechen-Ingush, Daghistanis, Georgian*, and *Hemshin* groups are predominantly Islamic. Circassians are the largest among the Caucasian groups (1,150,000). Most of them are bilingual but in urban areas many of the younger generations are monolingual in Turkish. *Adighes* and *Abhazas* are the two major sub-groups of Circassians. As opposed to Circassians, Chechens and Ingush people do not have certain concentration areas. Present figures show around 10,000 Chechens and Ingush in Turkey but recent conflicts in Chechnya resulted in forced emigration of many Chechens to Turkey again. Apparently, Chechens and other Caucasian groups see Turkey as a safe-haven to escape oppression. *Avar, Lak,* and *Lezghian* sub-groups constitute the main Daghistani group. Like other Caucasian groups, their group identity is based on a common sense of exile from their homeland. Daghistanis are known for their strong language maintenance and material culture, but in recent times, as for all other language groups, this has been changing. Younger generations move to larger cities for better opportunities and education, and Turkish becomes the main vehicle of communication. After the Circassians, the *Georgians* are the largest Caucasian group. According to Grimes (1996), about 91,000 Muslim Georgians live in Turkey. As a result of the increase of out-group marriages, first language maintenance has been weakened amongst them. Georgian still seems to be widely used in the domestic domain, while Turkish is used in contacts with the outside world and for schooling. Nevertheless, younger generations are more assimilated to the mainstream community.

2.3.7.   Non-Muslim language groups

Apart from local populations of Armeniansand Greeks, there are other Christian groups who were either deported from their homeland or came at their own will to Turkey. There are small groups of *Estonians, Germans, Poles, Cossacks, Arameans,* and *Christian Arabs*. There are around 4,000 Greeks, mainly concentrated in Istanbul. Like the Greeks, the 20,000 *Ladinos* (Judea-Spanish) live mainly in Istanbul. Christian groups have their own schools and places of worship. The Greek Orthodox Church contributes to the strong linguistic and cultural maintenance of Greek people. In the same vein, the Armenian Apostolic Church promotes the linguistic and cultural development of Armenians. They have special schools, trusts for welfare, and opportunities to use and print the Armenian language. Like Jews and Greeks, Armenians enjoy the privilege of an officially recognised minority status. As opposed to Armenians outside Turkey, Turkish-Armenians are more inclined to peaceful co-existence with the Muslim majority in Turkey (Andrews 1989).

2.4. Language maintenance and shift

As documented in Yağmur (2001), Atatürk's principle of nationalism assumes that anyone who is a citizen of the Republic of Turkey is Turkish, which does not suggest any allusion to ethnic identity. Many people recognise and accept the ethnic and linguistic differences amongst them. Most of all, a sense of a common homeland and a common destiny unites all Armenians, Greeks, Kurds, Tatars, Turks and others, irrespective of their ethnic or religious backgrounds. Ethnic differences are more prevalent among rural populations but much less so among urban populations. With the strong effect of Turkish media and educational institutions, the rate of assimilation to Turkish among all groups in urban areas is very high, with the exception of some southeastern towns, where Kurdish (mainly Kurmanji), Zaza and Arabic are the languages of communication next to Turkish.

There are some factors that accelerate the pace of linguistic assimilation of various language groups to the mainstream society. The main agent of assimilation is education. The principle of nationalism aims at linguistic absorption of all people into Turkish. Local languages other than Turkish cannot be taught at regular schools. Only Armenian, Greek, and Hebrew are exceptions to this constitutional rule. Secondly, domestic migration from rural to urban areas speeds up the assimilation of younger generations of all language groups. The rate and speed of linguistic assimilation in urban areas among all groups is much stronger than in rural areas. Mass media are other strong agents of linguistic absorption. All information and news is transmitted in Turkish. There are more than 100 national television stations, both private and public, and also local TV stations, which only broadcast in Turkish. Apart from domestic migration, education, and media, military service is another agent of linguistic absorption. In remote parts of the country, especially in the mountainous east and northeast, not everyone receives adequate schooling. Those who could not learn Turkish in schools are destined to do so during their military service when they are 20 years old. Every male citizen of Turkey is required to do the military service, and if someone who joins the army is illiterate, he receives literacy training in Turkish. There have been special classes for this purpose, but because the rate of literacy has become much higher, these classes are not prevalent anymore. Finally, socio-economic upward mobility and job opportunities require a good command of Turkish. Families want a good education and good jobs for their children, and a good command of Turkish is essential to achieve that goal.

As a matter of fact, the number of speakers per language group, and the language use and choice patterns of these groups are not known. As long as there are no well-documented sociolinguistic and ethnographic investigations on language maintenance and shift patterns of language groups in Turkey, not much can be said about these patterns. Turkish policies concerning language groups are absorption-oriented. The "unitarian" or "melting pot" approach as practiced in some other countries is also the approach taken by Turkish policy makers. Like the concept and practice of laicism, the unitarian approach was also borrowed from France. Language policies, westernisation, de-Ottomanism, de-Islamitism, and all other concepts of shift from Islamic civilisation to western civilisation reflect the historical dilemma experienced by Turkish people. Atatürk not only embraced westernisation and modernisation of the nation-state against religious conservatism, but he also reformed all institutions in the country. In doing so, his models were Western European institutions. What he achieved in the early 1920s is a "revolution" for many foreign and Turkish historians. Turkish reforms should be evaluated considering the circumstances and options available in the period immediately after World War I.

Because Turkey wants to join the EU, the country has to make radical policy changes. EU-Turkey relations have been very influential in recent policy changes implemented in Turkey. The European Parliament suggested to Turkey that the nation should "ensure cultural diversity and guarantee cultural rights for all citizens irrespective of their origin". Accordingly, any legal provision preventing these rights is to be abolished, including in education (Eraydin Virtianen 2003: 34). In return, in the National Parliament of Turkey, it was declared that Turkey would accede to all relevant international conventions and take the necessary measures to be on the same level with EU nation-states concerning democratic human rights. In the section on "Cultural life and Individual Freedoms" of the Constitution amendments (Eraydin Virtianen 2003: 34), it was stated that "the official language and the formal education language of Turkey is Turkish. This, however, does not prohibit the free usage of different languages, dialects and tongues by Turkish citizens in their daily lives. This freedom may not be abused for the purposes of separatism and division". On the basis of this declaration, private schools offering instruction in Kurmanji have been set up mostly in southeast Anatolia. Yet, Article 42 of the Turkish Constitution remains intact, which says: "No language other than Turkish shall be taught as a mother tongue to Turkish citizens at any institutions of training or education. Foreign languages to be taught in institutions of training and education and the rules to be followed by schools conducting training and education in a foreign language shall be determined by law. The provisions of international treaties are reserved".

On the whole, Turkey takes concrete steps to liberalise its language policy but the strong roots of the nation-state ideology and the Turkish Constitution do not allow for minority language instruction in mainstream schools. Nevertheless, the potential EU membership idea has led to many positive developments with respect to the use of minority languages.

3.   A case study on Austria

The rich diversity observed in the Turkish emigration context is partly reflected in the immigration context as well. In the chapter of Extra and Yağmur, this Volume, findings on the Turkish group represent the linguistic diversity among Turkish immigrant children in Western Europe. In this section, a different approach to mapping linguistic diversity in the immigration context is presented.

3.1.   Challenging questions

Official census figures regarding the Austrian population with an immigrant background are highly incomplete. This is particularly true for the second and third generation, as descendants of immigrants are only identified when still holding a foreign citizenship or having been naturalised after birth. Persons being descendants of immigrants but born as Austrian citizens, however, cannot be identified on the basis of official figures, since no statistical information is available connecting these persons to their parents' immigrant background (Herzog-Punzenberger 2003: 1126). Concerning the Turkish community in Austria, one has to rely on estimated figures that mount up to about 200,000 persons (i.e., roughly 2.5% of Austria's resident population). Persons with a Turkish immigrant background can be said to represent the country's second-largest immigrant group, after immigrants from the successor states of the former Yugoslavia (Herzog-Punzenberger 2003: 1127).

We are not only confronted with inconsistencies with respect to the Turkish group's size but also to its linguistic composition. According to ethnographic data, about 40 minority languages in addition to Turkish have to be expected in this group, the largest one being Kurdish. Even though there are no actual statistical figures available in Austria, Six-Hohenbalken (2001) claims that up to 30% of the Turkish immigrants in Austria speak Kurdish. The *Wiener Schulma-trik* (Viennese Pupils' Evidence) (Knapp 2006), based on routine inquiries by the schools as part of the enrolment process, reflects only very few of Turkey's minority languages. In this database Kurdish is reported to be spoken only by around 2% of the Viennese primary school children with Turkish backgrounds. This discrepancy between ethnographic and official figures in Austria concerns not only official sources, but also linguistic, educational and sociological migration research, where data collection, tests and analyses are often based on the assumption of exclusively Turkish-speaking immigrants, not at all considering the existence of smaller and/or stigmatised languages (e.g., Weiss et al. 2006).

Not only documenting but also explaining language-related issues is difficult for the Turkish case in Austria, given the low school success and incomplete language acquisition among Turkish pupils (Herzog-Punzenberger 2003; Esser 2006). The only Austrian longitudinal study on immigrant primary school children's language acquisition (Vienna 1999–2003, Peltzer-Karpf et al. 2006) confirmed this *status quo*: from the very first to the last year of primary schooling the Turkish group showed a remarkably weak proficiency in the tested school language (i.e., German) as well as, even more surprisingly, in the tested family language (i.e., Turkish). So far, educational migration research has not contributed any satisfactory explanations for this well-documented phenomenon (Esser 2006).

Many questions emerge from the difficulties in documenting and explaining the Turkish group's specific language background and profile. The present study's sample (Brizić 2007) consisted of those 60 second-generation primary school children aged 9–10 with former-Yugoslavian (N = 37) and Turkish (N = 23) background who had already been participants in the Peltzer-Karpf study.

3.2.   Goals and methods of the study

It was decided to focus on two methodological considerations. With a small sample of 60 children, it was feasible to aim at high data quality; and in consideration of the sociolinguistic and educational topic, it was a central task to build on interdisciplinarity.

To start with the methodological challenge of documenting language diversity, and thus with data quality: to obtain as reliable information on language use as possible, data were intended to be collected by means of in-depth interviews with at least one of each of our 60 childrens' parents. The interviewers should stimulate the parents to openly talk about their language use at home by creating a familiar and open sphere, taking into account the probable existence of multilingual settings, smaller and/or stigmatised languages, and patterns of language shift. However, the interviews themselves could only be prepared and conducted in a rather "monolingual" way, i.e., in Turkish (or Bosnian/Croatian/Serbian, respectively), due to the fact that the country of origin's majority language had been the only language mentioned by the parents in the official school enrolment inquiry. The parents' apparently majority-language oriented behaviour at the official inquiry in fact confirmed our assumption that the resulting *Wiener Schulmatrik*'s could be expected to represent only a very rough, maybe even distorting glance at linguistic reality.

The second challenge, i.e., the weak performance question, leads us further to the demand for interdisciplinarity, as sociology and linguistics both agree on this weak performance but tend towards contradictory explanations for this phenomenon. The question of how these contradictions may be linked to different data collection approaches to language mapping has been of greatest interest for the study. However, not only different methods, but also heterogeneous theoretical approaches can in fact be assumed to provide an explanation for the communication gap between the macrocosm of large-scale quantitative surveys and the microcosm of small-scale linguistic studies. A broad consensus has been reached in most areas of migration research that children's individual abilities can by no means be regarded as responsible for collective failure, in the same way as individual parental attitudes and career aspirations (Kronig 2003: 126). For the *Language Capital Model* (LCM) developed within the present study, both macro- and micro-level considerations have been taken into consideration in terms of the linguistic capital acquired by the parents in the countries of origin (following Bourdieu 1983) and in terms of the inter-generational capital transmission to the children (following Nauck, Diefenbach, and Petri 1998: 720).

Whereas sociology contributes to our central theme by special consideration of the macro-level, it shows a certain lack of differentiation: all country-of-origin-related as well as all language-related macro-factors (like language planning) are still largely missing in recent models (e.g., in Esser 2006). An approach able to complete sociology in this respect is research on language shift or, more precisely, Sasse's (1992: 19) Gaelic-Arvanitika Model, which the LCM is therefore strongly geared towards. For sociolinguistics, with its general lack of models, this means a considerable enrichment too, as well as for mapping sociolinguistic reality in general – as in our case language shift had to be strongly assumed to constitute at least partly our Turkish sample's linguistic reality. However, research on language shift in turn also needs amendment because of its almost exclusive focusing on proficiency in the shifting "old" language – which brings us back again to psycholinguistics, which is in fact the only discipline exhaustively investigating pupils' concrete command not only in the shifting, but also in the dominant, newly acquired (school and/or family) language.

3.3.   Outcomes

The extensive and time-consuming interviews with the children's parents made all the difference: with every new angle the sample's "linguistic face" changed.

What had been a homogeneous group with a Turkish family language according to the school enrolment inquiry (*Wiener Schulmatrik*) turned in the interviews out to be in fact a group using Turkish, Kurdish and/or Greek. The minority proportion (Kurdish, Greek) had thus increased from zero to at least 13% and at most 39% in the Turkish sample. Furthermore, what had been defined as a group with "L1 use" (Turkish) turned out to be actually a group with extensive language shift (from Kurdish or Greek to Turkish; from Turkish or Kurdish to German). Moreover, some of the investigated families were in fact plurilingual (e.g., Kurdish-Turkish-German) and would never have taken a self-definition of Turkish only if this had not been requested at school enrolment.

In the course of the interviews, specific differences with respect to parental "answering behaviour" emerged between our two groups of origin: the Turkish and the Yugoslavian one. Whereas the Yugoslavian sample's parents enjoyed talking offensively about their languages, dialects and varieties, the Turkish parents tended towards a sort of "hedging" both in regard to their dialectal Turkish (attaching much more importance to German) and especially in regard to minority languages which they seemed to consider as an almost untouchable topic. Actually, the specific categorisation of "unknown linguistic background" had to be implemented for those cases where parental answers to the family language question just represented a general and official language-oriented statement rather than providing any exact information. The "unknown" category was thus established to strictly avoid any overhasty, eventually false classification and is also the reason for the relatively wide margin (13–39%) between definite and possible/probable minority language backgrounds in the Turkish sample.

The highly origin-specific parental response behaviour leads us further to an interdisciplinary approach, as such behaviour can hardly be understood without considering the language policies of the countries of origin and the resulting macro-variables (like affiliation to a majority/minority, higher/lower average educational level, (non-)mother-tongue instruction at school, mother tongue as (un)official language, and higher/lower prestige of the minority/majority language in the country of origin). The linguistic conditions in Turkey differ greatly from those in former Yugoslavia (Bugarski 1999). In the latter case, some population groups suffered from strong educational discrimination (e.g., Albanians), but at the same time enjoyed far-reaching linguistic rights (e.g., a whole minority language school system, cf. Bachmaier 1982: 40–42), resulting in a relatively strong minority language vitality. Turkey, in contrast, can be characterised as aiming explicitly at educational integration of all population groups, including linguistic unification, affecting most of the minority languages and leading to their exclusion from the educational system.

These macro-conditions' impact on parental linguistic capital as well as transmission behaviour turned out to be highly significant: the better the conditions for parental language acquisition in the country of origin were (i.e., a low threshold between family language and language of instruction), the higher their proficiency in the family and school language(s), and the less their tendency towards language shift. As hypothesised, this leads to a higher language shift proportion in the Turkish sample (35% partial, 17.4% total shift, e.g., from Kurdish to Turkish [not including the "unknown" group] or from Turkish to German) than in the Yugoslavian sample.

As further hypothesised, the macro-level's significant dominance was mirrored at the micro-level as well: the better macro-conditions were in parental language acquisition, the higher children scored in the tested family language *and* in German. This result becomes transparent via the parental meso-level: those children whose families have not shifted to whatever new and dominant language but have maintained the parental (minority or majority) language(s) score particularly well, both in the tested family language as well as in dominant German. Language shift turned out to represent a heavy capital loss, occurring predominantly under stigmatising macro-conditions and inhibiting the next generation's proficiency not only in the family language(s) but also in the tested school language.

3.4. Discussion

It has been clearly shown that focusing on data quality makes all the difference. Without extensive and time-consuming interviews, most of the Turkish sample's smaller or stigmatised languages as well as the many other facets of multilingual language use, from multiple linguistic affiliations to language shift, would have remained largely undetected. The question remains whether data quality would increase when interviews with Turkish parents were conducted not only in the majority language, but also in the respective minority languages or even in several varieties of both. However, it will be difficult to find practicable new solutions for two reasons. Firstly, it is in the nature of stigmatised affiliations that people tend to hide them; researchers therefore hardly ever know before the interviews which languages are actually spoken in a sample. Secondly, in samples comparable to ours we have to expect a highly complex context: considering only our sample's Turkish section, about 40 larger and smaller minority languages (comprising highly different varieties) have to be kept in mind, in addition to a rather complex majority language situation. Obviously, people equipped for any conceivable challenge in such a complex context are few in number, if they exist at all. Eventually, a collaborative system could be taken into consideration with a main interviewer forwarding the interviewed persons, if necessary, to a further interviewer proficient in the ascertained minority language(s) or varieties. In any case, such a forwarding system would disturb the familiar atmosphere in the main interview. Any interviewer has to be highly sensitive and aware of the multiple preconditions, experiences, variants and facets of language use, allowing languages to emerge during an interview as well as looking out for the possibility that languages – and particularly language shift – sometimes simply remain hidden, subconscious or even unknown.

The many facets of a complex context like the Turkish one clearly show that any request for the probands' "first language" is highly questionable (cf. the example of the *Wiener Schulmatrik*), as such a question can be assumed to be unanswerable for a great deal of immigrant families. This has led and will probably continue to lead to the fact that the phenomenon of language shift can be assumed to be completely under-estimated. This seems to be the case in many linguistic and non-linguistic fields of research, in regard to dimensions as well as consequences of language shift, and it can be assumed to concern the country of origin just as much as the country of immigration. Many further questions are bound to the handling of this fact, for example the current European debate whether immigrant family language maintenance is a "luxury" or not. Esser's (2006) quantitative sociologically oriented meta-study arrives at the conclusion that maintaining immigrant family languages is not necessarily conducive to the children's educational success – as especially those pupils who mainly speak the parental language at home, i.e., pupils without shift to the dominant language show a particularly weak proficiency in the dominant school language (Bacher 2005). The very few qualitative linguistically oriented studies which have explicitly focused on proficiency in a newly acquired "first language" after shift regularly arrive at the contrary result, thus coinciding with the present study's outcomes: a particularly weak proficiency in the dominant language is found especially together with shift to this language due to, e.g., a lack of adequate input in this "new L1" (Lasimbang, Miller, and Otigil 1992: 344; Wodak and Rindler-Schjerve 1985: 14–16). The future of immigrant family language teaching in European schools will strongly depend on how research will answer the above-mentioned methodological and theoretical challenges. How able are we to investigate the benefit of immigrant family language teaching when the actual family languages remain undetected in far too many studies? And how do we investigate the pros and cons of language maintenance or shift when language shift itself is hardly ever uncovered in educational research?

It seems that all these questions should particularly with regard to the Turkish context provoke: mistrust with respect to any official census figures (see also Andrews 1989: 53) as well as with respect to any results in educational research based on far too superficially ascertained language use patterns (as, e.g., in Esser's 2006 meta-study); an impulse for a broad improvement of data collection methods, wherever they are located on the quantitative-qualitative continuum; and a substantial opening up for interdisciplinary research.

4. Conclusions

Concerning language mapping in the contexts of Turkey and Austria, we have presented two different approaches. In the context of Turkey, we have focused on the availability and challenges of large-scale (census) data on home language use. In the context of Austria, we have focussed on small-scale data on home language repertoires, derived from in-depth parental interviews. Both types of approaches could lead to complementary information on language repertoires. In quantitative large-scale surveys, at least multiple questions on home language use should be incorporated, including questions on multiple home language repertoires. In the qualitative language mapping method, much more detailed information can be obtained on individual families; yet, the findings reported will always be based on a limited set of informants. The findings presented should above all draw the attention to the receiving society's language policies with respect to immigrant languages. Irrespective of the home language(s) spoken, many immigrant children fail in the educational system due to language-related problems. Offering instruction in home languages would considerably improve the status of these languages and would also promote children's acquisition of the mainstream language.

References

Andrews, P.
  1989   *Ethnic Groups in the Republic of Turkey.* Wiesbaden: Dr. Ludwig Reihart Verlag.

Bacher, J.
  2005   Bildungsungleichheit und Bildungsbenachteiligung im weiterführenden Schulsystem Österreichs. Eine Sekundäranalyse der PISA 2000-Erhebung. *SWS-Rundschau* 45 (1): 37–62.

Bachmaier, P.
  1982   *Aspekte der Bildungs- und Wissenschaftspolitik Jugoslawiens 1944–1979.* Wien: Österreichisches Ost- und Südosteuropainstitut.

Balım, Ç.
1996   Turkish as a symbol of survival and identity in Bulgaria and Turkey. In:
        Y. Suleiman (ed.), *Language and Identity in the Middle East and North
        Africa*. Surrey: Curzon Press.

Bourdieu, P.
1983   Ökonomisches Kapital, kulturelles Kapital, soziales Kapital. In: R. Kre-
        ckel (ed.), *Soziale Ungleichheiten*, 183–198. Göttingen: Schwartz.

Brizić, K.
2006   The secret life of languages. Origin-specific differences in L1/L2 acquisi-
        tion by immigrant children. *International Journal of Applied Linguistics*
        16 (3): 339–362.
2007   *Das geheime Leben der Sprachen. Gesprochene und verschwiegene Spra-
        chen und ihr Einfluss auf den Spracherwerb in der Migration*. Interna-
        tionale Hochschulschriften 465. Münster/New York: Waxmann.

Bugarski, R.
1999   Language and state: the Yugoslav experience. *Wiener linguistische Gazette*
        66: 3–11.

Dündar, F.
1999   *Türkiye Nüfus Sayımlarında Azınlıklar*. (Minorities in Turkish Censuses).
        Ýstanbul: Doz Yayıncılık.

Eraydin Virtianen, O.
2003   *Recent Changes in Turkey's Language Legislation*. Working Papers, No.
        11, Barcelona: Ciemen-Mercator.

Esser, H.
2006   *Sprache und Integration. Die sozialen Bedingungen und Folgen des
        Spracherwerbs von Migranten*. Frankfurt/New York: Campus.

Grimes, B.F. (ed.)
1996   *Ethnologue: Languages of the World*. (Internet edition:
        http://www.sil.org/ethnologue/)

Herzog-Punzenberger, B.
2003   Ethnic segmentation in school and labour market? 40 years legacy of
        Austrian guestworker policy. In: M. Crul and H. Vermeulen (eds.), *The
        future of the second generation. The integration of migrant youth in six
        European countries* (International Migration Review 37: 4), 1120–1144.
        New York: Center for Migration Studies.

Kirisci, K.
2003   Turkey: A Transformation from Emigration to Immigration.
        http://www.migrationinformation.org/Feature/display.cfm?ID=176
        (viewed on 7/9/2006).

Knapp, A.
2006   *Wiener Schulpflichtmatrik, Stand Juni 2005.* Wien: Stadtschulrat für Wien.

Kronig, W.
2003   Das Konstrukt des leistungsschwachen Immigrantenkindes. *Zeitschrift für Erziehungswissenschaft* 6 (1): 126–141.

Lasimbang, R., C. Miller and F. Otigil
1992   Language competence and use among coastal Kadazan children. In: W. Fase, K. Jaspaert and S. Kroon (eds.), *Maintenance and Loss of Minority Languages*, 333–355. Amsterdam: Benjamins.

Lewis, G.
1999   *The Turkish Language Reform: A Catastrophic Success.* Oxford University Press.

Nauck, B., H. Diefenbach and K. Petri
1998   Intergenerationale Transmission von kulturellem Kapital unter Migrationsbedingungen. Zum Bildungserfolg von Kindern und Jugendlichen aus Migrantenfamilien in Deutschland. *Zeitschrift für Pädagogik* 44 (5): 701–722.

Peltzer-Karpf, A., V. Wurnig, B. Schwab, M. Griessler, R. Akkuþ, K. Lederwasch, D. Piwonka, T. Blažević and K. Brizić
2006   *A kući sprecham Deutsch. Sprachstandserhebung in multikulturellen Volksschulklassen: bilingualer Spracherwerb in der Migration.* Wien: Austrian Ministry of Education (BMBWK).

Sasse, H.-J.
1992   Theory of language death. In: M. Brenzinger (ed.), *Language Death. Factual and Theoretical Explorations with Special Reference to East Africa*, 7–30. Berlin/New York: Mouton de Gruyter.

Six-Hohenbalken, M.
2001   *Migrantenfamilien aus der Türkei in Österreich. Wohnen, Verortung und Heimat; mit einem Exkurs über die Wohnsituation im Aufnahmeland.* Wien: Österreichisches Institut für Familienforschung.

Weiss, H., P. Gapp, R. Strodl, A. Unterwurzacher, M. Wittmann-Roumi Rassouli
2006   *Leben in zwei Welten. Zur sozialen Integration ausländischer Jugendlicher der zweiten Generation. Eine empirische Untersuchung in Österreich.* Research report, Department of Sociology, University of Vienna.

Wodak, R. and R. Rindler-Schjerve
1985   *Funktionen der Mutter beim Sprachwechsel: Konsequenz für die Primärsozialisation und Identitätsentwicklung.* Wiesbaden: Vieweg.

Yağmur, K.
    2001   Languages in Turkey. In: G. Extra and D. Gorter (eds.), *The other languages of Europe. Demographic, Sociolinguistic and Educational Perspectives*, 407–426. Clevedon: Multilingual Matters.

The *Linguistic Atlas of South Africa:*
Mapping diversity in space and time

Izak J. van der Merwe and Johannes H. van der Merwe

1. Introduction: Language atlases as scientific genre

The "mapping" of languages is an established geographical research focus with its roots in the age of modernity when large-scale political and cultural changes affected Europe. Traditionally the emphases in this research domain have been on themes such as cartography and languages; on exploring the links between language and identity; and on the more practical questions of language planning (Desforges and Jones 2001). The *Linguistic Atlas of South Africa* focuses on the time-space dimension of South Africa's remarkable linguistic diversity. It casts the geography of language within the conceptual framework of Geolinguistics.

Apart from its symbolic value, the main function of language is to provide individuals of a particular population group with a mode of communication. Within a multi-ethnic society language is frequently the means through which particular groups seek to consolidate their social identity. In this process linguistic differences can also enrich the cultural fabric of society. On the other hand, language diversity may cause friction between different communities. An ethno-linguistic group is usually characterised by common descent and traditions, specific cultural traits and a strong awareness of common identity and togetherness. A host of geolinguistic concepts underpin the theoretical framework and the empirical content of the *Linguistic Atlas of South Africa* (2006), among which the role of language in space and place, spatial convergence and competition, regional expansion and dominance, segregation and assimilation, ethnicity, social ecology, language identity, social interaction, migration patterns, as well as the institutional environment within which languages function (Van der Merwe 1995).

Geolinguistic studies as conceptualised in Figure 1 may be undertaken at different resolutions (i.e., global, national, subregional and urban); may focus on various research attributes (i.e., language typology, its spatial patterns, the social and economic profile, and the institutional environment). The temporal

```
        ┌──── Geolinguistic research ────┐
        │         │         │            │
        ▼         ▼         ▼            ▼
     Global   National  Subregional    Urban   ◀------- Spatial resolution
        │         │         │            │
        │         ▼         ▼            │
        │    ┌──────────────────────────┐◀┘
        └───▶│ • Language typology       │◀┘
             │ • Location and            │
             │   distribution            │
             │ • Concentration and       │
             │   segregation             │◀------------------ Research focus
             │ • Speaker profile         │
             │ • Institutional           │
             │   environment             │
             └──────────────────────────┘
                 │         │         │
                 ▼         ▼         ▼
               Past     Present   Future
              pattern    status  projection   ◀------------ Temporal dimension
```

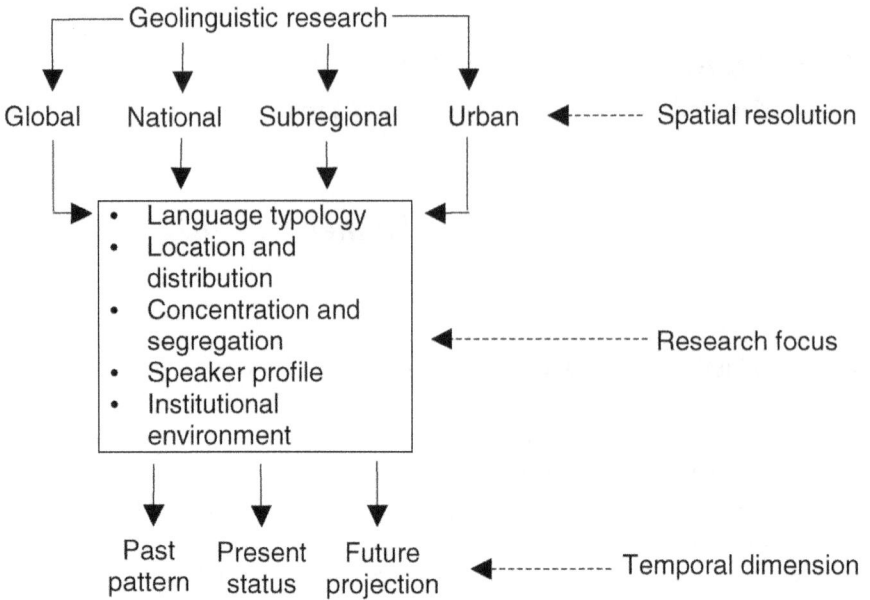

Figure 1. Geolinguistic framework for language mapping

dimension embraces the present static form of language attributes against its past and future dynamic change (Van der Merwe 1996; Williams and Van der Merwe 1996). Therefore, the *Linguistic Atlas of South Africa* (2006) mainly develops from two general geolinguistic concepts, i.e., the spatial outcome of language location and language change in a time-space context. As the main analytical research foci it portrays language (i) at the national (South Africa), regional (Western Cape province) and urban (Cape Town metropolis) spatial scales; (ii) in a temporal focus on the present condition as well as the evolving patterns from the past; and (iii) in its location, distribution and speaker profile.

Linguistic mapping and the compilation of language atlases are widely practiced internationally. Many countries have had atlases compiled at national or subregional levels, to record their spatial language patterns, for example Italy, Germany, the Netherlands, France, Switzerland, China, Japan, Brazil, Mexico, U.S.A., Canada, Nigeria and Kenya (Comrie et al. 1996). The UNESCO *Atlas of the World's Languages in Danger of Disappearing* (Wurm 1996) portrays graphically and lists languages worldwide endangered by eminent demise.

The first full scale linguistic atlas in South Africa was the *Language Atlas of South Africa* (LASA) prepared in the late 1980s (Grobler et al. 1990) by the Human Sciences Research Council's Institute for Research into Language and

Arts, and the Institute for Cartographic Analysis at Stellenbosch University. It utilised 1980 population census data and considered the role of language in education, regional development, officialisation of languages, commerce and communication as crucial performance areas for language mapping. This pioneering effort inevitably excluded the former apartheid-era "Bantustans" not incorporated in the earlier population censuses, which skewed the portrayal towards an Afrikaans and English focus (Braam et al. 2005). The subsequent *Language Atlas of South Africa* (Van der Merwe and Van Niekerk 1994), as a follow-up to the LASA project, used 1980 and 1991 population census information to compare and illustrate changes in the distribution of the eleven official languages of South Africa. The *Education Atlas of South Africa* (Krige 1994) and the *Socio-Economic Atlas of South Africa* (Tait 1996) were similarly aligned to the 1991 census data to provide ancillary maps on the distribution of the official languages by province and magisterial districts.

By the late 1990s the South African National Language Service of the Department of Arts and Culture was approached by UNESCO (2000) to participate in a survey for a world language report. The project covered all the official languages of South Africa as well as the Khoe, San and Nama languages. A wealth of information on a wide variety of aspects on the different language groups of South Africa was gathered, such as geographical location, linguistic varieties, the number of speakers of each language, migration impacts, economic activities of language communities, language attitudes, literary traditions and bodies responsible for language policy and planning.

Because geolinguistic information usually supports informed language planning and policy frameworks in multilingual societies, post-apartheid South African language planning needs similar research support for its crucial role in the national agenda for social transformation.

2. Language policy framework of South Africa

South Africa has been the meeting ground of speakers of languages belonging to several major linguistic families, viz the Khoesan, Bantu and Indo-European clusters (Mesthrie 2002). The Black languages, linked to the wider Eastern Bantu Group, are numerically predominant in the country, comprising essentially the following:

– Nguni cluster (iziZulu, IsiXhosa, isiNdebele, siSwati);
– Sotho cluster (Sepedi, Sesotho, Setswana); and
– Xitsonga and Tshivenda.

The *Indo-European* linguistic family in South Africa has members of the Germanic branch (i.e., English, Afrikaans, and German), the Indic branch (Hindi, Urdu, Gujarati and Konkani among others) and the Romance branch (chiefly Portuguese, spoken to varying degrees by immigrants from Angola, Mozambique and other parts of Africa but also Dutch, Italian and French to some extent). South Africa is also receiving a substantial number of refugees and immigrants from central and southern Africa. This has brought several new African languages into the country, as well as varieties of French and Portuguese. Other language families of note in South Africa include the Dravidian group (Tamil and Telugu) and the Polynesian languages (e.g., Malay, Malagasy). Chinese, Arabic, Hebrew and Greek languages are also present in limited numbers. The *Khoesan* linguistic family (called Hottentot/Khoe and Bushman/San) are now virtually on the verge of extinction (Mesthrie 2002).

Up to the 1990s, a functional profile of South African languages was hierarchical with English dominant in commerce, higher education and industry, while Afrikaans was dominant in civil service and government. African languages had been used mainly in local communities and as media of instruction in many schools. The country's constitution (Republic of South Africa 1996) specifically emphasises the link between language, culture and human development. South African language policy is based on the broad acceptance of principles such as linguistic diversity, social justice, the principle of equal access to public services, and respect for language rights. The policy defined in the constitution recognises eleven official languages with equal status. This is unique internationally and makes South Africa one of the most multilingual countries in the world. The language policy reflects the democratic nature of the national constitution that recognizes the right of people to express themselves in their own languages.

Article 6 of the constitution emphasises the *status of the languages* in the following stipulations:

(1) The official languages of the Republic are Sepedi, Sesotho, Setswana, siSwati, isiNdebele, isiXhosa, isiZulu, Tshivenda, Xitsonga, Afrikaans, and English.

(2) Recognising the historically diminished use and status of the indigenous languages of our people, the state must take practical and positive measures to elevate the status and advance the use of these languages.

(3) The national government and provincial governments may use any particular official languages for the purposes of government, taking into account usage, practicality, expense, regional circumstances and the balance of the needs and preferences of the population as a whole or in the province concerned, but the national government and each provincial government must use at least two

official languages. Municipalities must take into account the language usage and preferences of their residents.

(4) The national government and provincial governments, by legislative and other measures, must regulate and monitor their use of official languages. Without detracting from the provisions of subsection (2), all official languages must enjoy parity of esteem and must be treated equitably.

(5) A Pan South African Language Board established by national legislation must
    (i)   promote, and create conditions for the development and use of all official languages; the Khoi, Nama and San languages, and sign language;
    (ii) promote and ensure respect for all languages commonly used by communities in South Africa, including German, Greek, Gujarati, Hindi, Portuguese, Tamil, Telegu and Urdu; and Arabic, Hebrew, Sanskrit and other languages used for religious purposes in South Africa (Republic of South Africa 1996).

Article 29 of the constitution highlights the role of *language in education*:

Everyone has the right to receive education in the official language or languages of their choice in public education institutions where that education is reasonably practicable. In order to ensure the effective access to, and implementation of this right, the state must consider all reasonable educational alternatives, including single medium institutions, taking into account equity, practicability, and the need to redress the results of past racially discriminatory laws and practices. (Republic of South Africa 1996)

Articles 30 and 31 of the constitution emphasise the relation between *language and culture*:

Everyone has the right to use the language and to participate in the cultural life of their choice, but no one exercising these rights may do so in a manner inconsistent with any provision of the Bill of Rights.

Persons belonging to a cultural, religious or linguistic community may not be denied the right, with other members of that community to enjoy their culture, practice their religion and use their language; and to form, join and maintain cultural, religious and linguistic associations and other organs of civil society. These rights may not be exercised in a manner inconsistent with any provision of the Bill of Rights (Republic of South Africa 1996).

In line with the National Constitution's Article 6 (subsection 3) the *Constitution of the Western Cape* (Province of the Western Cape 1998) responded in its Article 5 as follows regarding the provincial language policy:

(1) For the purposes of provincial government the official languages Afrikaans, English and isiXhosa are to be used; and these languages enjoy equal status.

(2) The Western Cape government must through legislative and other measures, regulate and monitor its use of Afrikaans, English and isiXhosa.

(3) The Western Cape government must take practical and positive measures to elevate the status and advance the use of those indigenous languages of the people of the Western Cape whose status and use have been historically diminished.

Western Cape language patterns play a significant role in the *Linguistic Atlas of South Africa* (2006) under consideration. The key question for linguists and educators is to what extent the new constitutional flexibility towards language use can be affected in practice. Despite the praiseworthy language policy quoted above, the reigning language practice in South Africa is not congruent with it, as is apparent in most African countries (Du Plessis 2003). The former colonial languages (in particular English) are used for higher and specialised registers, and the mother tongue of speakers of Black African languages is used for the lower registers (e.g., in the family and in social circles). African languages are important markers of socio-cultural identity, while English functions as the higher register language and is therefore regarded as the language of upward mobility. A large section of the South African population also regards English as the language of empowerment, of progress, of transformation and of political correctness. As the second standard written language, Afrikaans is also available to the Afrikaans language community for use as a higher register language. For a language to really have status, it must have developed a higher register capacity. That the country has eleven official languages is regarded by some commentators as highly problematic and out of step with sociolinguistic realities.

Apart from the constitution, various policy instruments affecting language policy have been passed in South Africa, especially with regard to the establishment of a supporting infrastructure for languages. The Pan South African Language Board (PANSALB), which is instrumental for language development, the promotion of multilingualism and the protection of language rights, was constitutionally instituted in 1996. The Language Plan Task Group and the National Language Service have also been established to further strengthen the language infrastructure. Probably the most influential policy document since the 1996 constitution is the *National Language Policy Framework* (Department of Arts and Culture 2002). This framework creates measures for bringing about a more even distribution of the higher register in the official languages. The document contains actual plans for the implementation of the so-called rotation system, which should develop the use of the higher register in formerly disadvantaged official languages, and consequently raise their status.

It should be emphasised, however, that studies on the implementation of language policy in South Africa suggest that what is on paper does not necessarily happen in practice. Rather, one might experience it as a mismatch between South Africa's multilingual policies on the one hand, and language practices on the other. The language policy promotes additive multilingualism while language practices promote unilingualism towards English (Du Plessis 2003).

3. The Linguistic Atlas of South Africa

3.1. Objectives and use of the atlas

Various criteria could be used to measure and map diversity, e.g., nationality, race, religion, birth country, self-categorisation or home language. Home language is probably the most promising indicator for obtaining basic information on the increasingly multicultural composition of nation-states and societies. Mapping linguistic diversity offers valuable insights in the distribution and vitality of home languages across different population groups and thus raises the public and political awareness of multilingualism. Language is a significant marker of social structuring, cultural diversity and minority grouping. Apart from its symbolic value, the main function of language is to provide a mode of communication between individuals of a specific cultural or ethnic group. The spatial dimension of language is interwoven with political, economic, ethnic, religious and other social phenomena, as well as the natural environment and communication networks within which it functions.

The general aim of the set of maps in the *Linguistic Atlas of South Africa* is to provide a visual representation of the diverse geolinguistic realities in South Africa, the Western Cape province and the Cape Town metropolitan area, respectively. The specific choices of province and urban area represent mere case studies as examples of what could be replicated in other locations and situations. The regional concentrations and time-space changes of the eleven official languages are portrayed cartographically as a tool for language exploration to delimit possible service areas for institutional and commercial planning. In the process a dynamic image is created which may serve to inform and aid understanding of the role of language as a public utility in the strategic planning of language structures and associated infrastructure investment in a multilingual society. It further embraces the dissemination of geo-spatial realities of the complex South African language mosaic to planners, decision-makers, market analysts, researchers, as well as the local and foreign public interested in language issues. Education in South Africa, for example, is in dramatic and continuous flux, which necessitates scientific and adaptive strategic planning. The linguistic patterns in the atlas could, therefore, provide education authorities with spatial information for targeting service areas and community sectors in its efforts to comply with the requirements of the National and Provincial constitution, respectively. In this way the atlas could support decision-making on service delivery and market identification currently taking place at all levels of education. The broad aim of the atlas is to serve as a source of spatial linguistic information for national and international reference. The more specific objectives of the atlas, stemming from the conceptual framework in Figure 1, are to:

– clarify the *institutional and policy framework* underlying specific spatial and demographic language patterns;
– spatially identify *current language distributions and concentrations* at national (South Africa), subregional (Western Cape province), and metropolitan (Cape Town) scales to uncover regional patterns, language core areas and possible integration trends;
– spatially identify time-space dynamics of *change in language distribution* at the various resolution levels to show possible areas of language growth or decline;
– expose the *demographic profile* of language speakers at the different resolution levels, to indicate whether distinctive social markers and identities exist amongst the various language groups.

The spatial distribution patterns of the different language speakers of South Africa are portrayed cartographically to identify their regional proportional concentrations and time-space dynamic. In the process an image is created which may serve as a source of information to help understand and plan language communication in a multicultural South Africa. Amidst the linguistic diversity of South Africa, it is possible to demarcate spatially segmented patterns, which suggest underlying processes of social ecology, cultural interaction, ethnic segregation and assimilation. An understanding of the social space in which the people of South Africa live and work daily may stimulate social capital formation. In the context and spirit of the South African coat of arms and motto, the *Linguistic Atlas of South Africa* is an exhibition of societal "unity in diversity".

3.2.   Methodology and organisation of the atlas

Any map pattern should be assessed in the light of the context and nature of the data from which it has been created. Census data are not without limitations, yet it remains the most comprehensive official source of information relating to the population characteristics of a country. The maps in the *Linguistic Atlas of South Africa* (2006) are based on the 1991 and 2001 national population censuses. The extraction of data from the census records, obtained from *Statistics South Africa*, was based on the variable of first home language. In the relevant questionnaire the question is phrased: "Which language does the person speak most often in the household?" For the purposes of the atlas, language response was grouped to correspond with the eleven official languages according to the National Constitution, with the remainder labeled as "other languages". In this way the language data of 44.8 million people in 2001 (and 37.7 million in 1991) were linked to spatial units, utilising the ARCGIS Geographical Information System. The statistical, cartographic and query capabilities of this GIS platform facilitated intensive and versatile statistical and cartographic analyses. Unfortunately, the former "Bantustan" apartheid states were not represented in the computerised 1991 census databases. Therefore, the 6.7 million people residing there in 1991 could not be included in the detailed analyses. Since 1994 these regions have been reintroduced into the RSA records.

The 91 maps in the atlas were compiled according to strict cartographic and scientific procedures whereby the language characteristics of the South African population were analysed statistically, tabulated, portrayed visually and interpreted textually. In order to accommodate the language patterns at three regional levels, GIS technology was implemented at the most appropriate spatial unit level as defined by Statistics SA, i.e., 354 Magisterial Districts (for South Africa nationally), 30 Municipal Districts (for the Western Cape province), and 30 Main Place units (for the Cape Town metropolitan area). While magisterial and municipal district boundaries largely coincide, metropolitan main places have no such boundary consistencies. Statistical measures incorporate and reflect both absolute numbers and percentage ratios for each language group, as well as statistical tables, geographical centres of gravity, segregation indices and correlation coefficients. The language "names" used on the maps for the eleven official groups is the label given to them by the relevant native speakers themselves – the so-called autoglotonym (UNESCO 2000).

To introduce each regional level section, orientation maps facilitate the interpretation of the language maps that follow. The administrative maps identify and label the spatial mapping units in order to identify specific districts/wards, while the population and landscape maps add context to the language patterns. At each regional level introductory interpretation of the language composition provides further perspective on the quantitative prominence of the individual language groups. At all three regional levels the presentation order of the maps for each language group follows a similar thematic scheme:

(i)   National (South Africa)
   – *Language distribution* (2001) per "magisterial district" for each of the eleven national language groups, expressed as absolute number of speakers (circle symbols) and ratio (%) of total population in the magisterial district (shadings);
   – *Language change* (1991–2001) for each of the eleven languages expressed as absolute numbers as well as proportional (%) change;
   – *Preponderant language,* comparing the percentage share of each language per spatial unit to numerically determine the strongest group;
   – *Socio-demographic profiles* for each of the eleven official linguistic groups in the country.

(ii) Provincial (Western Cape)
   – *Language distribution* (2001) per "municipal district" for Afrikaans, English and isiXhosa-speakers expressed as absolute numbers (circle symbols) and ratio (%) of total population in the municipal district (shadings);
   – *Language change* (1991–2001) for each of the three languages expressed as absolute numbers and as proportional (%) change;
   – *Preponderant language,* comparing the percentage share of each language per spatial unit to numerically determine the strongest group;
   – *Socio-demographic profiles* for each of the three official language groups in the province.

(iii) Metropolitan (Cape Town)
   – *Language distribution* (2001) per urban "main place" (ward) for Afrikaans, English and isiXhosa-speakers expressed as absolute numbers (circle symbols) and ratio (%) of total population in the ward (shadings);
   – *Language change* (1991–2001) for each of the three language groups expressed as absolute numbers and as proportional (%) change;
   – *Preponderant language,* comparing the percentage share of each language per spatial unit to numerically determine the strongest group;
   – *Socio-demographic profiles* for each of the three official language groups in the metropole.

In the language distribution maps series, the total number of people who stated a particular language as their first home language (circle symbol) was also expressed as a percentage of the total population in that district/ward (shaded map). The values obtained in this way for each of the individual language groups were subsequently divided into five equal class intervals ranging from low to high. Five map shadings distinguish the degree of relative domination for each language on a comparative basis. The former Bantustan states, with census data absent for 1991, were left blank on the change maps. By utilising the centrographic procedure in the GIS, the geographical centre of gravity for each language group was calculated for 1991 and 2001 and displayed on the maps, indicating a general spatial redistributive trend for each group of language speakers at each regional level. Spatial patterns often reveal underlying cultural processes of language segregation or integration. The tendency among people with similar socio-cultural profiles to group together is measured statistically by means of a Segregation Index – the closer to 100 the value, the higher the level of grouping together separate from others (Shaw and Wheeler 1985).

The maps on preponderant language compare all the relevant languages simultaneously and serve to illustrate the linguistic diversity or homogeneity at the regional scale. The percentage share of each language total per spatial unit was compared to numerically determine the preponderant language in that district/ward in 2001. Comparison with similar 1991 values may reveal spatial units that have experienced a language shift (change in preponderant status) over the ten-year period. Brief interpretive text accompanies each map, providing helpful background information on the linguistic origin and historical traits of the specific language group, its salient distribution/concentration patterns, its demographic profile, as well as the relevant social segregation tendencies. However, in the final instance the effective utilisation of these maps rests in the hands of individual users and their specific needs.

In the following two sections the *Afrikaans* language will be utilised as a case study to illustrate the mapping recipe followed for all the other official languages at two of the three regional scale levels (national and metropolitan). This particular language presented itself as the choice of focus for several reasons:

– It is one of only two fully developed written languages in the country, with an active and proven functional record as medium in governance, science, business, academia, literature and civil society, and is one of three languages afforded official constitutional language status in the province of the Western Cape;
– It qualifies as an indigenous South African language that, while originating from European/Germanic (Dutch) root stock, was significantly shaped by the cosmopolitan influences of the South African cultural melting pot – a language truly of and for Africa;
– While being indisputably related to the Western European family of languages, it is also a language under threat from English hegemony similar to the current European experience and as such deserves nurturing attention

similar to the languages other than English in Europe – a case study par excellence.

4. National focus: South Africa

4.1. Language composition

One of the most striking characteristics of the South African population is its linguistic diversity. Table 1 depicts the national linguistic composition and change trends of the eleven official languages. Three language groups dominated the linguistic scene in 2001. Approximately 10.7 million people, constituting 24% of South Africa's total population, regarded isiZulu as their first home language. The almost 18% isiXhosa speakers comprised 7.9 million, while Afrikaans speakers totaled 6.0 million (13%). The other prominent languages are Sepedi, Setswana, English and Sesotho. The speakers of the nine Black African languages jointly constitute approximately three-quarters (78%) of the total population in the country. Oriental languages and European immigrant languages are used as a first home language by only a small fraction of the population. They were enumerated together in the census as "other". Except for Setswana, all the Black African languages demonstrated sharp proportional increases in their numbers between 1991 and 2001, Sesotho, Tshivenda and isiNdebele being the leaders.

Table 1. Language composition of South Africa

Language	1991		2001		Change 1991–2001	
	Number	%	Number	%	Number	%
isiZulu	8,343,590	22.1	10,677,306	23.8	2,333,716	28.0
isiXhosa	6,646,568	17.6	7,907,154	17.6	1,260,586	19.0
Afrikaans	5,702,535	15.1	5,983,426	13.3	280,891	4.9
Sepedi	3,530,616	9.4	4,208,982	9.4	678,366	19.2
Setswana	3,482,657	9.2	3,677,016	8.2	194,359	5.6
English	3,414,900	9.1	3,673,197	8.2	258,297	7.6
Sesotho	2,420,889	6.4	3,555,189	7.9	1,134,300	46.9
Xitsonga	1,439,809	3.8	1,992,207	4.4	552,398	38.4
siSwati	952,478	2.5	1,194,428	2.7	241,950	25.4
Tshivenda	673,540	1.8	1,021,759	2.3	348,219	51.7
isiNdebele	477,895	1.3	711,818	1.6	233,923	48.9
Other	630,927	1.7	217,297	0.5	− 413,630	− 65.6
Total	37,716,404	100.0	44,819,779	100.0	7,103,375	18.8

4.2.   Regional preponderant language

The maps on preponderant language compare the number of speakers from the eleven official languages simultaneously and illustrate linguistic diversity or homogeneity at a national scale (Maps 1a and 1b). The term "preponderant", being the language recording a numerical majority, should be interpreted very carefully. In this analysis it merely indicates a generalised relative and spatial concentration pattern. The percentage share of each language per spatial unit was calculated to determine the numerically strongest language in each magisterial district in 2001. Comparison with the similar values for 1991 reveals spatial language shifts (change in preponderant status) having occurred over the ten-year period. The distribution pattern reveals that each individual language numerically dominates a clearly identifiable core region in South Africa, while some share a secondary node of concentration with other contact languages. Districts where the 2001 preponderant home languages differ from their 1991 status demonstrate the process of language shift.

The links between language, culture and historical settlement patterns remain spatially paramount, since especially the African languages clearly reflect a legacy of historical settlement patterns and being the dominant home language in a particular region of the country. Afrikaans dominated in the largest area depicted on the distribution map, but its heartland in the west is largely barren and thinly populated in comparison to the northern and eastern parts of the country. On the other hand, English was the preponderant home language in very few small districts, but all these were densely populated metropolitan areas. Although increasingly represented in the first-world "apartheid cities", Black African languages tend to concentrate in single-language rural regions. The traditional territorial base of each African language coincides largely with a historical "homeland".

The Nguni languages (isiXhosa, isiZulu, siSwati, isiNdebele) occur as a contiguous zone in the naturally more favourably endowed regions of the east and along the coast, while the Sotho languages (Sesotho, Setswana, Sepedi) occupy a contiguous zone in the west and on the inland plateau. Tshivenda and Xitsonga are interspersed in the far north and in the east of the Limpopo province. Only the English language lacks a spatially concentrated core because of its urban orientation. Metropolitan areas display a unique cosmopolitan character with a diverse variety of languages sharing a common urban space. That these unique regional patterns of the eleven official languages show relatively minimal spatial correlation is confirmed by a Pearson Inter-Correlation analysis on the various language distributions. The highest correlation reached -0,33 (between

Preponderant Language Distribution (2001)

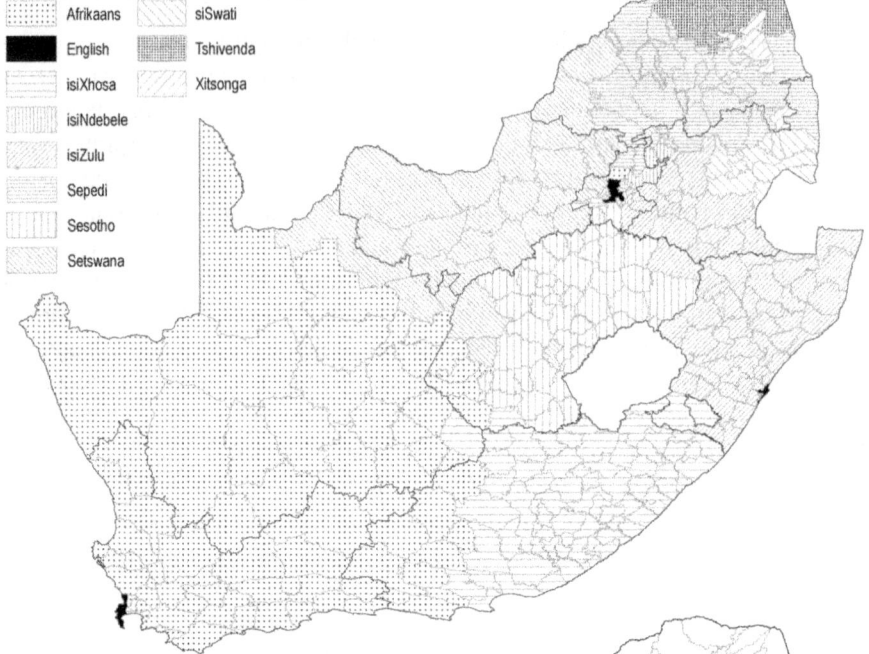

Afrikaans	siSwati
English	Tshivenda
isiXhosa	Xitsonga
isiNdebele	
isiZulu	
Sepedi	
Sesotho	
Setswana	

Preponderant Language Shift (1991 - 2001)

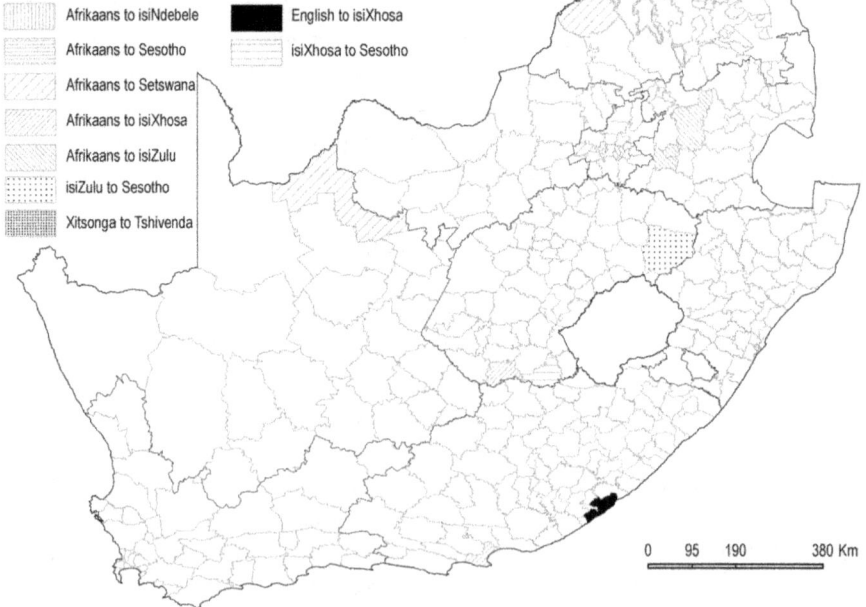

Afrikaans to isiNdebele	English to isiXhosa
Afrikaans to Sesotho	isiXhosa to Sesotho
Afrikaans to Setswana	
Afrikaans to isiXhosa	
Afrikaans to isiZulu	
isiZulu to Sesotho	
Xitsonga to Tshivenda	

0   95   190   380 Km

Maps 1a and 1b. Preponderant language in South Africa – Distribution and shift

isiZulu and Afrikaans), indicating virtually no resemblance or correspondence in general distribution pattern on a national scale.

Some provinces show considerable multilingual heterogeneity, while others appear more monolingual in character. North West (Setswana), Northern Cape (Afrikaans and Setswana), Eastern Cape (isiXhosa and Afrikaans), KwaZulu/ Natal (isiZulu and English) and Free State (Afrikaans and Sesotho) are dominated by one or two languages, while Limpopo (Sepedi, Xitsonga and Tshivenda), Mpumalanga (isiZulu, siSwati and isiNdebele), Western Cape (Afrikaans, English and isiXhosa) and Gauteng (isiZulu, Sepedi, Afrikaans, Setswana, English and Sesotho) are more diverse in their language composition. The latter profile illustrates the extent to which metropolinisation acts as a cultural "melting pot" regarding language speaker integration.

A mere 18 magisterial districts recorded preponderant language change between 1991 and 2001. Districts that experienced a shift in first home language are scattered throughout the country – thirteen of these representing Afrikaans losses to African languages: isiZulu (5), Setswana (3), isiXhosa (2), Sesotho (2) and Ndebele (1). From this general picture the study now zooms into the specific profile and national spatial patterns of the Afrikaans language group.

4.3.   Afrikaans patterns

The current status of the Afrikaans language is the result of an evolutionary process over three centuries in which it became a fully-fledged mode of communication. The linguistic origin of this Germanic language can be traced to 1652 when the Dutch dialect of Hollands was transplanted by colonists and subsequently gave birth to Afrikaans (Deumert 2004). Since the mid-1800s, people started using Afrikaans as a written language. Initially it had to compete for recognition, first against its "pure" Dutch parent, and later also against English during the British imperial rule of the 19th century and beyond. In 1925 it attained the status of second official language in South Africa, alongside English. Since 1996, it shares this status equally with ten other languages. Three population groups were primarily responsible for the birth of Afrikaans, i.e., the European settlers, the indigenous Khoe and the enslaved peoples of African and Asian provenance (Mesthrie 2002). Mingling of languages and assimilation inevitably took place within the multicultural society of South Africa. This holds for *Khoe*, Malay, Dutch, Portuguese, German, French and the powerful English language. During this process, the cultural heterogeneity and localised strengths of indigenous languages contained Afrikaans dominance to the south-western one third of South Africa (Van der Merwe 1989).

Speakers of Afrikaans as first home language totaled approximately 5,984,000 in 2001 (Table 2), comprising 13% of the total South African population. In absolute terms, most Afrikaans speakers live in the urban metropoles – Cape Town and Gauteng being the main centres, while Port Elizabeth, Bloemfontein and Kimberley are secondary foci (Maps 2a and 2b). A somewhat alternative pattern emerges when the relative concentration relates Afrikaans speakers to the total population of the respective districts. The Western Cape and Northern Cape provinces are conspicuous as a contiguous core area with most districts containing more than 80% Afrikaans speakers. In relative terms these rural areas rate highly as Afrikaans core areas, but not so in terms of absolute numbers. A large number of districts experienced a significant decrease in Afrikaans speakers (Maps 3a and 3b). These districts are scattered throughout South Africa, but the greatest impact was evident in the metropoles and eastern parts of the country. The Afrikaans centre of gravity is located close to the geographical centre of South Africa, reflecting a fairly even distribution of Afrikaans throughout the country. This evident spatial integration process is confirmed by a segregation index of 62,0 for this language group (the lowest value among the eleven official languages, indicating a relatively strong integration tendency). Related to this feature, the urbanisation level is quite high at 85% of Afrikaans speakers living in urban areas. The Afrikaans language profile (Table 2) in generalised terms characterises this linguistic group as mainly belonging to the Brown and White population groups, adhering to Christian religions, while this language group has an older age and a higher education profile than the South African norm.

5.   Metropolitan focus: Cape Town

The finest resolution for geolinguistic mapping is usually obtained at the individual city level. Cape Town is the oldest urban settlement in South Africa and holds the second position in the country's urban hierarchy, after Johannesburg. It represents the demographic, economic and socio-cultural core of the Western Cape province. The structural remnants of colonial and apartheid policies and post-apartheid restructuring processes, so prominent in South African cities, are also manifested in the geolinguistic patterns within the Cape Town urban space.

5.1.   Language composition

The Cape Town metropolitan language composition is recorded in Table 3. The city's language composition offers a classic close-up view of the regional concentration patterns manifested at the national scale. The eleven official languages are not equally represented in all the regions and cities of South Africa, and only

Table 2. Afrikaans language profile of South Africa

Variable	Afrikaans	South Africa	Variable	Afrikaans	South Africa
Segregation index	62,0	–	% Urbanised	85.4	56.8
Total Number (2001)	5,983,427	44,819,778	*Gender*		
			% Female	51.5	52.2
% of total	13.3	100.0	*Age*		
% Change (1991–2001)	4.93	18.8	Average (years)	30.4	26.8
Population Group			< 15 (%)	26.2	32.1
% Black African	4.2	79.0	15–60 (%)	64.1	60.6
% White	42.4	9.6	> 60 (%)	9.7	7.3
% Brown	53.4	11.4	*Education (≥ 25 years)*		
Religion			% No schooling	6.6	20.2
% Christian	90.6	79.8	% Grade 12	25.4	18.1
% Non-Christian	3.1	3.7	% Diploma/ Certificate	9.0	6.1
% No Affiliation	4.6	15.1	% Degree	6.5	3.3

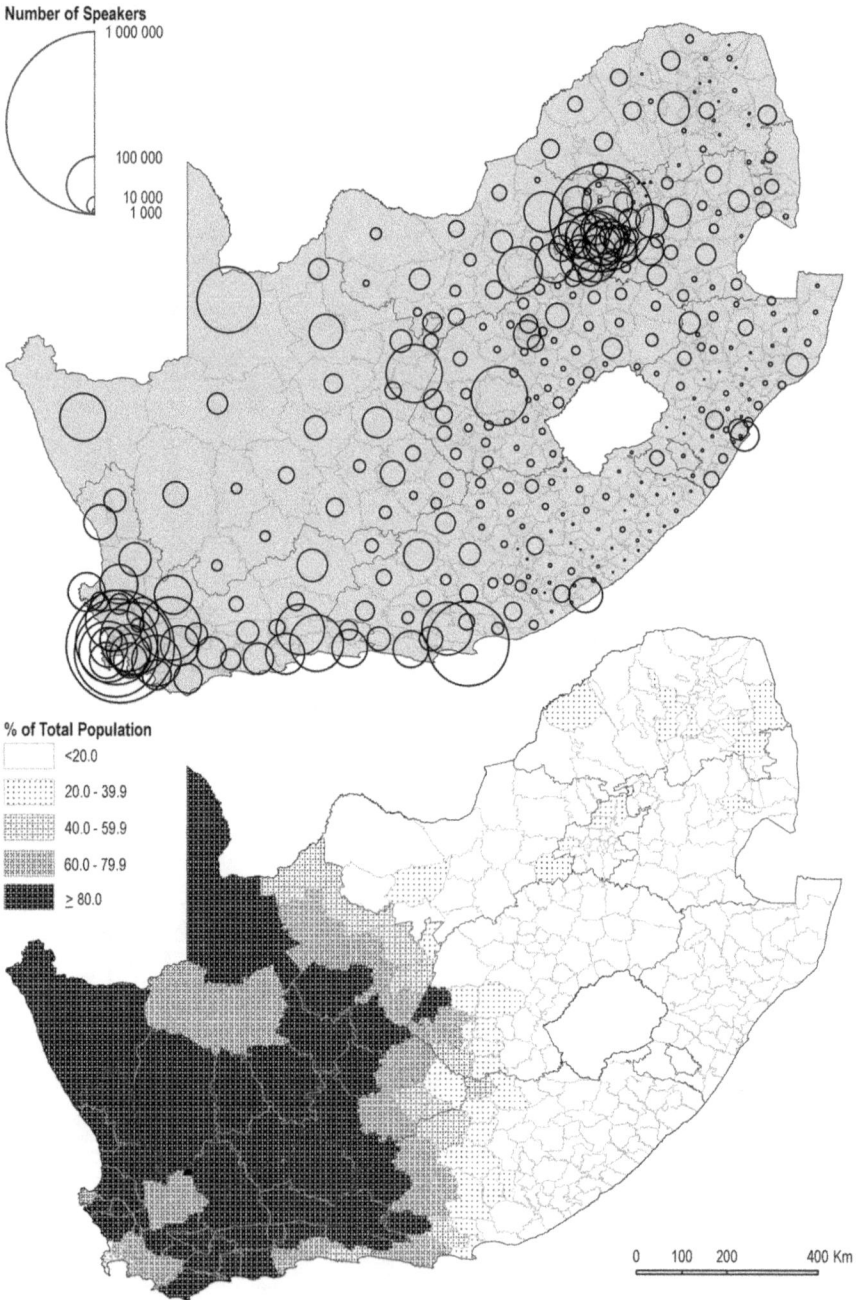

Maps 2a and 2b. Afrikaans language distribution in South Africa (2001)

Change in Number of Speakers

1 000 000

100 000

10 000
1 000

○ Increase

◉ Decrease

No Data

% Change in Number of Speakers

< - 30.0

-10.1 to -30.0

-10.0 to +10.0

+10.1 to +30.0

> +30.0

■ Centre of Gravity (1991)

★ Centre of Gravity (2001)

0   100   200   400 Km

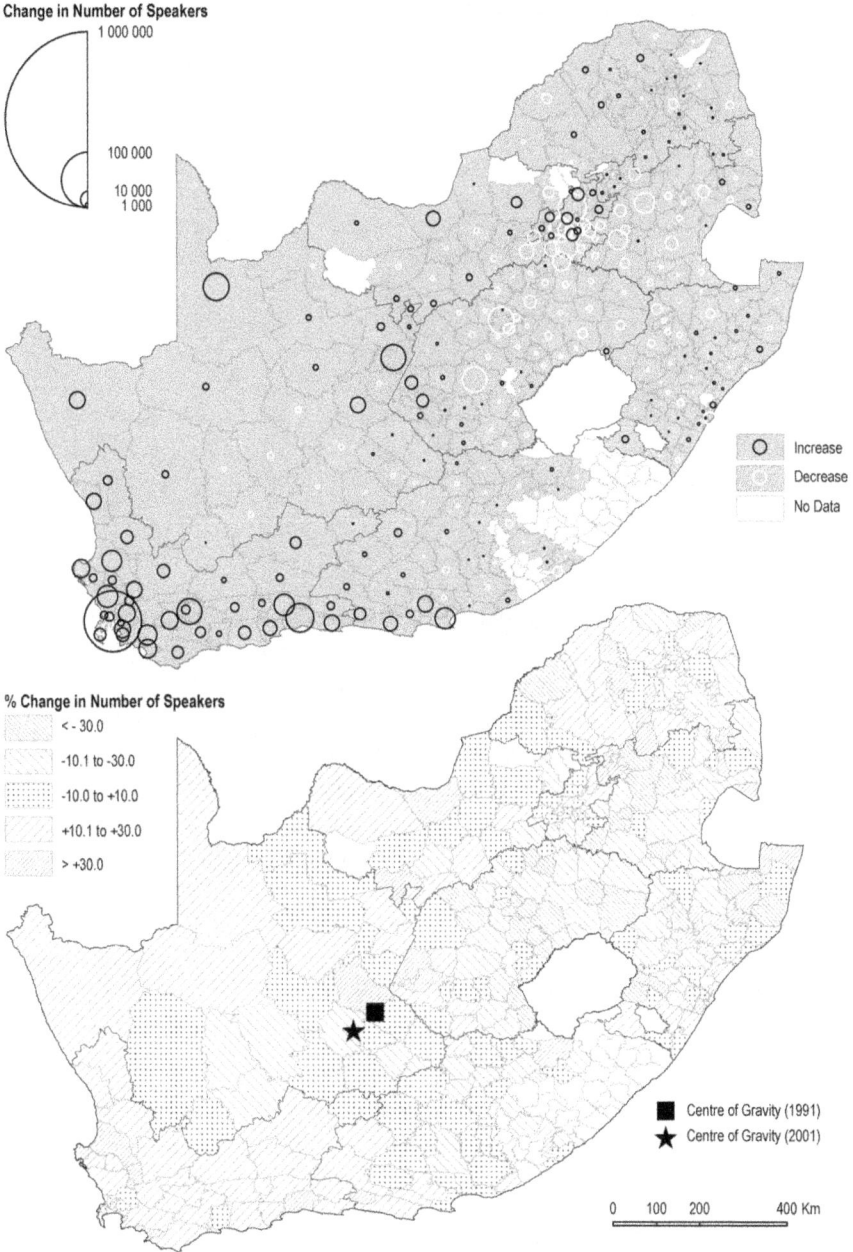

Maps 3a and 3b. Afrikaans language change in South Africa (1991–2001)

Table 3. Language composition of Cape Town

Language	1991		2001		Change 1991–2001	
	Numbers	%	Numbers	%	Numbers	%
Afrikaans	1,012,771	48.4	1,128,250	40.1	115,479	+11.4
English	643,459	30.8	802,069	28.5	158,610	+24.6
isiNdebele	45	0.1	1,990	0.1	1,945	>+100.0
isiXhosa	403,844	19.3	825,288	29.3	421,444	+104.4
iziZulu	1,172	0.1	7,567	0.2	6,395	>+100
Sepedi	1,030	0.1	1,506	0.1	476	+46.2
Sesotho	4,871	0.2	18,637	0.6	13,766	>+100.0
Setswana	897	0.1	4,139	0.2	3,242	>+100.0
siSwati	132	0.1	1,408	0.1	1,276	>+100.0
Tshivenda	91	0.1	995	0.1	904	>+100.0
Xitsonga	259	0.1	1,412	0.1	1,153	>+100.0
Other	20,422	0.9	15,911	0.6	-4,511	-22.1
Total	2,088,993	100.0	2,809,169	100.0	720,176	+34.5

three languages dominated the Western Cape and Cape Town linguistic scene in 2001. The three official languages in the Western Cape overwhelmingly dominated the metropolitan linguistic scene in 2001: more than 1,1 million people, constituting 40% of the total urban population, reported Afrikaans as their first home language. The isiXhosa group with 825,000 speakers (29%) was almost on par with the 28% (802,000) English speakers in the city population. Except for "other" (mainly European and Oriental) language speakers, the remaining Black African language numbers were very small. Although Afrikaans and English experienced increases in their numbers between 1991 and 2001, they lost ground proportionally to the total city population growth. IsiXhosa filled this niche with a very strong increase of 104% (10,4% p.a.), a sure sign of significant in-migration by this language group.

5.2.   Spatially preponderant language

The same "preponderant language" methodology applied at the national level was also implemented towards the three official languages of the Cape Town metropolitan area. Each language's percentage share of the total population was compared per spatial unit to numerically determine the majority language in that Main Place (ward) in 2001 (Maps 4a and 4b). Afrikaans was the preponderant language in 15 wards. English was preponderant in nine units and isiXhosa in six units. The general distribution reveals a rather sharp division between an English-orientated Southern and Western seaboard, and Afrikaans-orientated

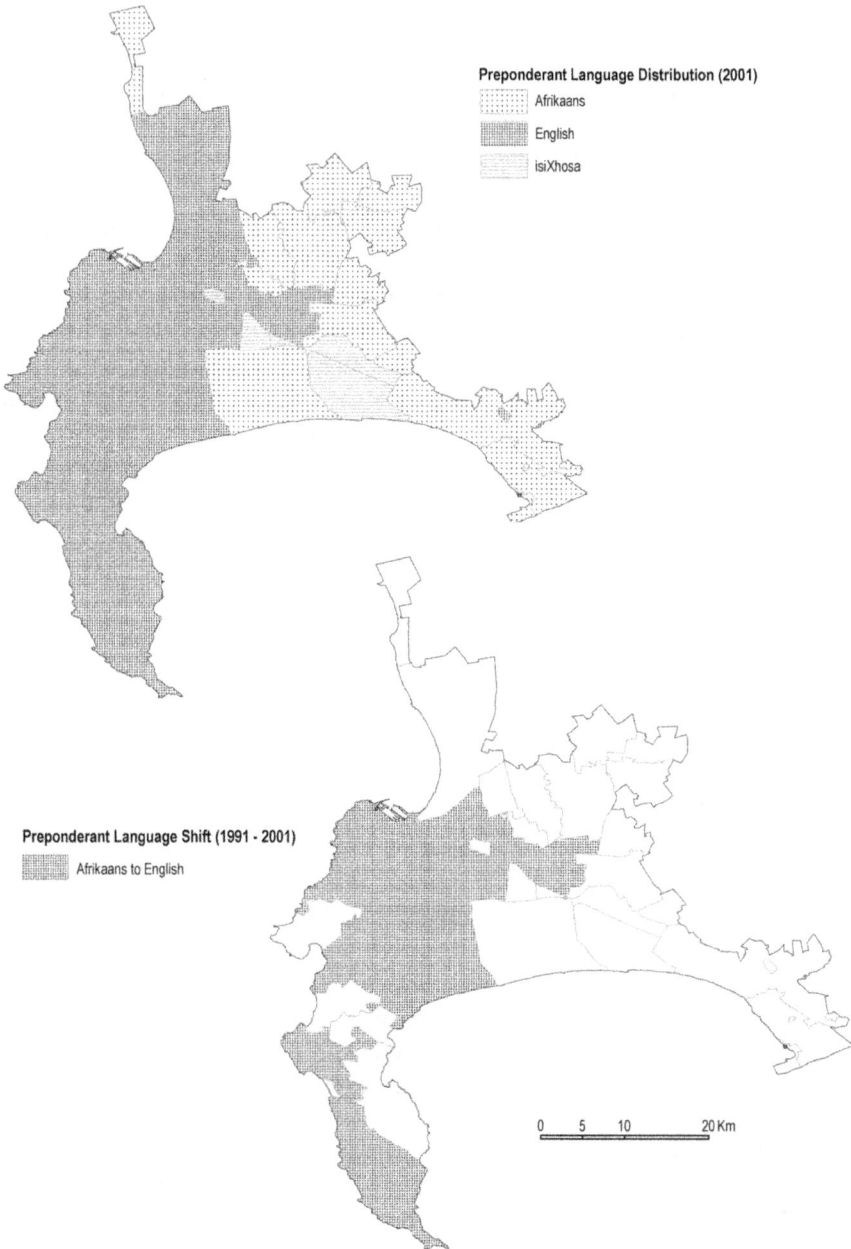

Preponderant Language Distribution (2001)

  Afrikaans

  English

  isiXhosa

Preponderant Language Shift (1991 - 2001)

  Afrikaans to English

0   5   10   20 Km

Maps 4a and 4b. Preponderant language in Cape Town – Distribution and shift

Northern and Eastern False Bay sectors. Crossroads, Guguletu, Khayelitsha, Langa, Mfuleni and Lwandle stand out as urban-cultural isiXhosa enclaves on the map. The spatial correlation coefficients of isiXhosa with Afrikaans (-0,7) and with English (-0,6), respectively, stress the fact that there is little correspondence between the three map patterns – each language developed a unique metropolitan locational image. In summary, the metropolitan spatial structure displays two distinct developmental axes: an English sector in a southerly direction parallel to the Table Mountain range and an Afrikaans sector along the N1 and N2 transport routes. Former Brown and Black group-areas on the Cape Flats fill the zone in between. Only two shifts in language dominance between 1991 and 2001 were observed (Maps 4a and 4b): in the large Cape Town ward and Goodwood, respectively. However, the Afrikaans majorities in Durbanville, Melkbosstrand and Mitchell's Plain are marginal when compared to either English or isiXhosa. In sum, whether at a national, provincial or metropolitan scale, language differentiation in South Africa demonstrates unique spatial identities within a multicultural context.

5.3.   Afrikaans patterns

The 1.13 million Afrikaans first home language speakers in 2001 represented 40% of the total Cape Town metropolitan population. The spatial distribution of Afrikaans speakers (Maps 5a and 5b) is heavily concentrated in three wards, namely Blue Downs, Mitchell's Plain and the Cape Town ward, where 56% of the city's Afrikaans population were accommodated. The location of centres of gravity is also determined by these nodal concentrations (Maps 6a and 6b). The two first mentioned suburbs were prominent Brown group areas in the apartheid era before 1994. When mapped in proportional terms relative to their total population, most wards carry Afrikaans speakers of more than 60%, e.g., Bellville, Eersterivier, Elsiesrivier, Gordons Bay, Kuilsrivier, Parow, and Somerset West. Regarding the temporal change in language numbers (Maps 6a and 6b), the large Cape Town ward recorded a substantive decrease in Afrikaans numbers between 1991 and 2001. On the other hand, Blue Downs had the strongest increase, raising the question whether a mobile population phenomenon or a language shift is manifested. The other wards showed changes within a rather narrow range of variation. Although Afrikaans is numerically still the strongest language in Cape Town, it lost substantial ground (from 48% in 1991 to 40% in 2001) in proportion to the city's total population.

The average socio-demographic profile of Afrikaans speakers (Table 4) characterises the language as overwhelmingly spoken by Brown (78%) and to a lesser extent White (19%) population groups, strongly associated with Chris-

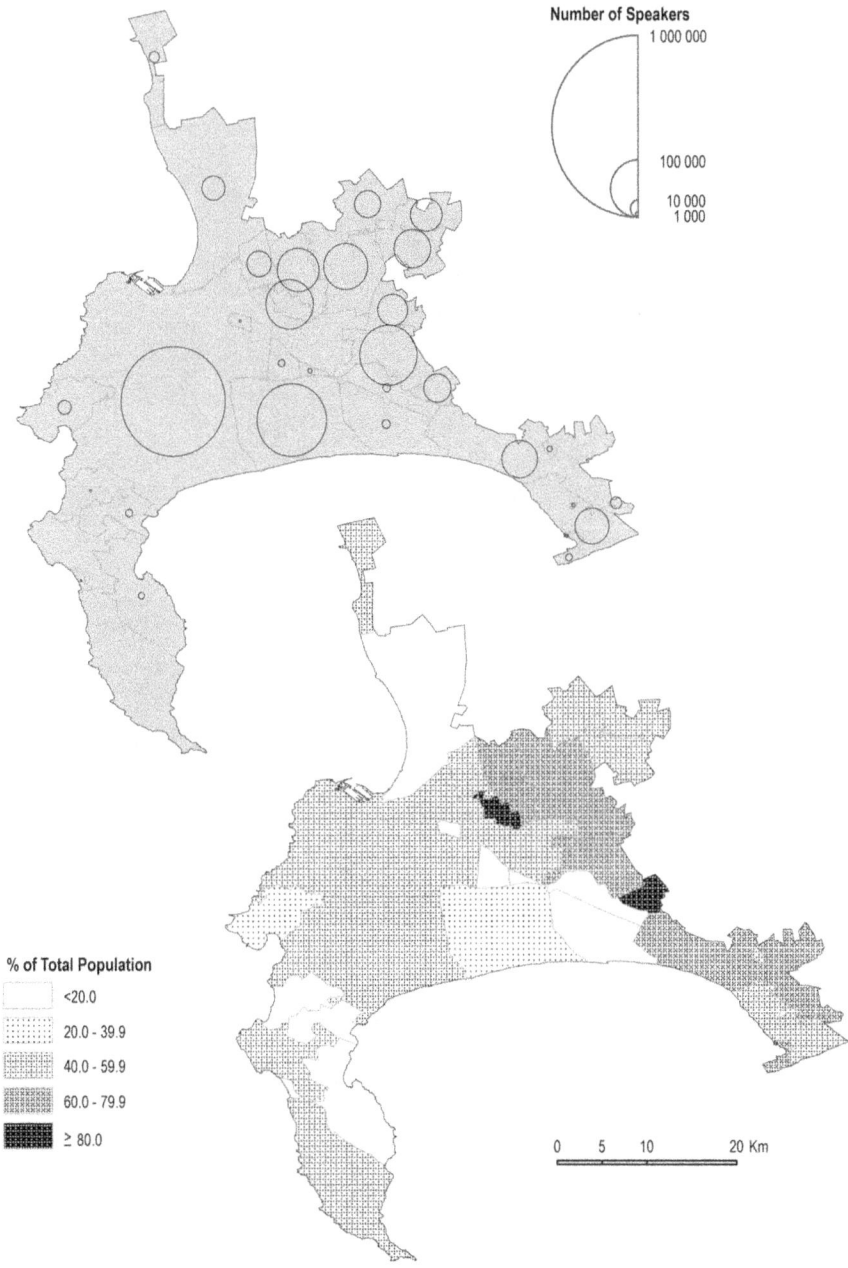

Maps 5a and 5b. Afrikaans language distribution in Cape Town (2001)

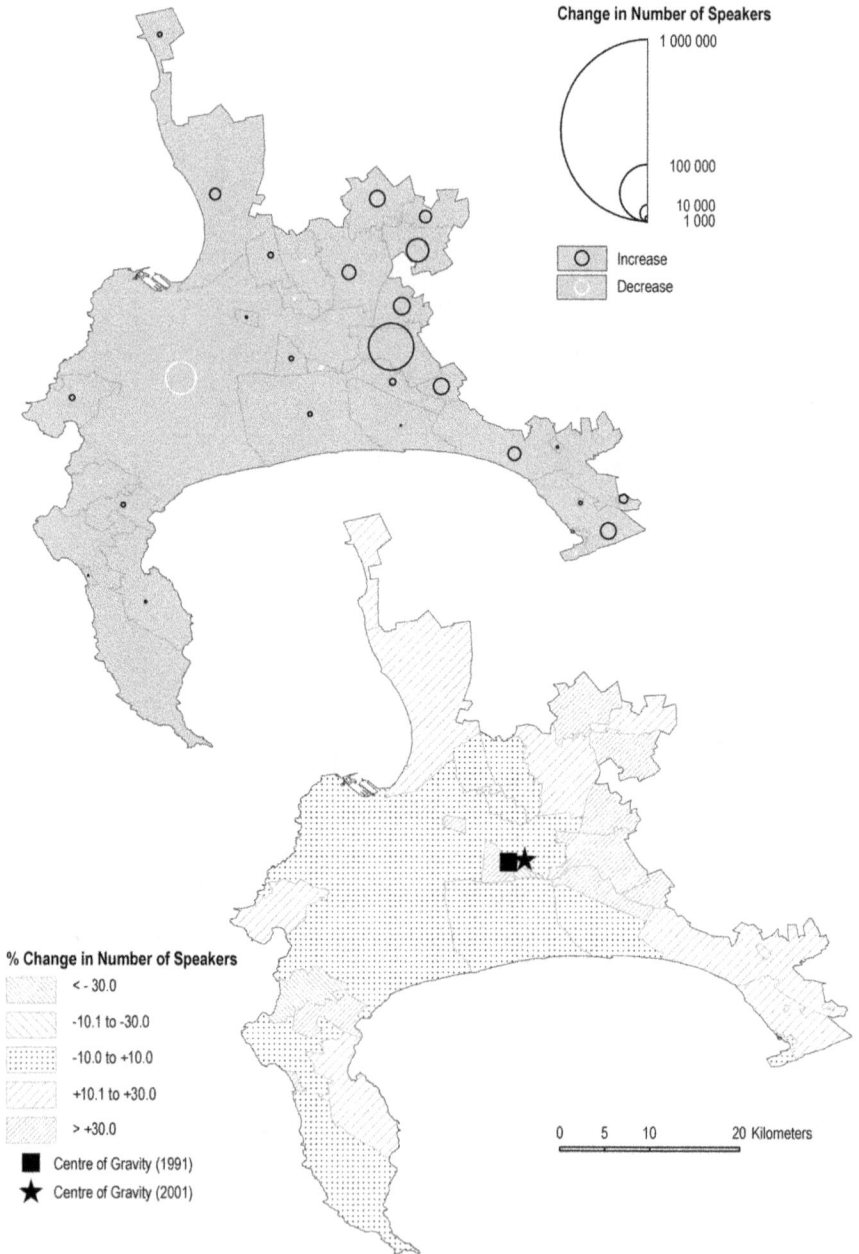

Maps 6a and 6b. Afrikaans language change in Cape Town (1991–2001)

Table 4. Afrikaans language profile of Cape Town

Variable	Afrikaans	Cape Town	Variable	Afrikaans	Cape Town
Segregation index	38,8	–	*Gender*		
Total Number (2001)	1,128,250	2,809,169	% Female	52.3	52.0
% of total	40.2	100.0	*Age*		
% Change (1991–2001)	11.4	34.5	Average (years)	29.0	29.0
			< 15 (%)	26.7	26.5
Population Group			15–60 (%)	65.2	65.9
% Black African	2.0	32.3	> 60 (%)	8.1	7.6
% White	19.6	19.2	*Education (≥ 25 years)*		
% Brown	78.4	48.5	% No schooling	3.6	4.5
			% Grade 12	19.2	23.0
Religion			% Diploma/Certificate	6.0	8.0
% Christian	82.0	76.1	% Degree	4.7	6.2
% Non-Christian	11.6	11.3			
% No Affiliation	4.8	10.8			

tian religions, suffering education levels below the city average, but with an age composition coinciding with the metropolitan averages. The Segregation Index value of 38,8 indicates quite significant degrees of integration at the broad urban Main Place scale. However, in the residential neighbourhoods segregation levels are expected to be high still (0 indicates full integration, and 100 full segregation).

6. Synthesis

On a regional level, the selection of a suitable language medium for effective communication in public management, health delivery, commerce, marketing, newspapers and television/radio, or as a teaching medium, is usually dependant on the preponderant language distribution and spatial changes which take place within a country's or city's subregions. The evidence presented shows that South African society is diverse rather than homogeneous in its ethnolinguistic structure. The respective distribution patterns show substantial elements of concentration and segregation within specific core regions of the country. Language planning in South Africa has lead to a policy of constitutionalising eleven national official languages, together with the possibility of localised official languages at the provincial level. Such a strategy will have to be sensitive to the patterns of preponderance and change of certain languages in specific regions. The same pattern repeats itself at the metropolitan regional scale.

The links between socio-cultural boundaries, cultural traditions, historical memory, and the formation of linguistic landscapes should be investigated further in the South African multicultural context. Ethno-linguistic identity, through the geography of language, remains a highly topical and fascinating focus for research. As an academic subdiscipline it provides various research opportunities in South Africa and internationally. Although our exploratory attempts may have added to the knowledge of geolinguistics in South Africa, many gaps remain, and unanswered questions need to be explored. Geographers, cartographers, sociologists and linguists are urged to take up the opportunities of interdisciplinary partnerships in the search for a universal corpus of sound conceptual and empirical geolinguistic information at global, national, regional and urban scale.

References

Braam, D., M. October and P. Plüddeman
    2005   *Realising policy: Mapping language to access education.* Proceedings of the Africa GIS Conference. Pretoria: Geo-Information Society of SA.

Comrie, B., S. Matthews and M. Polinsky (eds.)
    1996   *The Atlas of Language: The Origin and Development of Languages throughout the World.* London: Quarto.

Department of Arts and Culture
    2002   *National Language Policy Framework.* Pretoria.

Desforges, L. and R. Jones
    2001   Geographies of language/Languages of geography. *Social & Cultural Geography* 2 (3): 261–264.

Deumert, A.
    2004   *Language Standardization and Language Change. The Dynamics of Cape Dutch.* Amsterdam: John Benjamins.

Du Plessis, T.
    2003   Taalbeleidsontwikkeling in Suid-Afrika – Twee treë vorentoe, een terug? *Tydskrif vir Filosofie en Kultuurkritiek* 12/13: 47–57.

European Science Foundation
    2006   SCH *Exploratory Workshop Guidelines.*
            Available at *http://www.esf.org/workshops*.

Grobler, E., K.P. Prinsloo and I.J. van der Merwe
    1990   *Language Atlas of South Africa.* Pretoria: Human Sciences Research Council.

Krige, D. (ed.)
    1994   *The Education Atlas of South Africa.* Durban: Education Foundation.

Mesthrie, R.
    2002   South Africa: A sociolinguistic overview. In: R. Mesthrie (ed.), *Language in South Africa.* Cambridge: Cambridge University Press.

Province of the Western Cape
    1998   *Constitution of the Western Cape,* Act No 1 of 1998. Cape Town: Government Printer.

Republic of South Africa
    1996   *Constitution of the Republic of South Africa,* Act 108 of 1996. Pretoria: Government Printer.

Shaw, G. and D. Wheeler
    1985   *Statistical Techniques in Geographical Analysis.* Chichester: John Wiley.

Tait, N. (ed.)
   1996   *A Socio-Economic Atlas of South Africa.* Pretoria: Human Sciences Research Council.

UNESCO
   2000   *World Language Survey: Official Languages of South Africa.* Dept. of Arts & Culture. Available at *http://www.dac.gov.za.*

Van der Merwe, I.J.
   1989   The geography of the Afrikaans language in South Africa. *South African Geographical Journal* 71 (2): 89–93.
   1995   Language change in South Africa: A geographical perspective. *GeoJournal* 37 (4): 513–523.
   1996   Geolinguistics of European minority groups in Cape Town. *Tijdschrift voor Economische en Sociale Geografie* 87 (2): 146–160.

Van der Merwe, I.J. and J.H. van der Merwe (ed.)
   2006   *Linguistic Atlas of South Africa: Language in Space and Time.* University of Stellenbosch: Sun Press.

Van der Merwe I.J. and L.D. van Niekerk
   1994   *Language in South Africa: Distribution and Change.* University of Stellenbosch: Department of Geography.

Williams, C.H. and I.J. van der Merwe
   1996   Mapping the multilingual city: A research agenda for urban geolinguistics. *Journal of Multilingual and Multicultural Development* 17 (1): 49–66.

Wurm, S.A.
   1996   *Atlas of the World's Languages in Danger of Disappearing.* London: UNESCO Publishers.

Community languages in Australia

Sandra Kipp

1. Introduction

While multilingualism has always been a national reality in Australia, it is a reality that has been addressed in many different ways over the last 200 years or so. The rich diversity of aboriginal languages present at the time of the arrival of the First Fleet in 1788 has been decimated, and the languages this paper will focus on, imported at and after the time of European settlement, have seen changing and varied fortunes.

2. Immigration and language policy

2.1. From European settlement until the Second World War

Languages other than English were brought to Australia by the First Fleet (1788), and added to by the arrival of many other free settlers in the early years of settlement. Economic hardship, religious persecution and political upheaval in Europe provided the growing cities (and rural centres) in Australia with energetic and resourceful citizens from many countries, as evidenced by the vibrant multilingual press that was established during the course of the 19th century (Gilson and Zubryzycki 1967). The late 18th century and much of the 19th century were characterised first by an accepting but *laissez faire* attitude towards languages other than English (LOTEs), then by a tolerant but rather more restrictive approach, which Clyne (1991) attributes largely to the advent of state compulsory education in the late 19th century. This had the effect of mainstreaming monolingual education at the expense of the LOTE or bilingual models established by a number of different groups, particularly German-speaking Lutherans living in rural enclaves, but also speakers of languages such as French, Gaelic and Hebrew (Clyne 1988). The gold rushes of the mid to late 19th century brought in their wake a further wave of migration from all over the world, including many people from China. A backlash against the surge in Asian migration became evident in restrictive practices introduced by some colonies. For example, unreasonably large landing taxes imposed on Chinese travelling by ship to Victoria led to the overland trekking of Chinese miners from coastal South Australia to the Victorian goldfields. This anti-Asian bias was to be further institutionalised at the time of the Federation of colonies into the Commonwealth of Australia in 1901.

1901 ushered in a period of aggressive monoculturalism and monolingualism, with immigration policies severely restricting the immigration of "non-white" persons. The *White Australia Policy* (administered via the infamous *Dictation Test* which required a prospective settler to successfully complete a dictation test in a European language with which (s)he was not necessarily familiar) was not completely dismantled until the mid 1970s, when a new reformist government introduced a selection system based on "points",[1] under which all applicants could compete on a common basis. English monolingualism was promoted in the period following Federation, both as a symbol of British heritage and increasingly also as a symbol and marker of Australia's national identity (Clyne 1991). Assimilationist views replaced the *laissez faire* attitudes of the 19th century, and, while some European migration continued to occur, the major source country was Britain. Immigration policies promoted the image of an essentially British-Australian people, fitting easily into a prosperous and relatively egalitarian society (Jupp 1966: 5). While there was a minor influx of Southern European migrants in the 1920s (brought about largely by changes in US immigration policy), this was met with a significant degree of negative reaction, both by the workers' unions and the population at large. The ensuing public debate led to the Immigration (Amendment) Act of 1925, making it possible to proclaim limits or bans on the admission of any national group (Jupp 1966: 6).

2.2.   The post-war immigration boom

An extremely ambitious immigration policy was launched in the wake of the Second World War, one which was to fundamentally change the demographic face of Australia. Its goals were twofold: to provide a buffer against the perceived military threat from Australia's northern neighbours, and to man the greatly expanding secondary industry (Clyne 1991; Kipp et al. 1995). It was presented to the population as a scheme which would import mostly Britons (thus maintaining the status quo of the 20th century to date), but this was never going to be feasible, given the numbers required and Britain's own shortage of manpower. The government's first "alternative" source was the refugee camps of Europe, and some 170,000 "displaced persons" were brought to Australia between 1947 and 1954 (Lack and Templeton 1995). From the early 1950s the net was cast ever more widely, to include economic migrants from all parts of Europe, starting with the north and west (including Germany, despite initial misgivings from some sectors of the Australian population) and eventually including Italy, Greece, Malta, Cyprus and former Yugoslavia. By the late 1960s these sources were beginning to dry up, and agreements were signed with Syria, Turkey, then Lebanon. From the early to mid 1970s, as the *White Australia Policy* was being dismantled and a refugee crisis was developing in Indo-China, the numbers of settlers from Asian sources increased dramatically, most recently through the "business" component of the immigration program (Kipp 2007).

Within a generation or two, the "bold experiment" (Lack and Templeton 1995) of the post-war years, marketed as the only way to secure a "white and British" Australia, had led to an unarguably multicultural society. In 1947 the population of Australia was 7.5 million, with almost 90% of British origin and the rest mainly European. Less than 1% was of Asian origin (Jordens 1995). In 2001 the population was almost 19 million, with some 28% born overseas, and nearly 5% born in Asia (south, southeast, north and northeast) (Australian Bureau of Statistics).

2.3.   Policy directions since the Second World War

The assimilationist policies of the early part of the 20th century were still strongly in place at the time of the post-war immigration boom, and the expectation was that the settlers would assimilate as quickly as possible to monolingual Australia. There were laws in place in some states (dating from the First World War) prohibiting bilingual education, and there were laws severely restricting the amount of broadcasting in "foreign languages". The mainstream education system offered little opportunity to acquire or develop a language other than English, and those that were taught (most commonly French and Latin) were restricted to the secondary sector and strongly conceptualised as "foreign" language programs. Teachers advised parents to use only English at home (regardless of the standard of said English), otherwise their children would never achieve in the school system. There is a wealth of anecdotal evidence documenting the abuse immigrants of the time received if they dared to use "their" language in public places.

As foreshadowed above, there was a change of government in 1972, with the reformist Whitlam government elected after 23 years of conservative rule. Apart from the dismantling of the White Australia Policy, other enabling changes came about, such as increased space on radio airwaves and the devolution of school governance to the local level, which greatly enhanced the profile of community languages in Australia as they were now called, in preference to "foreign languages" (Clyne 1991). Language services were provided, notably the innovative Telephone Interpreter Service (TIS) in 1973, to cater for the rapidly expanding range of languages in which assistance was needed. The establishment of Schools of Languages (after-hours government schools now in Victoria, New South Wales, South Australia and the Northern Territory) provided a flexible framework for the teaching of a wide range of languages to students who were not able to access programs in their day schools. Ethnic community schools, hitherto entirely self-funded, now received government support. Multilingual community and government radio and television stations established in the 1970s still broadcast in a large number of languages, and the ethnic press has proliferated.

Australia's first official policy on languages (Lo Bianco 1987) grew out of, and reflected, the reformist energy and concern for issues of social justice that moved a coalition of academic linguists, language teachers, ethnic, Aboriginal and deaf groups to lobby for just such a policy (Clyne 1997). It stressed the complementarity of English and community languages. However, by the late 1980s the political climate had shifted to one of economic rationalism, as revealed in the next policy initiative, laid out in Dawkins (1991). In place of the underlying concern for social justice that had driven Lo Bianco (1987), the emphasis was now on the economic value of languages to the nation. The issue of literacy (but only in English) was also fore-grounded. A further development (Rudd 1994), prioritising a small number of Asian languages nationally (Mandarin, Korean, Indonesian and Japanese), reflected this economic bias and also continued the shift of emphasis away from Australian language communities. While the population of Mandarin speakers was growing rapidly, for example, numbers speaking Korean, Japanese and Indonesian were still relatively small, and all four communities were at any rate completely disregarded in the initiative. "Other" Asian languages with significant Australian communities of speakers, such as Vietnamese (and increasingly Filipino) were not included at all.

3.   The Australian National Census

1976 saw the beginning of an invaluable longitudinal resource for the study of Australian language ecology, namely the introduction of a question on language in the 5-yearly National Census. The initial question (1976) targeted "regular use" of a language other than English, there was no question on language use in 1981, and since 1986 the question has been the same: "Does this person speak a language other than English *in the home*? [my italics], and if so, which one? If more than one language is used, which is the most frequently used?" Those who answer this question in the affirmative are then asked to grade their (spoken) English on a scale of *very well – well – not well – not at all*. While a question on home language use is a good basis on which to predict the ongoing potential for transmission to further generations, it clearly understates language use within the community, ignoring as it does language use patterns in the homes of extended family and community members and in public settings and at community functions.

According to the 2001 National Census, more than 200 languages were used in Australian homes at that time, with 16% of the population speaking a LOTE at home. This proportion rose to 29% and 27% respectively in Sydney and Melbourne, Australia's largest cities and the ones in which immigration has been concentrated (Clyne and Kipp 2002). Although, as stated above, the language question was somewhat different in 1976, Table 1 illustrates in broad terms the changes that have occurred over nearly 30 years of large-scale data collection on language use.

Especially notable from Table 1 is the complete absence of Asian speakers in any numbers in 1976, and the subsequent rapid growth of speakers of Vietnamese and the Chinese varieties, but also Filipino. Arabic, while already reasonably widely spoken in 1976, also continues to increase its numbers, forming the largest single community language group in Sydney. While Italian (1950s) and Greek (1960s) are still relatively strong nationally, other languages of the post-war years, such as German (1940s, 1950s) and Dutch (1950s) are declining rapidly, as are a further range of languages not shown in this table, such as Latvian, Ukrainian, Lithuanian and Polish (largely 1940s and early 1950s, with Polish spread over a number of "vintages"). And even the position of Italian and Greek looks a little shaky when one focuses on statistics for younger speakers – see Table 2.

3.1. Language maintenance and language shift

Census data reflects not only new migration, and language used by overseas-born, it also reflects the relative success of different community language groups in maintaining their languages. Language shift can be calculated by cross-tabulating language use figures with birthplace figures. For example, in 2001 11.4% of persons born in Italy now speak only English at home, yielding a language shift rate of 11.4%. Using birthplace as a surrogate for "language first spoken" is clearly far from satisfactory, particularly for birthplaces with multiple ethnicities (such as Egypt, former Yugoslavia and Vietnam), but it does have the benefit of objectivity. An "Ancestry" question, trialled in 1986 and reintroduced in 2001, may help with some of these difficulties (for example, separating the ethnic Chinese from the ethnic Vietnamese for the Vietnam-born), but the concept of "ancestry[2]" is highly subjective and of course potentially multiple for any individual.

Table 1. Top 10 community languages in Australia, 1976–2001 (Australian Bureau of Statistics)

Language	1976	Language	1986	Language	1996	Language	2001
Italian	444,672	Italian	415,765	Italian	375,752	Italian	353,606
Greek	262,177	Greek	277,472	Greek	269,770	Greek	263,718
German	170,644	Serbo-Croatian	140,575	Cantonese	202,270	Cantonese	225,307
Serbo-Croatian	142,407	Chinese	139,100	Arabic	177,599	Arabic	209,371
French	64,851	Arabic	119,187	Vietnamese	146,265	Vietnamese	174,236
Dutch	64,768	German	111,276	German	98,808	Mandarin	139,288
Polish	62,945	Spanish	73,961	Mandarin	91,911	Spanish	93,595
Arabic	51,284	Polish	68,638	Spanish	91,254	Tagalog (Filipino)	78,879
Spanish	48,343	Vietnamese	65,856	Macedonian	71,347	German	76,444
Maltese	45,922	Dutch	62,181	Tagalog	70,444	Macedonian	71,994

Table 2. Use of selected languages by speakers 0–14 years old in Sydney and Melbourne, 2001 (Australian Bureau of Statistics)

Language	Melbourne	Sydney
Vietnamese	15,395	15,242
Greek	14,446	10,464
Arabic	12,404	37,217
Cantonese	10,241	21,199
Italian	9,434	5,699
Mandarin	6,540	11,320
Spanish	3,349	6,128

From 1976 to 1996, language shift in the second generation has been calculated on the basis of *birthplace of child (Australia) x birthplace of mother (full range of birthplaces) x birthplace of father (full range of birthplaces)*. That is, the proportion of Australian-born persons, with one or more parents born in a particular birthplace, who now speak only English in the home. To continue with the Italian example, this was 57.9% in 1996. This was not possible in 2001 (or 2006) due to a change in the question related to parental birthplace – instead of a full range of birthplaces only a binary choice is provided: parent born in Australia/parent born overseas. The ancestry question now included, and designed to provide "background" information on individuals born outside their "ancestral" country or in countries with multiple ancestries, does not allow us to distinguish between second, third (or sixth) generation Australian-born and does not provide any reliable link with language background. The 1996 shift rates (G1 and G2) and the 2001 shift rates (G1) for selected languages are presented in Table 3.

As Table 3 shows, the most retentive language communities at the time of the 2001 Census were newly arrived groups from Asia, Africa and the Middle East, although Greek is still relatively well-maintained, and Macedonian even more so. Both of these languages were part of the post-war immigration boom, although Macedonian has since been revitalised by further migration from former Yugoslavia (most of the earlier migrants were from northern Greece). And there are some newer migrations from the Indian subcontinent and the Philippines that are notable for their rapid shift, a shift that may be at least partially explained by their pre-existing experience with English and the status and function of English in the homeland. A particularly high exogamy rate for the Philippines-born may also contribute to the considerable shift in both generations for this group.

Table 3. Language shift in Australia, 2001 (first generation) and 1996 (first and second generation) (based on data from the Australian Bureau of Statistics)

Birthplace	% shift (G1 2001)	% shift (G1 1996)	% shift (G2 1996) Endogamous[a]	Exogamous[b]	Aggregated G2
Austria	54.4	48.3	80.0	91.1	89.7
Chile	12.2	9.8	12.7	62.3	38.0
France	36.8	37.2	46.5	80.4	77.7
Germany	54.0	48.2	77.6	92.0	89.7
Greece	7.1	6.4	16.1	51.9	28.0
Hong Kong	10.3	9.0	8.7	48.7	35.7
Hungary	35.0	31.8	64.2	89.4	82.1
Italy	15.9	14.7	42.6	79.1	57.9
Japan	16.9	15.4	5.4	68.9	57.6
Republic of Korea	11.1	11.6	5.4	61.5	18.0
Lebanon	6.2	5.5	11.4	43.6	20.1
Macedonia	4.7	3.0	7.4	38.6	14.8
Malta	38.2	36.5	70.0	92.9	82.1
Netherlands	62.6	61.9	91.1	96.5	95.0
Other South America	18.4	17.2	15.7	67.1	50.5
Poland	22.3	19.6	58.4	86.9	75.7
PRC	4.3	4.6	17.1	52.8	37.4
Spain	25.1	22.4	38.3	75.0	63.0
Taiwan	3.8	3.4	5.0	29.2	21.0
Turkey	7.1	5.8	5.0	46.6	16.1

[a] Where both parents were born in birthplace x.
[b] Where one parent was born in birthplace x and the other parent was born elsewhere.

Large-scale census data is very useful in providing us with the "big picture" of language maintenance differential between community language groups, and sometimes two sets of statistical data (such as marriage patterns and language use) can provide some insight into possible reasons for this differential behaviour. However, factors established on a statistical base do not always behave predictably – for example, geographical concentration appears generally to promote language maintenance (Clyne and Kipp 1997), but individual cases do not always comply. One need only look at the very high geographical concentrations within Melbourne (and Sydney) of Macedonian and Maltese speakers (Clyne and Kipp 1998). Macedonian is extremely well maintained, Maltese much less so. And we have already seen that period of residence is not directly or unproblematically related to language maintenance or shift. In order to better understand the ways in which factors work together, as well as to learn more about the language behaviour of groups *outside* their homes (given the limitations of the Census question), small-scale studies are vital. Even within the home domain, the Census does not attempt to address questions such as frequency of use or complexity of language, or to establish literacy levels in either English or a community language.

A number of researchers have supplemented Australian Census data with smaller case studies. The following is just a sample of the issues (and language groups) that have been researched:

- *Standard/Dialect*, and the ways in which situations of pre-existing diglossia between varieties may affect language maintenance efforts in a country of migration. See for example Pauwels (1986) (for Dutch and German); and Bettoni and Rubino (1996), Rubino (2006) (for Italian);
- *Pluricentricity*, or differing national norms. See Clyne and Kipp (1999) (for Arabic from Lebanon and Egypt, Spanish from Spain and Chile, Mandarin from Taiwan and Cantonese from Hong Kong);
- *Migration vintage* – what are the factors involved in period of residence (including language and social policies at home and in the country of migration)? See for example Clyne and Kipp (1999) (for Arabic, Chinese and Spanish), Clyne and Fernandez, (2006) (for Hungarian), Borland (2006) (for Maltese), Søndergaard and Norrby (2006) (for Danish);
- *Gender*. See for example Pauwels (1995), Winter and Pauwels (2000, 2006);
- *Codification and status of L1*. See Clyne and Kipp (2006) (for Macedonian, Somali and Filipino);
- *Language and religious practice*. See for example Woods (2004);
- *New technologies*. See for example Fitzgerald and Debski (2006) (for Internet use by Polish migrants).

Two issues of the *International Journal of the Sociology of Language* (72 and 180) have been devoted to Australian community languages, with most articles reporting on small-scale studies.

4. Languages other than English in education: how does provision match demography?

4.1. Who provides language programs in Australia?

There are three main providers of language programs for school-age students in Australia:

- *Regular day schools, at both primary and secondary levels*. Apart from State schools, there are Catholic schools and "Independent" schools, the latter largely affiliated with a Christian denomination other than the Roman

Catholic Church, or with another religious or ethno-religious group (Islamic, Jewish, etc.). Some of these schools have links with a particular language, and give special weight to the teaching of that language – for example, Arabic in Islamic, Coptic and Maronite schools, Hebrew in Jewish schools, Modern Greek in Greek Orthodox schools and to some extent German in Lutheran schools (Clyne and Fernandez 2008). Over one-third of Australian school children attend non-government schools, the proportion being greater at the secondary than at the primary level.

– *Schools of Languages.* These are government schools in a number of states and territories[3] which run out-of-hours classes (generally on a Saturday morning) for students who cannot study the language of their choice in their regular day school. They offer a wide range of languages, and are open to introducing new ones after a number of base criteria are met (demonstrated demand, availability of teachers and resources).

– *After-hours ethnic schools run by communities or private individuals.* Many of these are subsidised by the Federal and State governments, and some are partially or fully funded from overseas.

Both the Schools of Languages and the ethnic schools, taking place as they do largely on Saturday, compete against sporting and other extracurricular activities. Small enrolments in some languages may also result in the combining of a number of age and/or proficiency levels in one classroom, particularly at primary and junior secondary levels. In addition, the relative emphasis of language *vs.* culture *vs.* religious instruction may vary widely across the ethnic school network. This network is, however, under its umbrella organisation of Community Languages Australia, becoming increasingly important as a national lobby group for community language learning, as well as the instigator of national conferences and a site for the promotion and application of local applied linguistic research (Clyne and Fernandez, 2008).

4.2.   An historical overview of language provision in the Australian education system

Up to and including the 1950s and 1960s languages other than English (LOTEs) were generally not taught in primary schools, and by far the most commonly taught modern language in the secondary sector was French, with German available as an additional language in a limited number of schools and Italian and Russian also available in a very minor way (Clyne et al. 2004). All of these programs were clearly intended for those without a home background in the language, and there were subtle means of discriminating against students with such a background in the matriculation examinations in some languages (Clyne 2005: 118–119). The range of languages available at universities was generally wider than that available in secondary schools. French and German were taught at virtually all universities, and some institutions also offered Italian, Greek, Indonesian and Russian. Dutch, Swedish, Chinese and Japanese were available in a more limited way. While the European languages offered were becoming more and more widely spoken in the Australian community due to the post-war immigration program, the same could not be said for Asian languages, as racially restrictive immigration policies were still in place (see above). However, all of the languages were taught as intellectual exercises for cultural enrichment rather than as a means of developing or maintaining a community language (Clyne and Fernandez 2008; Pauwels 2007).

Various groups, including state modern language teachers associations, university departments and community language groups lobbied from the 1960s for the availability of German and Italian (in some states also Greek) as alternatives to French, particularly in areas where these languages were widely used (Clyne et al. 2004). From about this time Asian languages (Indonesian, and to a lesser extent Japanese and Mandarin) also began to be introduced into some schools. However it was in 1972, with the election of a reformist labour government (see above), that a new era in language-in-education could be said to have begun, against the background of the rapid change from assimilation to multiculturalism as the dominant policy and the final dismantling of the *White Australia Policy*. Migrant education conferences and lobbies in a number of state capital cities, which received considerable input from academics in relevant fields, produced sets of demands which included the teaching of community languages in secondary schools. Ethnic schools began to receive government funding (Clyne and Fernandez 2008).

The comprehensive language policy introduced in 1987 (see above) saw the continued expansion of language offerings. The devolution of decision making to local school communities meant that many schools opted for community languages of significance in their local communities. Italian, the most widely used community language in Australia, was very popular, particularly since the community had decided to direct its ethnic school funding in most states to Italian programs in Catholic and state schools, taught by teachers provided by the community (Clyne and Fernandez 2008). Several other community languages, including Turkish and Serbo-Croatian, were introduced in a more limited number of schools, in areas where there were concentrations of speakers of these languages. The National Policy on Languages (Lo Bianco 1987) secured federal funding for innovations in language maintenance as well as second language acquisition programs.

By 2006 the number of languages examinable in the last year of schooling stood at 43[4] (with two more under discussion), and with provision arrangement between the state authorities for low candidature languages to be examined nationally. Asian languages received a further boost via the NALSAS[5] program (see above – Rudd 1994), which continued to be funded until the end of 2002. It was a very selective boost, however, in its prioritisation of Chinese (Mandarin), Japanese, Indonesian and Korean, and it took no account of the presence of local communities speaking even those languages.

While the situation outlined in the previous paragraph, at least in terms of breadth of languages offered, is a far cry from the one pre-1987, and particularly pre-1970s, the direction of language-in-education policy continues to evolve, and not in a way that emphasises the language communities of Australia. The emphasis of the NALSAS program already demonstrates this. Lo Bianco (2001), in his review of Australian language policy, shows how governments since the 1970s have progressively distanced community involvement from policy, preferring a "managed" top-down approach, marginalising both the input of professional networks of language advocates as well as the interests of community groups.

4.3.   The situation in 2001

Table 4 sets out the relative ranking of languages by student numbers in Australian schools in 2001, and compares this both with their ranking in the top 20 languages nationally and in the top 20 languages in the 0–14 age group nationally.

The strong position of Japanese in Australian schools over all educational sectors clearly owes more to the position of Japan as the nation's biggest trading partner than it does to any significant community presence (28,317 speakers nationally). In contrast, Italian's position as a long-established, as well as the most widely spoken community language in Australia is reflected in its strong position in schools, although it is better represented in the state and Catholic systems than in independent schools. As already noted above, this is largely due to the decision of a federation of Italian community organizations in the 1970s to devote their resources to teaching Italian in mainstream schools, especially primary schools, as distinct from out-of-hour ethnic schools.

With the exception of Italian, significant community languages in the Australian context are generally not well represented in the school sector. This is demonstrated most clearly by the cases of Arabic, Greek and Vietnamese. The positions of Arabic and Vietnamese are particularly weak in light of the numbers of school age children who use these languages at home (see Table 3). For

Table 4. The top 10 community languages in Australian schools (from Clyne et al. 2004: 7)

Ranking/Language	Number of students	Ranking in top 20 languages nationally	Ranking in top 20 0–14 years nationally
1. Japanese	402,882	*	17
2. Italian	394,770	1	5
3. Indonesian	310,363	20	13
4. French	247,001	18	20
5. German	158,076	9	15
6. Chinese (Mandarin)	111,464	6	6
7. Arabic	31,844	4	1
8. Greek	28,188	2	4
9. Spanish	24,807	7	7
10. Vietnamese	22,428	5	2

* Not in top 20 languages nationally

both Greek and Arabic, there has been less emphasis on "mainstreaming" the language, and more on language maintenance, leading to a larger presence in ethnic schools and the Schools of Languages. This also applies to Vietnamese, whose arrival in the late 1970s was in any case too late to benefit from the push for community languages in mainstream schools during that period (Clyne et al. 2004).

The position of "Chinese" is an interesting one, given the significant presence of at least two Chinese varieties in Australia (see Table 1). While the number of Mandarin speakers is certainly significant, and growing, there are still more speakers of Cantonese in Australia than speakers of Mandarin. However, in spite of the significance of Cantonese as a community language in Australia, and a *lingua franca*, trade language and media language in South-East Asia, it is one of the few community languages that are not examined and barely taught in Australia, registering fewer than 400 students nationally (Clyne et al. 2004). At present the only variety available for study at mainstream (and most "ethnic") schools is Mandarin. This means that children of Cantonese-speaking backgrounds learning "Chinese" in school are in effect learning a second language.

This issue of L1 and L2 speakers is becoming increasingly important, particularly with relation to Asian languages and particularly in the context of assessment. While there is a discourse which declares "non-background" learners to be disadvantaged in a mixed classroom, there is also evidence that "background" speakers and their families are being discouraged from maintaining or developing their language by the prospect of more stringent assessment measures (Clyne et al. 1997; Clyne and Kipp 1999; Clyne 2005). It is also clear that there is a long continuum of what one might term "background" – from passive competence (but little or no productive competence) in the home sphere in a vernacular variety to substantial secondary education experience in the Standard or codified variety – and the various classificatory schemes that have been devised to counter the perceived advantage have been seen as discriminatory and unfair by community groups (Clyne and Fernandez 2008). The context of migration, often undertaken for the upward mobility of the children, renders the issue of assessment particularly sensitive.

The pluricentricity of Arabic, with Standard Arabic existing alongside a large number of national vernaculars (for example, Arabic from Egypt, Lebanon, Syria and Iraq), also has implications for education, with "home background" not necessarily equating with competence in the school target language. This issue has also arisen for Italian, where most immigrants spoke an Italian dialect as their L1.

Finally, the closure of language programs at the tertiary level, due to declining public funding, is having a direct impact on schools, as universities have hitherto provided language teachers with advanced language skills (Clyne 2005: 117). The continuing attitudinal shift at the policy making level towards a monolingual mindset (although this does vary across states) is also contributing to a "status" problem for languages in all educational sectors. Clyne and Fernandez (2008) predict that this mindset could lead to a sidelining of the teaching of all but the top six or so languages other than English away from mainstream schools into ethnic schools or Schools of Languages, although with some official financial support.

5.   Concluding remarks

In terms of data collection, while the language question remains secure for the 2006 Census, allowing for a continuing longitudinal view of the first generation, there is no indication that the parental birthplace question will be reinstated. This effectively precludes a similarly longitudinal view of the second generation.

In terms of continuing linguistic diversity, it has been argued that the rich diversity of languages brought to Australia from all over the world is not always harnessed as it could be, and that language services and educational opportunities do not always keep pace with a changing linguistic demography (Clyne et al. 2005). This has been further demonstrated in this paper by the comparison of school language offerings with Australia's evolving demographic profile. In particular, the movement of language and language-in-education policy away from a community-based agenda towards an economically driven one that espouses monolingualism and monoculturalism is having an impact on the way in which languages are valued in Australia, and subsequently the ways in which they are offered over the education systems. An examination of the migration trends over the last decade also reveals an overall downturn in numbers and an emphasis on English-speaking source countries (Kipp 2007), and this has its own implications for Australia's future linguistic profile.

However, gains made and institutions put in place during the halcyon days of language policy making and implementation are still making a significant contribution to multilingualism in Australia. In particular, open-ended systems such as the Special Broadcasting Service (ethnic media), the Telephone Interpreter Service and the Schools of Languages are very effective models for the provision of services to a wide and constantly changing range of language groups. The inclusion of a question on language use in the National Census is still providing an excellent large-scale picture of linguistic demography (if no longer intergenerational language transmission) as well as the basis for a growing amount of fascinating smaller scale research.

Notes

[1]   With respect to categories such as age, skills and qualifications, occupational demand in Australia, work experience, English proficiency, etc.

[2]   The Census question read: "What is the person's ancestry?" The respondent was then told that (s)he could enter up to but not exceeding two ancestries, and was given the choice of: English, Irish, German, Chinese, Scottish, Australian and "other", which needed to be specified in the space provided.

[3]   New South Wales, Victoria, South Australia and the Northern Territory.

[4]   As of January 2006 five of these are under suspension due to low enrolments.

[5]   National Asian Languages and Studies in Australian Schools (strategy).

References

Bettoni, C. and A. Rubino
    1996   *Emigrazione e comportamento linguistico. Un'indagine sul trilinguismo dei siciliani e dei veneti in Australia.* Galatina: Congedo Editore.

Borland, H.
    2006   Intergenerational language transmission in an established Australian migrant community: What makes the difference? *International Journal of the Sociology of Language* 180, 23–41.

Clyne, M.
  1988   Bilingual Education - What can we learn from the past? *Australian Journal of Education* 32 (1): 95–114.
  1991   Community Languages. The Australian Experience. Cambridge: Cambridge University Press.
  1997   Language policy and education in Australia. In: R. Wodak and D. Corson (eds.), *Language Policy and Political Issues in Education* (Encyclopaedia of Language & Education, Volume 1), 127–135, Dordrecht: Kluwer.
  2005   *Australia's Language Potential*. Sydney: University of New South Wales Press.

Clyne, M. and S. Kipp
  1997   Trends and changes in home language use and shift in Australia. *Journal of Multilingual & Multicultural Development* 18: 451–73.
  1998   Language concentrations in metropolitan areas, *People and Place* 6 (2): 50–60.
  1999   *Pluricentric Languages in an Immigrant Context*. Berlin: Mouton de Gruyter.
  2002   Australia's changing language demography, *People and Place* 10 (3): 29–35.
  2006   *Tiles in a Multilingual Mosaic: Macedonian, Somali and Filipino in Melbourne*. Canberra: Pacific Linguistics.

Clyne, M., S. Fernandez, I. Chen and R. Summo-O'Connell
  1997   *Background Speakers*. Canberra: Language Australia.

Clyne, M., S. Fernandez, and F. Grey
  2004   Languages taken at school and languages spoken in the community – a comparative perspective. *Australian Review of Applied Linguistics* 27: 1–17.

Clyne, M., F. Grey and S. Kipp
  2005   Matching language policy implementation with demography, *Language Policy* 3 (3): 241–270.

Clyne, M. and S. Fernandez
  2006   Period of residence as a factor in language maintenance: Hungarian-English bilinguals in Australia as a case study. *ITL International Journal of Applied Linguistics* 149/150: 1–20.
  2008   Community language learning in Australia. In: N. Van Deusen-Scholl and N. Hornberger (eds.), *The Encyclopedia of Language and Education*, 169–181. New York: Springer-Verlag.

Dawkins, J.
  1991   *Australia's Language: The Australian Language and Literacy Policy*. Canberra: Australian Government Publishing Service.

Fitzgerald, M. and R. Debski
    2006   Internet use of Polish by Polish Melbournians: Implications for mainte-
            nance and teaching. *Language Learning and Technology* 10 (1): 87–109.

Gilson, M. and J. Zubryzycki
    1967   *The Foreign-language Press in Australia 1848–1964.* Canberra: Australian
            National University Press.

Jordens, A.-M.
    1995   *Redefining Australians. Immigration, Citizenship and National Identity.*
            Sydney: Hale and Iremonger.

Kipp, S.
    2007   Community languages and the 2001 Australian Census. In: A. Pauwels,
            J. Winter and J. Lo Bianco (eds.), *Maintaining Minority Languages in
            Transnational Contexts*, 13–29. New York: Palgrave Macmillan.

Kipp, S. and M. Clyne
    2003   Trends in the shift from community languages: Insights from the 2001
            Census. *People and Place* 11 (1): 33–41.

Kipp, S., M. Clyne and A. Pauwels
    1995   *Immigration and Australia's Language Resources.* Canberra: Australian
            Government Publishing Service.

Lack, J. and J. Templeton (eds.)
    1995   *Bold Experiment. A Documentary History of Australian Immigration since
            1945.* Melbourne: Oxford University Press.

Lo Bianco, J.
    1987   *National Policy on Languages.* Canberra: Australian Government Pub-
            lishing Service.
    2001   From policy to anti-policy: How fear of language rights took policy-
            making out of community hands. In: J. Lo Bianco and R. Wickert (eds.),
            Australian Policy Activism in Language and Literacy, 13–44. Canberra:
            Language Australia.

Pauwels, A.
    1986   *Immigrant Dialects and Language Maintenance in Australia.* Dordrecht:
            Foris.
    1995   Linguistic practices and language maintenance among bilingual women
            and men in Australia. *Nordlyd* 11: 21–50.
    2005   Maintaining the community language in Australia: Challenges and roles
            for families. *International Journal of Bilingual Education and Bilingual-
            ism* 8 (2 & 3): 124–131.

2007   Maintaining a language other than English through higher education. In: A. Pauwels, J. Winter and J. Lo Bianco (eds.), *Maintaining Minority Languages in Transnational Contexts*, 107–123. New York: Palgrave Macmillan.

Rubino, A.
2006   Linguistic practices and language attitudes of second-generation Italo-Australians. *International Journal of the Sociology of Language* 180: 71–88.

Rudd, K.M.
1994   *Asian Languages and Australia's Economic Future*. Brisbane: Queensland Government Printer.

Søndergaard, B. and C. Norrby
2006   Language maintenance and shift in the Danish community in Melbourne. *International Journal of the Sociology of Language* 180: 105–122.

Winter, J. and A. Pauwels
2000   Gender and language contact research in the Australian context. *Journal of Multilingual and Multicultural Development* 21 (6): 508–522.
2006   Language maintenance in friendships: second generation German, Greek and Vietnamese migrants. *International Journal of the Sociology of Language* 180: 123–139.

Woods, A.
2004   *Medium or Message? Language and Faith in Ethnic Churches*. Clevedon: Multilingual Matters Ltd.

The linguistic landscape of Tokyo

Peter Backhaus

1. Introduction

The world is a multilingual place. The coexistence of two or more languages, both in individuals and societies, is no exceptional state but an almost unnoticed reality to the better part of the people living on this planet. All the same, multilingualism has popularly been considered as though it was a deviation from some god-given *one nation – one language* condition. It is generally known that this ideology is a result of modern nation building processes and their transformation of formerly multilingual societies into monolingual nation states. It is due to these processes that linguistic homogeneity today is often seen as an important precondition for the general functioning of a society, at least for those nations traditionally assumed to be linguistically homogeneous.

Japan is a case in point here. It is well known as a country with strong self-beliefs in ethnolinguistic homogeneity, where being Japanese to many people means speaking Japanese. Nevertheless, like in most other countries subscribing to an apparently monolingual tradition, multilingualism is no phenomenon completely absent from Japan. Though the share of non-Japanese people in comparison with most other post-industrialised countries is rather small, linguistic diversity is increasingly becoming an issue in Japan as well. The aim of this chapter is to provide an overview of Japan's nascent multilingualism and introduce a research tool for its closer examination.

A more detailed account of the linguistic situation in Japan is given in section 2. It includes the latest official data on the nationalities of Japan's foreign population. Though this is anything but a reliable tool for the mapping of linguistic diversity, it is the only source of information available so far. Section 3 introduces the research object examined in this study, language on signs, and formulates three questions that are to be addressed. An introduction to the empirical study conducted in central Tokyo and some methodological remarks follow in section 4, before the basic results of the study are presented in section 5.

The three subsequent sections discuss one of the three research questions each. Section 6 takes a closer look at the geographic distribution of multilingual signs in Tokyo, thereby revealing some characteristic patterns as to the visibility of languages other than Japanese in given parts of the city. Questions concerning the target group of multilingual signs are addressed in section 7, which identifies two basic types of multilingual formats that allow some conclusions about the sign readers. Focusing on the coexistence of older and newer versions of a given type of sign, section 8 analyses the overall development of Tokyo's linguistic landscape in the past few years. Concluding section 9 summarises the main findings of the survey and critically reflects on the usefulness of the suggested approach to the mapping of linguistic diversity.

2.   Multilingualism in Japan

Both in domestic and international contexts, Japan has long stressed its unity of nation, culture, and language. That present-day Japan is among the most frequently quoted examples of societal monolingualism is a by-product of the nation building process that started in the second half of the 19th century (Carroll 2001; Lee 1996). Taking European nations as a model, the spread of a standard language in order to promote a sense of national allegiance was considered a key factor in the country's modernisation. Linguistic homogeneity was seen as a source of national power and social stability. Regional varieties and minority languages, including Ainu and Ryukyuan, were actively discouraged and discriminated against.

While national language policies and monolingual ideology in the past two centuries succeeded in eliminating much of the archipelago's former linguistic heterogeneity, recent years have seen the advent of new linguistic diversification. This development is being brought about by the growing presence of people with non-Japanese backgrounds. Two linguistic minority groups with a relatively long migration history are Chinese and Korean residents. Commonly referred to as "old-comers," they came before and during the Pacific War and have been living in Japan for several generations. Chinese and Korean communities are a characteristic component of larger Japanese cities, such as Nagasaki, Kobe, Yokohama, Osaka, and Tokyo. Many of the younger generations speak Japanese as their first language (Maher 1995).

The country's economic boom in the second half of the 20th century has attracted people from various other parts of the world, particularly from Southeast Asia and South American countries. The total number of non-Japanese nationals resident in Japan almost doubled from 0.78 million in 1980 to 1.68 million in 2000. Figures by the Ministry of Justice on 2006 give a total number of 1,973,747 foreign residents, which is around 1.5% of the total population (FPCJ 2006: 21).

Since these figures include only officially registered foreigners, the overall number of non-Japanese nationals in Japan can be assumed to be much higher. The majority of Japan's foreign population comes from Asian countries, particularly North and South Korea (30.8%), China (24.7%), and the Philippines (10.1%). Foreign residents from South American countries (18.1%) are a second major group. Many of them are so-called *Nikkeijin*, the offspring of Japanese nationals who emigrated at the beginning of the 20th century. The majority comes from Brazil (14.5%). People from North America (3.3%), Europe (3.0%), Oceania (0.8%), and Africa (0.5%) make up for less than ten percent of Japan's foreign population (MIC 2005: 55).

Though the share of Japan's foreign population appears small in comparison with most European countries, migration is likely to become an ever more important issue in Japan's near future. Most relevant to this development is the demographic transition of the country into an ageing society with low birth rates. According to a much quoted model calculation by the United Nations, Japan would have to admit some 600,000 labour migrants per year if it were to keep its workforce at the level of 1995, and some astronomical ten million annually in order to maintain the ratio between its working and non-working population (UNESA 2001). Unrealistic as these figures may be, they unmistakably reveal that Japan's non-foreign population is going to be on the rise.

The number of Japanese people abroad has been increasing as well. According to the Ministry of Foreign Affairs, more than 900,000 Japanese nationals in 2003 were living outside Japan for more than three months (MIC 2005: 56). Many of these are executives sent to overseas branches of their companies, who have to supervise and work together with local staff (Sakai 2000; Wah 1999). Their children grow up in non-Japanese environments and in many cases receive formal education in languages other than Japanese. Back home, these children constitute a linguistic minority group in their own right, whose situation has received increasing attention in recent years (Kanno 2003; Macdonald and Kowatari 1995).

To a nation where being Japanese used to be tantamount to speaking Japanese, such developments are a novel and highly remarkable experience. In the long run they are likely to break up the strong ties between ethnicity, culture, nation, and language, which have been taken for granted for a rather long time now. Recent years have paved the way for new perspectives on "multi-ethnic Japan" (Lie 2001), "multicultural Japan" (Denoon et al. 1996; also Douglass and Roberts 2000), and "multilingual Japan" (Maher and Yashiro 1995; also Coulmas and Heinrich 2005; Goebel Noguchi and Fotos 2001). Japanese society at the beginning of the 21st century thus finds itself in a period of transition. Not only is it facing demographic shifts likely to have dramatic impacts on its future population make-up, but, concomitantly, its very identity as a monolingual nation is being questioned.

3. Rationale and goals of research

The basic aim of this research has been to get a better understanding of Japan's new linguistic diversity, the actors involved, and the direction it is going to take. The research object chosen is language on signs, with a focus on the Japanese capital Tokyo. The study of language on signs is a relatively new sociolinguistic subfield referred to as "linguistic landscape" research (see Introductory Chapter to this Volume). The term was first used by Landry and Bourhis (1997) in a paper on ethnolinguistic vitality in Quebec. Though their study itself ironically does not include any empirical linguistic landscape research in the narrower sense, Landry and Bourhis's (1997: 23) definition of the term as "the visibility and salience of languages on public and commercial signs in a given territory or region" is quoted in most subsequent research on the topic. It can now be considered to be the standard definition.

Previous linguistic landscape research has been conducted in various urban regions around the world. Though these studies differ widely with regard to the linguistic make-up of the research environment, the underlying research perspective and the methodology applied, three basic questions can be identified to underlie most previous approaches to the topic. They refer to the sign writers, the sign readers, and the dynamics of the language contact situation as a whole:

(1) Linguistic landscaping by whom?
(2) Linguistic landscaping for whom?
(3) Linguistic landscape *quo vadis?*

The present study tries to provide some answers to these three questions with regard to Japan and its capital. A more general purpose is to reflect on the potential of linguistic landscape research for the mapping of multilingual diversity in urban contexts and what this type of research can and cannot achieve.

4. Methodology

Previous empirical studies about language on signs can be subdivided into qualitative and quantitative approaches. Studies of the former type have made various important observations about language use on signs and its instrumental, indexical and symbolic functions (e.g., Calvet 1990, 1994; Reh 2004; Scollon and Scollon 2003). Most of these studies do not rely on a clearly defined corpus of signs on which to base their observations. This is not necessarily a problem, but it is disadvantageous in so far as it doesn't provide any leeway for quantitative assessments of the observations made.

Quantitative approaches focus their chief attention on the representative strength of the languages in the linguistic landscape of a place (e.g., Monnier 1989; Rosenbaum et al. 1977; Wenzel 1996). To this end, they usually work with a clearly defined and systematically collected sample of signs. Analytical categories other than the language or languages contained are not, or only sporadically, considered. Most of the more recent approaches aim at combining a sound methodology of data collection with various types of qualitative analyses. Examples are Bagna and Barni (2007), Ben-Rafael et al. (2006), Cenoz and Gorter (2006), and Huebner (2006).

Collecting a sample of signs involves three major problems. It must be clarified how to determine (1) the survey area(s), (2) the survey items, and (3) the linguistic properties of (2). In my survey in Tokyo, the stations of the Yamanote Line, a circular railway line through the central parts of the city, served as basic orientation markers. A total of 28 areas were determined, each of them being part of a street between two consecutive traffic lights not too far off the stations. They range from 65 metres to 400 metres in length, with an average of 154 metres (for a full account see Backhaus 2007).

With regard to the second problem, all signs situated in the survey areas – and only those – were considered relevant survey items. A sign was defined to be any piece of written text within a spatially definable frame. This definition includes anything from lettered foot mats and inscribed litter boxes to huge commercial billboards and traffic guidance signage. Each sign was counted as one item, irrespective of its size. When signs identical in format appeared more than once, each item was counted separately.

All countable items were categorised as either mono- or multilingual. A multilingual sign was determined to be a sign (as defined above) containing at least one language in addition to, or instead of, Japanese. The group of multilingual signs according to this definition includes signs with only one language, provided that language is not Japanese. The term "multilingual sign" hereafter is used for the sake of terminological simplicity rather than with strict correspondence to a multiplicity of languages displayed. Some default rules were formulated for dealing with unclear cases.

The survey was conducted between February and May 2003, on working days between 11.00 am and 5.00 pm. Since shops often display parts of their commodities outside, only days with stable weather conditions were selected for research. In order to guarantee methodological consistency, I reiterated the procedure at all 28 areas before starting to analyse the data. All multilingual signs were recorded by digital camera. Signs categorised as monolingual were not taken into further consideration.

5.   Kernel results

In total, the 28 survey areas contained 11,834 countable items; 2,321 of them were categorised as multilingual on the basis of the definition given above. This is a ratio of 19.6%. If we generalise this finding, more than each fifth sign one encounters in central Tokyo thus is likely to contain a language other than Japanese. This outcome is in sharp contrast to the proportion of foreign residents, which even in Tokyo still is below 3% (TMG 2006). It reveals that the linguistic landscape has to be read with great care. It is not a faithful mapping of the linguistic make-up of the population of a place.

The 2,321 signs categorised as multilingual contain a total of 14 languages other than Japanese. As Table 1 shows, the predominant language is English. Contained on 97.6% of all signs, it is even more prominent than Japanese. With only 55 multilingual signs not containing English, the visibility of English is so salient that one may say that multilingualism in Tokyo's linguistic landscape is for the most part Japanese-English bilingualism. Other foreign languages make up a minor part of the sample only. Merely Chinese (2.7%) and Korean (1.7%)

Table 1. Languages on the signs of the sample

Language	Contained	% of cases
Japanese	1,674	72.1
English	2,266	97.6
Chinese	62	2.7
Korean	40	1.7
French	20	0.9
Portuguese	12	0.5
Spanish	8	0.3
Latin	6	0.3
Thai	5	0.2
Italian	4	0.2
Persian	2	0.1
Tagalog	2	0.1
German	2	0.1
Arabic	1	0.0
Russian	1	0.0
Total cases	2,321	100.0

have a ratio higher than one percent. Most other languages appear on less than ten signs of the sample.

The above analysis of the languages contained again shows that the visibility of a language in a given public space does not reflect the linguistic profile of the population in that space. In the present case, English is the native language of a tiny part of Tokyo's non-Japanese population only. Nevertheless, it has an incomparably stronger impact on the linguistic landscape than Chinese and Korean, even though these are the languages actually spoken by a sizeable number of people living in the city.

6. Geographic distribution: Linguistic landscaping by whom?

An important variable with regard to the visibility of languages other than Japanese in Tokyo's linguistic landscape is the geographic distribution of multilingual signs. Previous linguistic landscape studies have identified various characteristic patterns concerning the visibility of both indigenous and non-indigenous linguistic groups in a given part of a city. Some examples are French and Dutch in Brussels (Tulp 1978; Wenzel 1996), French and English in Montreal (CLF 2000; Monnier 1989), Arabic and Hebrew in Jerusalem and other Israeli locations (Ben-Rafael et al. 2006), and Arabic and Chinese in Paris (Calvet 1994). In all of these cases, the linguistic landscape of a city was found to reflect to some extent the spatial concentration of the speakers of these languages within that city.

In order to look for any comparable patterns in the geographic distribution of languages on signs in Tokyo, a brief outline of the geographic distribution of Tokyo's foreign population within the city's 23 wards needs to be given. Previous research has identified basically three tendencies (e.g., Tanaka 2000: 18; Yonehara 1997: 140): (1) People from Asia are concentrated in the wards situated in the north and northwest of central Tokyo. An overall trend here is that (2) long-term foreign residents are frequently found in the northern wards, particularly in Kita, Adachi, Arakawa, and Taitō, whereas people who have relatively recently come to Japan tend to live closer to the centre, in Shinjuku and Toshima Ward. (3) People from Western countries preferably settle in central or central-western wards such as Minato, Chiyoda, Shibuya, and Meguro.

To what extent do our data reflect any of these trends? Table 2 gives the spatial distribution of foreign languages for the 28 survey areas. Starting with the area around Yūrakuchō Station in the east of the Yamanote Line loop, the areas are arranged counter-clockwise in order of appearance. Eight areas do not contain any signs with languages other than English. Particularly noteworthy is a sequence of five English-only areas in the eastern part of the Yamanote loop

Table 2. Spatial distribution of languages other than Japanese

#	Survey area	Ward	English		Chinese		Korean	
1	Yūrakuchō	Chiyoda	53	(100.0)				
2	Tōkyō	Chiyoda	39	(100.0)				
3	Kanda	Chiyoda	85	(100.0)				
4	Akihabara	Chiyoda	137	(100.0)				
5	Okachimachi	Taitō	57	(100.0)				
6	Ueno	Taitō	27	(100.0)	1	(3.7)	1	(3.7)
7	Uguisudani	Taitō	68	(91.9)				
8	Nishinippori	Arakawa	55	(91.7)	1	(1.7)	1	(1.7)
9	Tabata	Kita	62	(100.0)			1	(1.6)
10	Komagome	Toshima	145	(100.0)	1	(0.7)		
11	Sugamo	Toshima	156	(100.0)	17	(10.9)		
12	Ōtsuka	Toshima	47	(100.0)				
13	Ikebukuro	Toshima	103	(99.0)	3	(2.9)		
14	Mejiro	Toshima	42	(97.9)	20	(46.5)		
15	Takadanobaba	Shinjuku	112	(96.6)	4	(3.4)		
16	Shin-Ōkubo	Shinjuku	112	(83.6)	3	(2.2)	34	(25.4)
17	Shinjuku	Shinjuku	79	(100.0)				
18	Yoyogi	Shibuya	28	(100.0)				
19	Harajuku	Shibuya	103	(96.3)	1	(0.9)		
20	Shibuya	Shibuya	163	(100.0)	6	(3.7)		
21	Ebisu	Shibuya	57	(100.00				
22	Meguro	Shinagawa	70	(97.2)				
23	Gotanda	Shinagawa	58	(92.1)			1	(1.6)
24	Ōsaki	Shinagawa	107	(97.3)	2	(1.8)	2	(1.8)
25	Shinagawa	Minato	75	(100.0)				
26	Tamachi	Minato	72	(100.0)				
27	Hamamatsuchō	Minato	84	(98.8)	1	(1.2)		
28	Shinbashi	Minato	70	(98.6)	2	(2.8)		

(#1–#5): Yūrakuchō, Tōkyō, Kanda, Akihabara, and Okachimachi. It comprises all survey areas situated in Chiyoda, one of the wards in which the presence of Western foreigners is known to be particularly high.

Despite their low frequency in total, some regularity in geographic distribution can be observed for languages other than English as well. Concentrating on those areas in which a language other than English is contained on at least ten percent of all multilingual signs, three locations are of relevance (#11, #14, #16), i.e., Sugamo (10.9% Chinese), Mejiro (46.5% Chinese), and Shin-Ōkubo (25.4% Korean). The three areas are situated in the west-north-western parts of the Yamanote loop, in Toshima Ward (Sugamo and Mejiro) and Shinjuku Ward (Shin-Ōkubo). As described above, these are two of the wards in which the share of foreign residents from Asian countries is known to be large. Particularly people who have only recently come to Japan settle in this part of the city. This suggests that the so-called "new-comers" leave a stronger impact on the linguistic landscape than their established "old-comer" compatriots. The same tendency has been observed by Kim (2003) in a recent linguistic landscape study in Osaka.

A closer analysis of the Chinese and Korean signs displayed in the three areas reveals some essential differences between the two. The Chinese signs in Sugamo and Mejiro are actually but one type of sign appearing in frequent repetition: a warning not to leave bicycles in the area. The originator of the sign is the Toshima ward administration. The same sign is used throughout Toshima Ward and was found several times in the survey area in Ikebukuro as well. The text on the sign is available in Japanese, English, and Chinese. The English version reads as follows (*sic*):

> This area is designated as a Bicycle & Motorbike NO Parking Area. Any bicycle left here will be impounded in accordance with TOSIMA CITY Ordinance. To retrieve your bicycle, you must pay a removal fee of ¥3,000 (bicycle) or ¥5,000 (Motorbike).
> NOTE: Chains may be cut if necessary.

The Korean signs in Shin-Ōkubo are of a completely different nature. Most of the signs have been set up by the local shopkeepers rather than by administrative agents. Thus we find Korean signs to indicate hairdressers and beauty parlours, opticians, Internet cafés, telephone shops, game centres, and various other businesses. The area even contains some handwritten messages offering jobs and services to the Korean community. In fact, only three of the 34 Korean signs in Shin-Ōkubo are signs with an official background.

Another difference between Korean in Shin-Ōkubo and Chinese in Sugamo and Mejiro becomes manifest in the way the two languages are combined with other languages. Bagna and Barni (2007) have referred to this problem as "autonomy." In contrast to the Japanese-English-Chinese parking prohibition for bicycles in Toshima ward, Korean in Shin-Ōkubo frequently occurs without any other language. In total, there are no less than eight Korean-only signs within the 175 metres of the Shin-Ōkubo area. The co-appearance of Korean and English on another seven signs that do not contain Japanese text is one more noteworthy pattern.

The absence of Japanese on Korean signs in Shin-Ōkubo is an interesting fact. These signs can be seen as what Calvet (1990: 175) has referred to as

Figure 1. Photo shop sign

a means of "marking the territory" by the Korean-speaking community. Thus we are witnessing first instances of how a non-Japanese population is about to take over parts of Tokyo's linguistic landscape. A telling example of this development is a series of prefabricated Japanese sign boards papered over by handwritten Korean text to serve the shopkeeper's more immediate needs. The original version of the sign, normally used by businesses offering photo developments, is given in Figure 1. Figure 2 shows the Shin-Ōkubo version of the sign.

To summarise, the spatial distribution of languages other than Japanese on the signs of the sample in fact seems to be indicative of larger concentrations of Tokyo's foreign population. Two general tendencies can be observed: (1) a sequence of English-only areas in the eastern parts of the Yamanote Line loop, including one of the central wards in which Western foreigners are known to concentrate; and (2) a higher visibility of signs containing Chinese and Korean in the north-western survey areas.

Figure 2. Photo shop sign papered over with Korean text

7. Availability of translation: Linguistic landscaping for whom?

A foreign language on a sign does not necessarily address a foreign target group. Previous linguistic landscape research has shown that signs containing foreign languages in many cases are used primarily to attract the attention of domestic readers. This is particularly salient with regard to the cosmopolitan flair and chic of English. The journal *English Today* has recently published a series of smaller linguistic landscape studies that demonstrate the growing prominence of English in non-English speaking locations around the globe (e.g., Griffin 2004; MacGregor 2003; McArthur 2000). Though these studies do not deny the utility of English as a language of international communication, their main tenor is that English signs in many cases address a non-foreign target group. Previous linguistic landscape research in Tokyo has made similar observations (Inoue 2000; Masai 1972; Someya 2002).

How to distinguish English signs intended to provide information to for-eigners from those that mainly address domestic readers is a problem of high complexity. A helpful analytical category has been developed by Reh (2004), who has drawn up a first taxonomy about the functional relationships of the languages included on a sign. The chief variable in this taxonomy is the availability of translation, for which, in most simple terms, there are basically two options: either the two or more languages on a sign are translations of each other or they are not. The former case according to Reh is indicative of a multilingual readership made up of monolingual individuals; the latter case presupposes a certain degree of multilingualism on the individual level as well, providing the message on the sign is to be understood in full.

An analysis centring on the availability of translation on the 2,266 signs of the sample containing English is a helpful tool in order to identify the target group of English texts in Tokyo's linguistic landscape. An example of each of the two types of sign is given in Figures 3 and 4.

The two litter boxes have in common that both display Japanese-English texts. With regard to the functional relationship between the two languages, however, they fundamentally differ. On the litter box in Figure 3, the same information is given in both Japanese and English: that this is a litter box reserved for combustible garbage. The two texts are mutual translations. On the litter box in Figure 4, by contrast, information about the type of garbage is available only in Japanese. The content of the English slogan "SAVE THE EARTH" is unrelated to the Japanese message and, important as it may be, without much immediate informative value.

The two signs illustrate in a nutshell the two basic functions that English texts in Tokyo's linguistic landscape fulfil. English is supplementary when providing a translation of a co-appearing Japanese message, as in the example in Figure 3. It is complementary when conveying contents unrelated to the Japanese text it accompanies, as is the case in Figure 4. With regard to the question of the target group, the following assumption can be made: When English is used in a supplementary way, it is intended to serve people without proficiency in Japanese; when used complementarily, it addresses the Japanese population. A basic rule of thumb then would be that those English signs providing a complete or partial translation of the texts contained are signs for the foreign population, while those not providing translations are signs for the Japanese reader.

The present sample of signs contains two groups of English signs not providing a translation: (1) signs with at least one language in addition to English, in most cases Japanese-English signs; and (2) English-only signs. A closer analysis of these signs reveals some characteristic patterns underlying the use of English. The most frequent pattern on the Japanese-English signs is a brief English slogan or catchphrase, in combination with more specific information in Japanese. Prototypical examples of this diglossia-like relationship are cigarette advertisements with English slogans like "SLOW DOWN. PLEASURE UP" or "Come

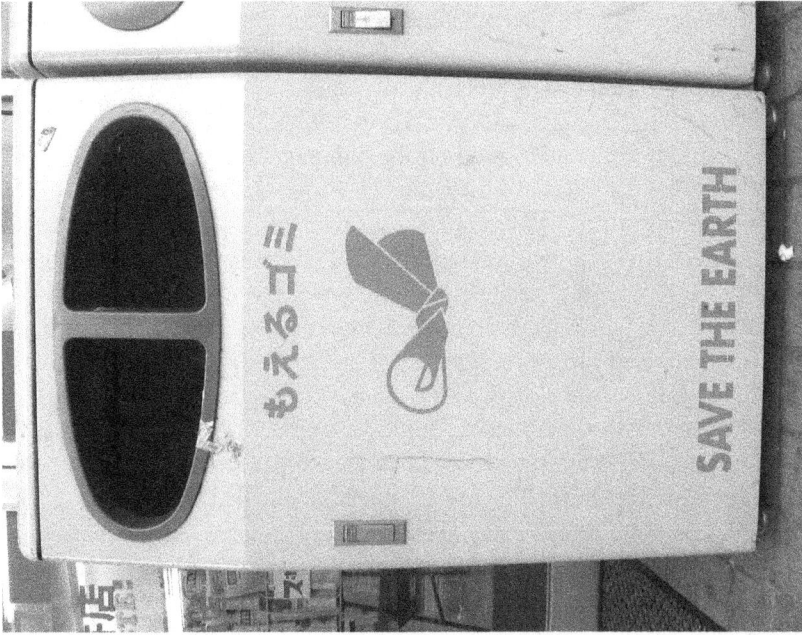

Figure 4. Litter box 2

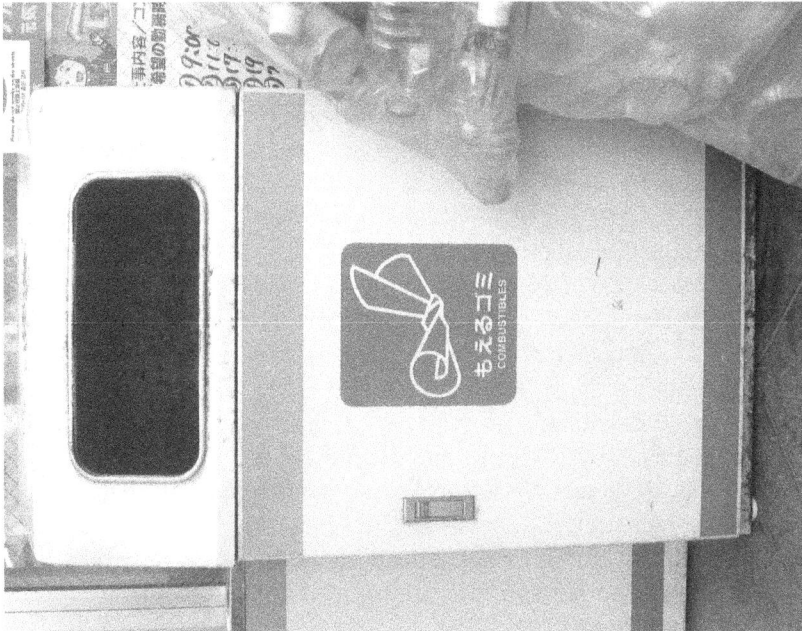

Figure 3. Litter box 1

to where the flavour is". The accompanying health warning, however, is given in Japanese. The text on the litter box in Figure 4 is another good example of this functional discrimination between global (English) and everyday (Japanese) contents.

Another pattern frequently found on the complementary Japanese-English signs is an English title like "Information", "Floor Guide", "PRICE LIST", or "Beauty Menu" in the headline of a sign that gives all subsequent information announced by that title in Japanese only. Obviously, the information value of this type of sign is relatively low to anyone who knows English but not Japanese. A third characteristic phenomenon on non-translating Japanese-English signs is mixed business names such as "COFFEE & RESTAURANT *jonasan*" [Jonathan], "Mansion & Hotel *sezāru*" [César], or "GAME *rasube-gasu*" [Las Vegas]. A possible motivation for these blends of the Roman alphabet with the Japanese Katakana script could be the desire to have foreign elements in a commercial name, while at the same time make sure that the Japanese background of the business remains recognisable. In quantitative terms, more than 85% of all Japanese-English signs without translation exhibit one of the three patters just described.

The texts on the English-only signs share many characteristics with the English part of the Japanese-English signs. English-only signs are for the most part signs with very short text. In many cases, only a single word is contained, such as "SALE", "Open", or "WELCOME". Another frequent type of messages displayed on English-only signs is brief slogans and catchphrases, for instance "Security & Safety" or "We make a difference in quality and freshness". A third characteristic type is signs announcing shops and other businesses. Some examples are "SHOES HAGIMOTO", "Textile Boutique TAKATOMI", and "FACTORY NAGATA". Again, over 85% of the English-only signs can be identified to follow one of the three above patterns.

Table 3 gives a quantitative analysis of all 2,255 signs of the sample that contain English (eleven missing values). As can be seen, over 58% of the items are signs on which the contents of the English text coincide with the co-occurring Japanese text, either partially (33.6%) or in full (25%). The residuary 41.4% do not provide a translation, either because the Japanese and the English text function complementarily or because they are English-only signs. Coming back on the above rule of thumb, it becomes clear that both types of English signs are of quantitative relevance.

Though various exceptions cannot be dealt with in this context (see Backhaus 2007), the analysis demonstrates that English texts in Tokyo's linguistic landscape address both a non-Japanese and a Japanese readership. To the former, English is used to provide supplementary information that otherwise would be

Table 3. Availability of translation

Type of sign	Cases	%
Translation available:		
(1) completely	564	25.0
(2) partially	757	33.6
Sum	1,321	58.6
No translation:		
(1) Japanese-English	333	14.8
(2) English-only	601	26.7
Sum	934	41.4
Total	2,255	100.0

available in Japanese only. To the latter, it frequently has a mainly decorative function ("SAVE THE EARTH"). However, the fact that English texts without a corresponding Japanese counterpart in many cases provide quite substantial information content ("Open", "PRICE LIST", "COFFEE & RESTAURANT") shows that English to the Japanese sign reader is more than a mere embellishment. Rather, it appears that a minimal degree of proficiency in English has become a basic requirement in order to understand a Japanese sign these days.

8.   Layering: Linguistic landscape *quo vadis*?

Our third question addresses the diachronic development of Tokyo's linguistic landscape. Generally speaking, two approaches are applicable when examining language in time. Ideally, one would conduct two or more successive surveys at different points in time and directly compare the results. This "real time" approach has also been applied by linguistic landscape researchers. An example is a series of empirical investigations by the Council of the French Language (CLF 2000) in Montreal, which reveals a growing visual prominence of English to the detriment of French throughout the 1990s.

An alternative way of examining diachronic changes in the linguistic landscape when data from only one point in time are available is to concentrate on the coexistence of older and newer editions of a given sign. Some earlier observations in this respect have been made in previous research as well. An example is Spolsky and Cooper's (1991: 5–8) survey in East Jerusalem, where co-occurring older and newer versions of a street sign were found to reflect recent changes in official sign writing policies. This way of investigation in diachronic linguistics is well known as "apparent-time" study. Borrowing a term from Scollon and Scollon (2003: 137), I have referred to the coexistence of older and newer versions of a given type of sign as "layering" (Backhaus 2005). An analysis of this phenomenon is a useful tool in order to explore the diachronic development of Tokyo's linguistic landscape.

Instances of layering are easiest to observe with regard to an increase in the number of languages used, particularly on official signs. Administrative agents usually replace older signs only on occasion, that is, when they have become hard to read, defaced, stolen, or are in any other need of restoration. In some cases, the newer version is simply attached next to the older one. Consequently, a great number of multilingual signs in the survey areas were found to coexist with Japanese-only counterparts of an older date: area maps, street block signs, information plates on traffic lights, and subway signs about train departures, among others. In most cases, the newer editions are Japanese-English signs. Occasionally, however, the latest version of a sign also includes Chinese and Korean text.

An illustrative example of this development is information boards about garbage collection. In Tokyo, where three types of garbage are regularly collected by the local garbage offices, these boards indicate the designated collection points and the days of the week on which what type of garbage is to be put out. The text on the boards for a long time used to be monolingual Japanese. According to the regularly published internationalisation reports by the Tokyo Metropolitan Government, the first Japanese-English versions of the sign were prepared in the early 1990s. Signs with additional texts in Korean and Chinese came into use around the end of the decade.

A closer look at this type of sign reveals that the increase in the number of languages is paralleled by an increase in amount of information these languages convey. Figure 5 shows two consecutive versions of the sign at once: the monolingual Japanese edition in the background and the newer Japanese-English edition that was fastened over it but has slightly come loose, thereby providing a brief glimpse at Tokyo's monolingual past. The Japanese-English sign contains all information one needs to know in order to properly understand the sign: that this is a "Recyclables and Waste Collection Point" (upper left), that one must not park here (upper right), that the originator of the sign is the "Shinjuku Waste collection Office" (bottom), and, most importantly, what type of garbage is collected on what days of the week (centre).

Texts available only in Japanese convey the following contents (top-down): an appeal that everyone should cooperate in recycling (below the English title line); additional information about the disposal of "Large-Sized Waste" (right-hand of the black text box); a request that garbage should be put out on the morning of the collection day (first asterisk); a reminder that garbage of commercial sources is charged with a fee (second asterisk); additional information about the

Figure 6. Information board on garbage collection 2

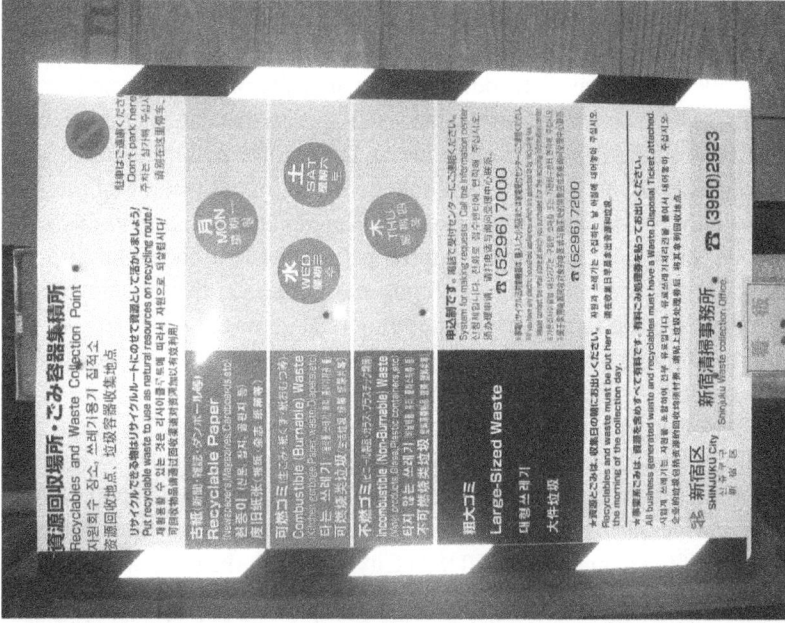

Figure 5. Information board on garbage collection 1

disposal of bottles and cans (third asterisk); and a prohibition to take away any part of the garbage that has been put out (bottom line).

An example of the sign with additional texts in Korean and Chinese is given in Figure 6. The high density of text on the sign suggests that considerable efforts must have been made in order to provide as much information as possible in all four languages. Even contents available on the bilingual version of the sign in Japanese only are translated into English, Korean and Chinese on this sign. They include the appeal to cooperate in recycling; the text about the disposal of "Large-Sized Waste"; the request to put out garbage in the morning of the collection day; and the reminder about commercial garbage.

It is interesting to observe that the days of the week are given in all four languages as well. As discussed elsewhere (Backhaus 2005), this piece of information was available only in Japanese and English on an earlier version of the quadrilingual sign. In the present example, the Japanese-English-Korean-Chinese format is even maintained where from a purely functional point of view it would be unnecessary. This can be observed in the left bottom, which identifies the originator of the sign as "SHINJUKU City". Though the Chinese version in fourth position is identical to the Japanese text on top, it has not been omitted. The only part of the sign not available in all four languages is the specification that the sign has been issued by the "Shinjuku Waste collection Office" (bottom line), which is given in Japanese and English only.

The three types of information boards thus exemplify both an increase in languages on public signs and an increase in functional weight assigned to these languages. Considering that the three types of signs have come into use in succeeding order, it becomes observable how a growing number of languages other than Japanese come to operate in Tokyo's linguistic landscape.

9.   Conclusions

In order to summarise the major findings of the linguistic landscape survey in Tokyo, let us come back to the three research questions about the producers of multilingual signs (by whom?), the assumed readership (for whom?) and the diachronic development (*quo vadis?*). Starting with the third question, the study has demonstrated that linguistic diversity in Tokyo is on the rise. We see that various sorts of monolingual signs are being exchanged by Japanese-English ones and, in some cases, even by signs additionally including Chinese and Korean text. Particularly this latter development deserves attention, because Chinese and Korean are the languages of Tokyo's and Japan's two largest linguistic minorities. In contrast to texts written in English, they do not address an anonymous "international" readership, but a clearly defined group of non-Japanese residents in Japan.

With regard to the first two questions, it could be seen that the visibility of languages and scripts other than Japanese in the streets of Tokyo is a product of three main factors: (1) official language policies aiming at an "internationalisation" of Tokyo; (2) larger concentrations of non-Japanese residents in some parts of the city; (3) and favourable attitudes towards the visibility of languages other than Japanese, particularly English, on the part of the Japanese host population. Thus we see how both Japanese and non-Japanese actors are involved in the making of Tokyo's multilingual landscape: Japanese produce multilingual signs for non-Japanese (1), non-Japanese produce multilingual signs for non-Japanese (2), and Japanese produce multilingual signs for Japanese (3).

The total of Tokyo's linguistic landscape reflects ongoing changes in the Japanese language regime (Coulmas and Heinrich 2005). It can be seen that the country's still much quoted monolingualism is about to lose relevance in a globalising world. The uncontested role of Japanese as the national language and its ideological underpinning as the essence of being Japanese now increasingly face pressure, both from outside and within. On the one hand, Japan's monolingual worldview is challenged by the power of English as the default language for all sorts of international communication (1) as well as the most prestigious foreign language domestically (3). On the other hand, a look at Tokyo's linguistic landscape also demonstrates that a growing number of people with non-Japanese backgrounds have started making their languages heard and seen (2).

What, then, does linguistic landscape research in Tokyo tell us about Japan's nascent multilingualism? It should be re-emphasised that there is no one-to-one mapping relationship between the languages visible in public space and the speakers who use them. In Tokyo, neither the ratio of multilingual signs nor the frequency of the languages contained reflects the city's linguistic make-up. For the mapping of linguistic diversity, linguistic landscape therefore is a tool to be applied with great care. Ideally, it should be used in combination with other research tools such as – if available – linguistic census data and large-scale home language surveys. Such research tools and their outcomes are presented elsewhere in this Volume. Nevertheless, it can be concluded that the linguistic landscape, if properly read, clearly does have something to say about linguistic diversity, the forces involved in its formation, and the direction it is likely to take.

References

Backhaus, P.
2005   Signs of multilingualism in Tokyo: A diachronic look at the linguistic landscape. *International Journal of the Sociology of Language* 175/176: 103–121.
2007   *Linguistic Landscapes: A Comparative Study of Urban Multilingualism in Tokyo*. Clevedon: Multilingual Matters.

Bagna, C. and M. Barni
2007   Per una mappatura dei repertori linguistici urbani. In: N. De Blasi and C. Marcato (eds.), *La Città e le sue Lingue: Repertori Lingustici urbani*. Napoli: Liguori Editore.

Ben-Rafael, E., E. Shohamy, M.H. Amara and N. Trumper-Hecht
2006   Linguistic landscape as symbolic construction of the public space: The case of Israel. *International Journal of Multilingualism* 3 (1): 7–30.

Calvet, L.-J.
1990   Des mots sur les murs: Une comparaison entre Paris et Dakar. In: R. Chaudenson (ed.), *Des Langues et des Villes* (Actes du colloque international à Dakar, du 15 au 17 décembre 1990), 73–83. Paris: Agence de coopération culturelle et technique.
1994   *Les Voix de la Ville: Introduction à la Sociolinguistique Urbaine*. Paris: Payot et Rivages.

Carroll, T.
2001   *Language Planning and Language Change in Japan*. Richmond: Curzon.

Cenoz, J. and D. Gorter
2006   Linguistic landscape and minority languages. *International Journal of Multilingualism* 3 (1): 67–80.

CLF (Conseil de la langue française)
2000   *La Langue de l'Affichage à Montréal de 1997 à 1999*. Québec: Conseil de la langue française.

Coulmas, F. and P. Heinrich (eds.)
2005   Changing Language Regimes in Globalizing Environments: Japan and Europe. *International Journal of the Sociology of Language* 175/176.

Denoon, D., M. Hudson, G. McCormack and T. Morris-Suzuki (eds.)
1996   *Multicultural Japan: Palaeolithic to Postmodern*. Cambridge/New York: Cambridge University Press.

Douglass, M. and G.S. Roberts (eds.)
2000   *Japan and Global Migration: Foreign Workers and the Advent of a Multicultural Society*. London/New York: Routledge.

FPCJ (Foreign Press Center of Japan)
    2006   *Facts and Figures of Japan 2006*. Tokyo: Foreign Press Center of Japan.

Goebel Noguchi, M. and S. Fotos (eds.)
    2001   *Studies in Japanese Bilingualism*. Clevedon: Multilingual Matters.

Griffin, J.L.
    2004   The presence of written English on the streets of Rome. *English Today* 20
            (2): 3–7, 47.

Huebner, T.
    2006   Bangkok's linguistic landscapes: Environmental print, codemixing and
            language change. *International Journal of Multilingualism* 3 (1): 31–51.

Inoue, F.
    2000   *Nihongo no nedan* [The Price of Japanese]. Tokyo: Taishūkan.

Kanno, Y.
    2003   *Negotiating Bilingual and Bicultural Identities: Japanese Returnees be-*
            twixt Two Worlds. Mahwah: Erlbaum.

Kim, M.
    2003   Gengo keikan kara mita nihon no taminzokuka [Japan's growing eth-
            nic heterogeneity seen from the linguistic landscape]. In: H. Shōji (ed.),
            Kokusai imin no jizon senryaku to toransunashonaru nettowāku no bunka
            jinruigaku [Cultural-ethnological Research on International Immigrants'
            Strategies of Independent Existence and Transnational Networks], 175–
            190. Osaka: National Museum of Ethnology.

Landry, R. and R.Y. Bourhis
    1997   Linguistic landscape and ethnolinguistic vitality. *Journal of Language and*
            Social Psychology 16 (1): 23–49.

Lee, Y.
    1996   *Kokugo to iu shisō: kindai nihon no gengo ninshiki* [The "kokugo" Ideol-
            ogy: Language Awareness in Modern Japan]. Tokyo: Iwanami.

Lie, J.
    2001   *Multiethnic Japan*. Cambridge: Harvard University Press.

Macdonald, G. and A. Kowatari
    1995   A non-Japanese Japanese: On being a returnee. In: J.C. Maher and G.
            Macdonald (eds.), *Diversity in Japanese Culture and Language*, 249–269.
            London and New York: Kegan Paul International.

MacGregor, L.
    2003   The language of shop signs in Tokyo. *English Today* 19 (1): 18–23.

Maher, J.C.
    1995   The Kakyo: Chinese in Japan. In: J.C. Maher and K. Yashiro (eds.), *Mul-*
            tilingual Japan, 125–138. Clevedon: Multilingual Matters.

Maher, J.C. and K. Yashiro (eds.)
  1995   *Multilingual Japan*. Clevedon: Multilingual Matters.

Masai, Y.
  1972   *Tōkyō no seikatsu chizu* [Living Map of Tokyo]. Tokyo: Jiji Tsūshinsha.

McArthur, T.
  2000   Interanto: The global language of signs. *English Today* 16 (1): 33–43.

MIC (Ministry of Internal Affairs and Communications)
  2005   *Dai gojūgo kai nihon tōkei nenkan* [Japan Statistical Yearbook 2005].
          Tokyo: Ministry of Internal Affairs and Communications.

Monnier, D.
  1989   *Langue d'Accueil et Langue de Service dans les Commerces à Montréal.*
          Québec: Conseil de la langue française.

Reh, M.
  2004   Multilingual writing: A reader-oriented typology – with examples from
          Lira Municipality (Uganda). *International Journal of the Sociology of
          Language* 170: 1–41.

Rosenbaum, Y., E. Nadel, R.L. Cooper and J.A. Fishman
  1977   English on Keren Kayemet Street. In: J.A. Fishman, R.L. Cooper and A.W.
          Conrad (eds.), *The Spread of English*, 179–196. Rowley, MA: Newbury
          House.

Sakai, J.
  2000   *Japanese Bankers in the City of London: Language, Culture and Identity
          in the Japanese Diaspora*. London: Routledge.

Scollon, R. and S.W. Scollon
  2003   *Discourses in Place: Language in the Material World*. London/New York:
          Routledge.

Someya, H.
  2002   *Kanban no moji hyōki* [Writing on signs]. In: Y. Tobita and T. Satō (eds.),
          Gendai nihongo kōza dai 6 kan: moji hyōki [Modern Japanese Course
          Vol. 6: Letters and Writing], 221–243. Tokyo: Meijishoin.

Spolsky, B. and R.L. Cooper
  1991   *The Languages of Jerusalem*. Oxford: Clarendon Press.

Tanaka, S.
  2000   *Tōkyō no kokusai seisaku to gengo sābisu* [Internationalisation policies
          and language services in Tokyo]. In: T. Kawahara (ed.), *Nihon no chihō
          jichitai ni okeru gengo sābisu ni kansuru kenkyū* [Research into Language
          Services of Japanese Local Governments], 18–25. Tokyo: Japan Associa-
          tion of College English Teachers, Language Policy Special Interest Group.

TMG (Tokyo Metropolitan Government)
  2006   *Jinkō no ugoki (Heisei* 17 *nen chū)* [Population Trends as of 2005]. Tokyo:
           Tokyo Metropolitan Government Bureau of General Affairs.
           http://www.toukei.metro.tokyo.jp/jugoki/2005/ju05qf0001.pdf

Tulp, S.M.
  1978   Reklame en tweetaligheid: Een onderzoek naar de geografische verspreid-
           ing van franstalige en nederlandstalige affiches in Brussel. *Taal en Sociale
           Integratie* 1: 261–288.

UNESA (United Nations, Department of Economic and Social Affairs)
  2001   *Replacement Migration: Is it a Solution to Declining and Ageing Popula-
           tions?* New York: United Nations.

Wah, W.H.
  1999   *Japanese Bosses, Chinese Workers: Power and Control in a Hong Kong
           Mega Store.* Richmond: Curzon.

Wenzel, V.
  1996   Reclame en tweetaligheid in Brussel: Een empirisch onderzoek naar de
           spreiding van Nederlandstalige en Franstalige affiches. In: Vrije Univer-
           siteit Brussel (ed.), *Brusselse Thema's* 3, 45–74. Brussels: Vrije Univer-
           siteit.

Yonehara, R.
  1997   *Tōkyōto: tayōsei ni michita shimin shakai* [Tokyo: Civil society full of di-
           versity]. In: H. Komai and I. Watado (eds.), *Jichitai no gaikokujin seisaku*
           [Policies Towards Foreigners by Local Administrations], 129–153. Tokyo:
           Akashi Shoten.

Contributing authors

Peter Backhaus
Research Fellow
German Institute for Japanese Studies
Tokyo, Japan
e-mail: backhaus@dijtokyo.org

Monica Barni
Associate Professor of Educational
Linguistics
Department of Science of Languages and
Cultures
Università per Stranieri di Siena
Italy
e-mail: barni@unistrasi.it

Katharina Brizić
Research Fellow
Institute for Linguistics
University of Vienna
Austria
e-mail: katharina.brizic@chello.at

Dominique Caubet
Professeur des Universités – arabe
maghrébin
Institut des Langues et Civilisations
Orientales
Paris, France
e-mail: caubet.dominique@yahoo.fr

Jasone Cenoz
Professor of Research Methods in
Education
Department of Research Methods in
Education
University of the Basque Country,
San Sebastian
Spain
e-mail: jasone.cenoz@ehu.es

Guus Extra
Professor of Language and Minorities
Department of Language and Culture
Studies
Tilburg University
The Netherlands
e-mail: guus.extra@utv.nl

Durk Gorter
Ikerbasque Research Professor
University of the Basque Country
Spain
e-mail: d.gorter@ikerbasque.org

Sandra Kipp
Research Fellow
School of Languages and Linguistics
University of Melbourne
Australia
e-mail: sandra.kipp@gmail.com

Georges Lüdi
Professor für Französische
Sprachwissenschaft
Institut für Franz. Sprach- und
Literaturwissenschaft
Universität Basel
Switzerland
e-mail: georges.luedi@unibas.ch

Izak J. van der Merwe
Professor and Research Fellow
Department of Geography and
Environmental Studies
University of Stellenbosch
South Africa
e-mail: ijvdm@sun.ac.za

Johannes H. van der Merwe
Professor of Geography and
Environmental Studies
University of Stellenbosch
South Africa
e-mail: jhvdm@sun.ac.za

Michel Poulain
Professor of Demography, Maître de
Recherche FNRS
GéDAP
Université catholique de Louvain
Belgium
e-mail: poulain@sped.ucl.ac.be

Massimo Vedovelli
Professor of Educational Linguistics
Department of Science of Languages and
Cultures
Università per Stranieri di Siena
Italy
e-mail: vedovelli@unistrasi.it

Colin H. Williams
Research Professor
School of Welsh
Cardiff University
United Kingdom
e-mail: williamsch@cardiff.ac.uk

Kutlay Yağmur
Associate Professor
Department of Language and Culture
Studies
Tilburg University
The Netherlands
e-mail: K.Yagmur@uvt.nl

Author index

Subject index

www.ingramcontent.com/pod-product-compliance
Lightning Source LLC
Chambersburg PA
CBHW022300280326
41932CB00010B/925